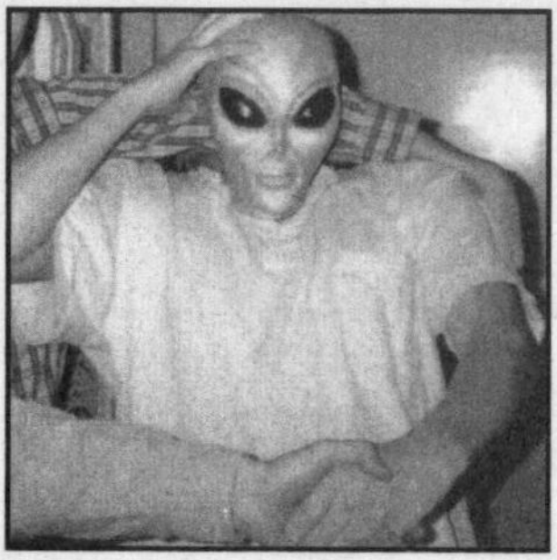

I've been gathering and reading a bunch of reference materials to do this "pirate story." However, the pirates that I admired so much in my youth hardly ever left written records of their history. I guess they were just too busy having fun with their own adventures and they forgot to leave their stories for future generations. That's just the trouble with those darned pirates.

—Eiichiro Oda, 1997

Author/artist Eiichiro Oda began his manga career in 1992 at the age of 17, when his one-shot cowboy manga **Wanted!** won second place in the coveted Tezuka manga awards. Oda went on to work as an assistant to some of the biggest manga artists in the industry, including Nobuhiro Watsuki, before winning the Hop Step Award for new manga artists. His pirate adventure **One Piece**, which debuted in **Weekly Shonen Jump** magazine in 1997, quickly became one of the most popular manga in Japan with sales of over 65 million copies.

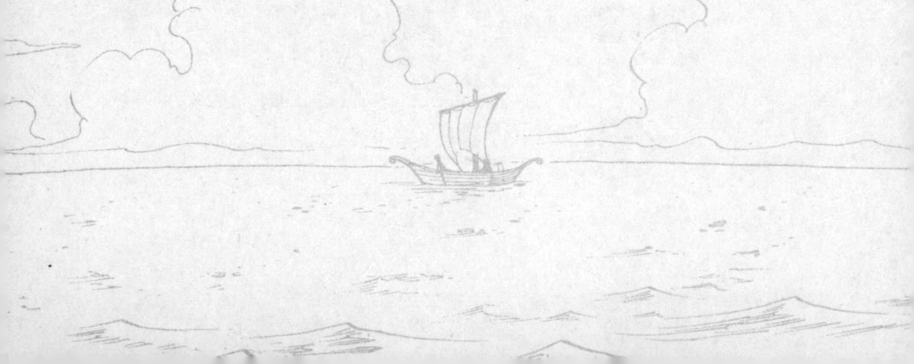

ONE PIECE VOL. 1
EAST BLUE PART 1

SHONEN JUMP Manga Edition

This graphic novel contains material that was originally published in English in **SHONEN JUMP** #1–4, plus the first **One Piece** episode in **SHONEN JUMP** #5.

STORY AND ART BY
EIICHIRO ODA

English Adaptation/Lance Caselman
Translation/Andy Nakatani
Touch-up Art & Lettering/Bill Schuch
Cover & Graphic Design/Sean Lee
Senior Editor/Jason Thompson

Printed in the U.S.A.

Published by VIZ Media, LLC
P.O. Box 77010
San Francisco, CA 94107

37
First printing, June 2003
Thirty-seventh printing, March 2023

VIZ MEDIA
viz.com

SHONEN JUMP

ratings.viz.com
RATED T TEEN

PARENTAL ADVISORY
ONE PIECE is rated T for Teen and is recommended for ages 13 and up. This volume contains fantasy violence and tobacco usage.

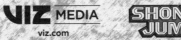

SHONEN JUMP MANGA

ONE PIECE

Vol. 1
ROMANCE DAWN

STORY AND ART BY
EIICHIRO ODA

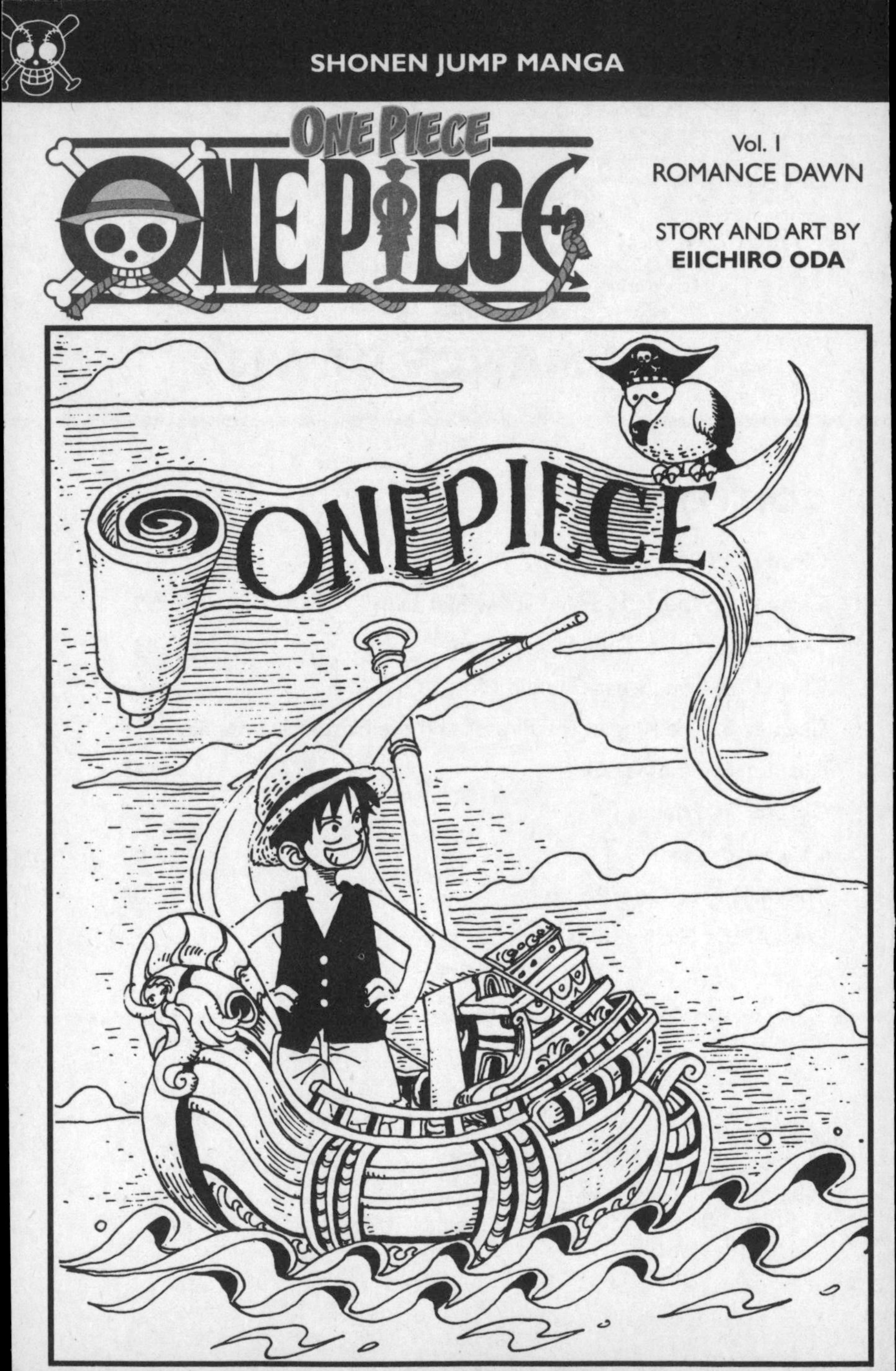
ONEPIECE

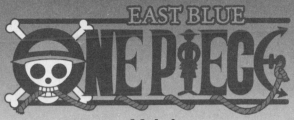

Vol. 1
ROMANCE DAWN

CONTENTS

Chapter 1: Romance Dawn	5
Chapter 2: They Call Him "Straw Hat Luffy"	59
Chapter 3: Enter Zolo: Pirate Hunter	83
Chapter 4: The Great Captain Morgan	105
Chapter 5: The King of the Pirates and the Master Swordsman	125
Chapter 6: Number One	145
Chapter 7: Friends	168
Chapter 8: Nami	189
The Making of **One Piece**	208
Facts About Eiichiro Oda	210

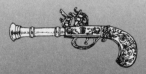

CHAPTER 1: ROMANCE DAWN

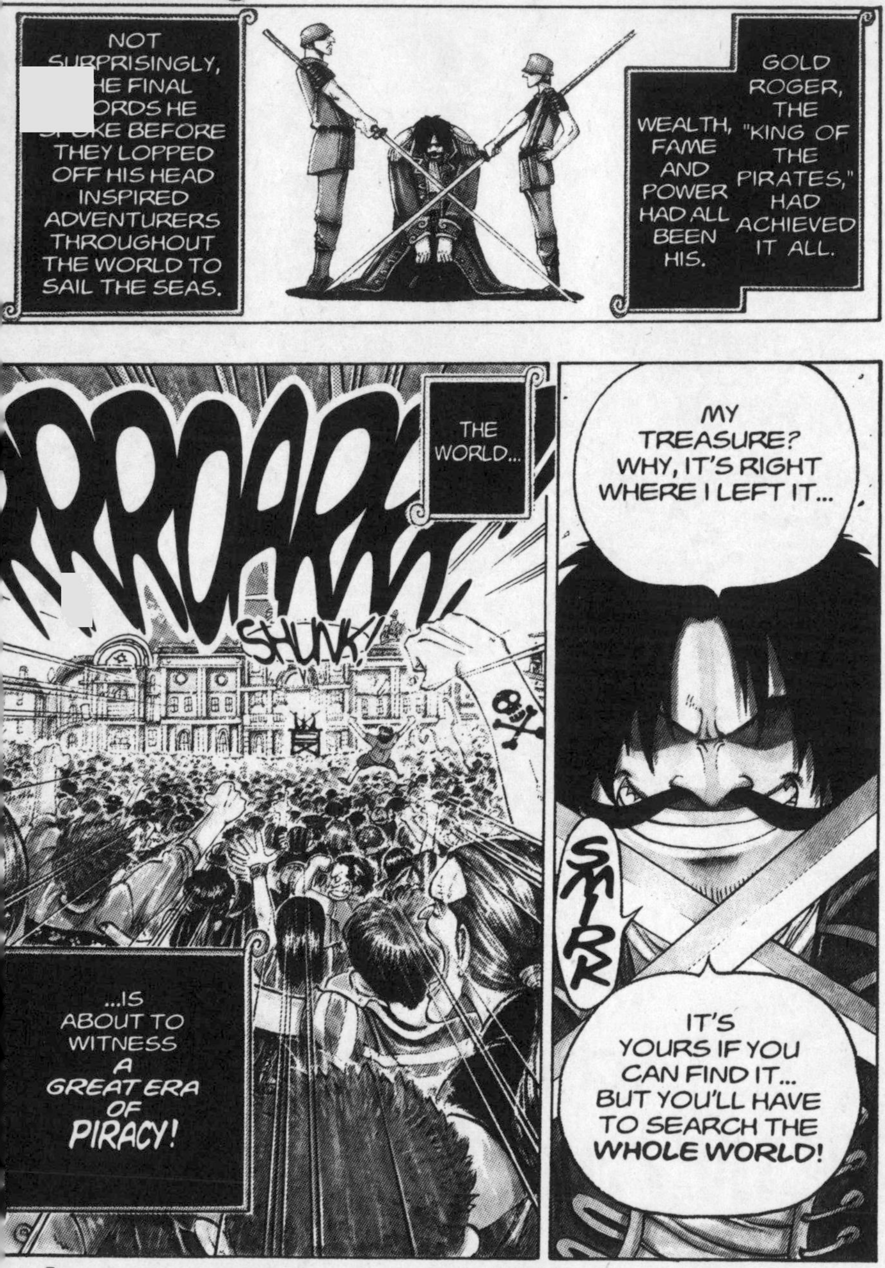
GOLD ROGER, THE "KING OF THE PIRATES," HAD ACHIEVED IT ALL.
WEALTH, FAME AND POWER HAD ALL BEEN HIS.
NOT SURPRISINGLY, HE FINAL ORDS HE OKE BEFORE THEY LOPPED OFF HIS HEAD INSPIRED ADVENTURERS THROUGHOUT THE WORLD TO SAIL THE SEAS.
MY TREASURE? WHY, IT'S RIGHT WHERE I LEFT IT...
SMIRK
IT'S YOURS IF YOU CAN FIND IT... BUT YOU'LL HAVE TO SEARCH THE WHOLE WORLD!
THE WORLD...
SHUNK!
...IS ABOUT TO WITNESS A GREAT ERA OF PIRACY!

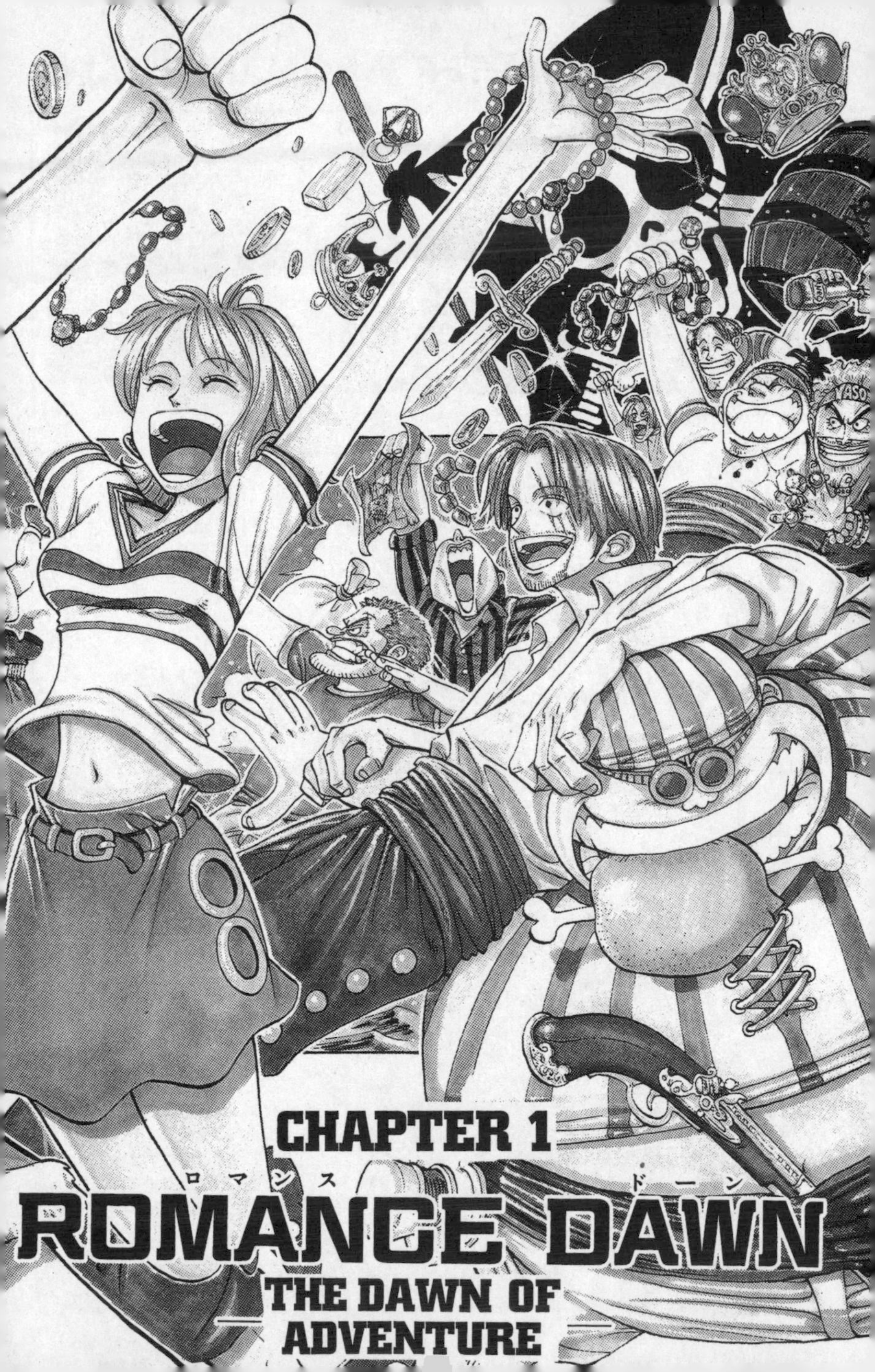
CHAPTER 1
ロマンス ドーン
ROMANCE DAWN
THE DAWN OF ADVENTURE

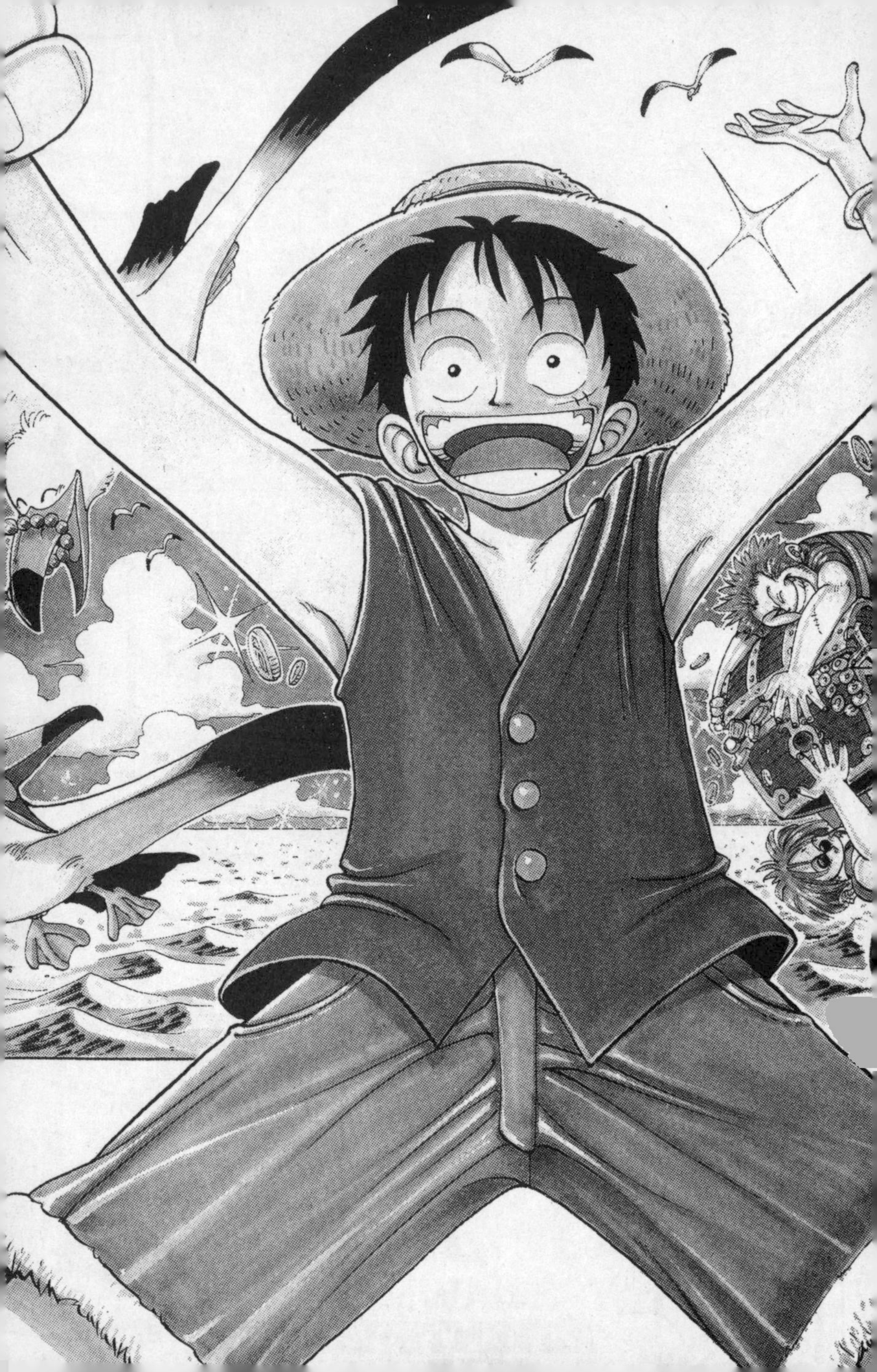

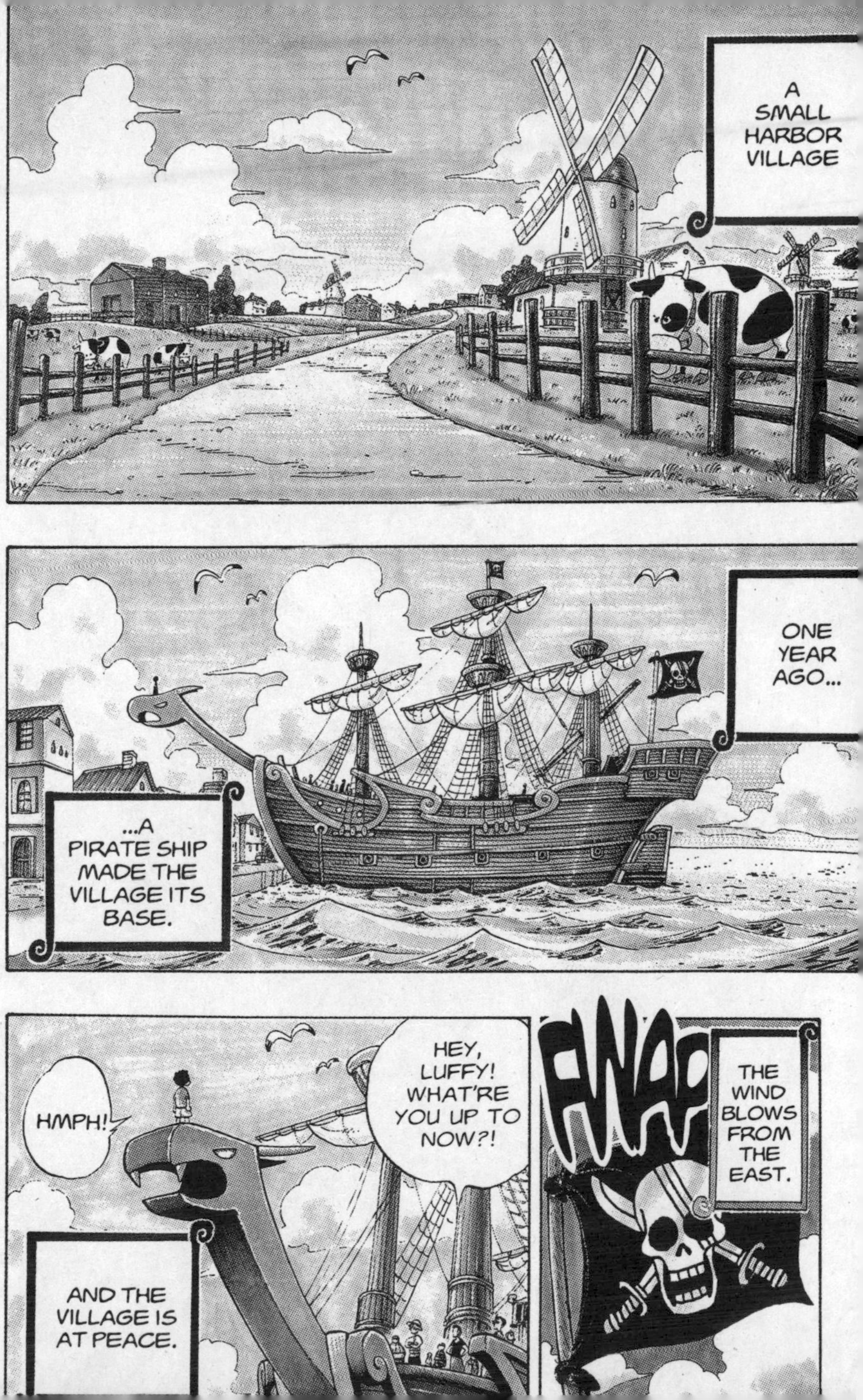
A SMALL HARBOR VILLAGE
ONE YEAR AGO...
...A PIRATE SHIP MADE THE VILLAGE ITS BASE.
FWAP
THE WIND BLOWS FROM THE EAST.
HEY, LUFFY! WHAT'RE YOU UP TO NOW?!
HMPH!
AND THE VILLAGE IS AT PEACE.

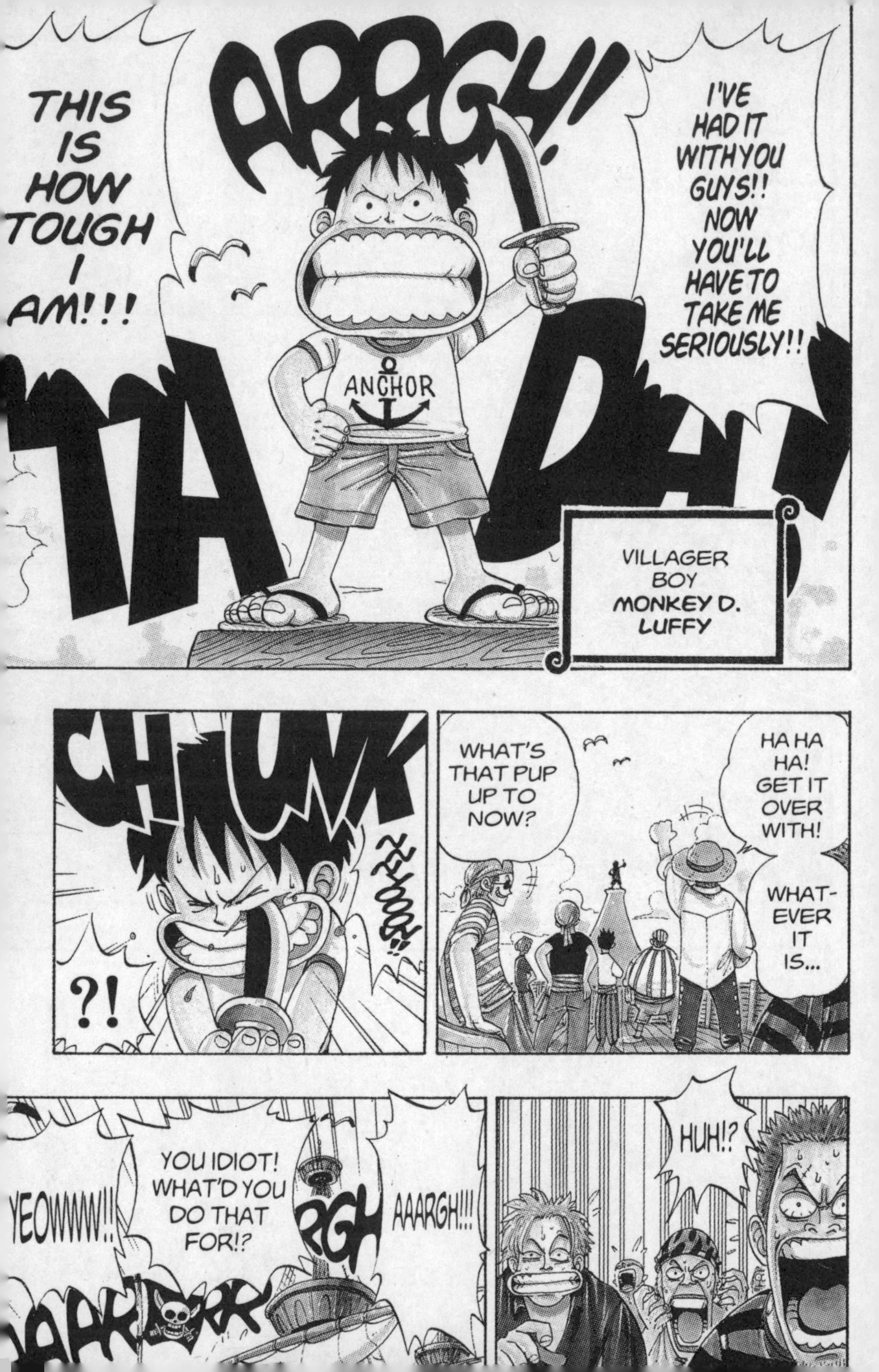
I'VE HAD IT WITH YOU GUYS!! NOW YOU'LL HAVE TO TAKE ME SERIOUSLY!!
ARRGH!
THIS IS HOW TOUGH I AM!!!
TA DA!
ANCHOR
VILLAGER BOY MONKEY D. LUFFY
HA HA HA! GET IT OVER WITH!
WHAT'S THAT PUP UP TO NOW?
WHAT-EVER IT IS...
CHUNK
?!
HUH!?
AAARGH!!!
RGH
YOU IDIOT! WHAT'D YOU DO THAT FOR!?
YEOWWW!!

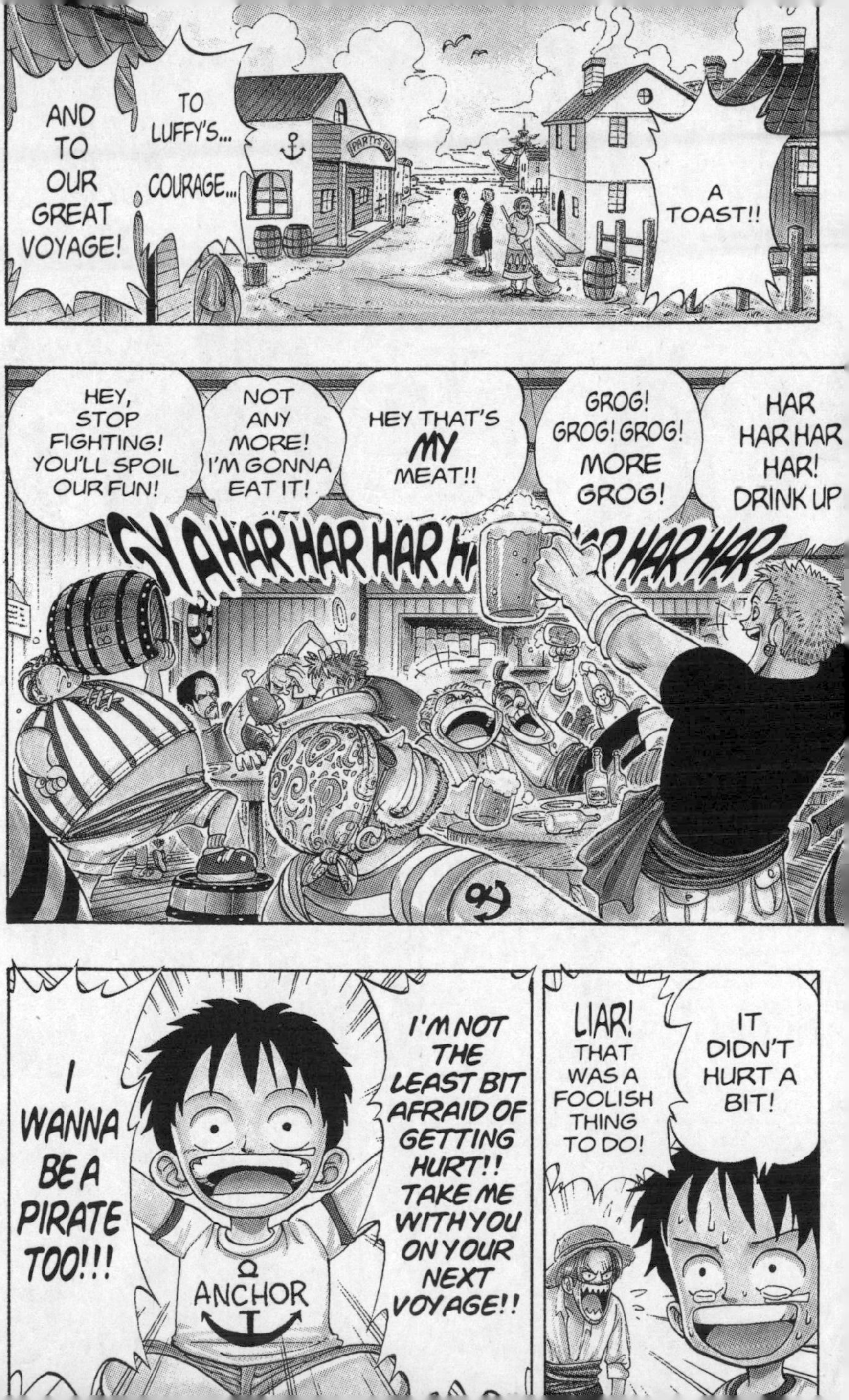
A TOAST!!
TO LUFFY'S... COURAGE...
AND TO OUR GREAT VOYAGE!
HAR HAR HAR HAR! DRINK UP
GROG! GROG! GROG! MORE GROG!
HEY THAT'S MY MEAT!!
NOT ANY MORE! I'M GONNA EAT IT!
HEY, STOP FIGHTING! YOU'LL SPOIL OUR FUN!
GYAHAR HAR HAR
HAR HAR HAR
IT DIDN'T HURT A BIT!
LIAR! THAT WAS A FOOLISH THING TO DO!
I'M NOT THE LEAST BIT AFRAID OF GETTING HURT!! TAKE ME WITH YOU ON YOUR NEXT VOYAGE!!
I WANNA BE A PIRATE TOO!!!
ANCHOR

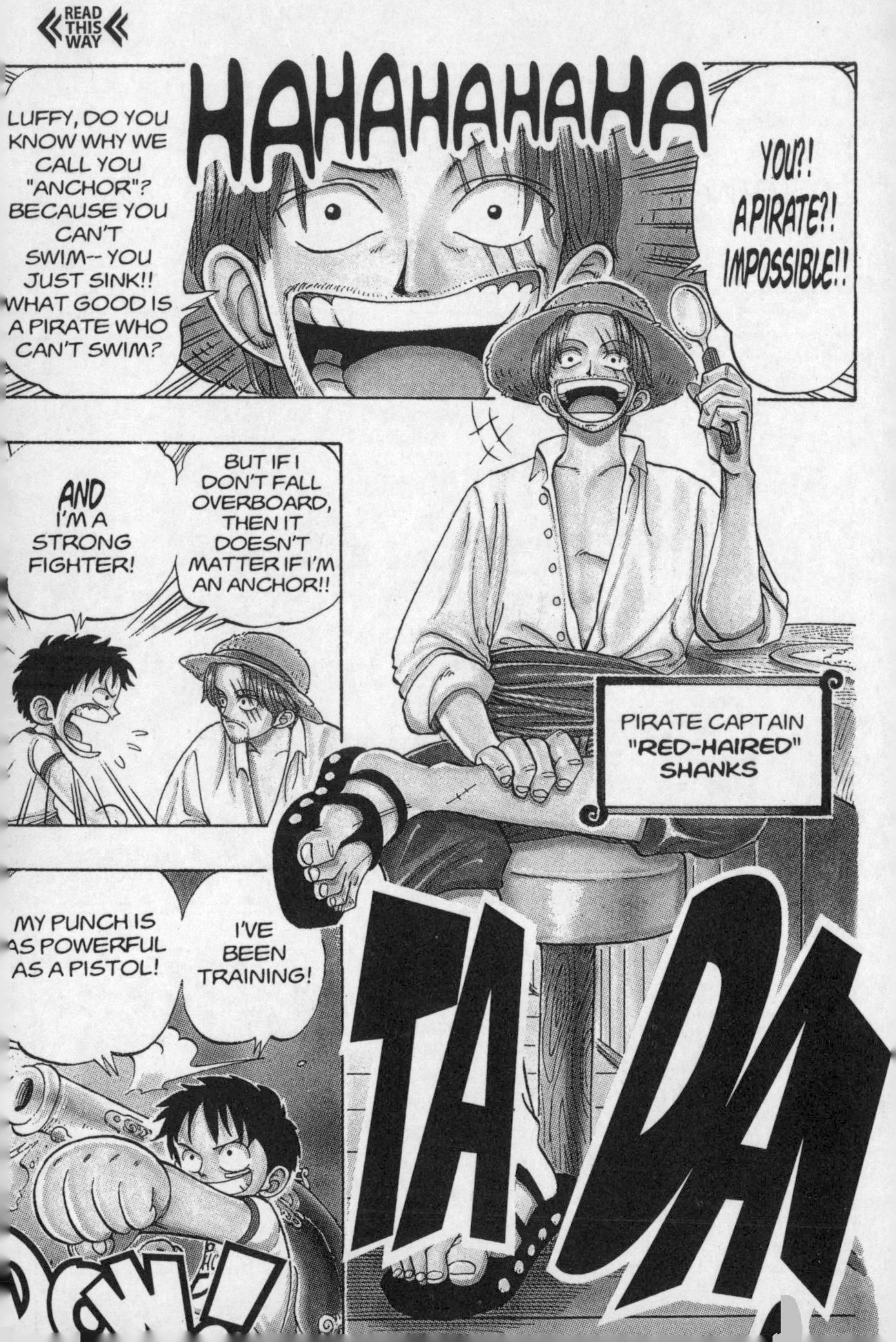
READ THIS WAY
HAHAHAHAHAHA
YOU?! A PIRATE?! IMPOSSIBLE!!
LUFFY, DO YOU KNOW WHY WE CALL YOU "ANCHOR"? BECAUSE YOU CAN'T SWIM-- YOU JUST SINK!! WHAT GOOD IS A PIRATE WHO CAN'T SWIM?
PIRATE CAPTAIN "RED-HAIRED" SHANKS
TADA!
BUT IF I DON'T FALL OVERBOARD, THEN IT DOESN'T MATTER IF I'M AN ANCHOR!!
AND I'M A STRONG FIGHTER!
I'VE BEEN TRAINING!
MY PUNCH IS AS POWERFUL AS A PISTOL!

READ THIS WAY

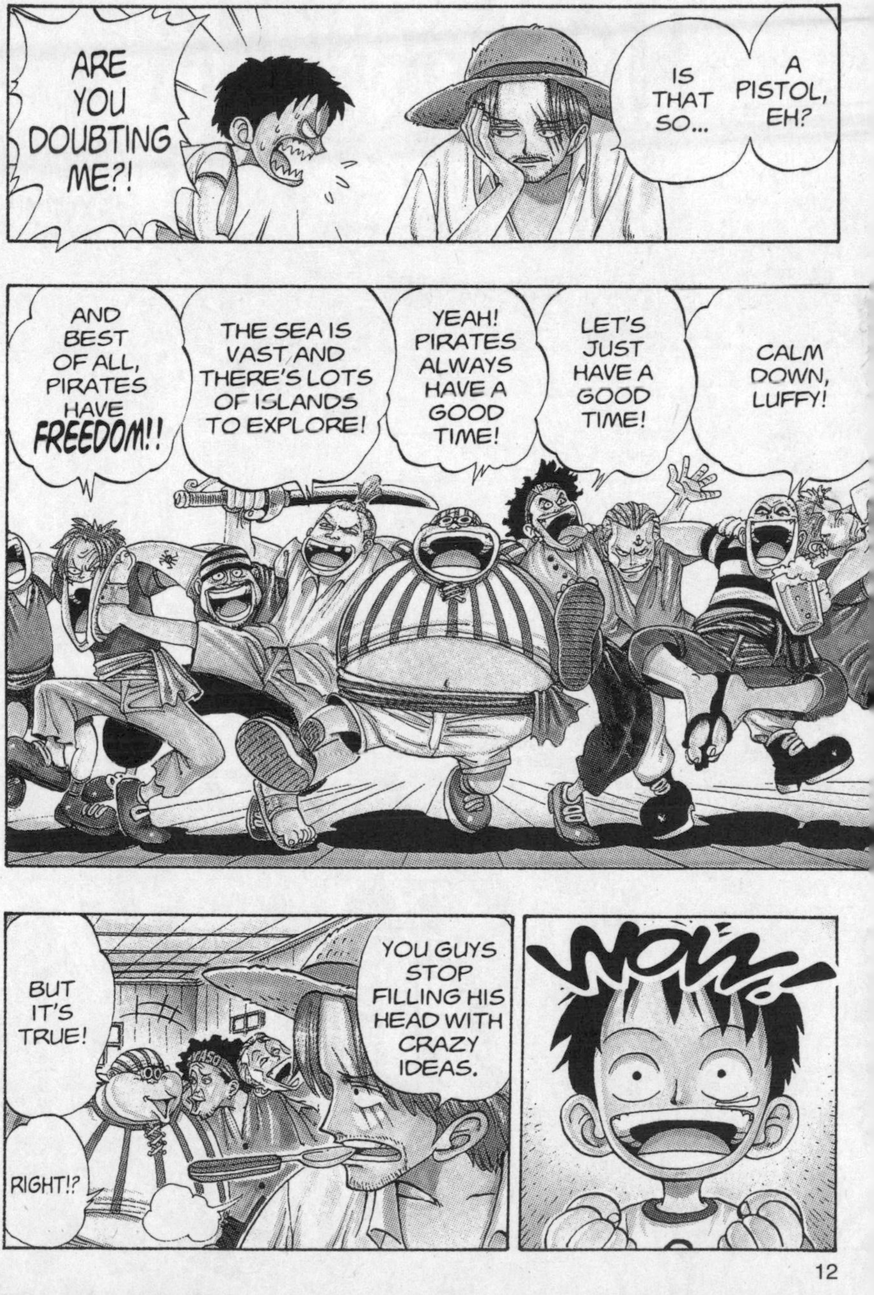
A PISTOL, EH?
IS THAT SO...
ARE YOU DOUBTING ME?!
CALM DOWN, LUFFY!
LET'S JUST HAVE A GOOD TIME!
YEAH! PIRATES ALWAYS HAVE A GOOD TIME!
THE SEA IS VAST AND THERE'S LOTS OF ISLANDS TO EXPLORE!
AND BEST OF ALL, PIRATES HAVE FREEDOM!!
WOW!
YOU GUYS STOP FILLING HIS HEAD WITH CRAZY IDEAS.
BUT IT'S TRUE!
RIGHT!?

READ THIS WAY

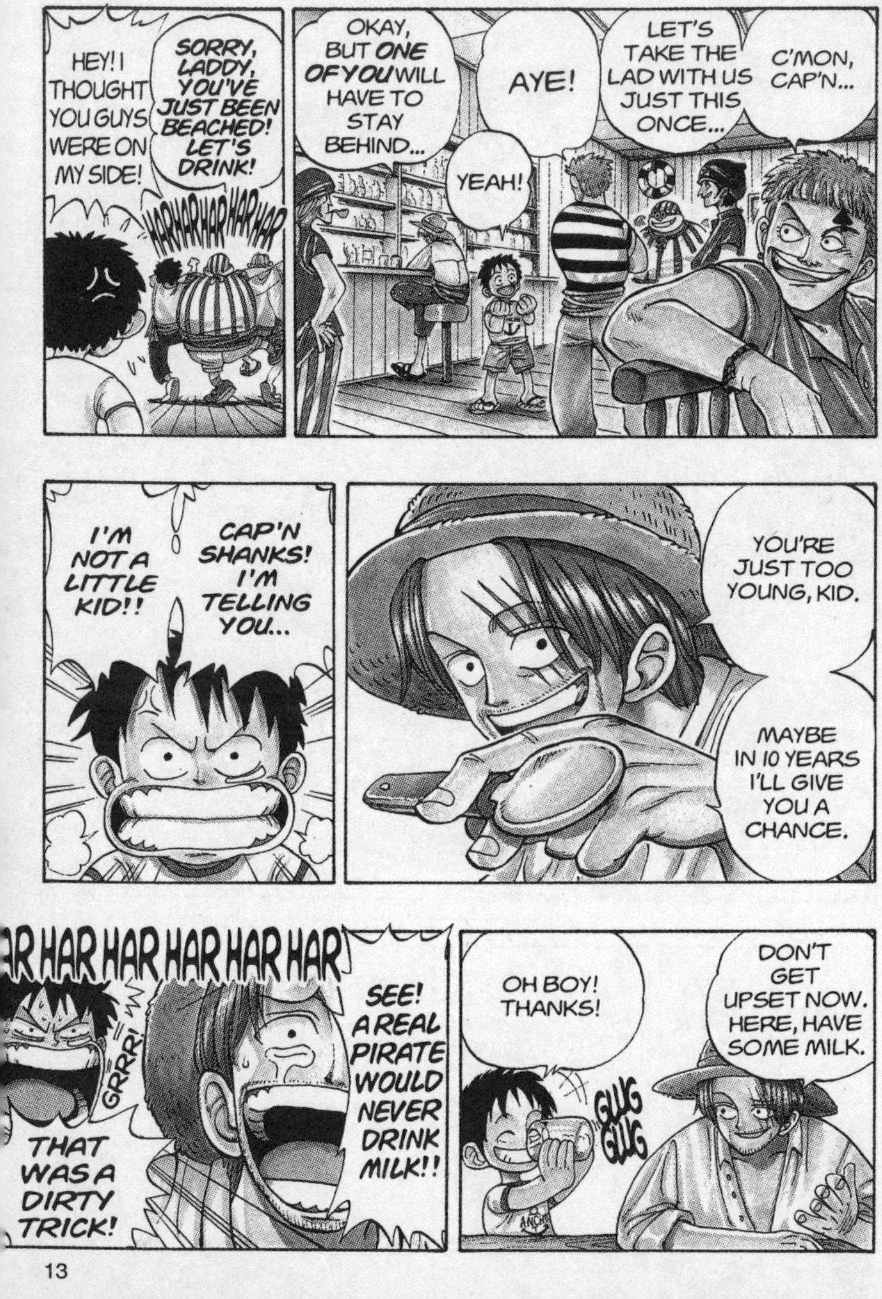
C'MON, CAP'N...
LET'S TAKE THE LAD WITH US JUST THIS ONCE...
AYE!
YEAH!
OKAY, BUT ONE OF YOU WILL HAVE TO STAY BEHIND...
SORRY, LADDY, YOU'VE JUST BEEN BEACHED! LET'S DRINK!
HEY!! I THOUGHT YOU GUYS WERE ON MY SIDE!
HARHARHAR HARHAR
YOU'RE JUST TOO YOUNG, KID.
MAYBE IN 10 YEARS I'LL GIVE YOU A CHANCE.
CAP'N SHANKS! I'M TELLING YOU...
I'M NOT A LITTLE KID!!
DON'T GET UPSET NOW. HERE, HAVE SOME MILK.
OH BOY! THANKS!
GLUG GLUG
AR HAR HAR HAR HAR HAR
SEE! A REAL PIRATE WOULD NEVER DRINK MILK!!
GRRR!
THAT WAS A DIRTY TRICK!

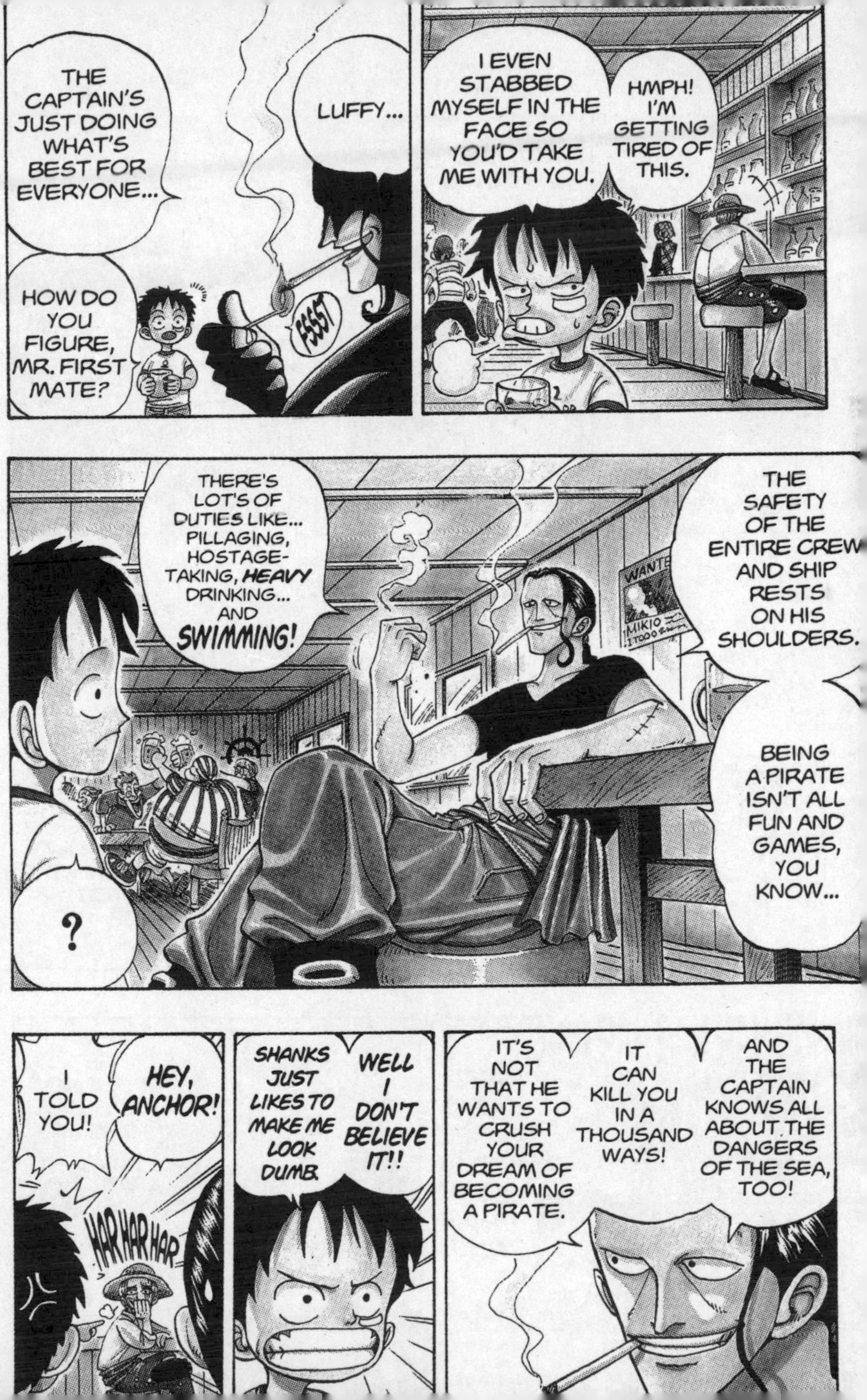
HMPH! I'M GETTING TIRED OF THIS.
I EVEN STABBED MYSELF IN THE FACE SO YOU'D TAKE ME WITH YOU.
LUFFY...
THE CAPTAIN'S JUST DOING WHAT'S BEST FOR EVERYONE...
FSSST
HOW DO YOU FIGURE, MR. FIRST MATE?
THE SAFETY OF THE ENTIRE CREW AND SHIP RESTS ON HIS SHOULDERS.
BEING A PIRATE ISN'T ALL FUN AND GAMES, YOU KNOW...
THERE'S LOT'S OF DUTIES LIKE... PILLAGING, HOSTAGE-TAKING, HEAVY DRINKING... AND SWIMMING!
?
AND THE CAPTAIN KNOWS ALL ABOUT THE DANGERS OF THE SEA, TOO!
IT CAN KILL YOU IN A THOUSAND WAYS!
IT'S NOT THAT HE WANTS TO CRUSH YOUR DREAM OF BECOMING A PIRATE.
WELL I DON'T BELIEVE IT!!
SHANKS JUST LIKES TO MAKE ME LOOK DUMB.
HEY, ANCHOR!
I TOLD YOU!
HAR HAR HAR

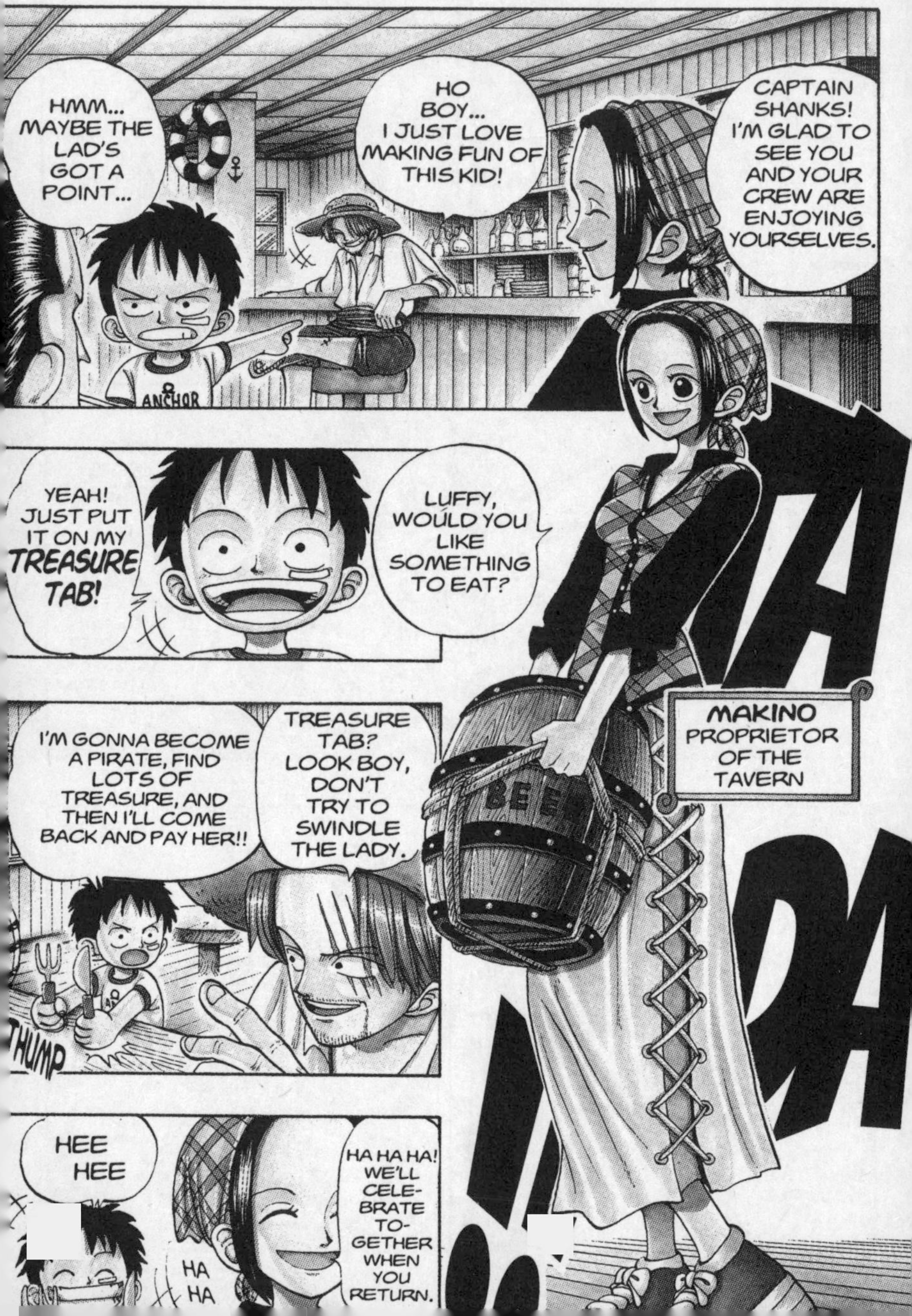
CAPTAIN SHANKS! I'M GLAD TO SEE YOU AND YOUR CREW ARE ENJOYING YOURSELVES.
HO BOY... I JUST LOVE MAKING FUN OF THIS KID!
HMM... MAYBE THE LAD'S GOT A POINT...
ANCHOR
MAKINO PROPRIETOR OF THE TAVERN
LUFFY, WOULD YOU LIKE SOMETHING TO EAT?
YEAH! JUST PUT IT ON MY TREASURE TAB!
TREASURE TAB? LOOK BOY, DON'T TRY TO SWINDLE THE LADY.
I'M GONNA BECOME A PIRATE, FIND LOTS OF TREASURE, AND THEN I'LL COME BACK AND PAY HER!!
THUMP
HA HA HA! WE'LL CELE-BRATE TO-GETHER WHEN YOU RETURN.
HEE HEE
HA HA

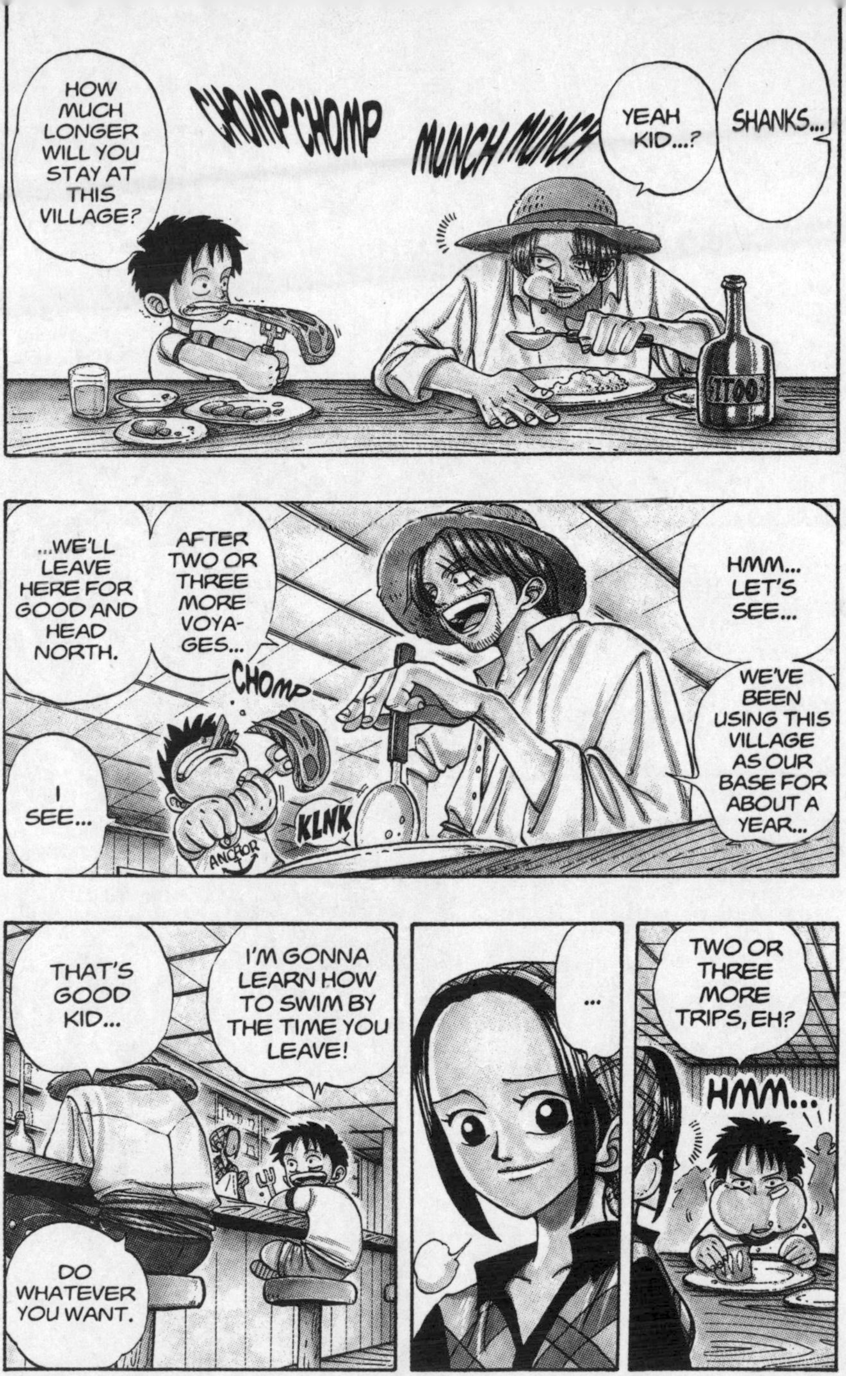
SHANKS...
YEAH KID...?
MUNCH MUNCH
CHOMP CHOMP
HOW MUCH LONGER WILL YOU STAY AT THIS VILLAGE?
HMM... LET'S SEE...
WE'VE BEEN USING THIS VILLAGE AS OUR BASE FOR ABOUT A YEAR...
AFTER TWO OR THREE MORE VOYAGES...
...WE'LL LEAVE HERE FOR GOOD AND HEAD NORTH.
CHOMP
KLNK
I SEE...
ANCHOR
TWO OR THREE MORE TRIPS, EH?
HMM...
...
I'M GONNA LEARN HOW TO SWIM BY THE TIME YOU LEAVE!
THAT'S GOOD KID...
DO WHATEVER YOU WANT.

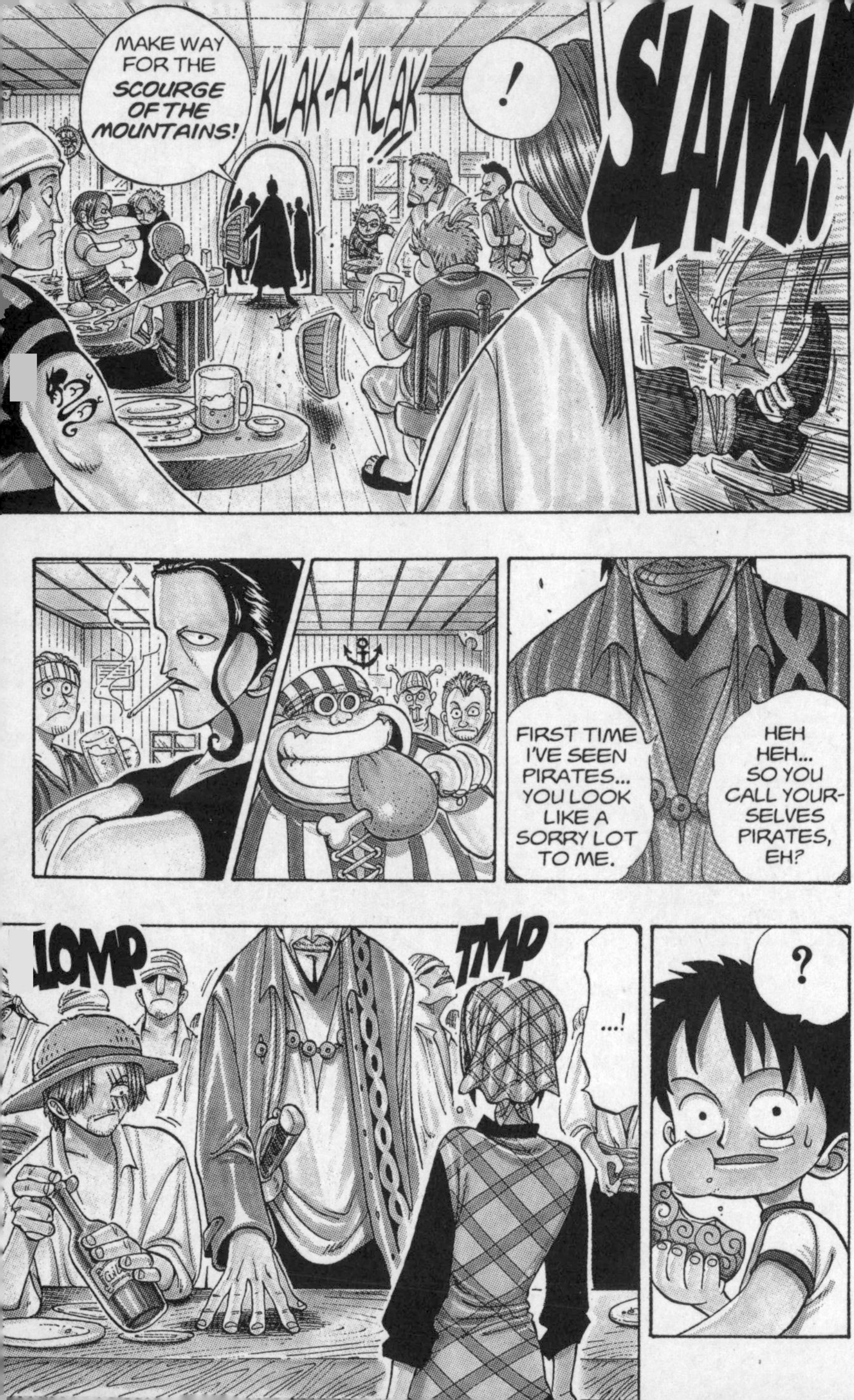
SLAM!!
!
KLAK-A-KLAK
MAKE WAY FOR THE SCOURGE OF THE MOUNTAINS!
HEH HEH... SO YOU CALL YOURSELVES PIRATES, EH?
FIRST TIME I'VE SEEN PIRATES... YOU LOOK LIKE A SORRY LOT TO ME.
?
...!
TMP
LOMP

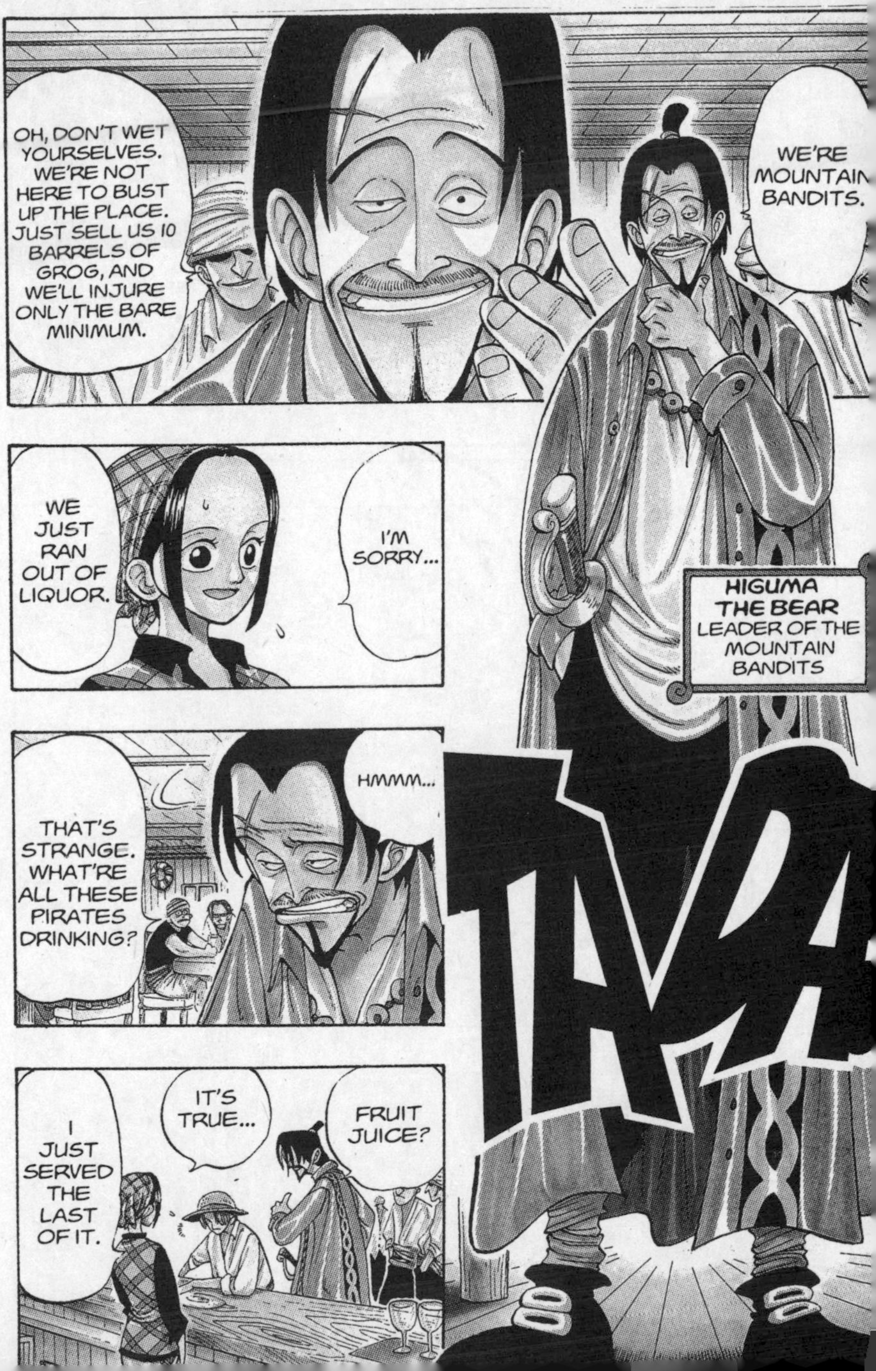
WE'RE MOUNTAIN BANDITS.
HIGUMA THE BEAR
LEADER OF THE MOUNTAIN BANDITS
TAP
OH, DON'T WET YOURSELVES. WE'RE NOT HERE TO BUST UP THE PLACE. JUST SELL US 10 BARRELS OF GROG, AND WE'LL INJURE ONLY THE BARE MINIMUM.
I'M SORRY...
WE JUST RAN OUT OF LIQUOR.
HMMM...
THAT'S STRANGE. WHAT'RE ALL THESE PIRATES DRINKING?
FRUIT JUICE?
IT'S TRUE...
I JUST SERVED THE LAST OF IT.

READ THIS WAY

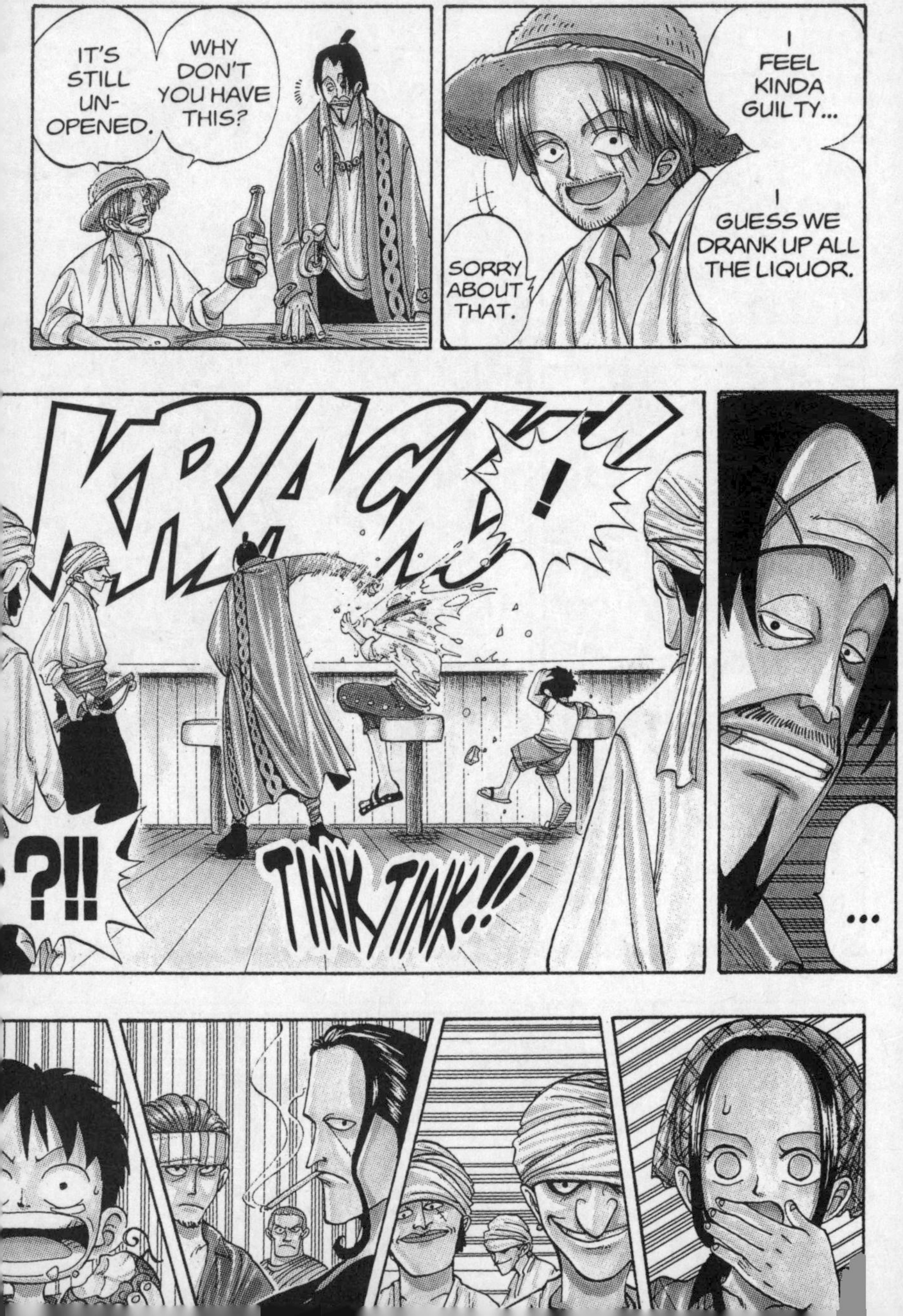
I FEEL KINDA GUILTY...
I GUESS WE DRANK UP ALL THE LIQUOR.
SORRY ABOUT THAT.
WHY DON'T YOU HAVE THIS?
IT'S STILL UN-OPENED.
...
KRACK!
TINK TINK!!
?!!

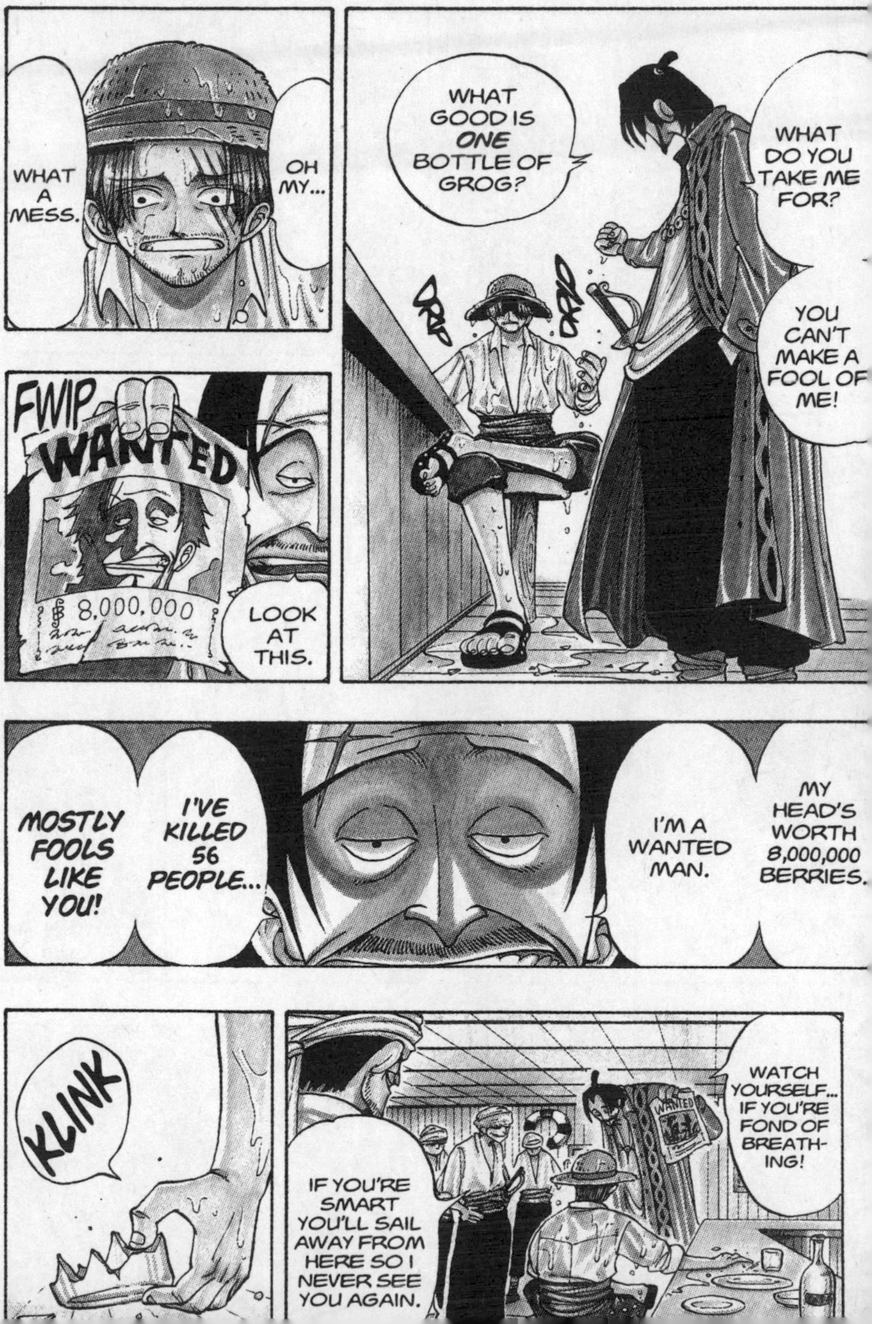
WHAT DO YOU TAKE ME FOR?
WHAT GOOD IS ONE BOTTLE OF GROG?
DRIP
DRIP
YOU CAN'T MAKE A FOOL OF ME!
OH MY...
WHAT A MESS.
FWIP
WANTED
8,000,000
LOOK AT THIS.
MY HEAD'S WORTH 8,000,000 BERRIES.
I'M A WANTED MAN.
I'VE KILLED 56 PEOPLE...
MOSTLY FOOLS LIKE YOU!
WATCH YOURSELF... IF YOU'RE FOND OF BREATH-ING!
IF YOU'RE SMART YOU'LL SAIL AWAY FROM HERE SO I NEVER SEE YOU AGAIN.
KLINK

READ THIS WAY

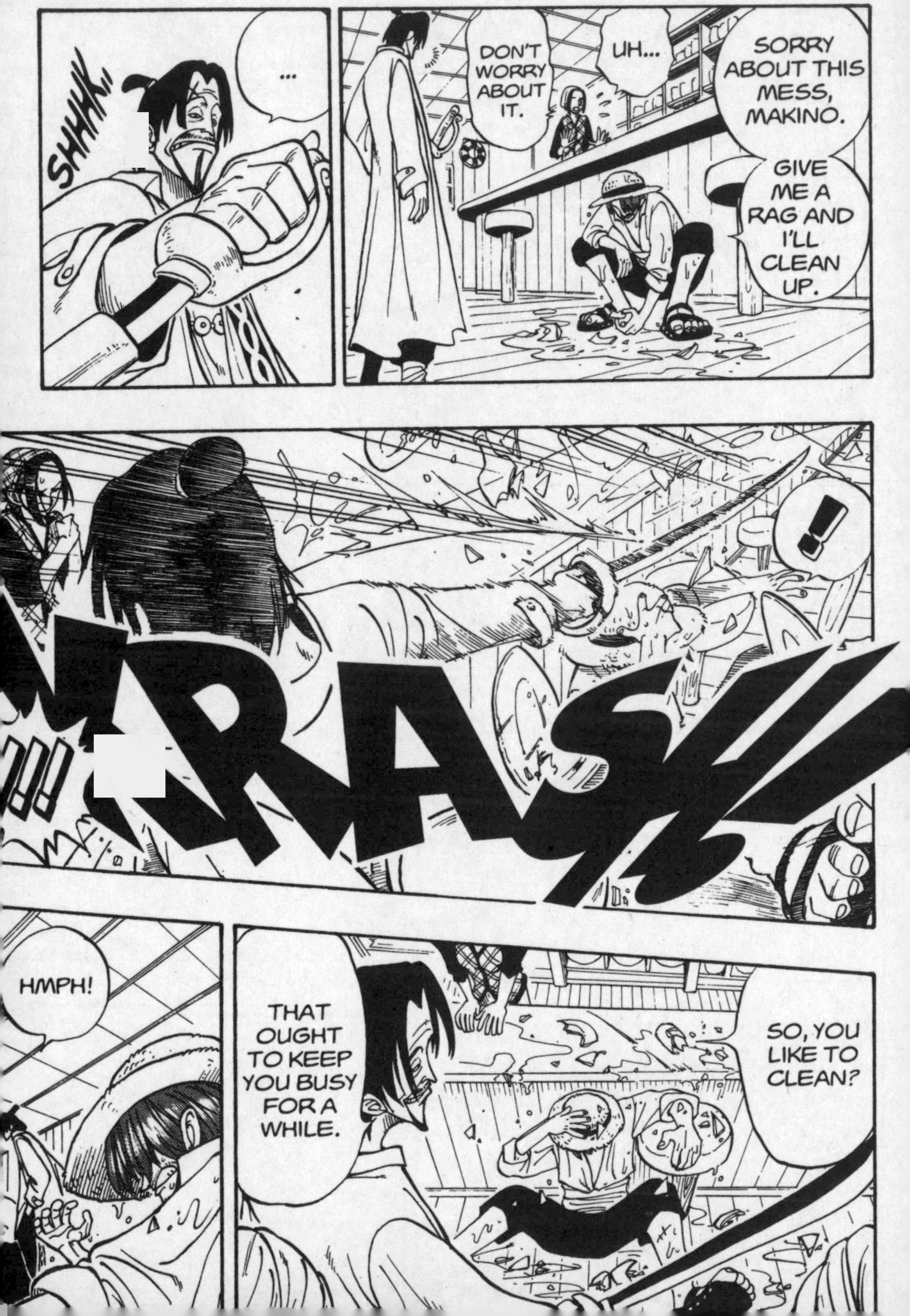
SORRY ABOUT THIS MESS, MAKINO.
GIVE ME A RAG AND I'LL CLEAN UP.
UH...
DON'T WORRY ABOUT IT.
...
SHHK!!
!
RASH!!
SO, YOU LIKE TO CLEAN?
THAT OUGHT TO KEEP YOU BUSY FOR A WHILE.
HMPH!

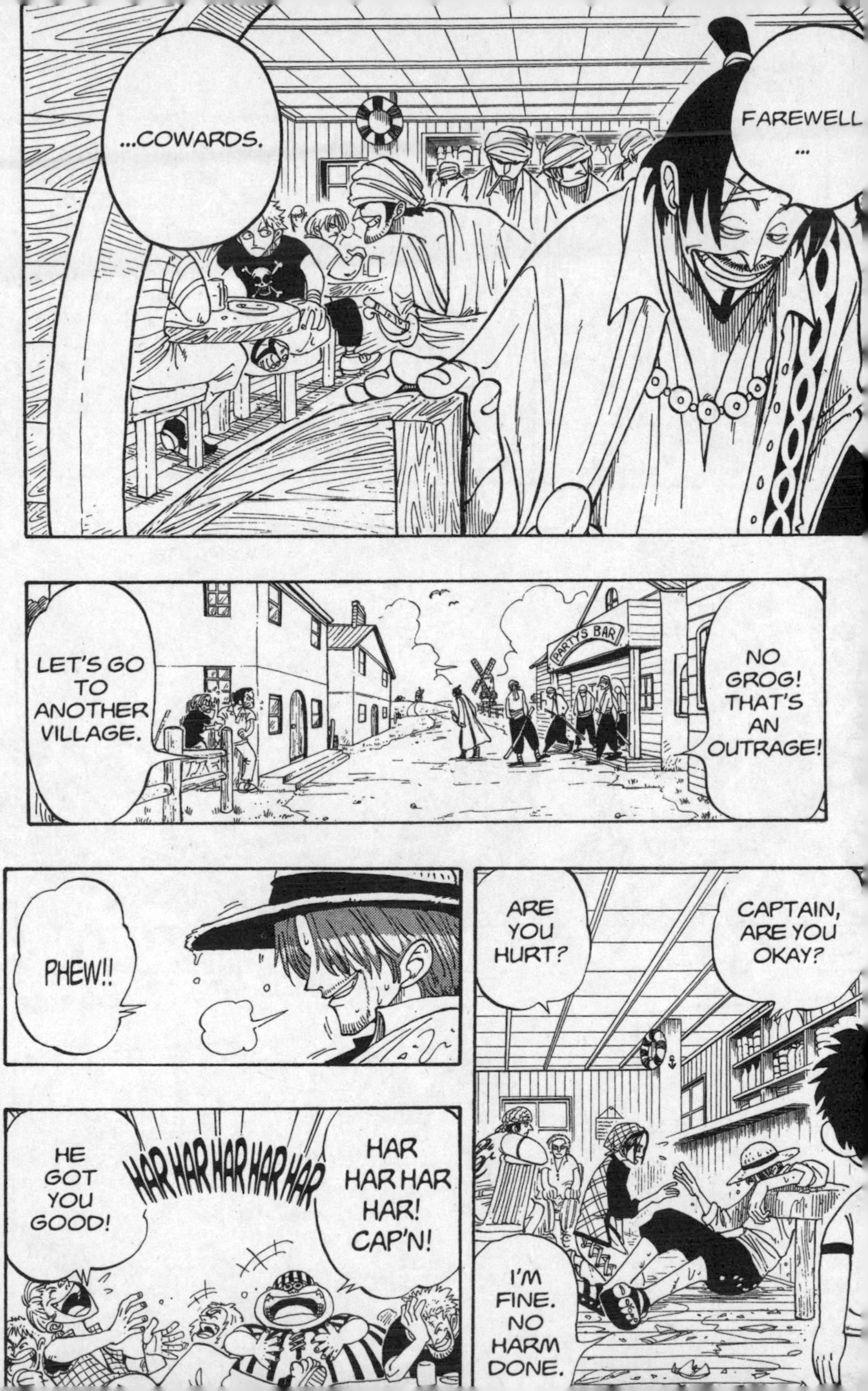
FAREWELL ...
...COWARDS.
NO GROG! THAT'S AN OUTRAGE!
PARTY'S BAR
LET'S GO TO ANOTHER VILLAGE.
CAPTAIN, ARE YOU OKAY?
ARE YOU HURT?
I'M FINE. NO HARM DONE.
PHEW!!
HAR HAR HAR HAR! CAP'N!
HAR HAR HAR HAR HAR
HE GOT YOU GOOD!

READ THIS WAY

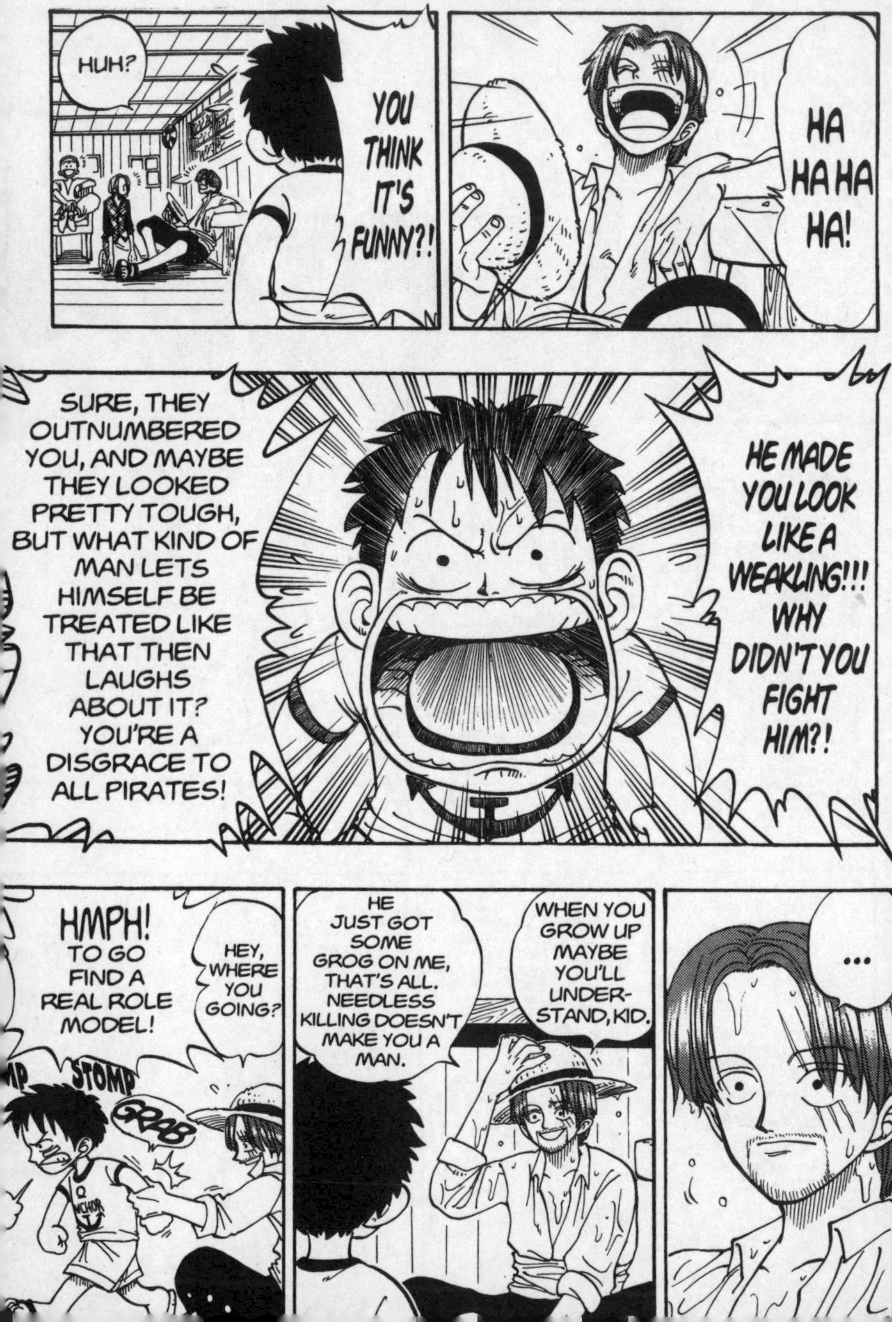

HA HA HA HA!
YOU THINK IT'S FUNNY?!
HUH?
HE MADE YOU LOOK LIKE A WEAKLING!!! WHY DIDN'T YOU FIGHT HIM?!
SURE, THEY OUTNUMBERED YOU, AND MAYBE THEY LOOKED PRETTY TOUGH, BUT WHAT KIND OF MAN LETS HIMSELF BE TREATED LIKE THAT THEN LAUGHS ABOUT IT? YOU'RE A DISGRACE TO ALL PIRATES!
...
WHEN YOU GROW UP MAYBE YOU'LL UNDERSTAND, KID.
HE JUST GOT SOME GROG ON ME, THAT'S ALL. NEEDLESS KILLING DOESN'T MAKE YOU A MAN.
HEY, WHERE YOU GOING?
HMPH! TO GO FIND A REAL ROLE MODEL!
STOMP
GRAB

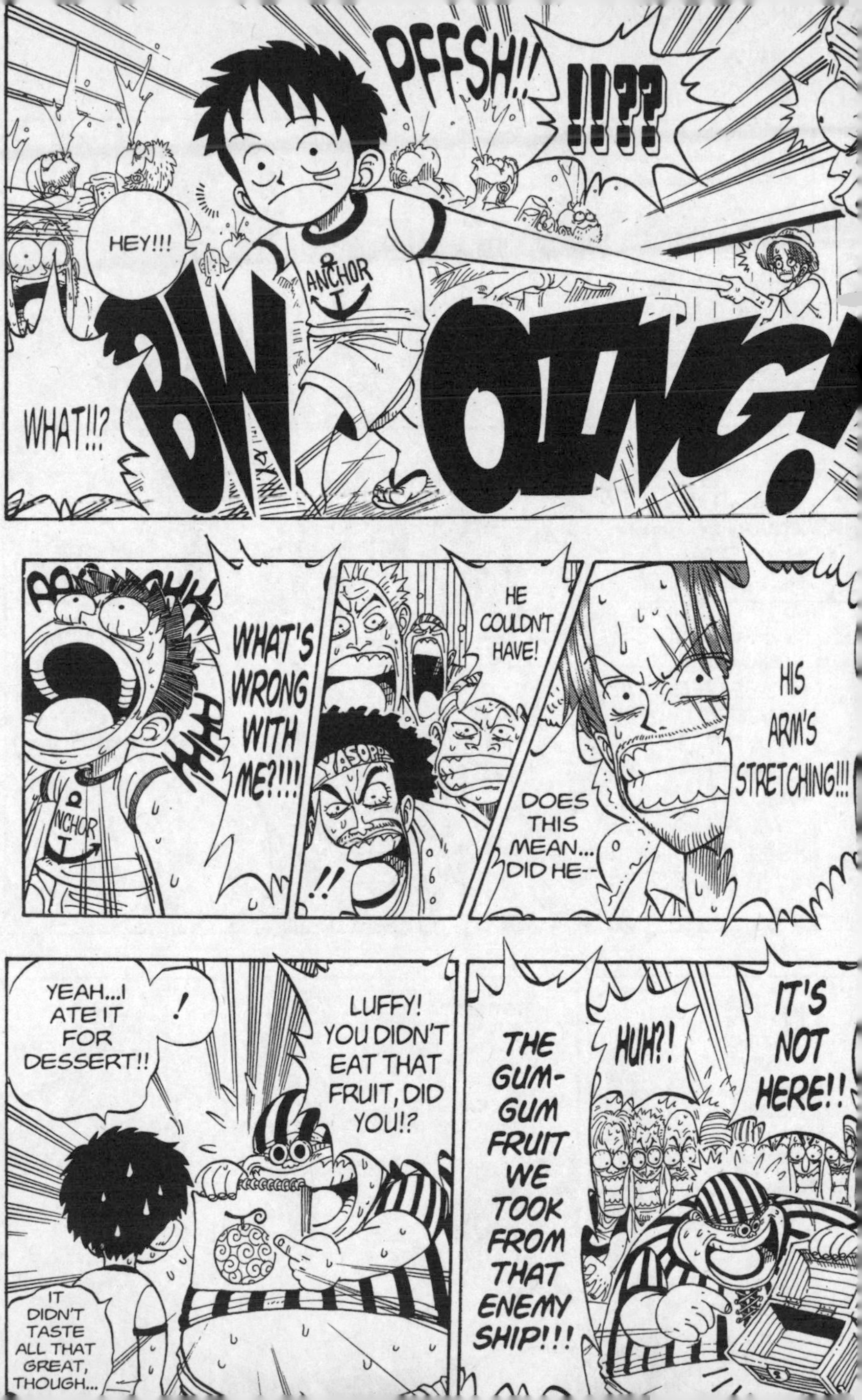
!!??
PFFSH!!
HEY!!!
BWOING!
WHAT!!?
HIS ARM'S STRETCHING!!!
DOES THIS MEAN... DID HE--
HE COULDN'T HAVE!
WHAT'S WRONG WITH ME?!!!
!!
IT'S NOT HERE!!
HUH?!
THE GUM-GUM FRUIT WE TOOK FROM THAT ENEMY SHIP!!!
LUFFY! YOU DIDN'T EAT THAT FRUIT, DID YOU!?
!
YEAH...I ATE IT FOR DESSERT!!
IT DIDN'T TASTE ALL THAT GREAT, THOUGH...

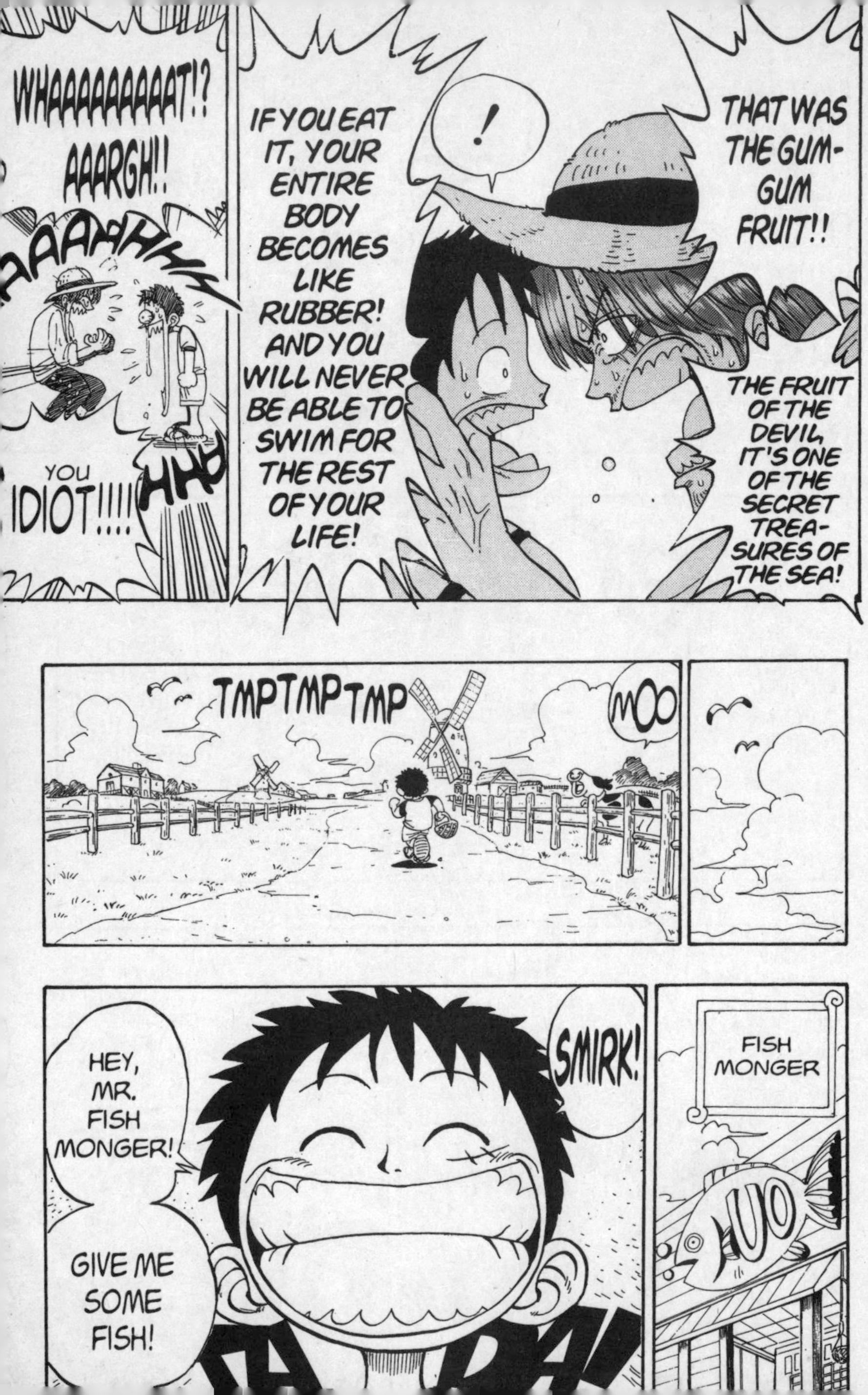
THAT WAS THE GUM-GUM FRUIT!!
THE FRUIT OF THE DEVIL, IT'S ONE OF THE SECRET TREA-SURES OF THE SEA!
!
IF YOU EAT IT, YOUR ENTIRE BODY BECOMES LIKE RUBBER! AND YOU WILL NEVER BE ABLE TO SWIM FOR THE REST OF YOUR LIFE!
WHAAAAAAAAAT!?
AAARGH!!
YOU IDIOT!!!!!....
MOO
TMPTMPTMP
FISH MONGER
UO
SMIRK!
HEY, MR. FISH MONGER!
GIVE ME SOME FISH!

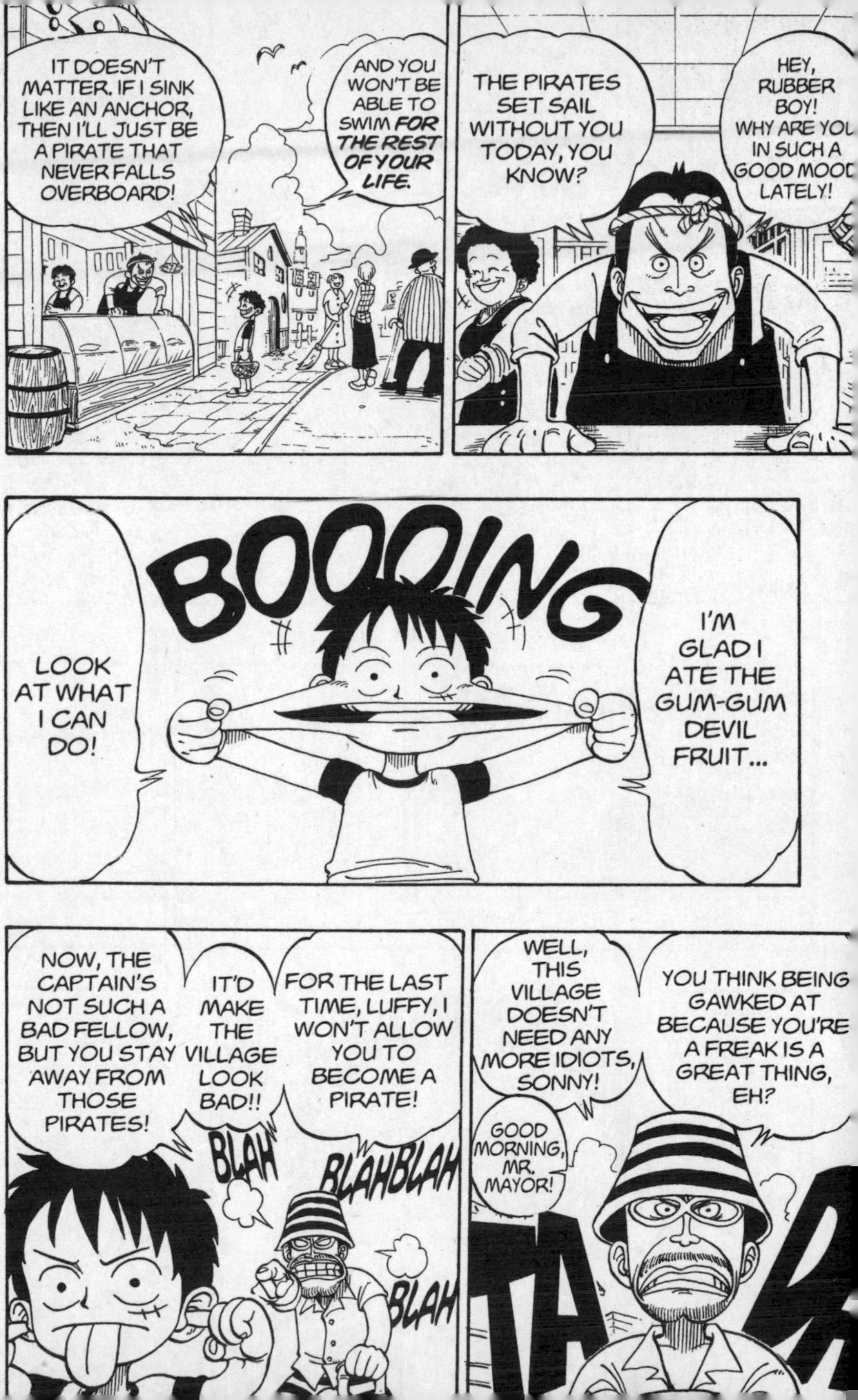
HEY, RUBBER BOY! WHY ARE YOU IN SUCH A GOOD MOOD LATELY!
THE PIRATES SET SAIL WITHOUT YOU TODAY, YOU KNOW?
AND YOU WON'T BE ABLE TO SWIM *FOR THE REST OF YOUR LIFE.*
IT DOESN'T MATTER. IF I SINK LIKE AN ANCHOR, THEN I'LL JUST BE A PIRATE THAT NEVER FALLS OVERBOARD!
I'M GLAD I ATE THE GUM-GUM DEVIL FRUIT...
BOOOING
LOOK AT WHAT I CAN DO!
YOU THINK BEING GAWKED AT BECAUSE YOU'RE A FREAK IS A GREAT THING, EH?
WELL, THIS VILLAGE DOESN'T NEED ANY MORE IDIOTS, SONNY!
GOOD MORNING, MR. MAYOR!
FOR THE LAST TIME, LUFFY, I WON'T ALLOW YOU TO BECOME A PIRATE!
IT'D MAKE THE VILLAGE LOOK BAD!!
NOW, THE CAPTAIN'S NOT SUCH A BAD FELLOW, BUT YOU STAY AWAY FROM THOSE PIRATES!
BLAH
BLAHBLAH
BLAH

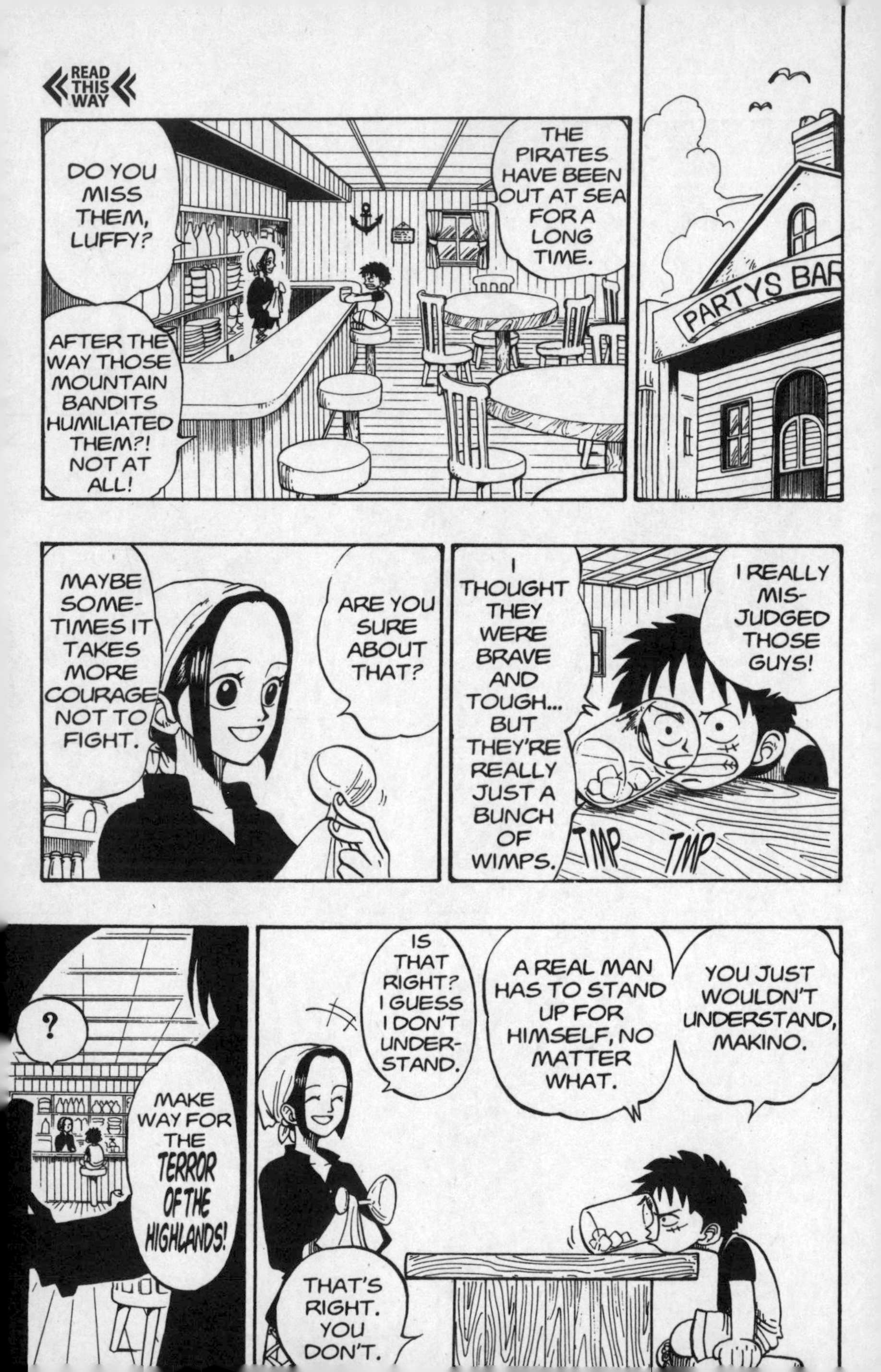
READ THIS WAY
PARTYS BAR
THE PIRATES HAVE BEEN OUT AT SEA FOR A LONG TIME.
DO YOU MISS THEM, LUFFY?
AFTER THE WAY THOSE MOUNTAIN BANDITS HUMILIATED THEM?! NOT AT ALL!
I REALLY MIS-JUDGED THOSE GUYS!
I THOUGHT THEY WERE BRAVE AND TOUGH... BUT THEY'RE REALLY JUST A BUNCH OF WIMPS.
TMP TMP
ARE YOU SURE ABOUT THAT?
MAYBE SOME-TIMES IT TAKES MORE COURAGE NOT TO FIGHT.
YOU JUST WOULDN'T UNDERSTAND, MAKINO.
A REAL MAN HAS TO STAND UP FOR HIMSELF, NO MATTER WHAT.
IS THAT RIGHT? I GUESS I DON'T UNDER-STAND.
THAT'S RIGHT. YOU DON'T.
?
MAKE WAY FOR THE TERROR OF THE HIGHLANDS!

READ THIS WAY

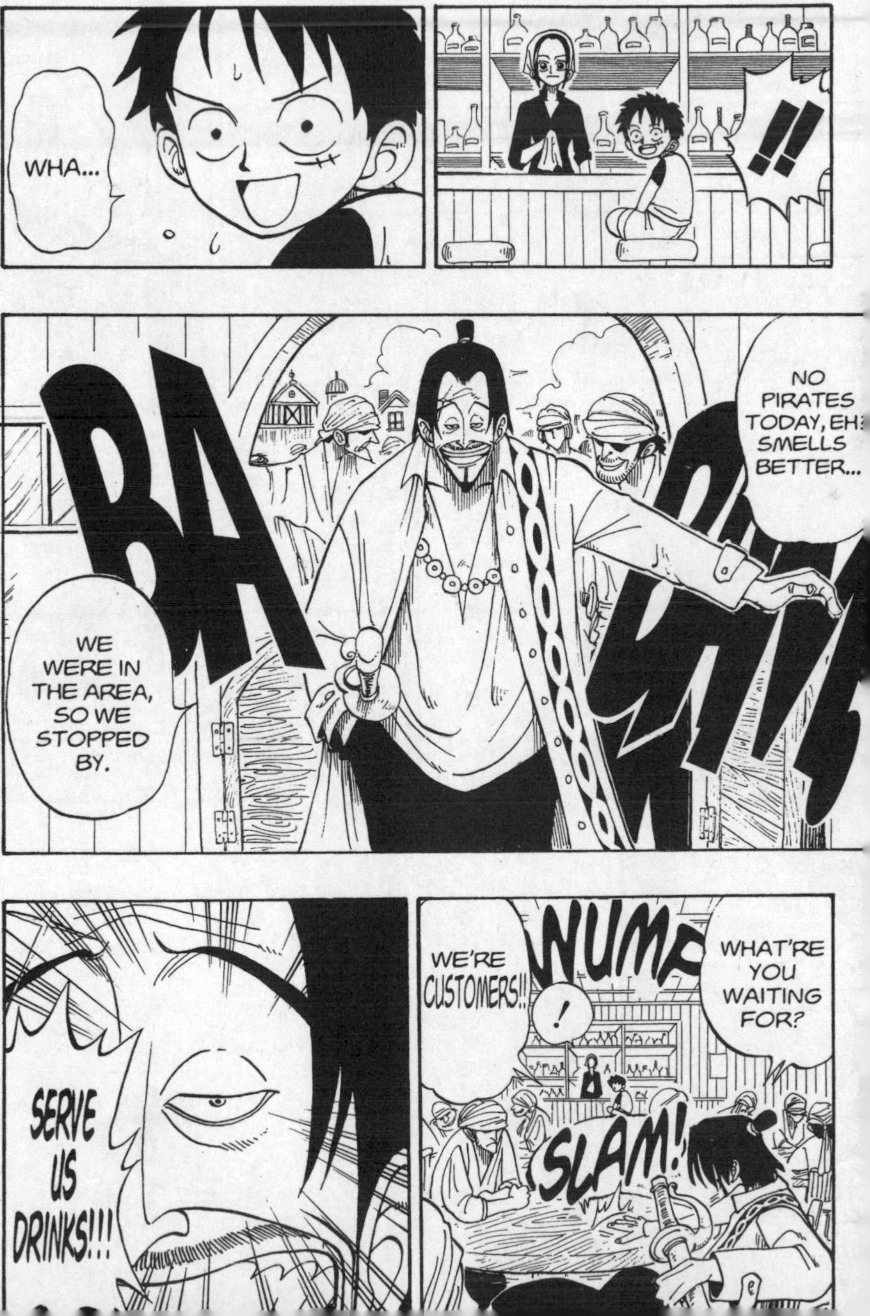
!!
WHA...
NO PIRATES TODAY, EH
SMELLS BETTER...
WE WERE IN THE AREA, SO WE STOPPED BY.
WHAT'RE YOU WAITING FOR?
WUMP
!
WE'RE CUSTOMERS!!
SLAM!
SERVE US DRINKS!!!

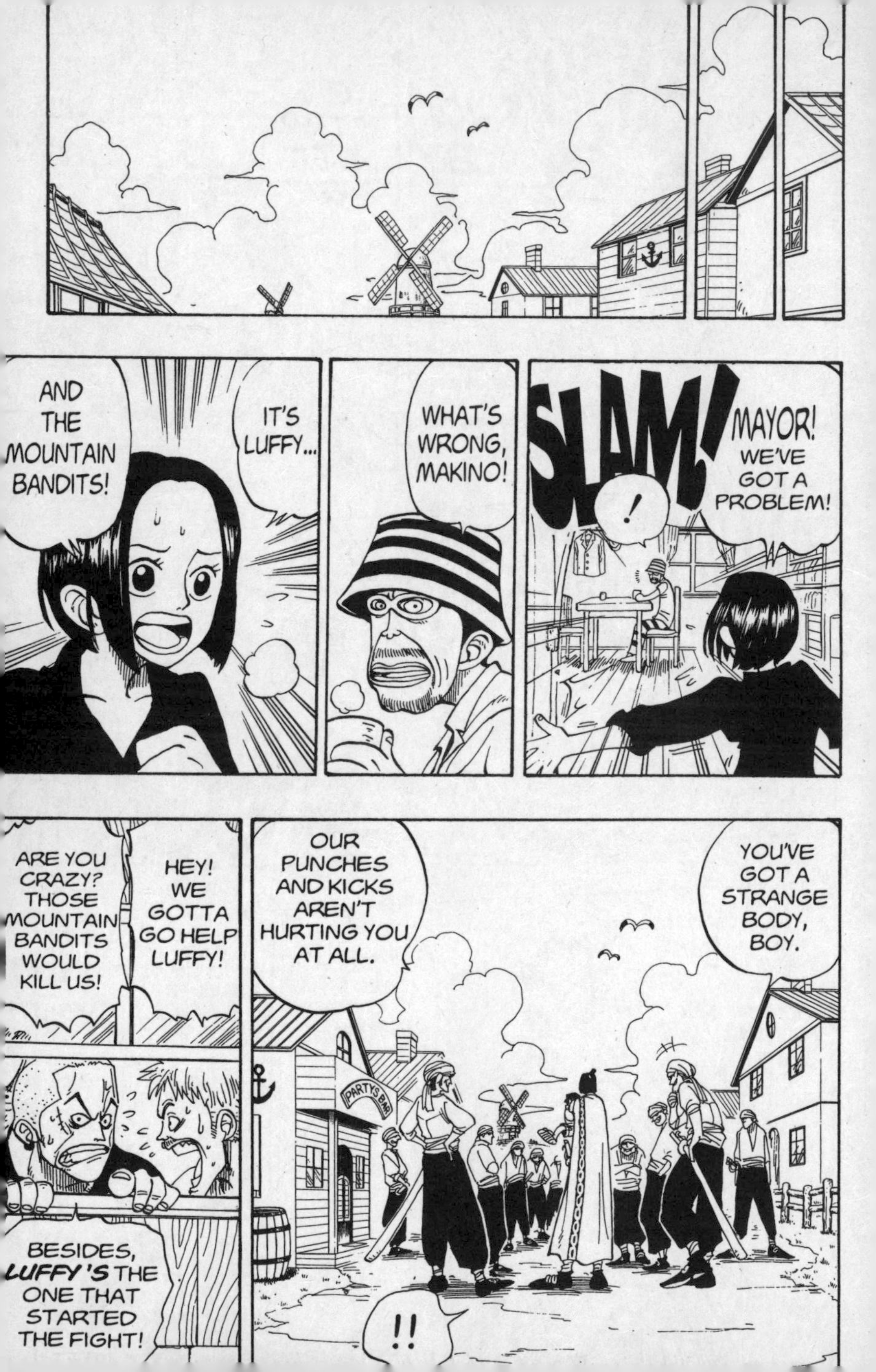
SLAM!
MAYOR! WE'VE GOT A PROBLEM!
!
WHAT'S WRONG, MAKINO!
IT'S LUFFY...
AND THE MOUNTAIN BANDITS!
YOU'VE GOT A STRANGE BODY, BOY.
OUR PUNCHES AND KICKS AREN'T HURTING YOU AT ALL.
PARTYS BAR
!!
HEY! WE GOTTA GO HELP LUFFY!
ARE YOU CRAZY? THOSE MOUNTAIN BANDITS WOULD KILL US!
BESIDES, LUFFY'S THE ONE THAT STARTED THE FIGHT!

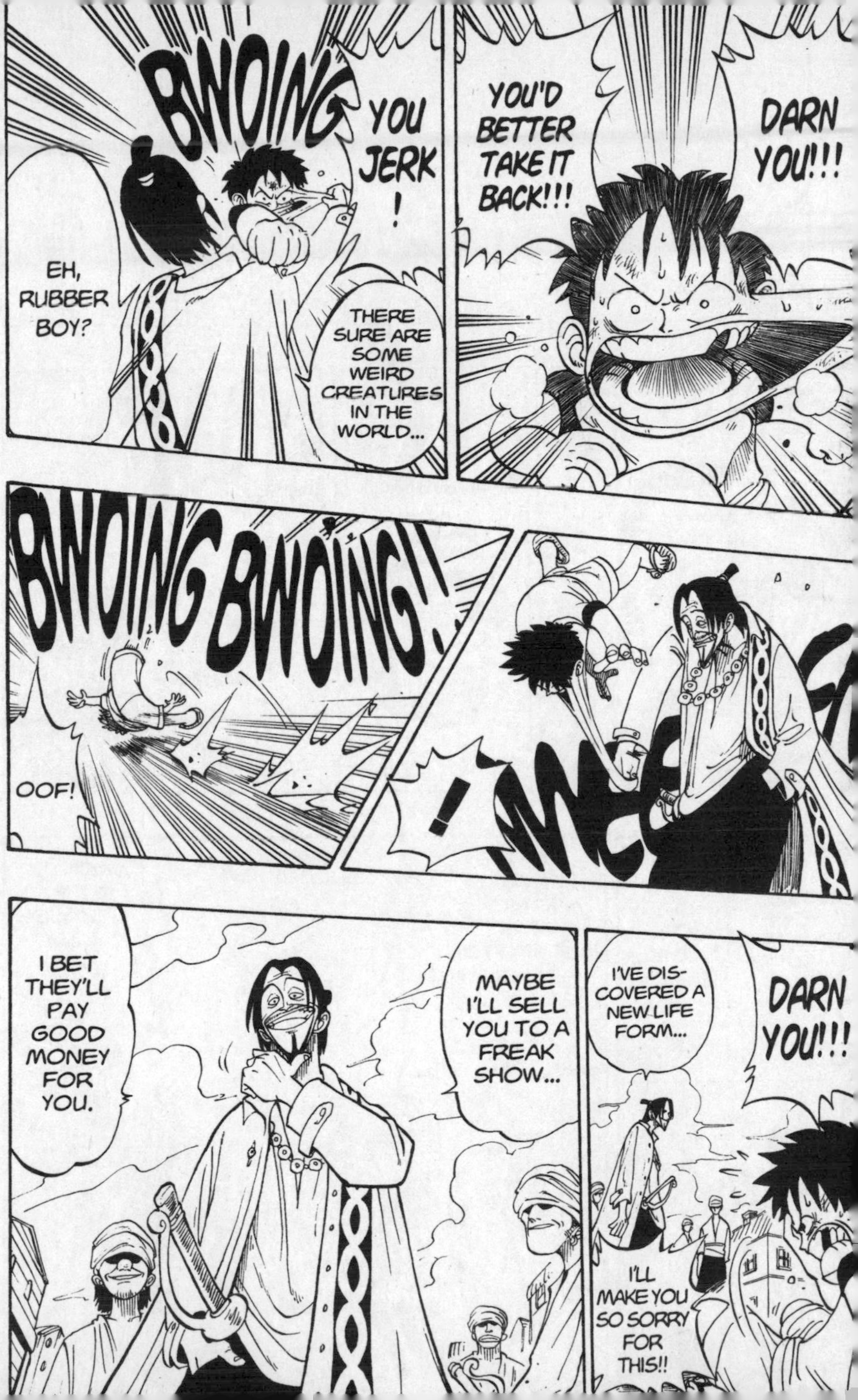
DARN YOU!!!
YOU'D BETTER TAKE IT BACK!!!
BWOING
YOU JERK!
THERE SURE ARE SOME WEIRD CREATURES IN THE WORLD...
EH, RUBBER BOY?
!
BWOING BWOING!!
OOF!
DARN YOU!!!
I'VE DIS-COVERED A NEW LIFE FORM...
I'LL MAKE YOU SO SORRY FOR THIS!!
MAYBE I'LL SELL YOU TO A FREAK SHOW...
I BET THEY'LL PAY GOOD MONEY FOR YOU.

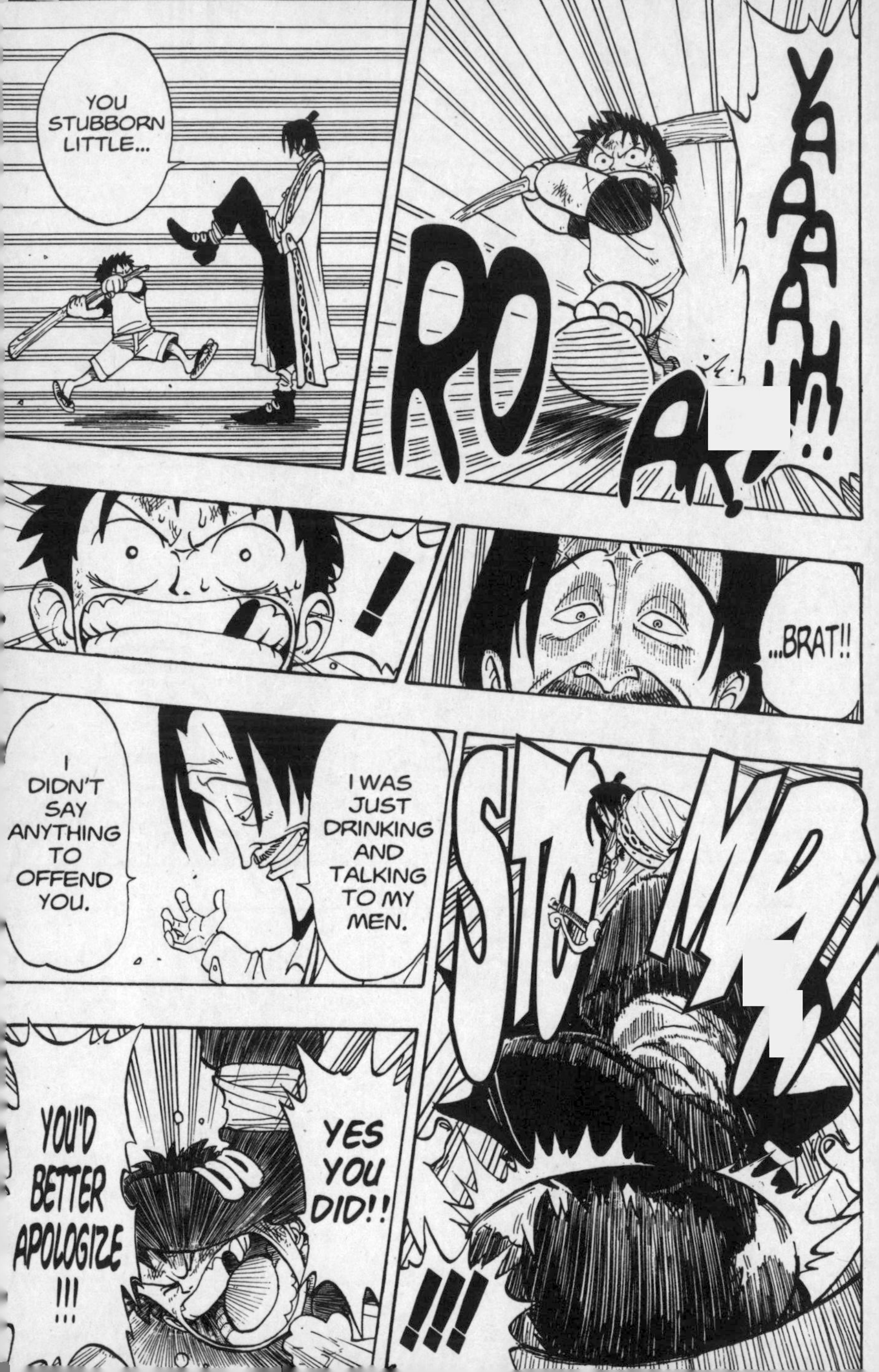
YAAAAH!!
ROAR!
YOU STUBBORN LITTLE...
...BRAT!!
!
STOMP
!!!
I WAS JUST DRINKING AND TALKING TO MY MEN.
I DIDN'T SAY ANYTHING TO OFFEND YOU.
YES YOU DID!!
YOU'D BETTER APOLOGIZE!!!

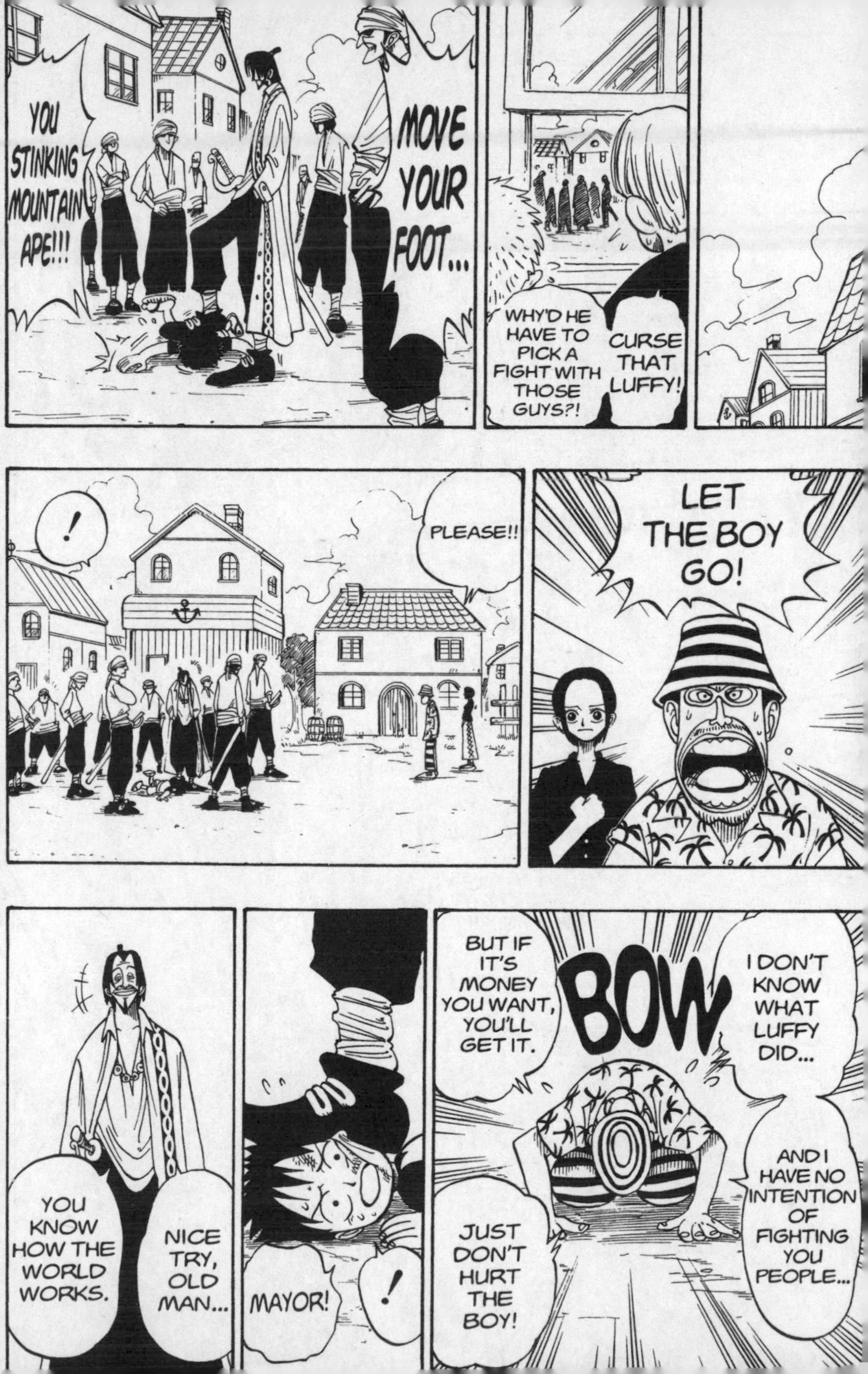
CURSE THAT LUFFY!
WHY'D HE HAVE TO PICK A FIGHT WITH THOSE GUYS?!
MOVE YOUR FOOT...
YOU STINKING MOUNTAIN APE!!!
LET THE BOY GO!
PLEASE!!
!
I DON'T KNOW WHAT LUFFY DID...
BOW
BUT IF IT'S MONEY YOU WANT, YOU'LL GET IT.
AND I HAVE NO INTENTION OF FIGHTING YOU PEOPLE...
JUST DON'T HURT THE BOY!
!
MAYOR!
NICE TRY, OLD MAN...
YOU KNOW HOW THE WORLD WORKS.

READ THIS WAY

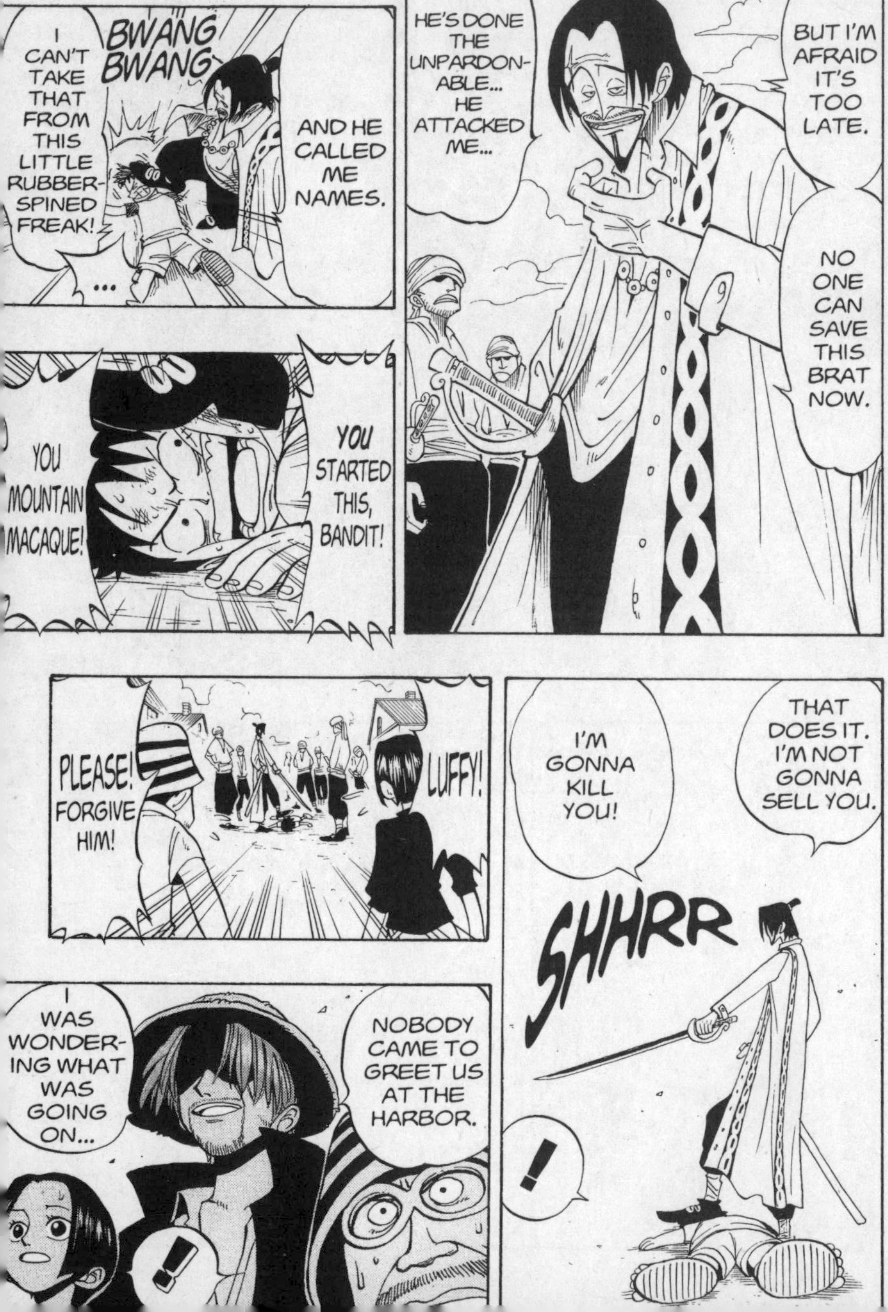
BUT I'M AFRAID IT'S TOO LATE.
HE'S DONE THE UNPARDON-ABLE... HE ATTACKED ME...
NO ONE CAN SAVE THIS BRAT NOW.
AND HE CALLED ME NAMES.
BWANG BWANG
I CAN'T TAKE THAT FROM THIS LITTLE RUBBER-SPINED FREAK!
...
YOU STARTED THIS, BANDIT!
YOU MOUNTAIN MACAQUE!
THAT DOES IT. I'M NOT GONNA SELL YOU.
I'M GONNA KILL YOU!
SHHRR
!
LUFFY!
PLEASE! FORGIVE HIM!
NOBODY CAME TO GREET US AT THE HARBOR.
I WAS WONDER-ING WHAT WAS GOING ON...
!

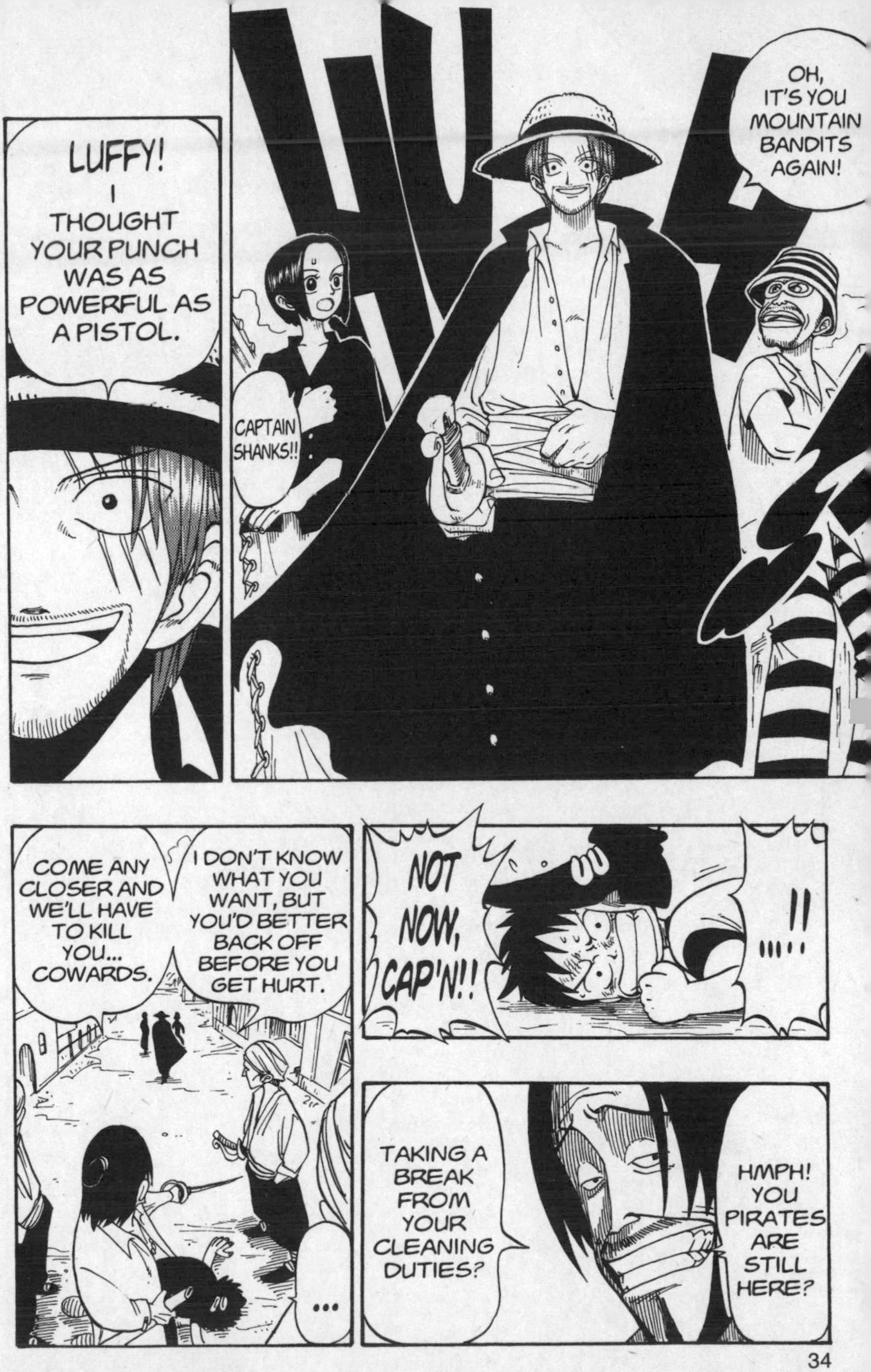
OH, IT'S YOU MOUNTAIN BANDITS AGAIN!
CAPTAIN SHANKS!!
LUFFY! I THOUGHT YOUR PUNCH WAS AS POWERFUL AS A PISTOL.
!!
NOT NOW, CAP'N!!
HMPH! YOU PIRATES ARE STILL HERE?
TAKING A BREAK FROM YOUR CLEANING DUTIES?
...
I DON'T KNOW WHAT YOU WANT, BUT YOU'D BETTER BACK OFF BEFORE YOU GET HURT.
COME ANY CLOSER AND WE'LL HAVE TO KILL YOU... COWARDS.

READ THIS WAY

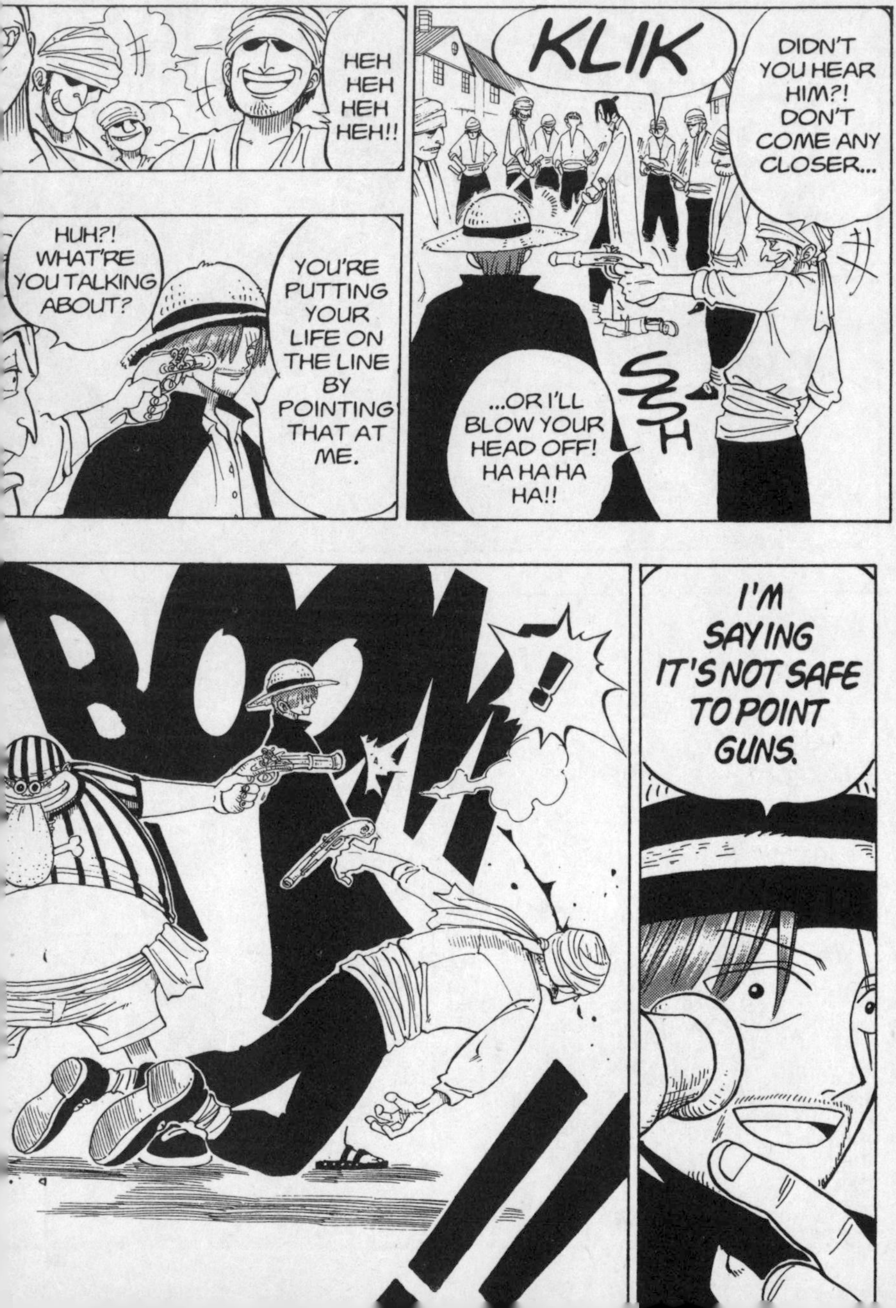
DIDN'T YOU HEAR HIM?! DON'T COME ANY CLOSER...
KLIK
...OR I'LL BLOW YOUR HEAD OFF! HA HA HA HA!!
SSH
HEH HEH HEH HEH!!
YOU'RE PUTTING YOUR LIFE ON THE LINE BY POINTING THAT AT ME.
HUH?! WHAT'RE YOU TALKING ABOUT?
I'M SAYING IT'S NOT SAFE TO POINT GUNS.
BOOM
!

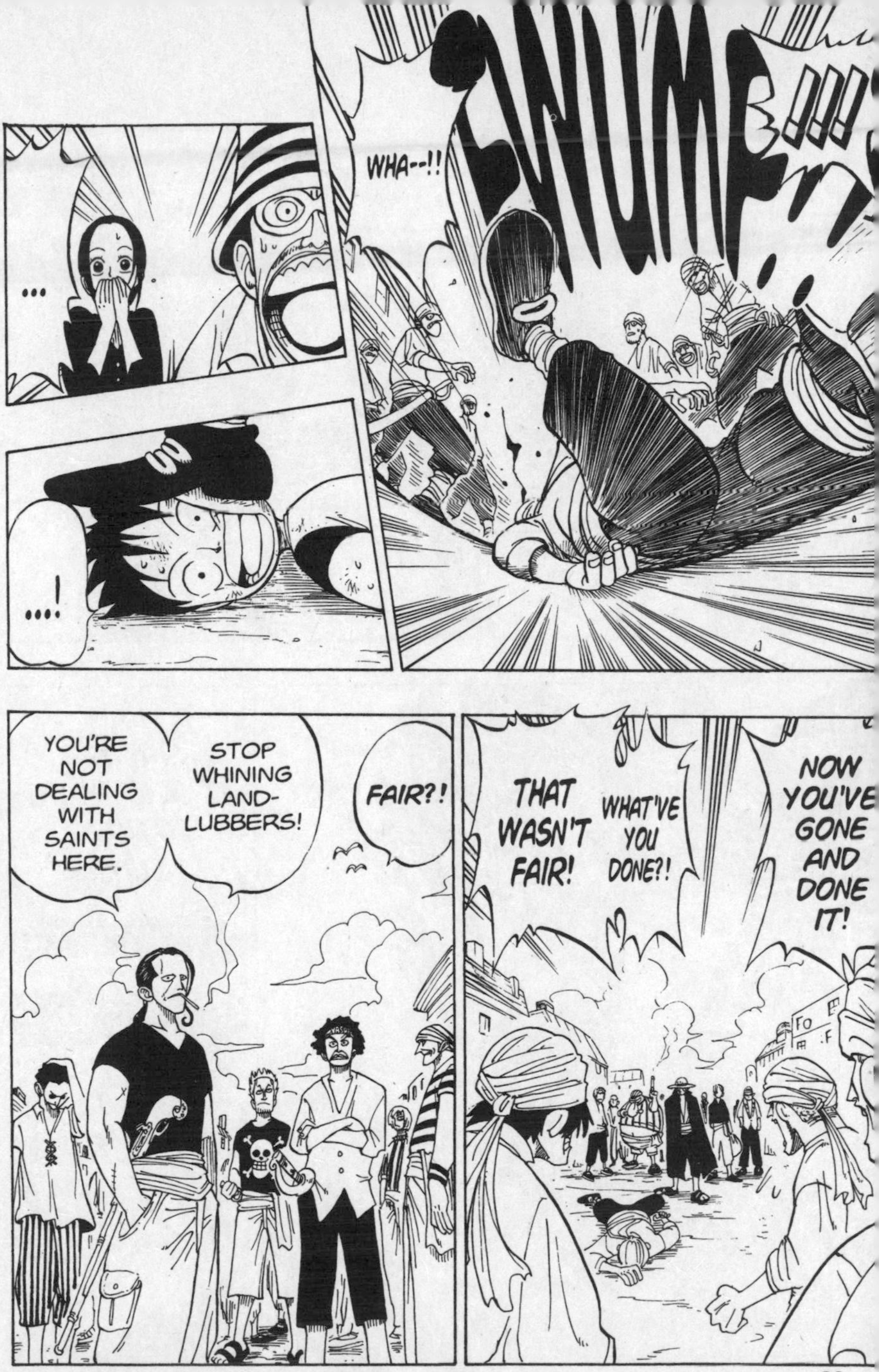
WHA--!!
...
...!
NOW YOU'VE GONE AND DONE IT!
WHAT'VE YOU DONE?!
THAT WASN'T FAIR!
FAIR?!
STOP WHINING LANDLUBBERS!
YOU'RE NOT DEALING WITH SAINTS HERE.

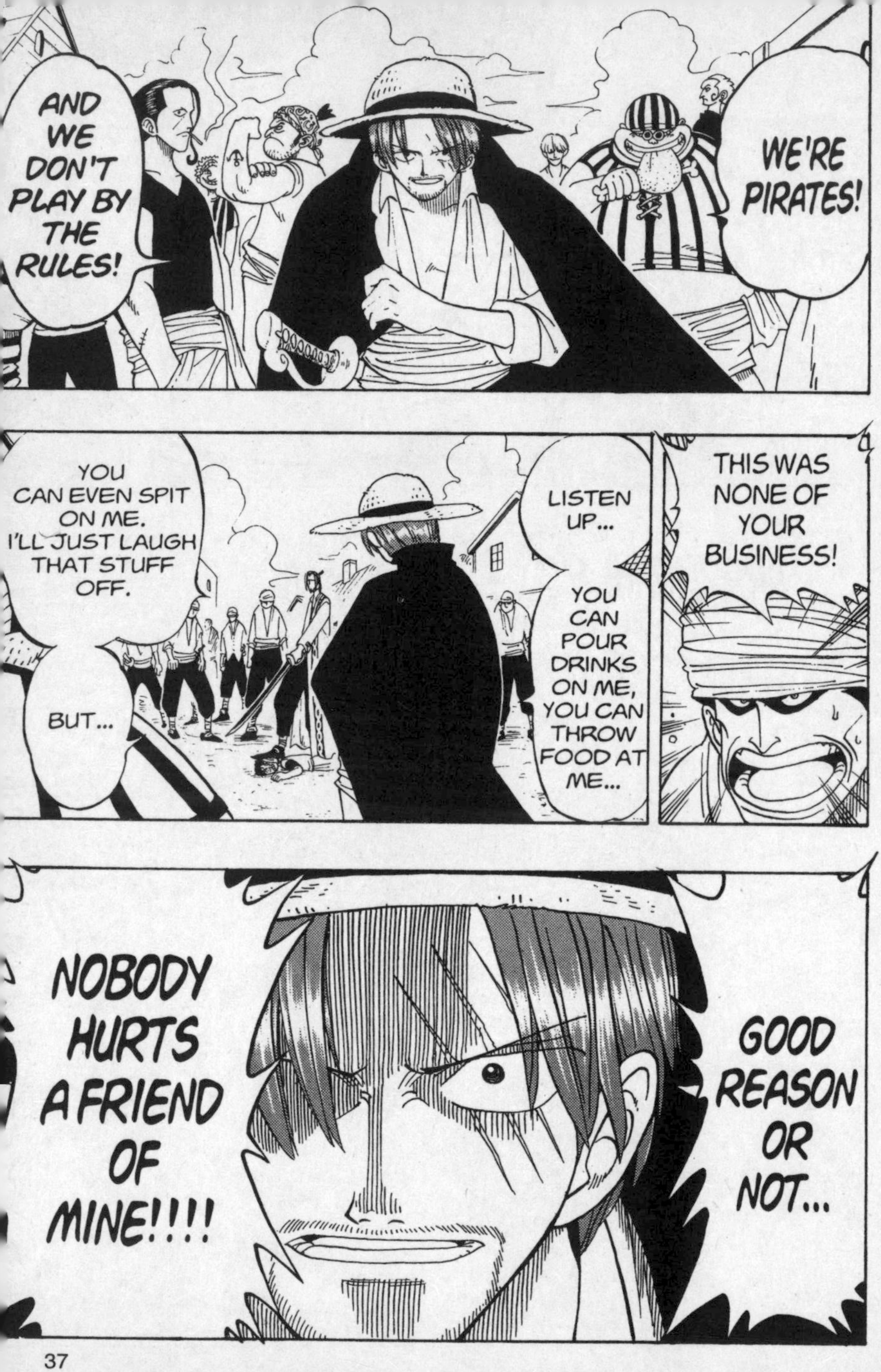
WE'RE PIRATES!
AND WE DON'T PLAY BY THE RULES!
THIS WAS NONE OF YOUR BUSINESS!
LISTEN UP...
YOU CAN POUR DRINKS ON ME, YOU CAN THROW FOOD AT ME...
YOU CAN EVEN SPIT ON ME. I'LL JUST LAUGH THAT STUFF OFF.
BUT...
GOOD REASON OR NOT...
NOBODY HURTS A FRIEND OF MINE!!!!

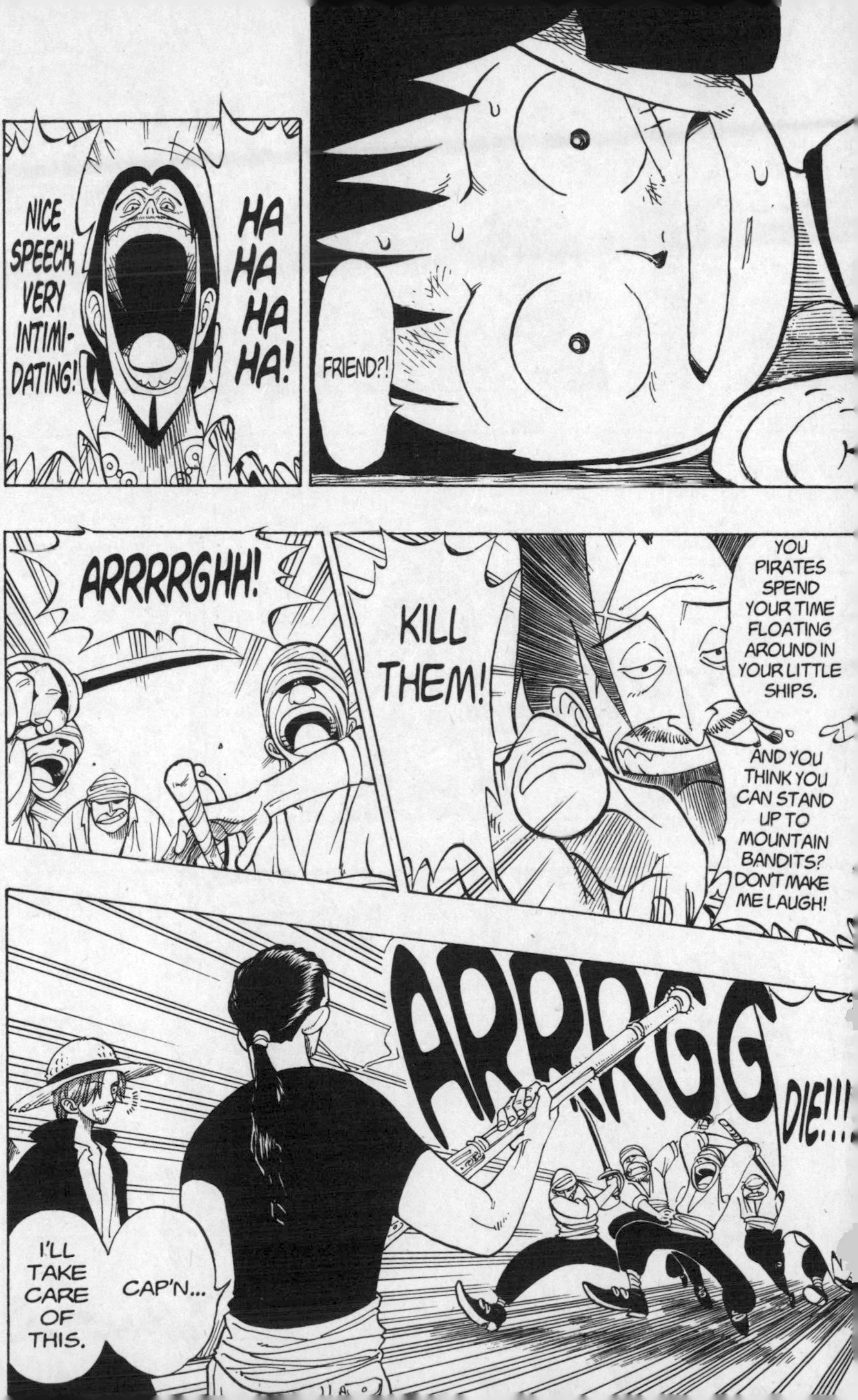
FRIEND?!
HA HA HA HA!
NICE SPEECH, VERY INTIMI-DATING!
YOU PIRATES SPEND YOUR TIME FLOATING AROUND IN YOUR LITTLE SHIPS.
AND YOU THINK YOU CAN STAND UP TO MOUNTAIN BANDITS? DON'T MAKE ME LAUGH!
KILL THEM!
ARRRRGHH!
ARRRGG
DIE!!!
CAP'N...
I'LL TAKE CARE OF THIS.

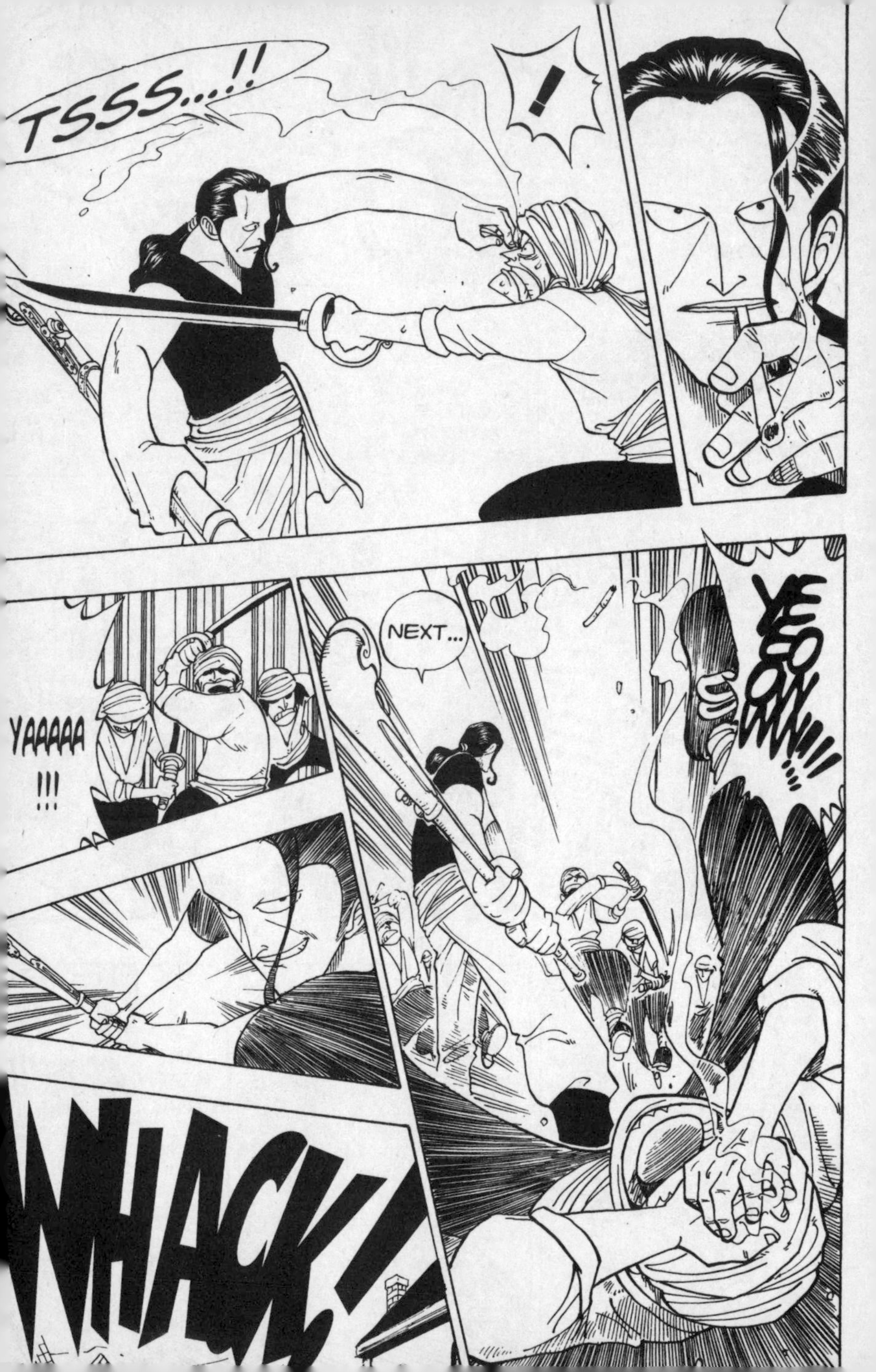
!
TSSS...!!
YEOOWW...!!!
NEXT...
YAAAAA !!!
WHACK!!

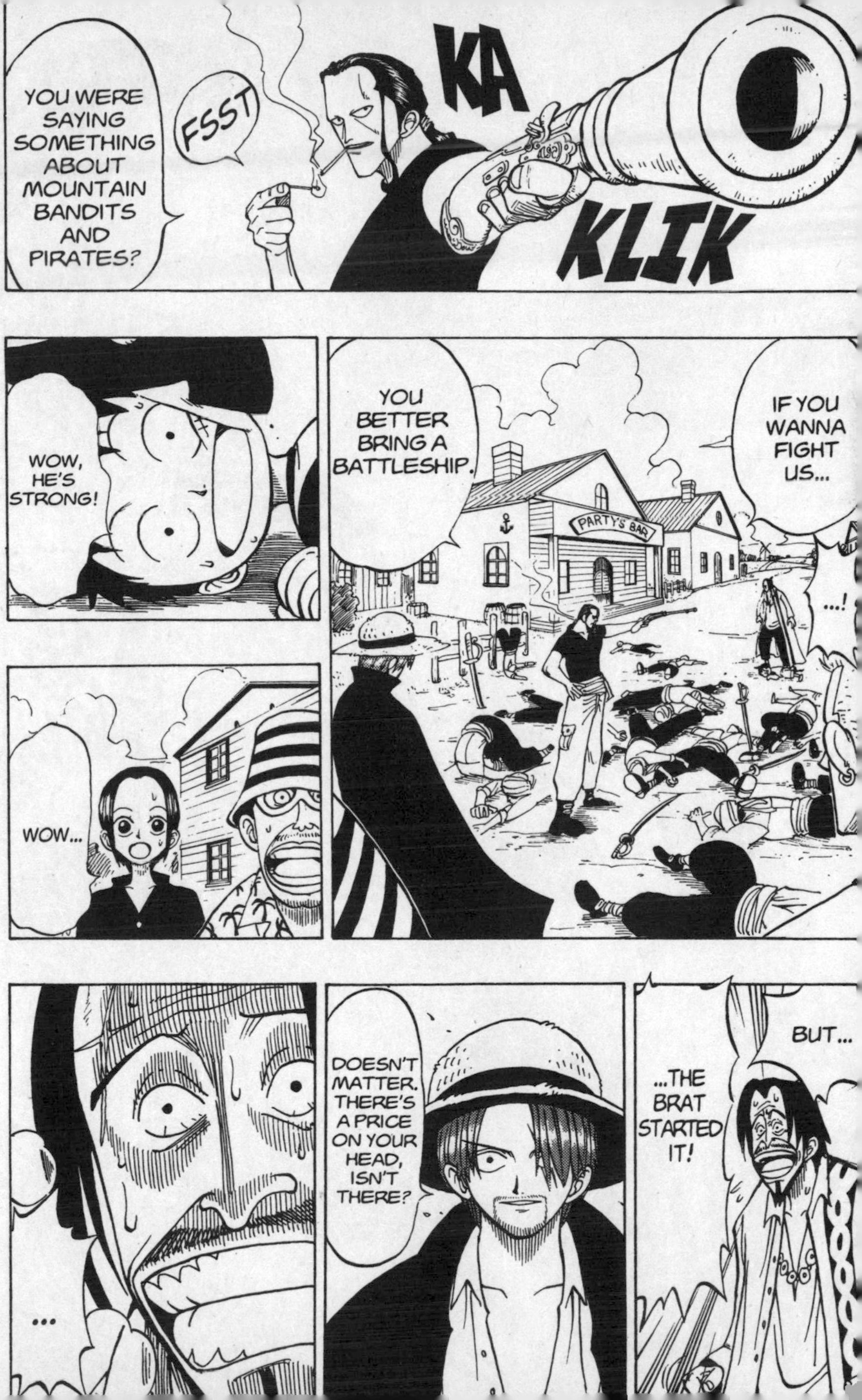
KA
KLIK
FSST
YOU WERE SAYING SOMETHING ABOUT MOUNTAIN BANDITS AND PIRATES?
IF YOU WANNA FIGHT US...
YOU BETTER BRING A BATTLESHIP.
...!
WOW, HE'S STRONG!
WOW...
BUT...
...THE BRAT STARTED IT!
DOESN'T MATTER. THERE'S A PRICE ON YOUR HEAD, ISN'T THERE?
...

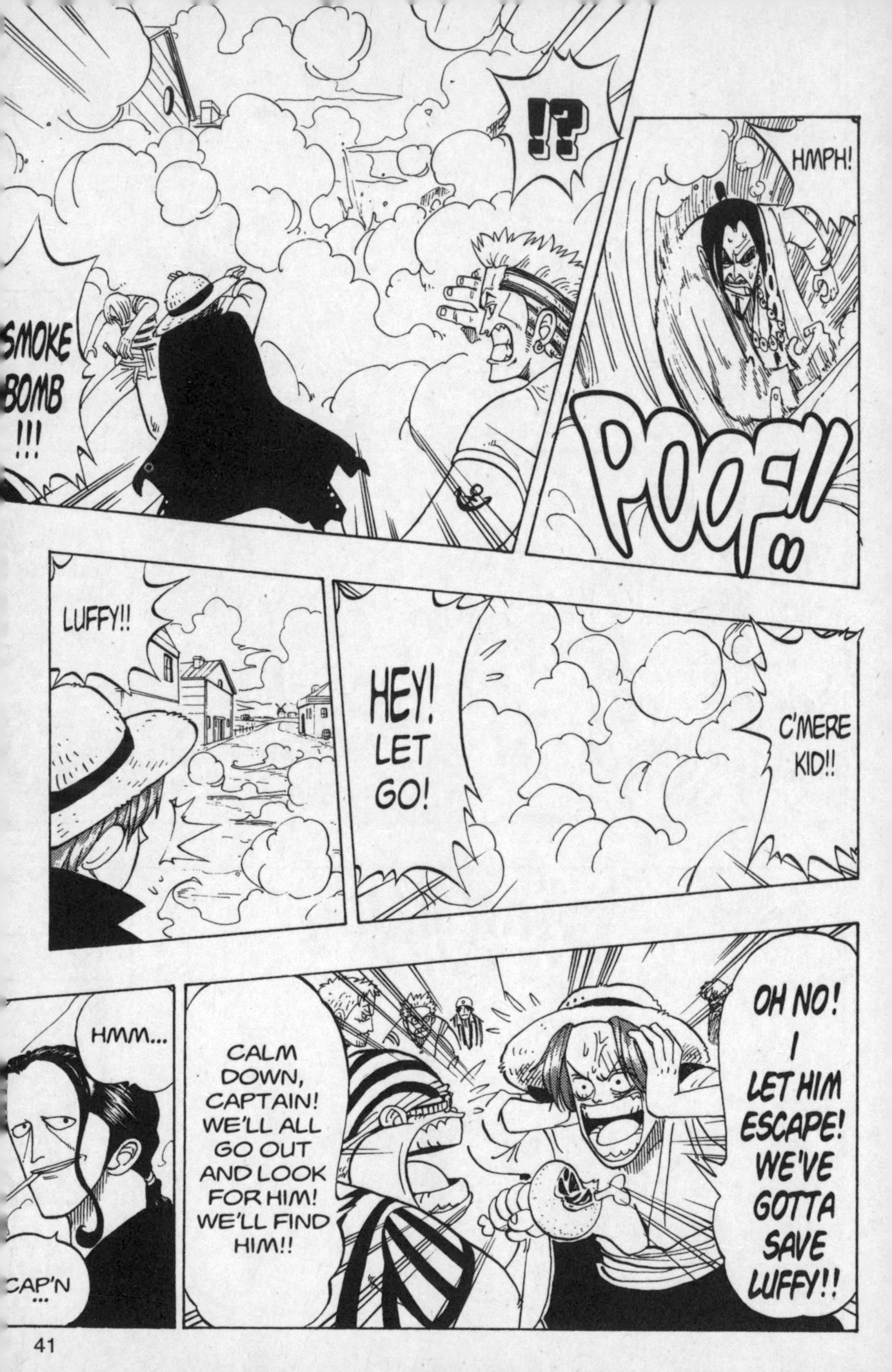
HMPH!
POOF!!
!?
SMOKE BOMB !!!
C'MERE KID!!
HEY! LET GO!
LUFFY!!
OH NO! I LET HIM ESCAPE! WE'VE GOTTA SAVE LUFFY!!
CALM DOWN, CAPTAIN! WE'LL ALL GO OUT AND LOOK FOR HIM! WE'LL FIND HIM!!
HMM...
CAP'N ...

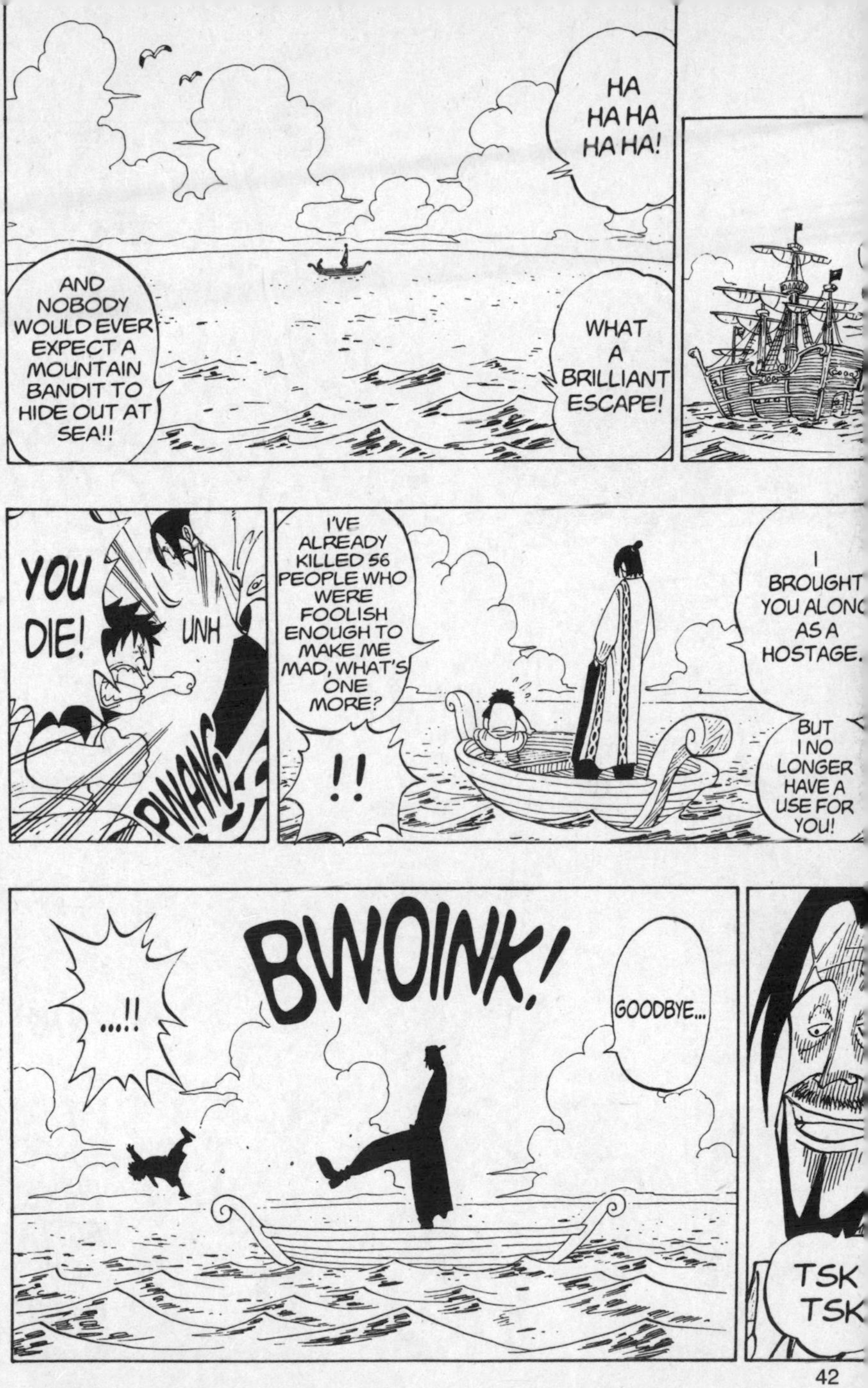
HA HA HA HA HA!
WHAT A BRILLIANT ESCAPE!
AND NOBODY WOULD EVER EXPECT A MOUNTAIN BANDIT TO HIDE OUT AT SEA!!
I BROUGHT YOU ALONG AS A HOSTAGE.
BUT I NO LONGER HAVE A USE FOR YOU!
I'VE ALREADY KILLED 56 PEOPLE WHO WERE FOOLISH ENOUGH TO MAKE ME MAD, WHAT'S ONE MORE?
!!
YOU DIE!
UNH
PWANG
TSK TSK
GOODBYE...
BWOINK!
....!!

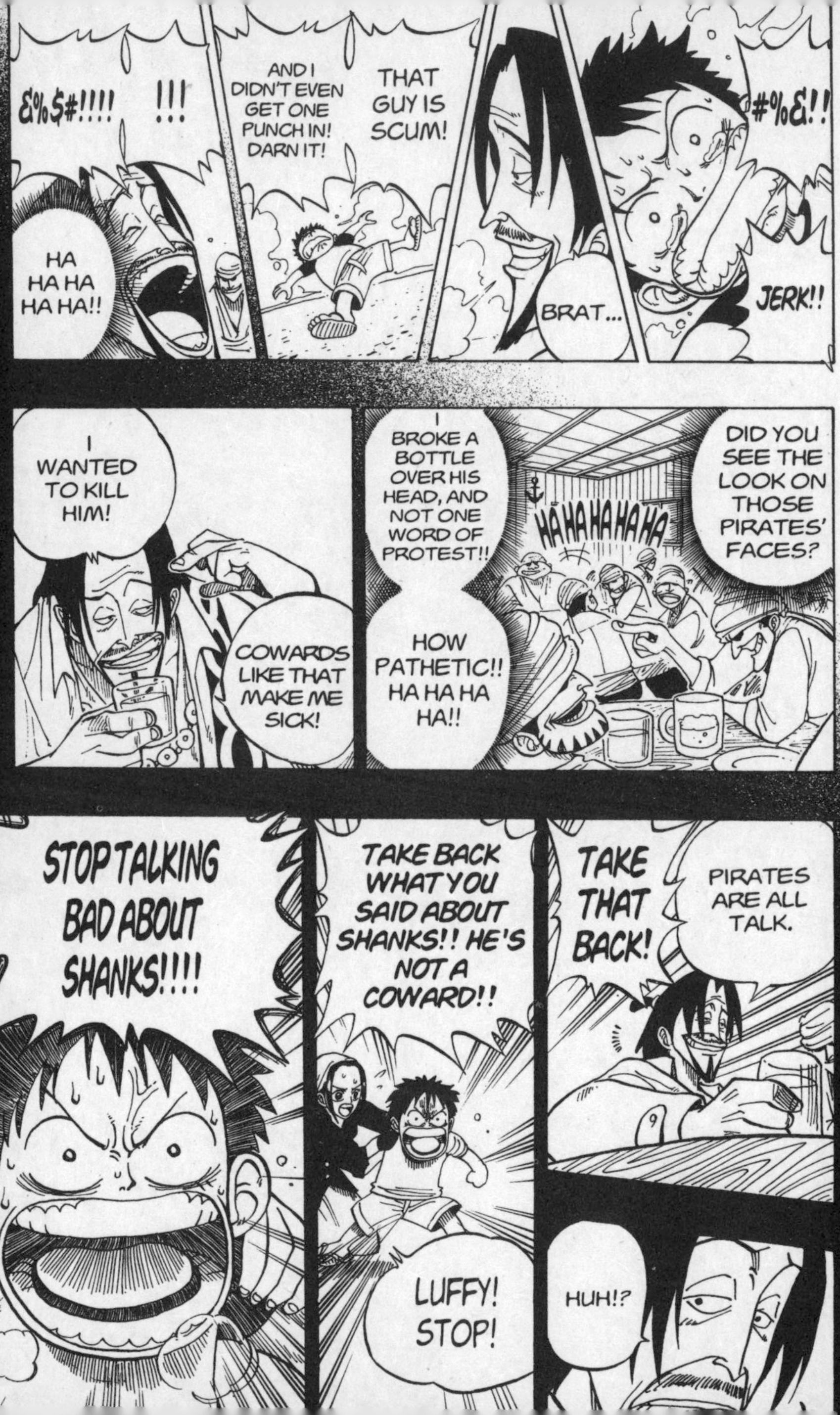
#%£!!
JERK!!
BRAT...
THAT GUY IS SCUM!
AND I DIDN'T EVEN GET ONE PUNCH IN! DARN IT!
!!!
£%$#!!!!!
HA HA HA HA HA!!
DID YOU SEE THE LOOK ON THOSE PIRATES' FACES?
HA HA HA HA HA HA
I BROKE A BOTTLE OVER HIS HEAD, AND NOT ONE WORD OF PROTEST!!
HOW PATHETIC!! HA HA HA HA!!
I WANTED TO KILL HIM!
COWARDS LIKE THAT MAKE ME SICK!
PIRATES ARE ALL TALK.
TAKE THAT BACK!
HUH!?
TAKE BACK WHAT YOU SAID ABOUT SHANKS!! HE'S NOT A COWARD!!
LUFFY! STOP!
STOP TALKING BAD ABOUT SHANKS!!!!

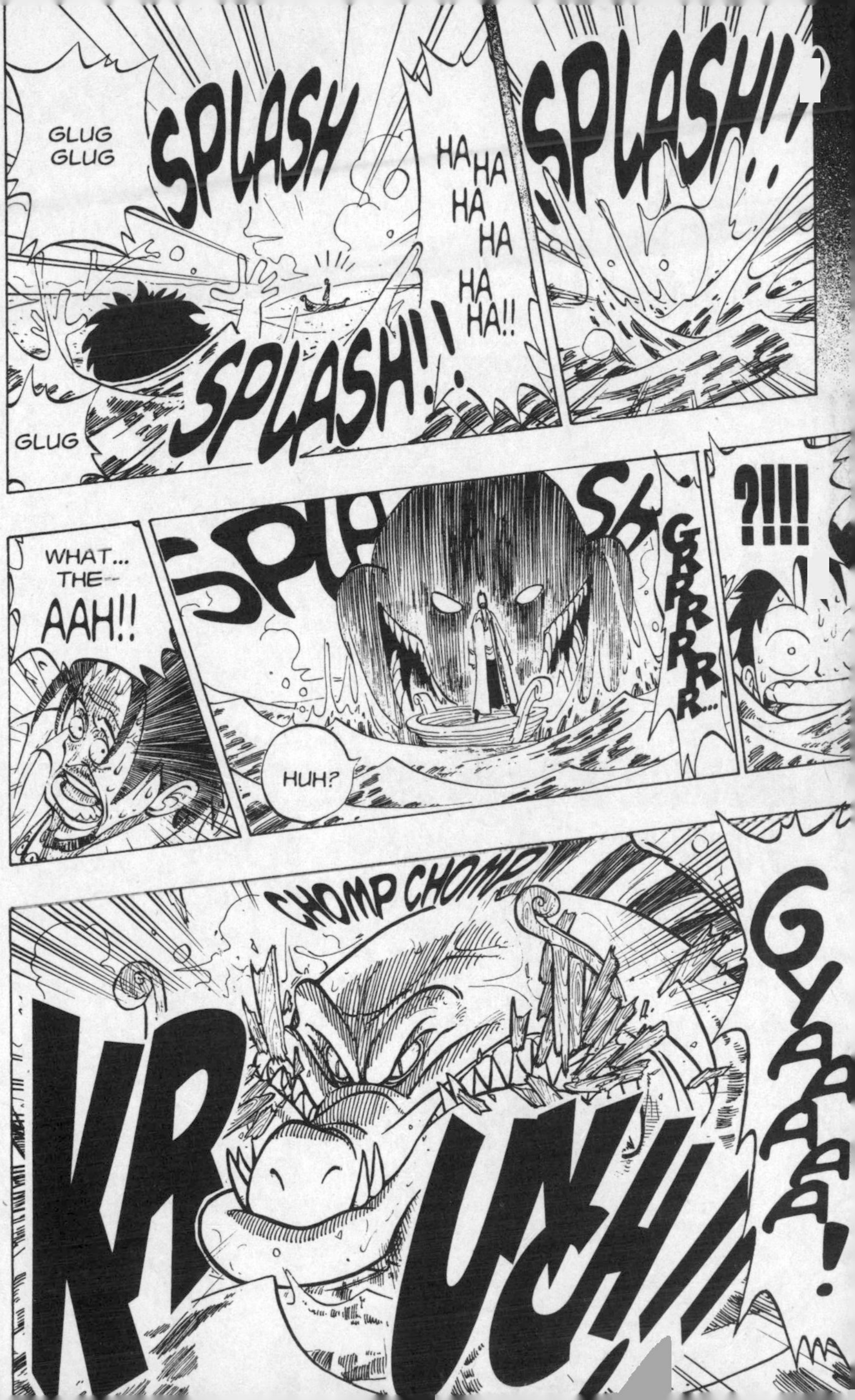
SPLASH!!
HA HA HA HA HA HA!!
SPLASH
GLUG GLUG
SPLASH!!
GLUG
?!!!
SPLASH
GRRRRRR...
HUH?
WHAT... THE--
AAH!!
GYAAAAA!
CHOMP CHOMP
KRUNCH!!

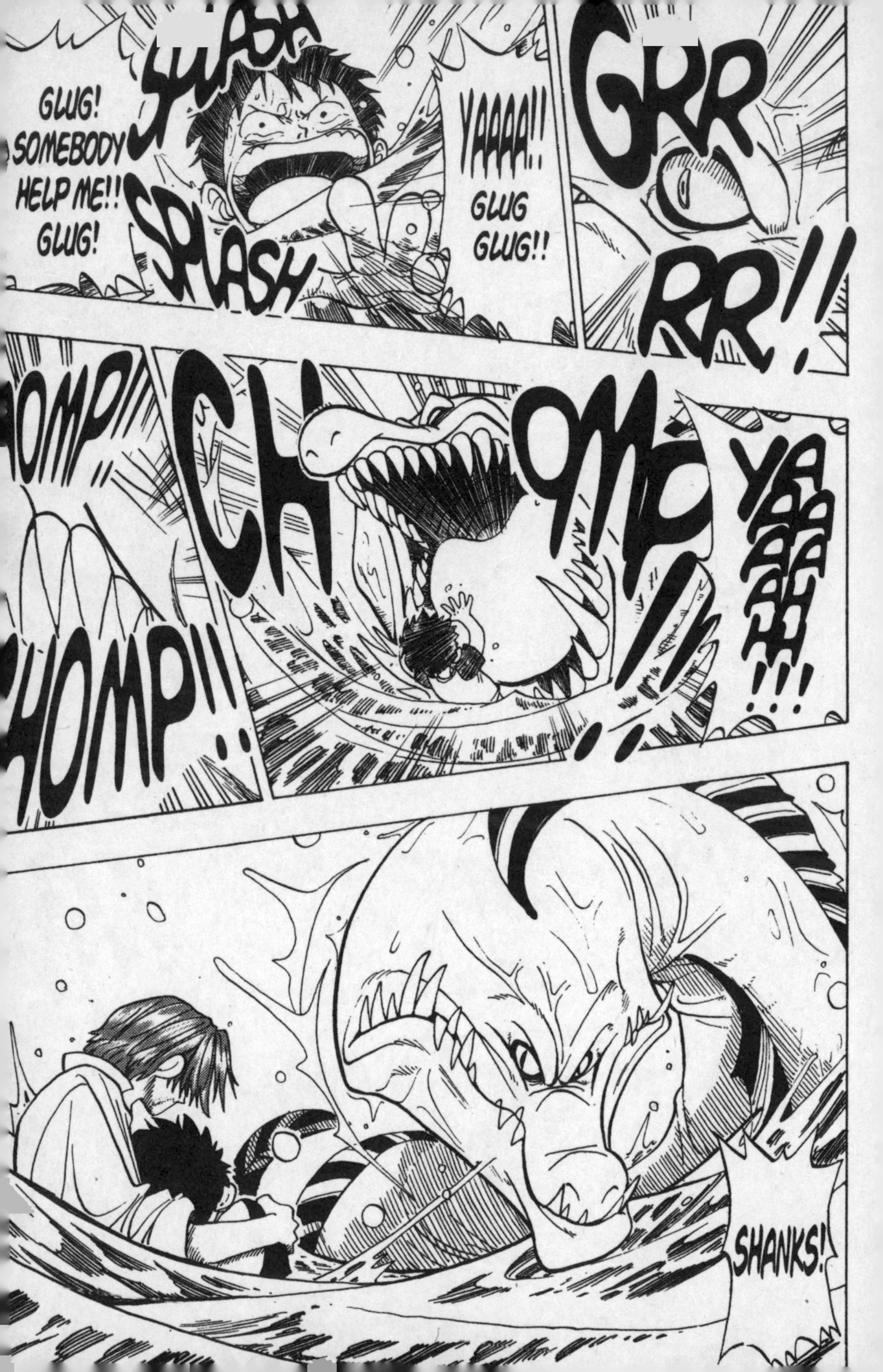
GRRRR!!
YAAAA!!
GLUG GLUG!!
SPLASH
GLUG! SOMEBODY HELP ME!! GLUG!
SPLASH
YAAAAAAH!!!
CHOMP!!
OMP!!
HOMP!!
SHANKS!

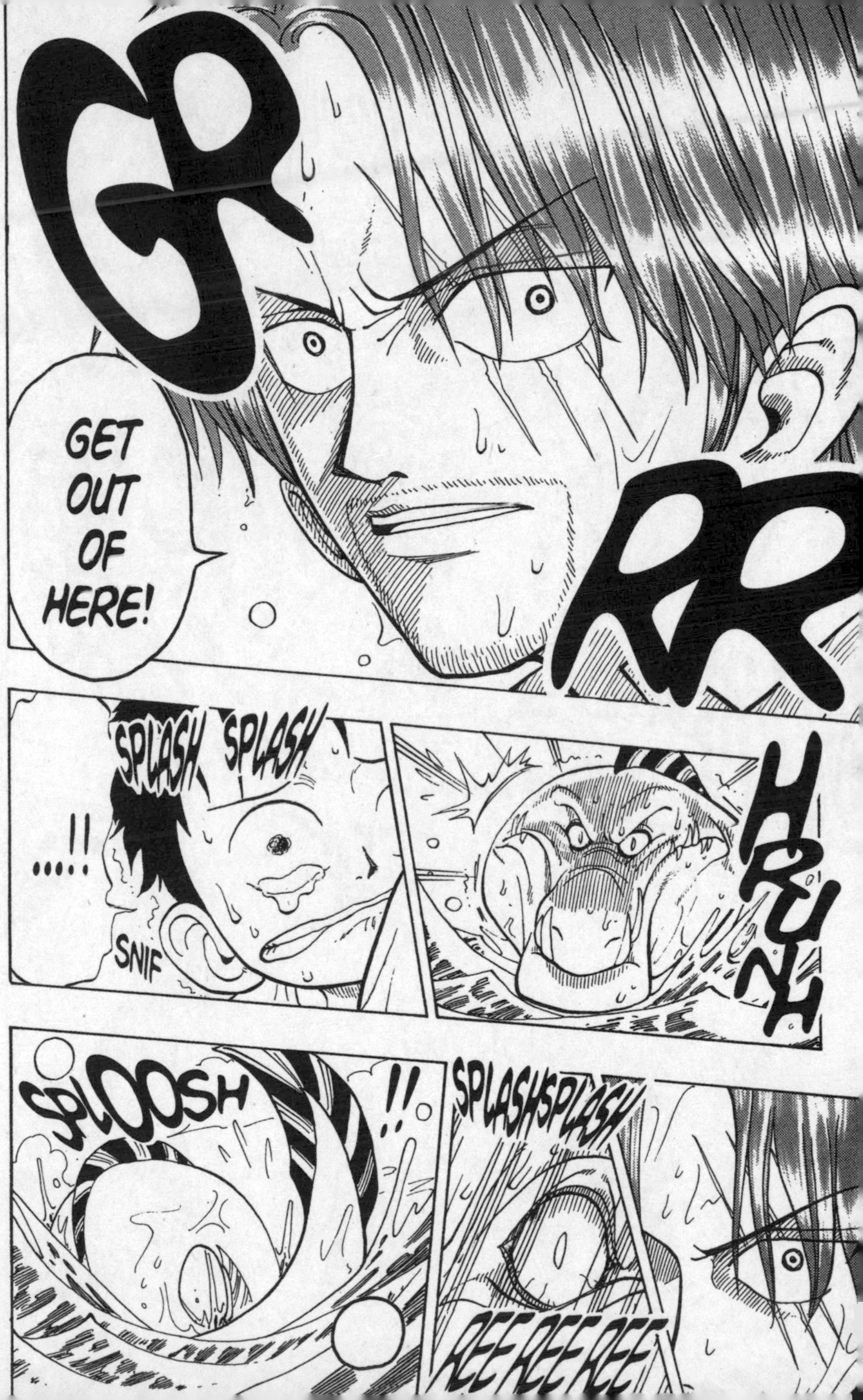
GRRR
GET OUT OF HERE!
HRUNCH
SPLASH SPLASH
....!!
SNIF
SPLASHSPLASH
REEREEREE
!!
SPLOOSH

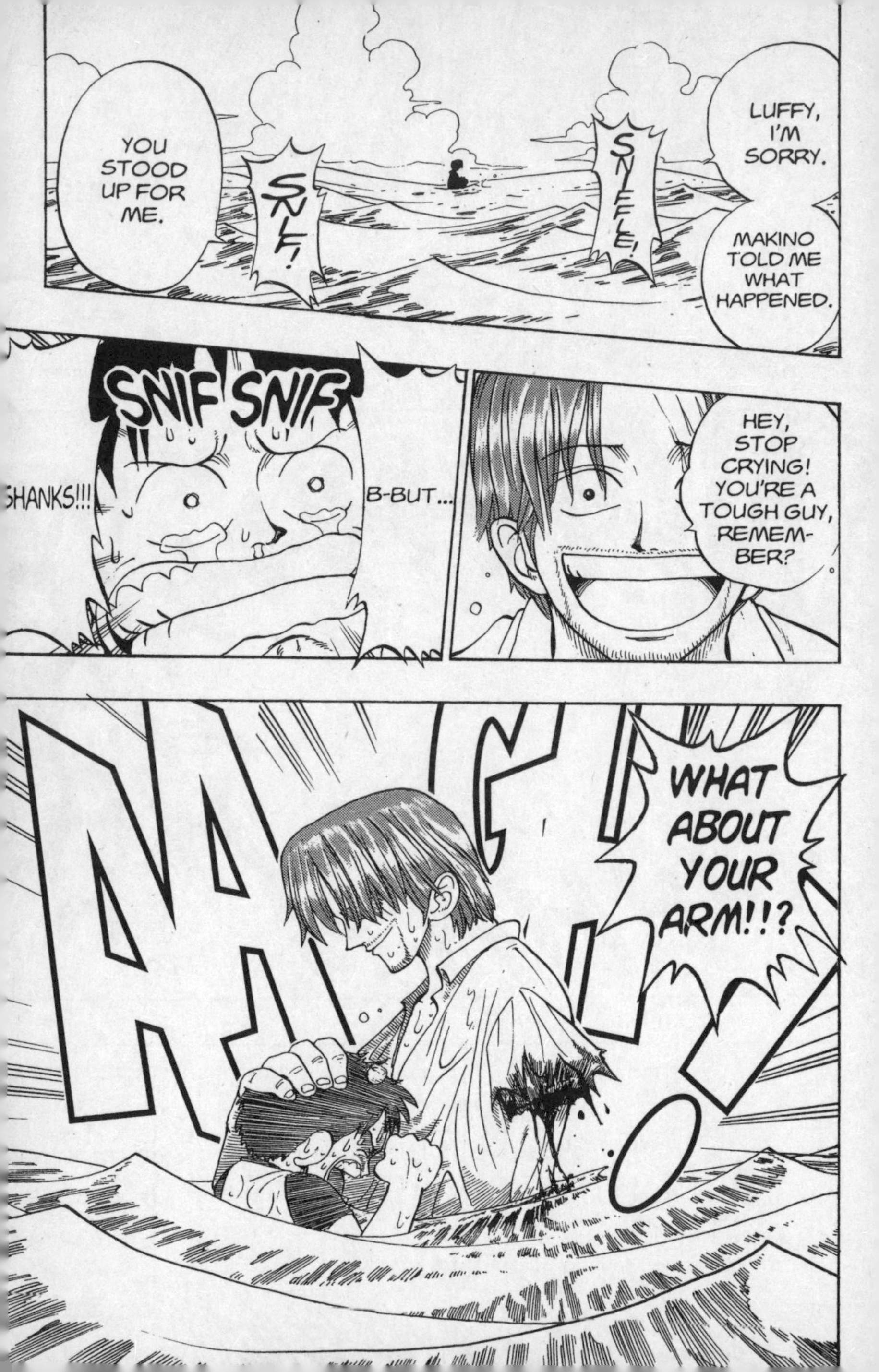
LUFFY, I'M SORRY.
MAKINO TOLD ME WHAT HAPPENED.
SNIFFLE,
SNIF!
YOU STOOD UP FOR ME.
HEY, STOP CRYING! YOU'RE A TOUGH GUY, REMEMBER?
SNIF SNIF
B-BUT...
SHANKS!!!
WHAT ABOUT YOUR ARM!!?

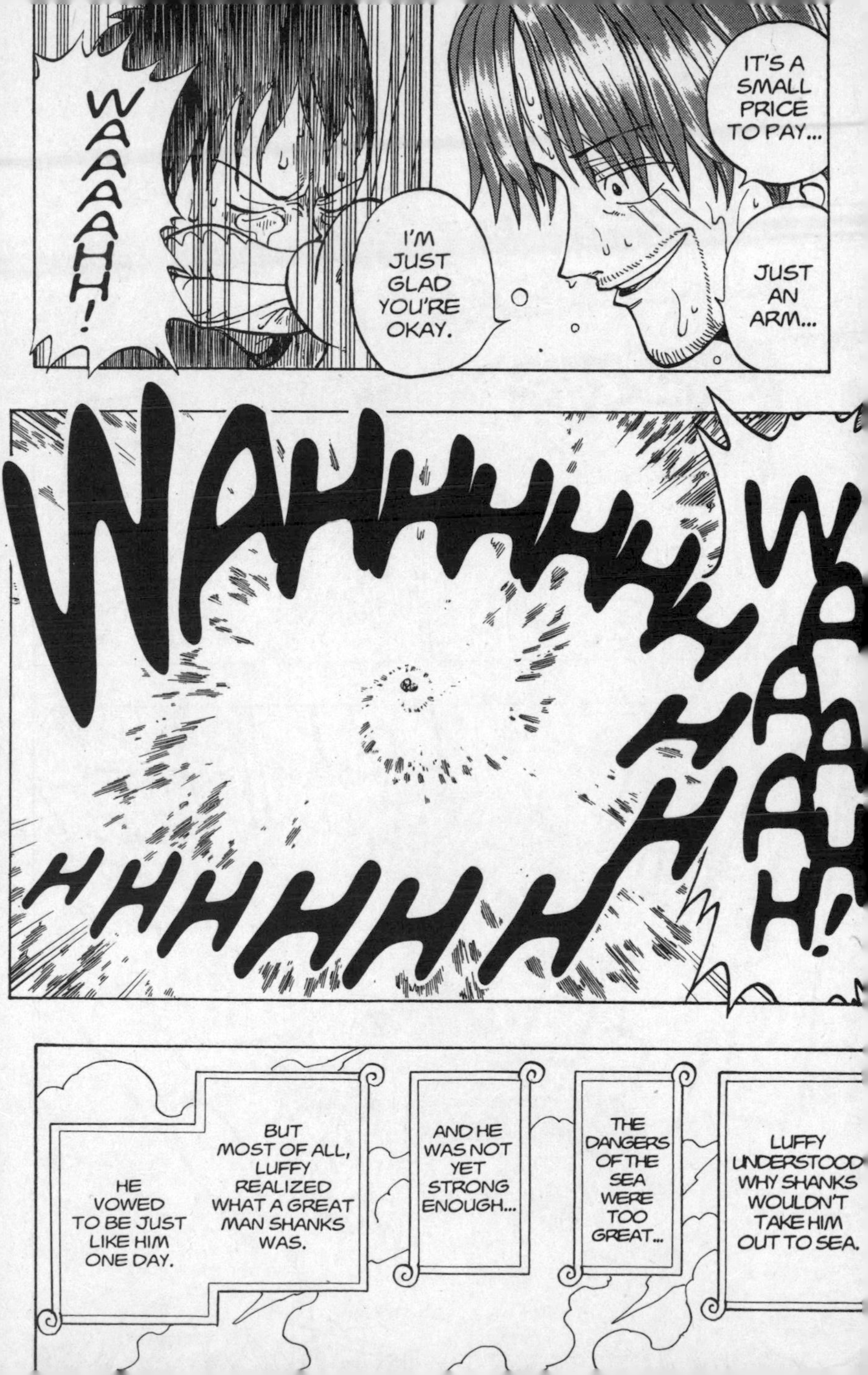
IT'S A SMALL PRICE TO PAY...
JUST AN ARM...
I'M JUST GLAD YOU'RE OKAY.
WAAAAAH!
WAHHHHHHHH HHHHHHH
WAAAAH!
LUFFY UNDERSTOOD WHY SHANKS WOULDN'T TAKE HIM OUT TO SEA.
THE DANGERS OF THE SEA WERE TOO GREAT...
AND HE WAS NOT YET STRONG ENOUGH...
BUT MOST OF ALL, LUFFY REALIZED WHAT A GREAT MAN SHANKS WAS.
HE VOWED TO BE JUST LIKE HIM ONE DAY.

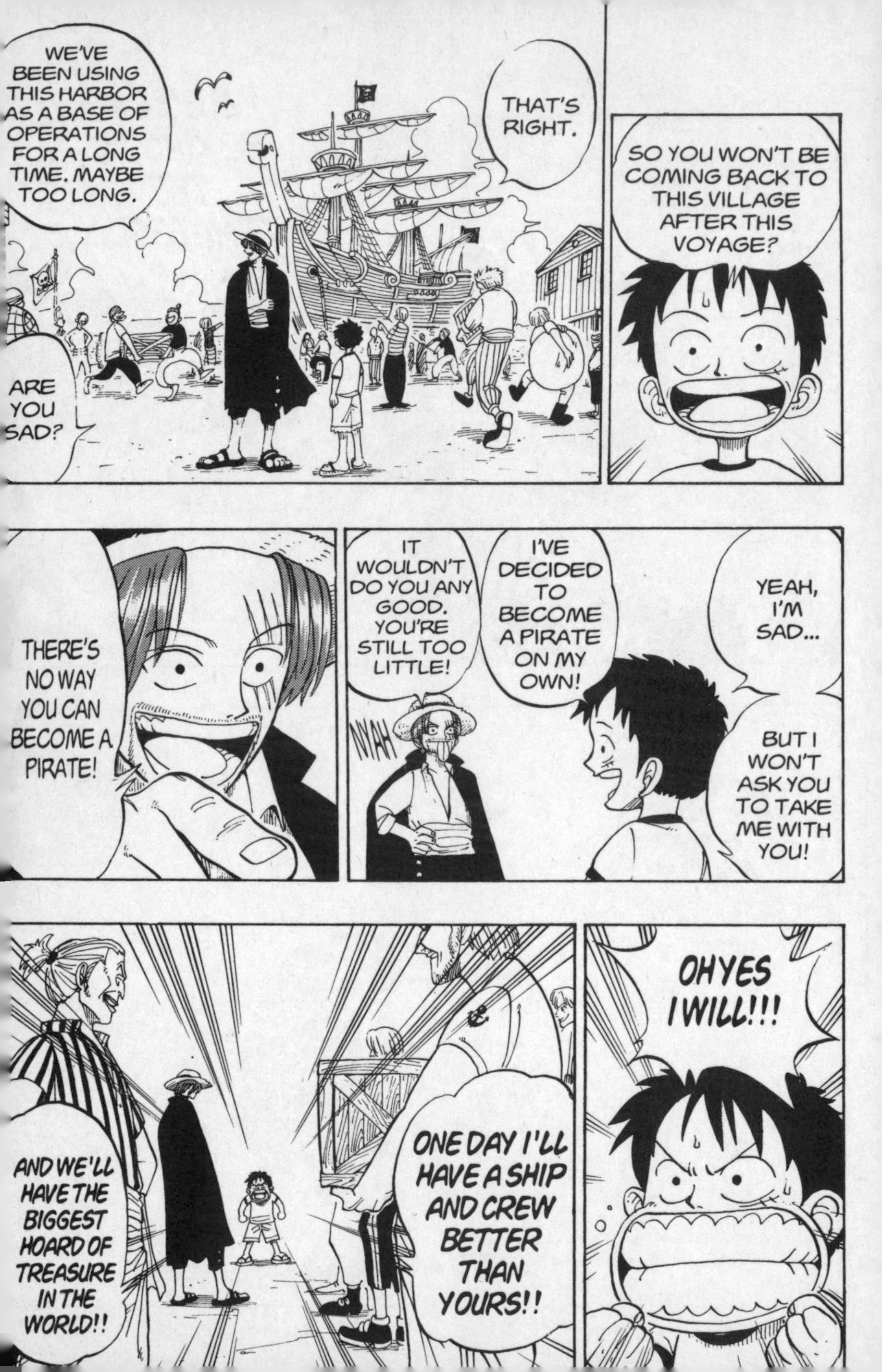
SO YOU WON'T BE COMING BACK TO THIS VILLAGE AFTER THIS VOYAGE?
THAT'S RIGHT.
WE'VE BEEN USING THIS HARBOR AS A BASE OF OPERATIONS FOR A LONG TIME. MAYBE TOO LONG.
ARE YOU SAD?
YEAH, I'M SAD...
BUT I WON'T ASK YOU TO TAKE ME WITH YOU!
I'VE DECIDED TO BECOME A PIRATE ON MY OWN!
IT WOULDN'T DO YOU ANY GOOD. YOU'RE STILL TOO LITTLE!
NYAH
THERE'S NO WAY YOU CAN BECOME A PIRATE!
OH YES I WILL!!!
ONE DAY I'LL HAVE A SHIP AND CREW BETTER THAN YOURS!!
AND WE'LL HAVE THE BIGGEST HOARD OF TREASURE IN THE WORLD!!

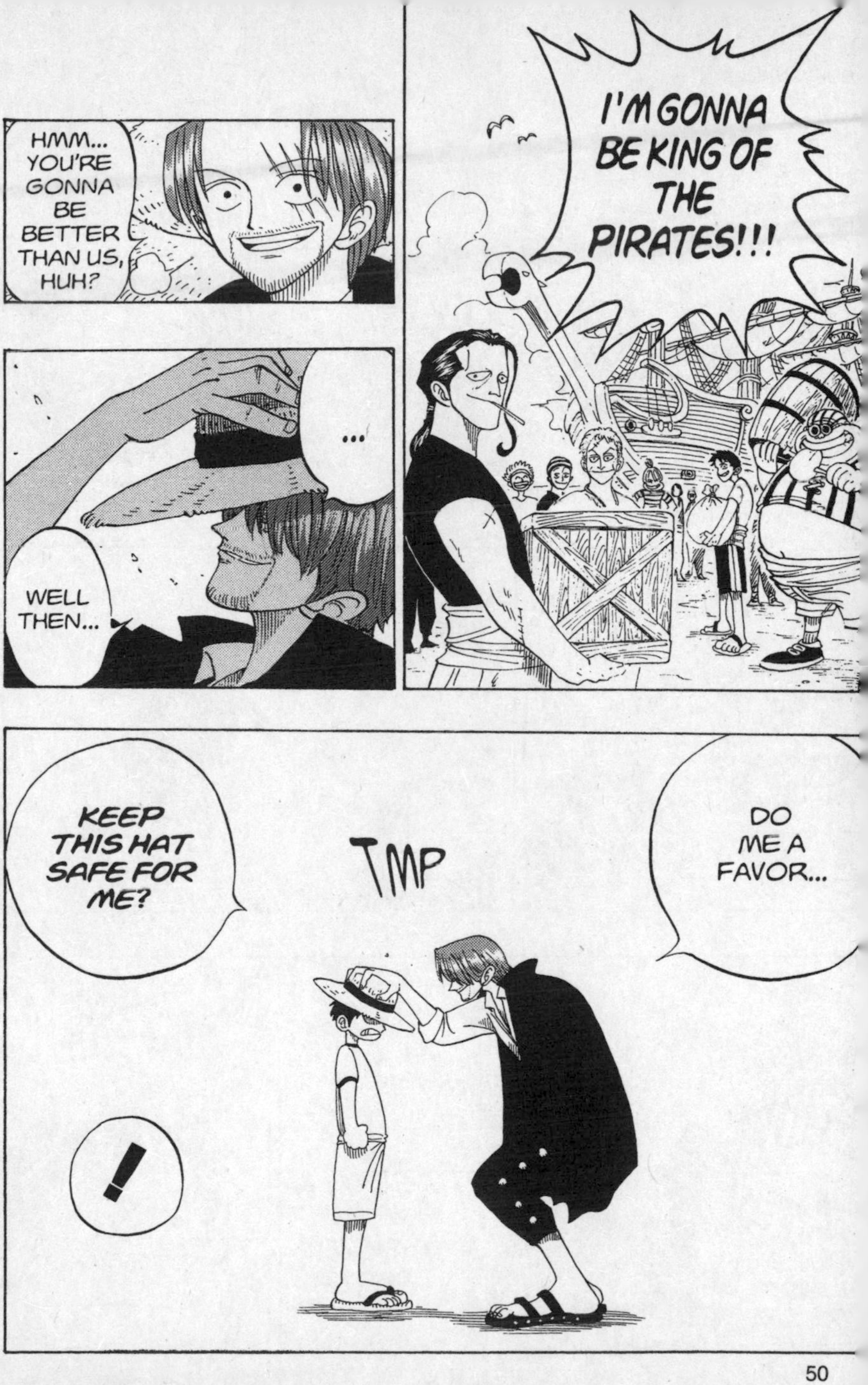

I'M GONNA BE KING OF THE PIRATES!!!
HMM... YOU'RE GONNA BE BETTER THAN US, HUH?
...
WELL THEN...
DO ME A FAVOR...
TMP
KEEP THIS HAT SAFE FOR ME?
!

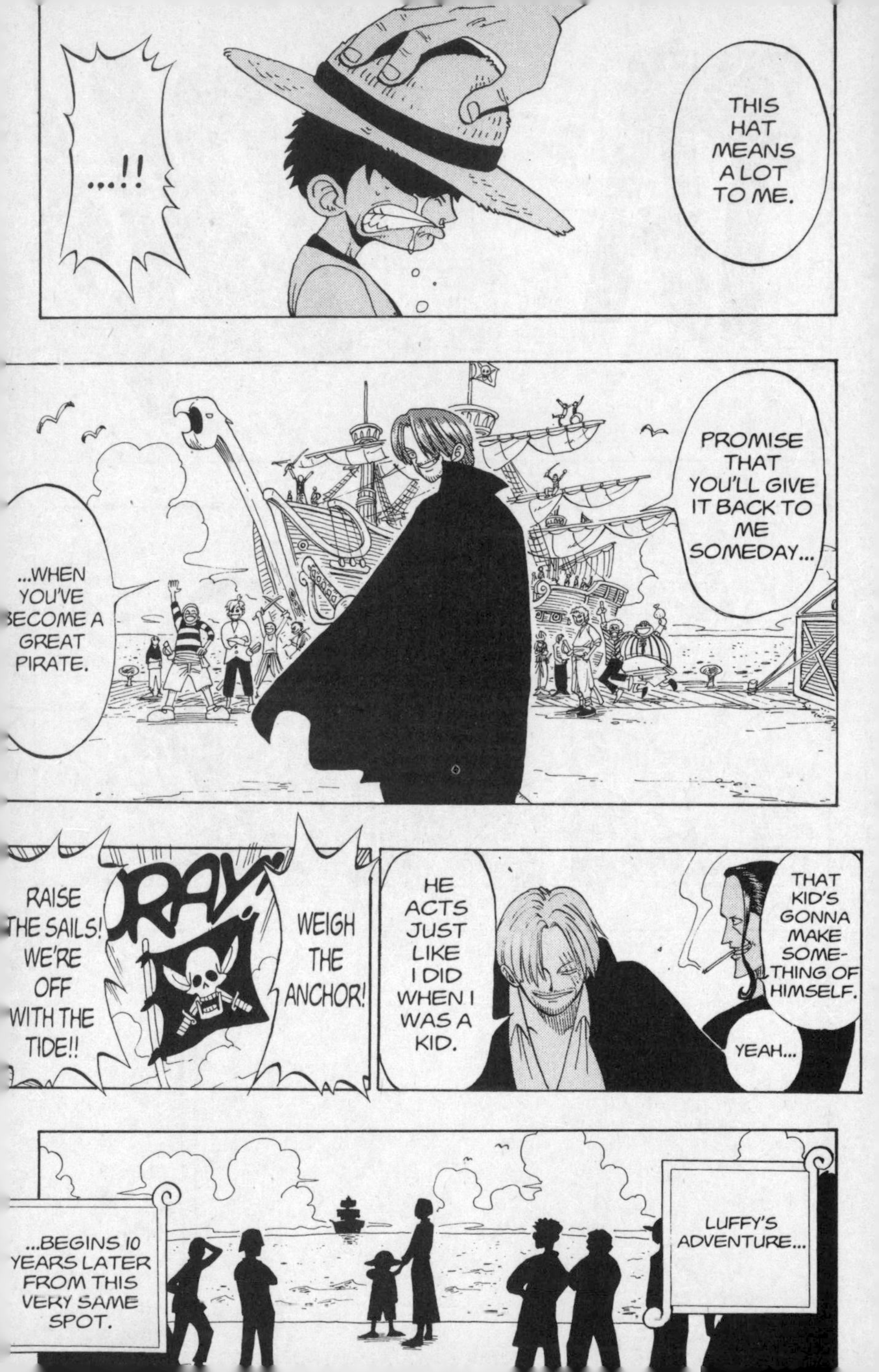
THIS HAT MEANS A LOT TO ME.
...!!
PROMISE THAT YOU'LL GIVE IT BACK TO ME SOMEDAY...
...WHEN YOU'VE BECOME A GREAT PIRATE.
THAT KID'S GONNA MAKE SOME-THING OF HIMSELF.
HE ACTS JUST LIKE I DID WHEN I WAS A KID.
YEAH...
WEIGH THE ANCHOR!
RAY!
RAISE THE SAILS! WE'RE OFF WITH THE TIDE!!
LUFFY'S ADVENTURE...
...BEGINS 10 YEARS LATER FROM THIS VERY SAME SPOT.

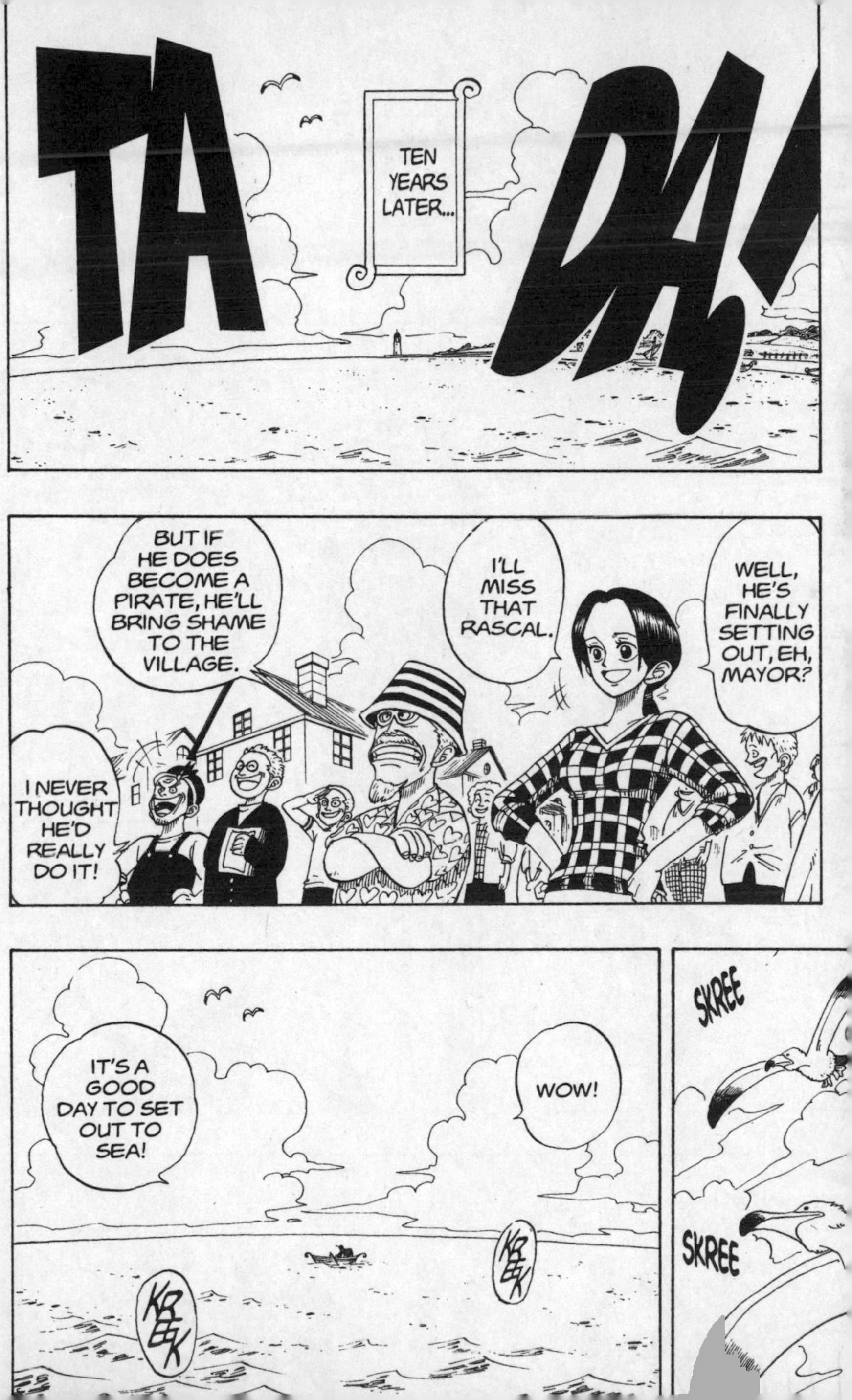
TEN YEARS LATER...
TA
DA!
WELL, HE'S FINALLY SETTING OUT, EH, MAYOR?
I'LL MISS THAT RASCAL.
BUT IF HE DOES BECOME A PIRATE, HE'LL BRING SHAME TO THE VILLAGE.
I NEVER THOUGHT HE'D REALLY DO IT!
SKREE
SKREE
WOW!
IT'S A GOOD DAY TO SET OUT TO SEA!
KREEK
KREEK

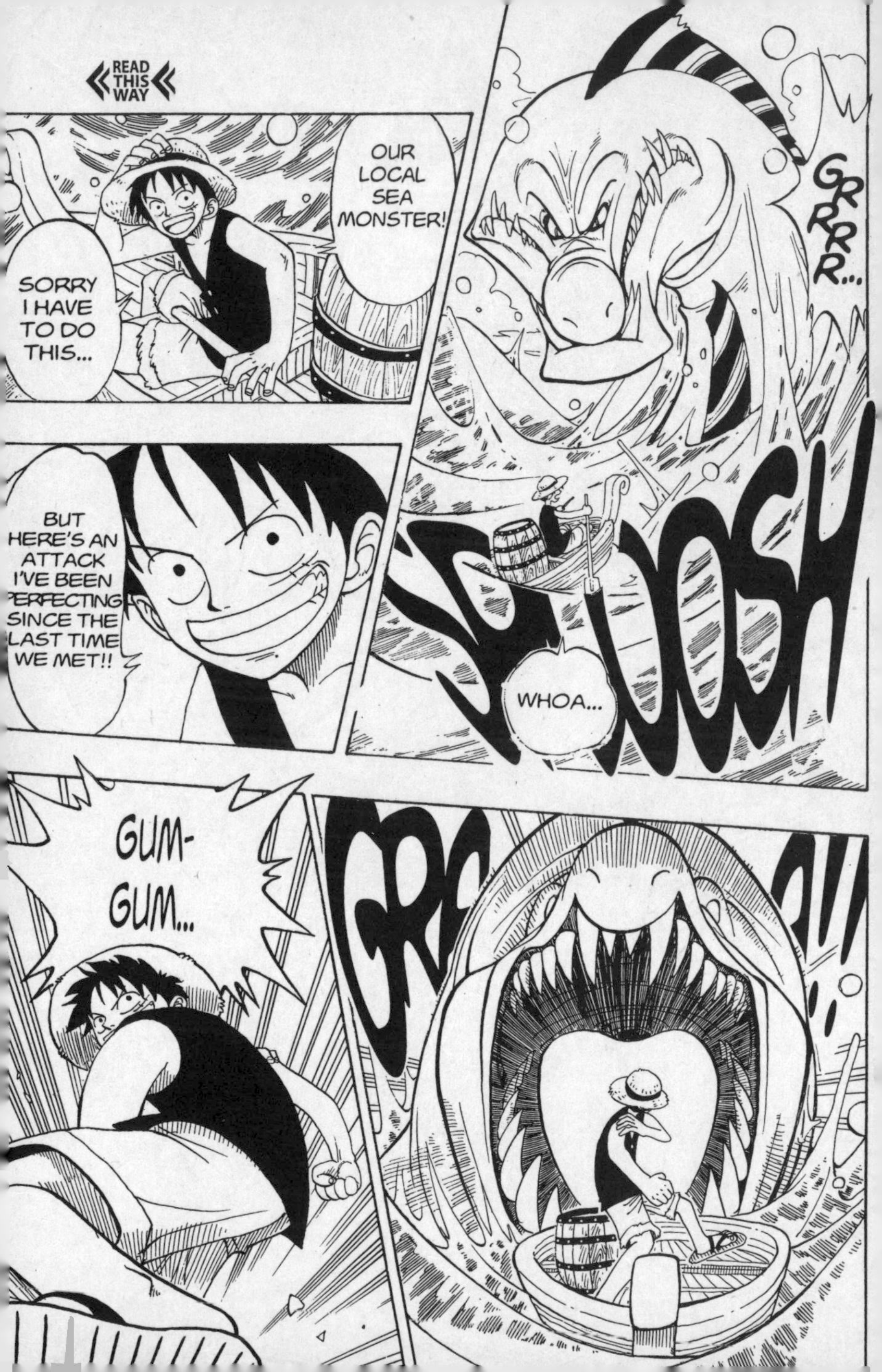
READ THIS WAY
GRRRR...
SWOOSH
WHOA...
OUR LOCAL SEA MONSTER!
SORRY I HAVE TO DO THIS...
BUT HERE'S AN ATTACK I'VE BEEN PERFECTING SINCE THE LAST TIME WE MET!!
GUM-GUM...

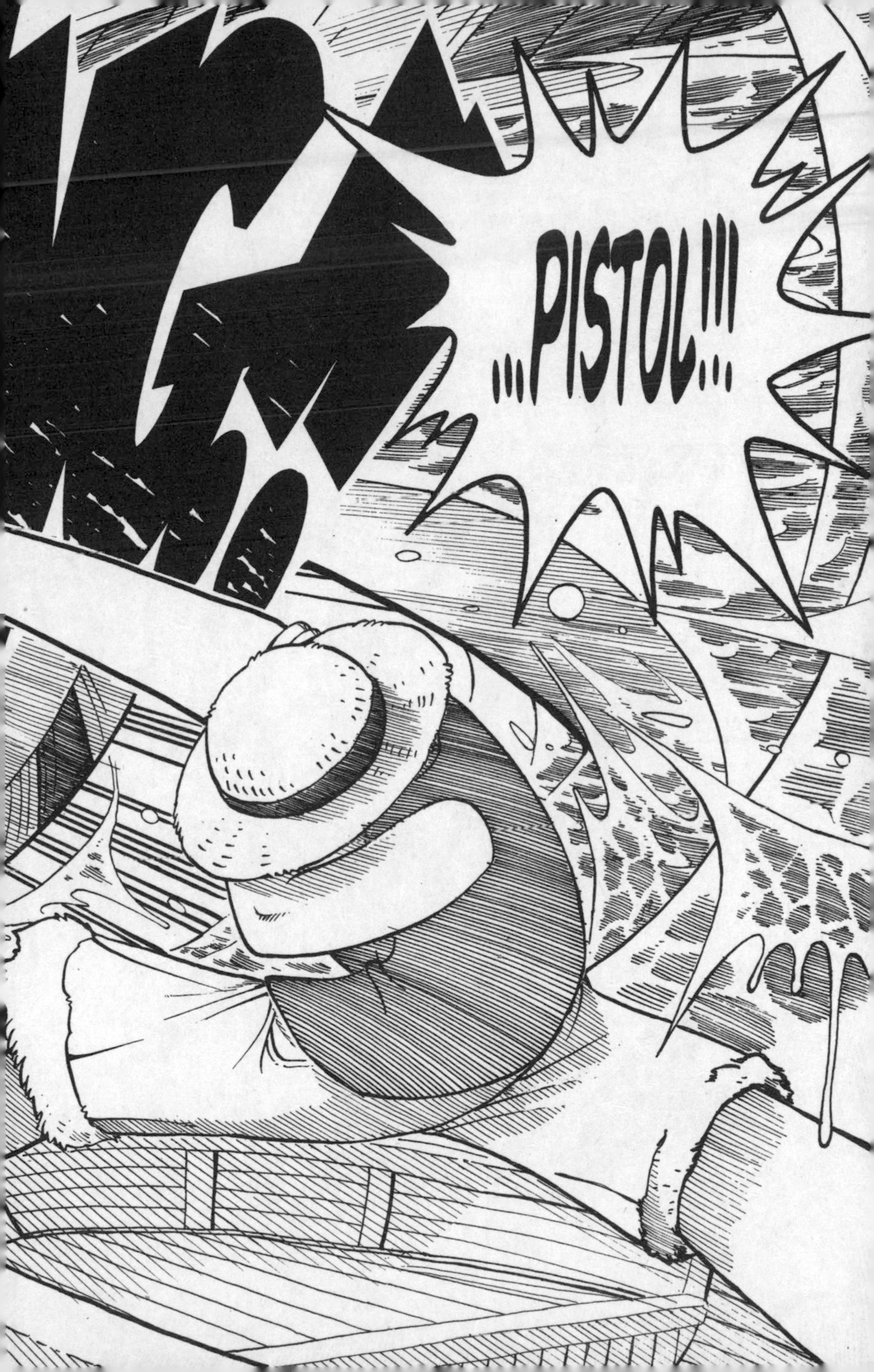
...PISTOL!!!

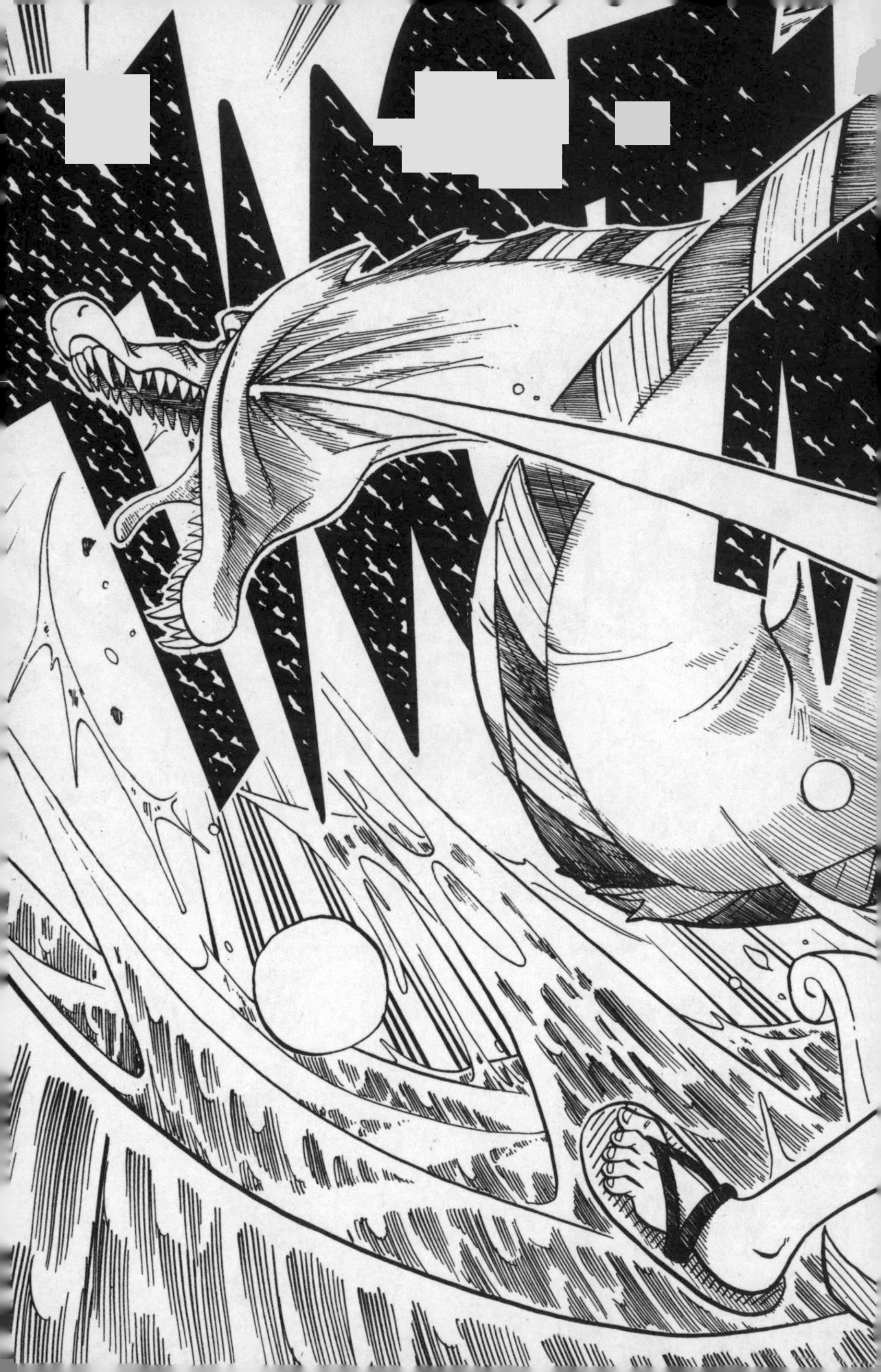

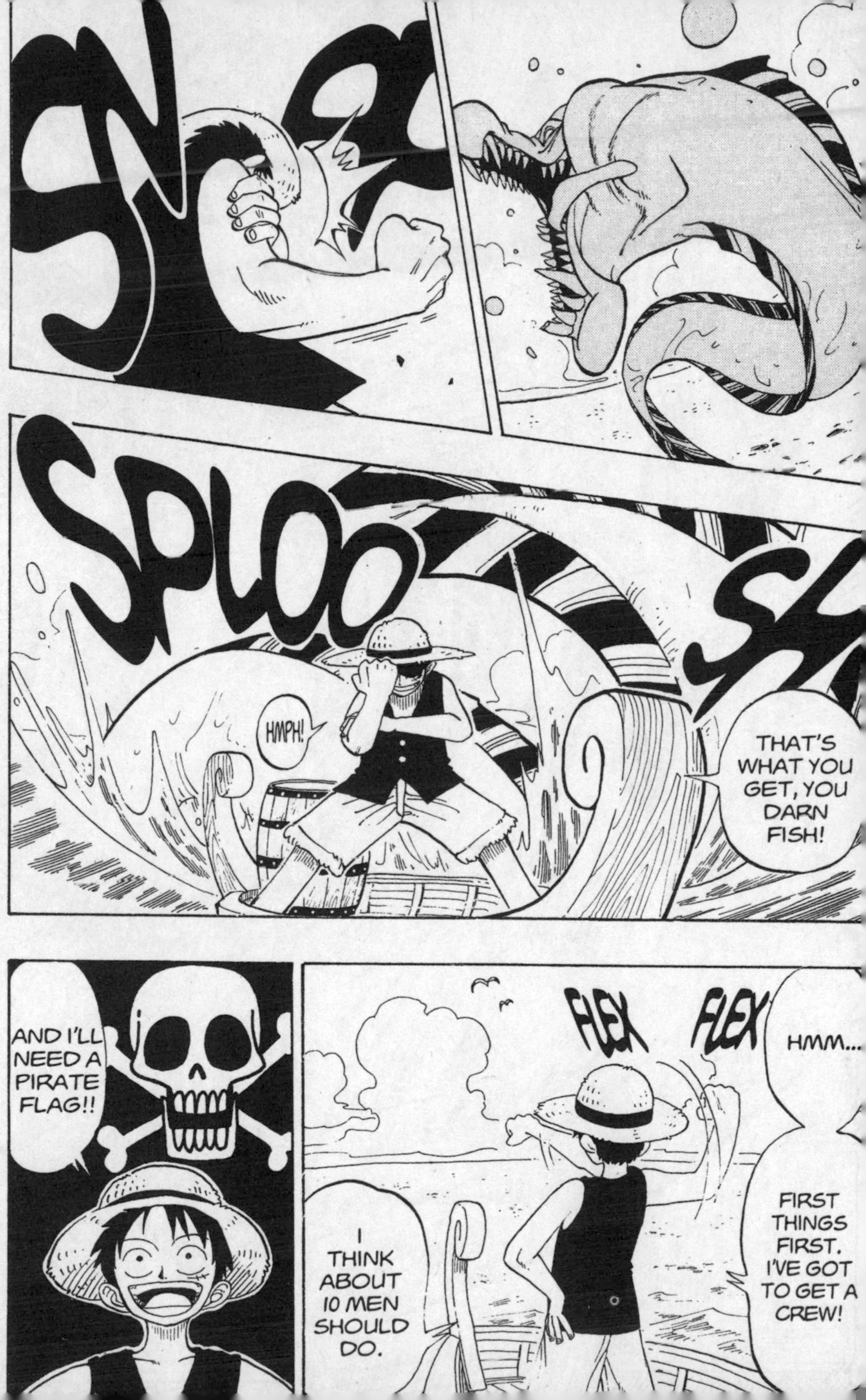
SPLOO
SH
THAT'S WHAT YOU GET, YOU DARN FISH!
HMPH!
HMM...
FLEX FLEX
FIRST THINGS FIRST. I'VE GOT TO GET A CREW!
I THINK ABOUT 10 MEN SHOULD DO.
AND I'LL NEED A PIRATE FLAG!!

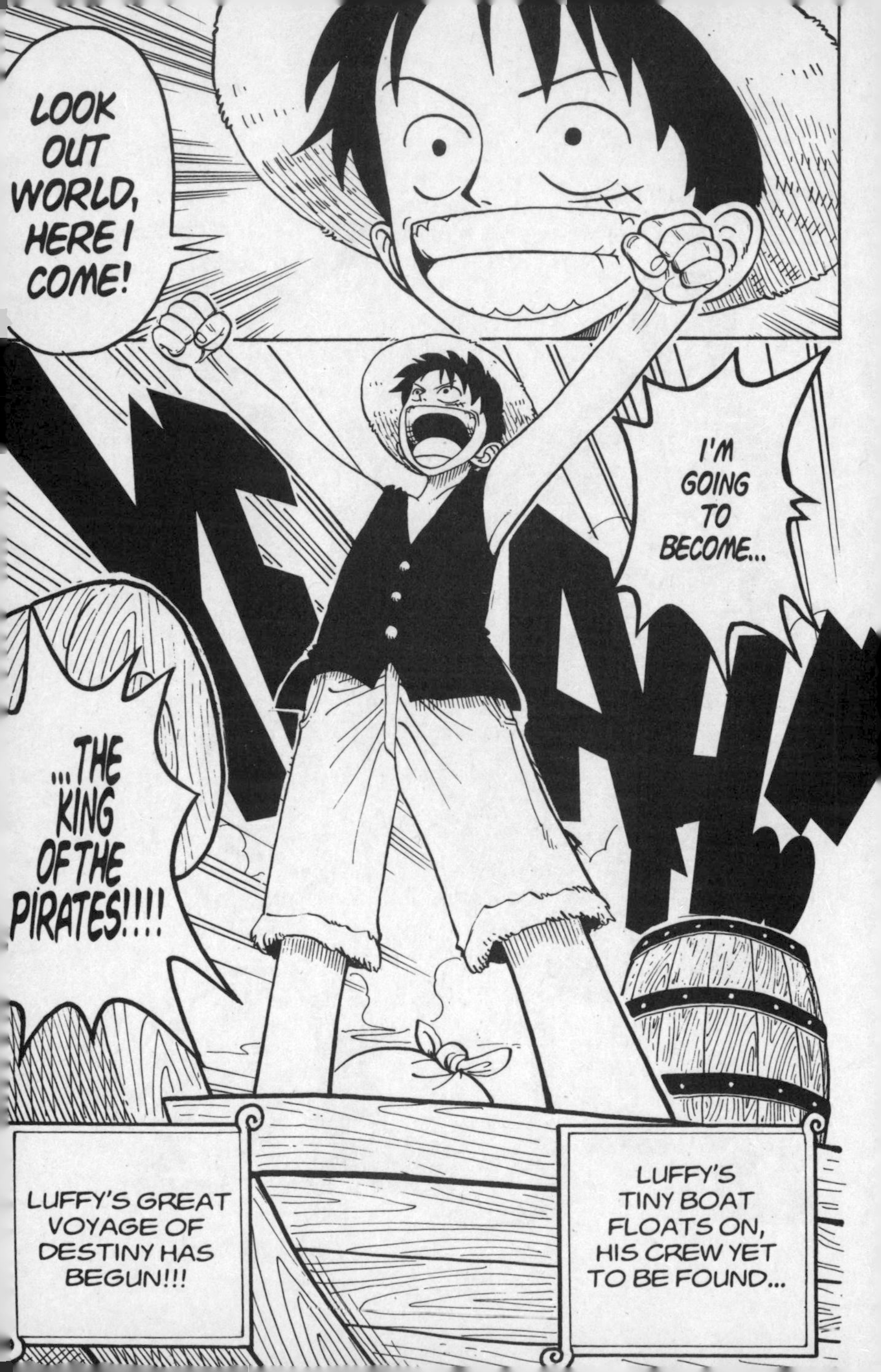
LOOK OUT WORLD, HERE I COME!
I'M GOING TO BECOME...
...THE KING OF THE PIRATES!!!!
LUFFY'S TINY BOAT FLOATS ON, HIS CREW YET TO BE FOUND...
LUFFY'S GREAT VOYAGE OF DESTINY HAS BEGUN!!!

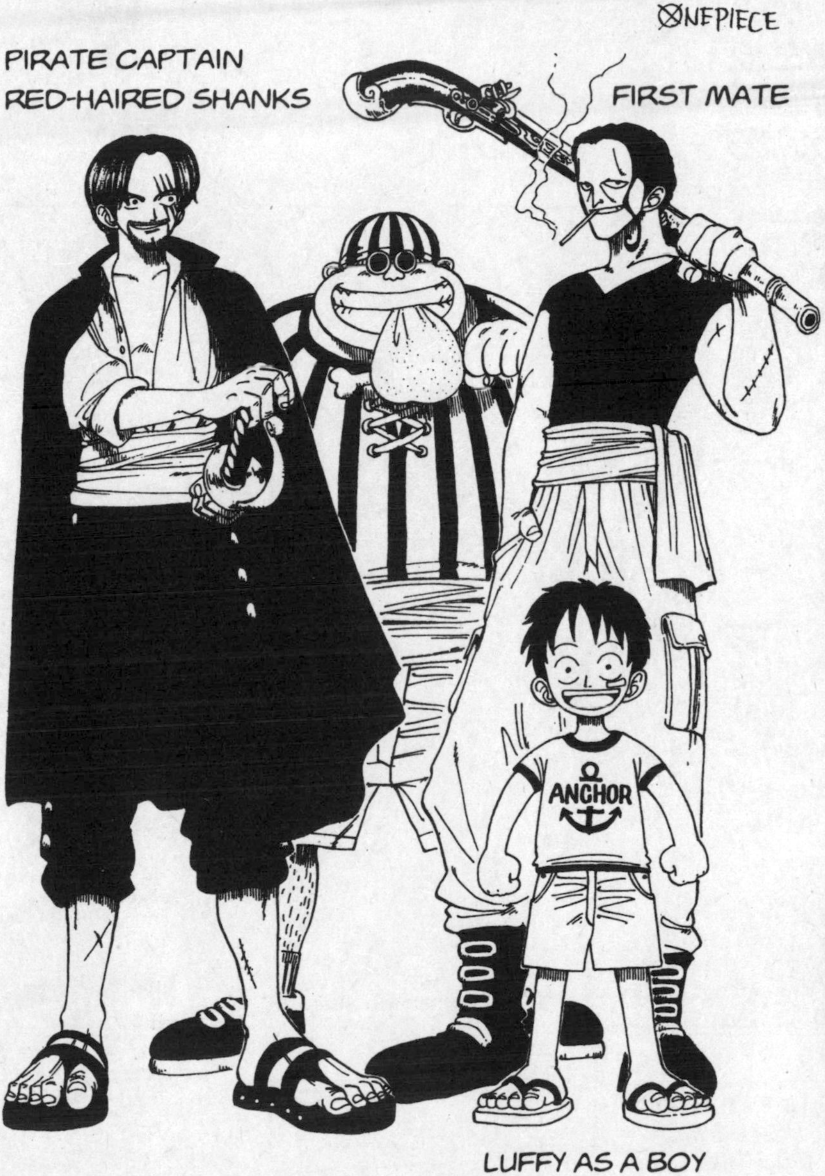

ONE PIECE
PIRATE CAPTAIN
RED-HAIRED SHANKS
FIRST MATE
ANCHOR
LUFFY AS A BOY

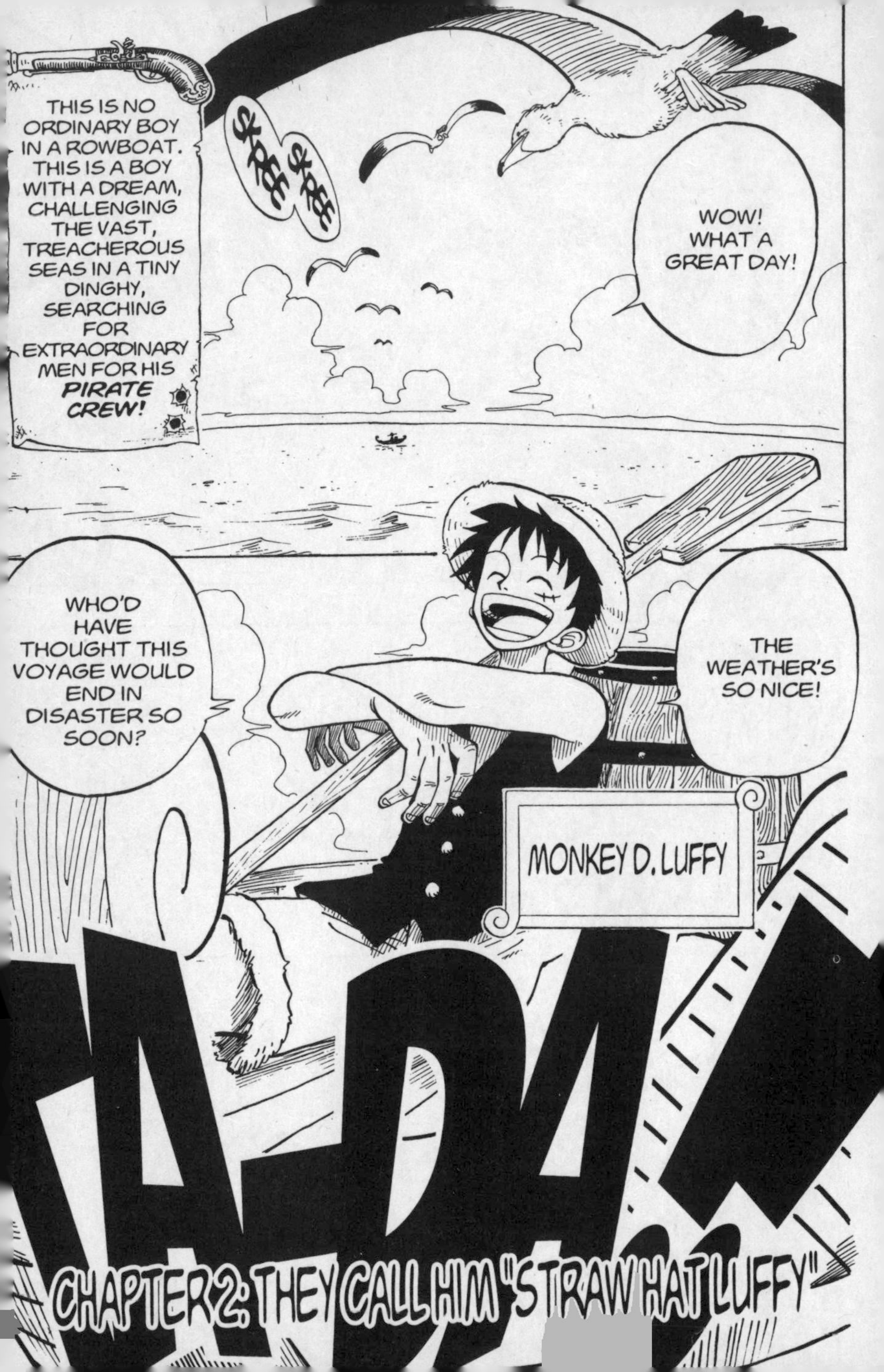
WOW! WHAT A GREAT DAY!
SKREE
SKREE
THIS IS NO ORDINARY BOY IN A ROWBOAT. THIS IS A BOY WITH A DREAM, CHALLENGING THE VAST, TREACHEROUS SEAS IN A TINY DINGHY, SEARCHING FOR EXTRAORDINARY MEN FOR HIS *PIRATE CREW!*
THE WEATHER'S SO NICE!
MONKEY D. LUFFY
WHO'D HAVE THOUGHT THIS VOYAGE WOULD END IN DISASTER SO SOON?
CHAPTER 2: THEY CALL HIM "STRAW HAT LUFFY"

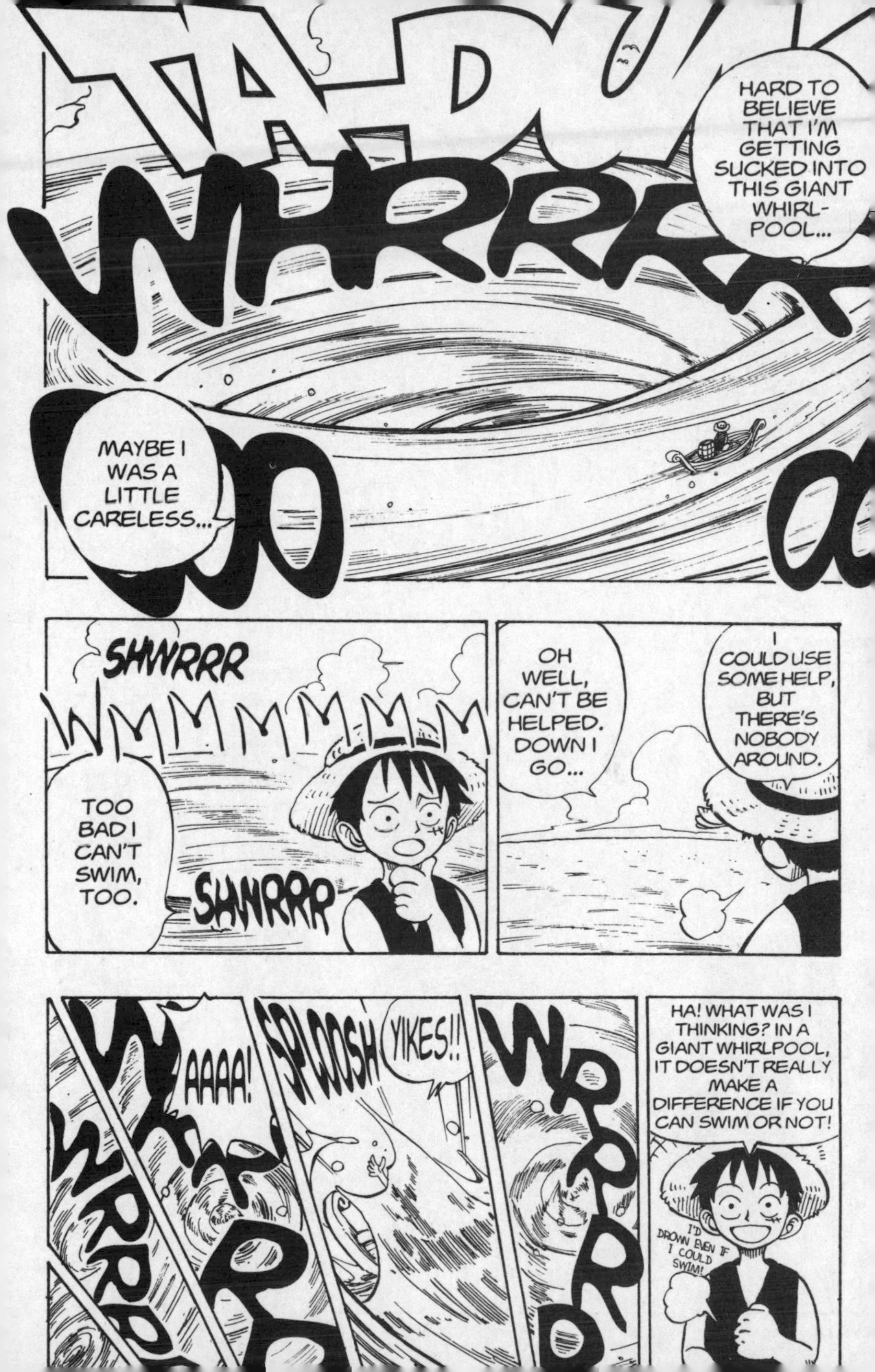
HARD TO BELIEVE THAT I'M GETTING SUCKED INTO THIS GIANT WHIRL-POOL...
MAYBE I WAS A LITTLE CARELESS...
I COULD USE SOME HELP, BUT THERE'S NOBODY AROUND.
OH WELL, CAN'T BE HELPED. DOWN I GO...
SHWRRR
TOO BAD I CAN'T SWIM, TOO.
SHWRRR
HA! WHAT WAS I THINKING? IN A GIANT WHIRLPOOL, IT DOESN'T REALLY MAKE A DIFFERENCE IF YOU CAN SWIM OR NOT!
I'D DROWN EVEN IF I COULD SWIM!
YIKES!!
SPLOOSH
AAAA!

CHAPTER 2:
THEY CALL HIM "STRAW HAT LUFFY"

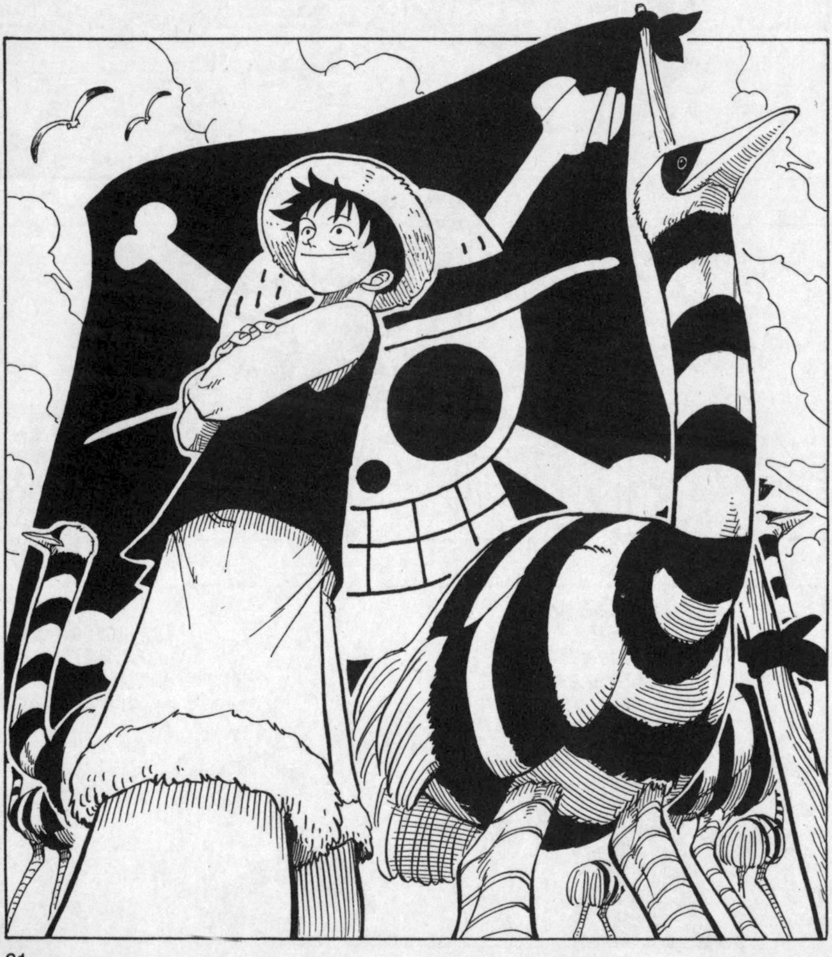

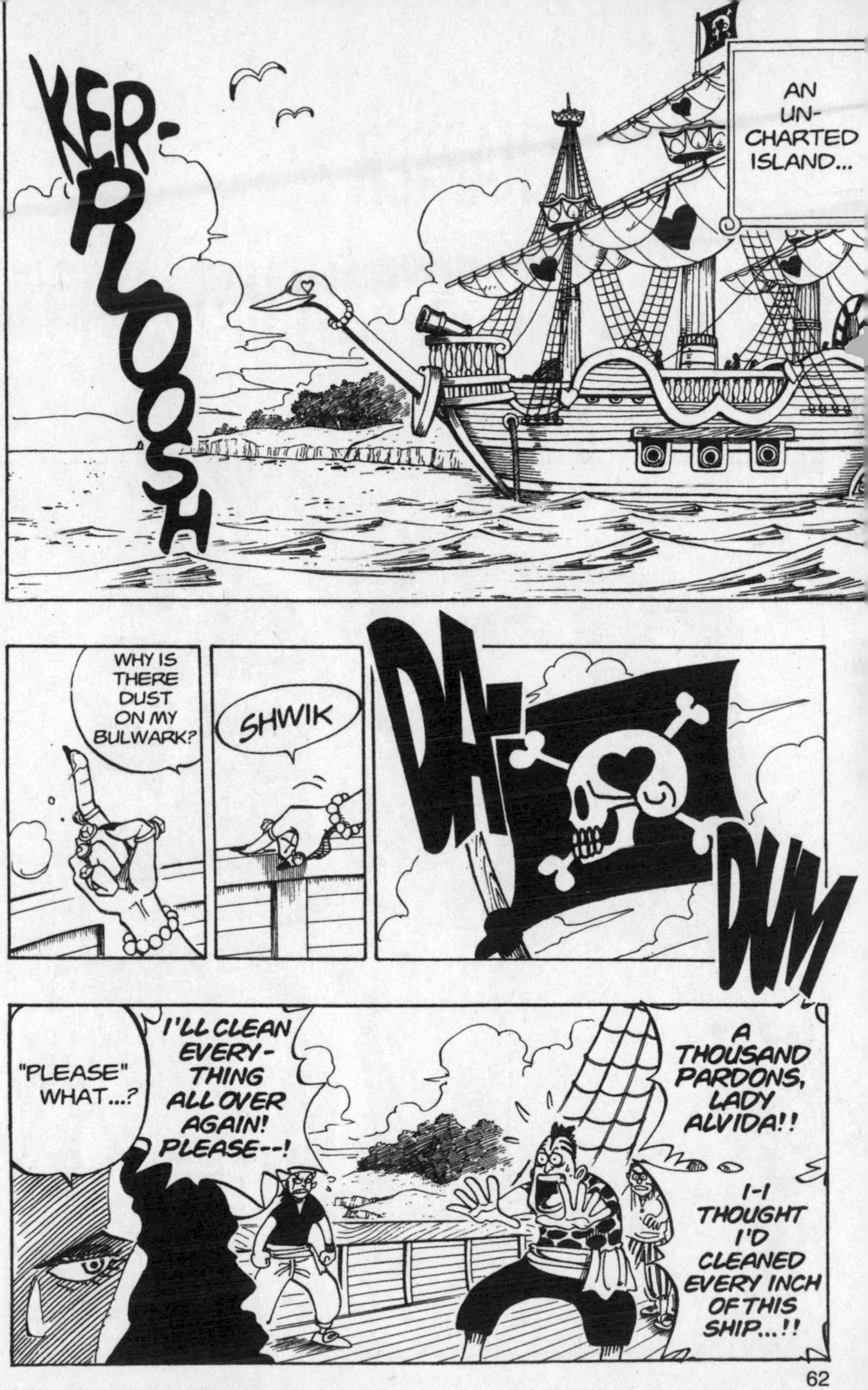
AN UN-CHARTED ISLAND...
KER-PLOOSH
DA-DUM
SHWIK
WHY IS THERE DUST ON MY BULWARK?
A THOUSAND PARDONS, LADY ALVIDA!!
I-I THOUGHT I'D CLEANED EVERY INCH OF THIS SHIP...!!
I'LL CLEAN EVERY-THING ALL OVER AGAIN! PLEASE--!
"PLEASE" WHAT...?

READ THIS WAY

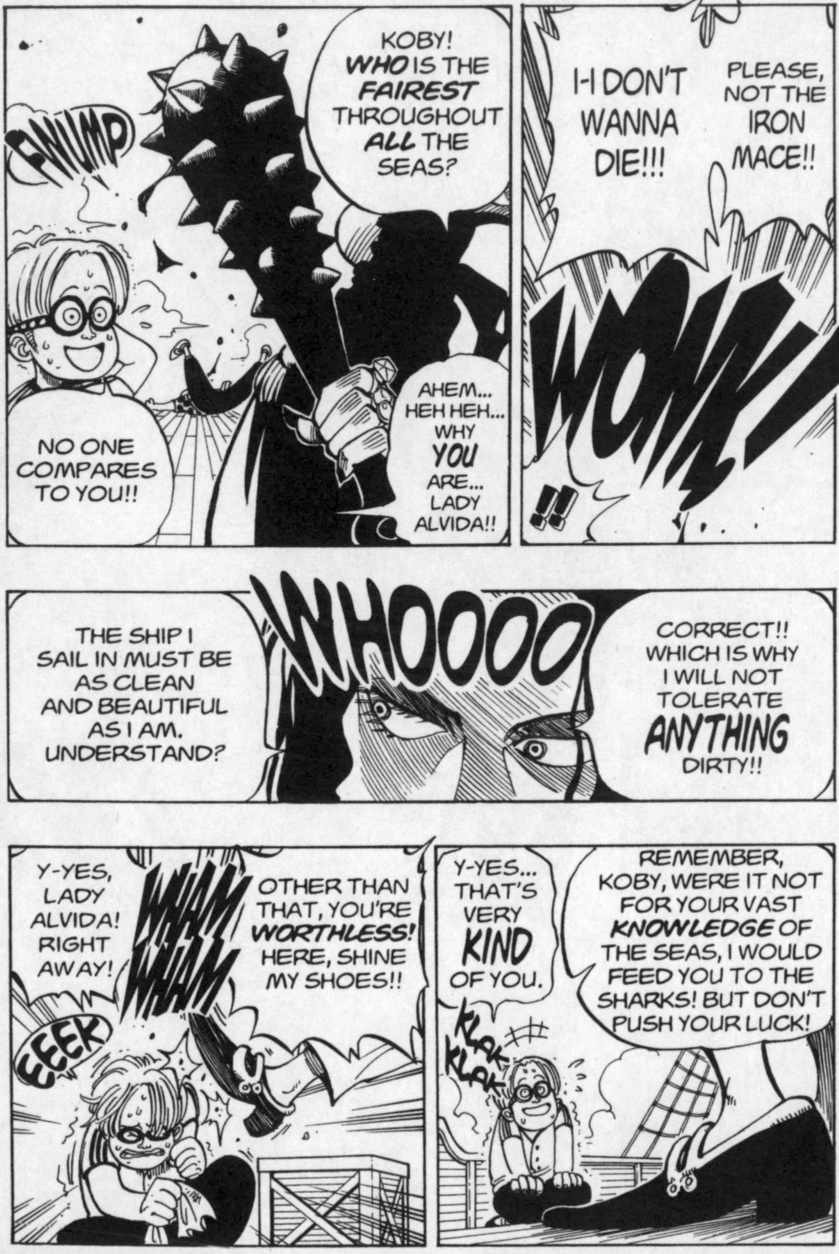

PLEASE, NOT THE IRON MACE!!
I-I DON'T WANNA DIE!!!
WOMP!!
KOBY! WHO IS THE FAIREST THROUGHOUT ALL THE SEAS?
AHEM... HEH HEH... WHY YOU ARE... LADY ALVIDA!!
SWUMP
NO ONE COMPARES TO YOU!!
CORRECT!! WHICH IS WHY I WILL NOT TOLERATE ANYTHING DIRTY!!
WHOOOO
THE SHIP I SAIL IN MUST BE AS CLEAN AND BEAUTIFUL AS I AM. UNDERSTAND?
REMEMBER, KOBY, WERE IT NOT FOR YOUR VAST KNOWLEDGE OF THE SEAS, I WOULD FEED YOU TO THE SHARKS! BUT DON'T PUSH YOUR LUCK!
Y-YES... THAT'S VERY KIND OF YOU.
KLAK KLAK
OTHER THAN THAT, YOU'RE WORTHLESS! HERE, SHINE MY SHOES!!
Y-YES, LADY ALVIDA! RIGHT AWAY!
EEEK

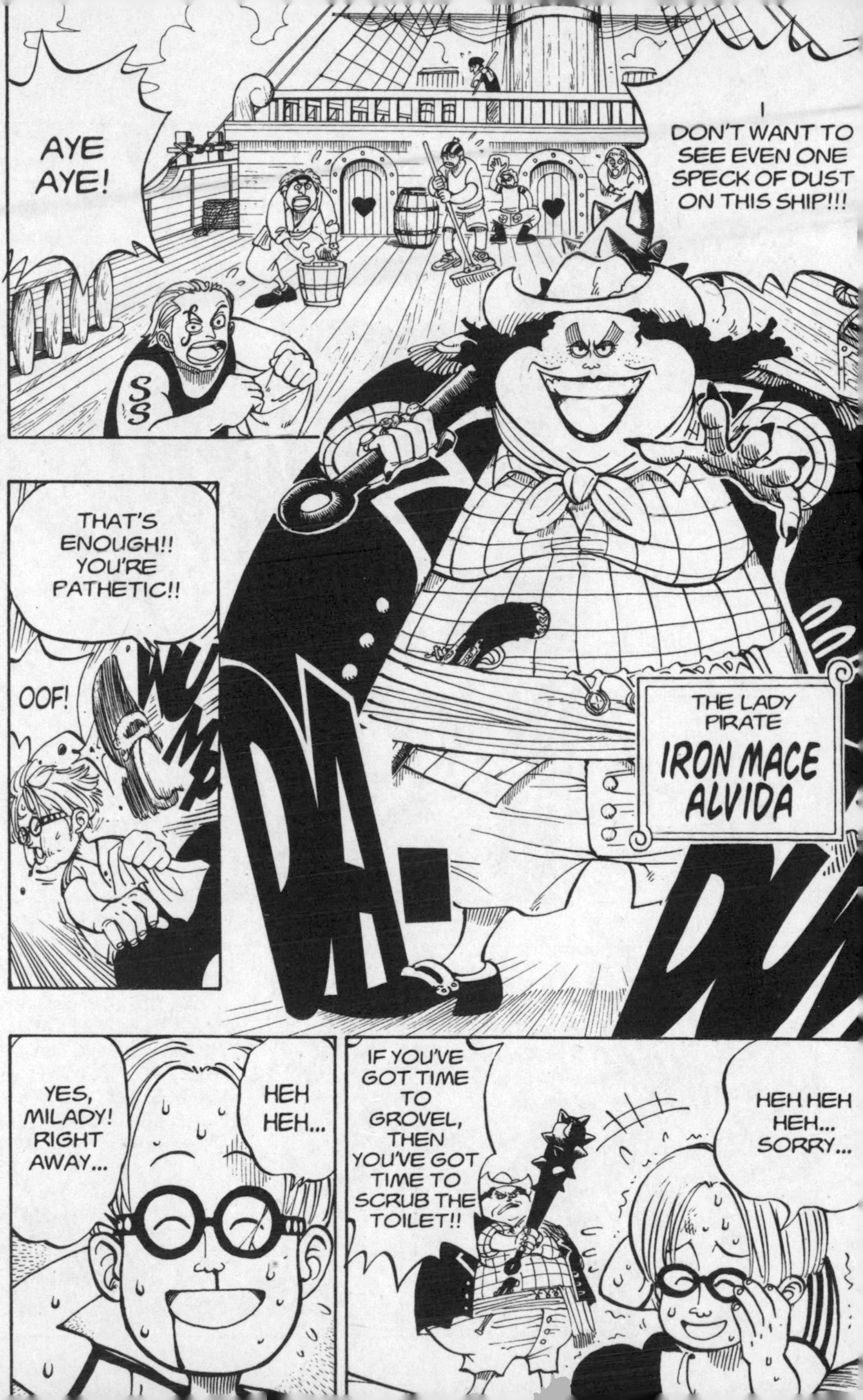
I DON'T WANT TO SEE EVEN ONE SPECK OF DUST ON THIS SHIP!!!
AYE AYE!
THE LADY PIRATE
IRON MACE ALVIDA
DA-
DA
THAT'S ENOUGH!! YOU'RE PATHETIC!!
WUMP
OOF!
HEH HEH HEH... SORRY...
IF YOU'VE GOT TIME TO GROVEL, THEN YOU'VE GOT TIME TO SCRUB THE TOILET!!
HEH HEH...
YES, MILADY! RIGHT AWAY...

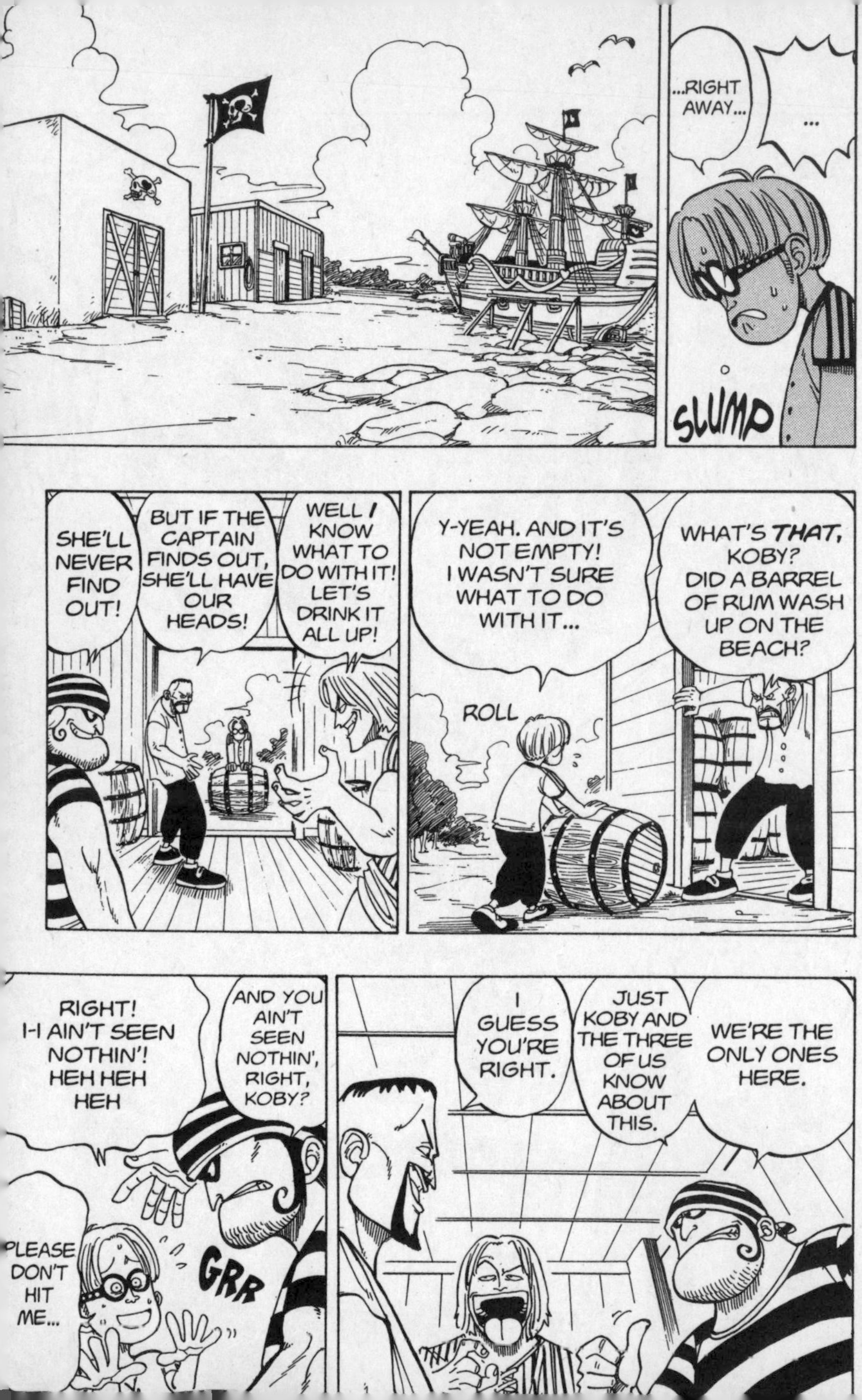
...RIGHT AWAY...
...
SLUMP
WHAT'S *THAT,* KOBY? DID A BARREL OF RUM WASH UP ON THE BEACH?
Y-YEAH. AND IT'S NOT EMPTY! I WASN'T SURE WHAT TO DO WITH IT...
ROLL
WELL *I* KNOW WHAT TO DO WITH IT! LET'S DRINK IT ALL UP!
BUT IF THE CAPTAIN FINDS OUT, SHE'LL HAVE OUR HEADS!
SHE'LL NEVER FIND OUT!
WE'RE THE ONLY ONES HERE.
JUST KOBY AND THE THREE OF US KNOW ABOUT THIS.
I GUESS YOU'RE RIGHT.
AND YOU AIN'T SEEN NOTHIN', RIGHT, KOBY?
RIGHT! I-I AIN'T SEEN NOTHIN'! HEH HEH HEH
GRR
PLEASE DON'T HIT ME...

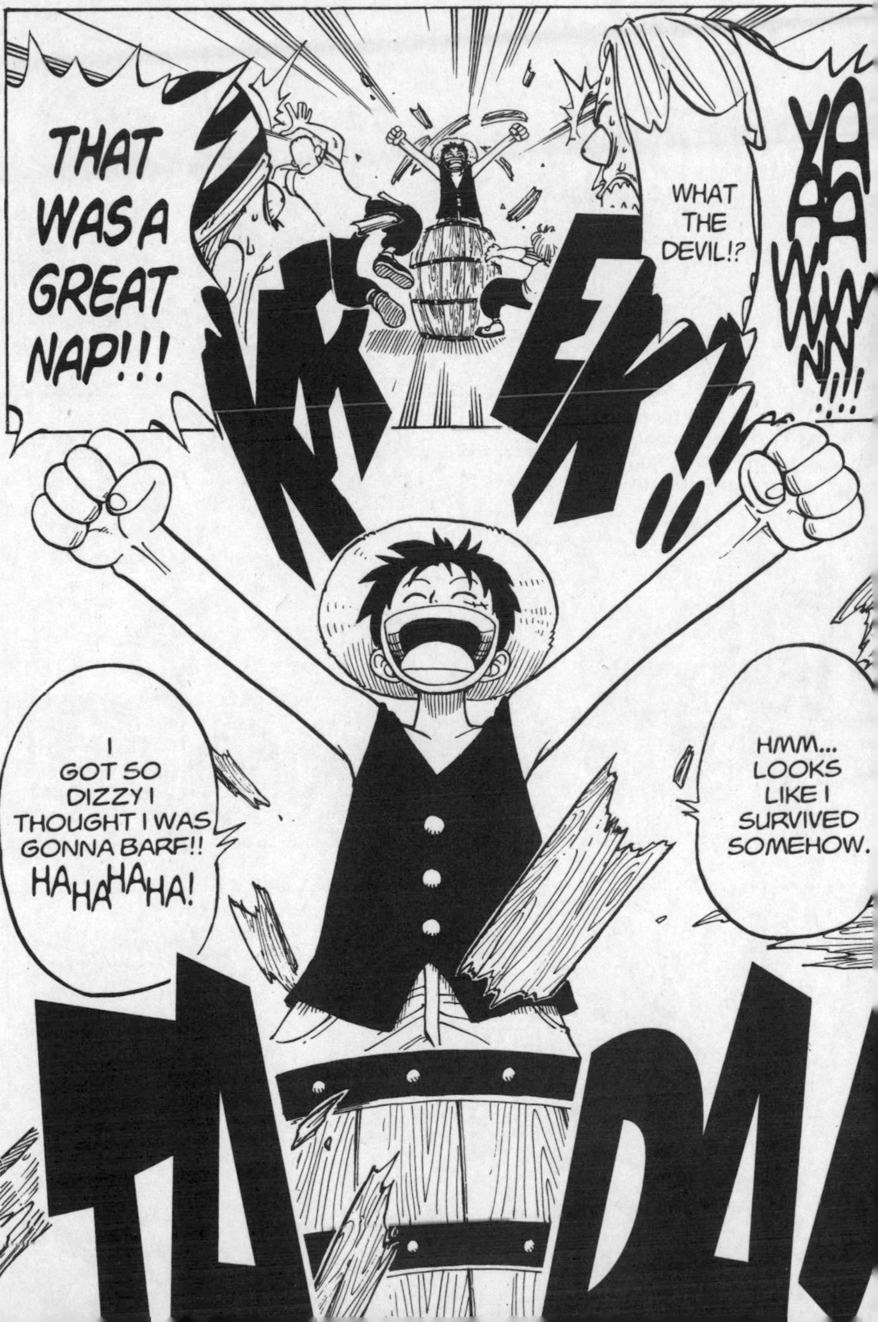
YAAAWWWN!!!!
WHAT THE DEVIL!?
THAT WAS A GREAT NAP!!!
HMM... LOOKS LIKE I SURVIVED SOMEHOW.
I GOT SO DIZZY I THOUGHT I WAS GONNA BARF!! HAHAHAHAHA!

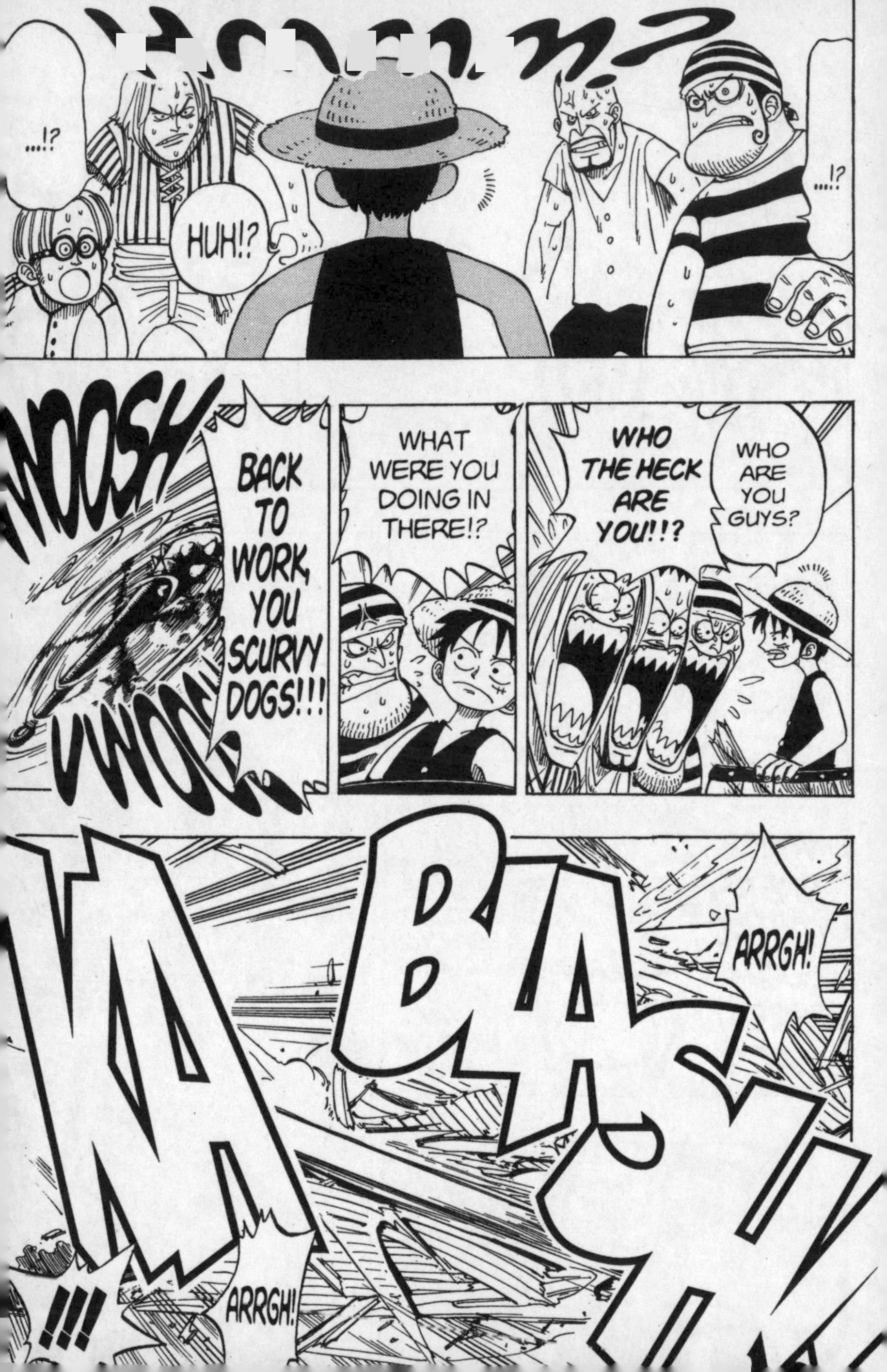

....!?
HUH!?
....!?
WHO ARE YOU GUYS?
WHO THE HECK ARE YOU!!?
WHAT WERE YOU DOING IN THERE!?
BACK TO WORK, YOU SCURVY DOGS!!!
WOOSH
ARRGH!
ARRGH!
!!!

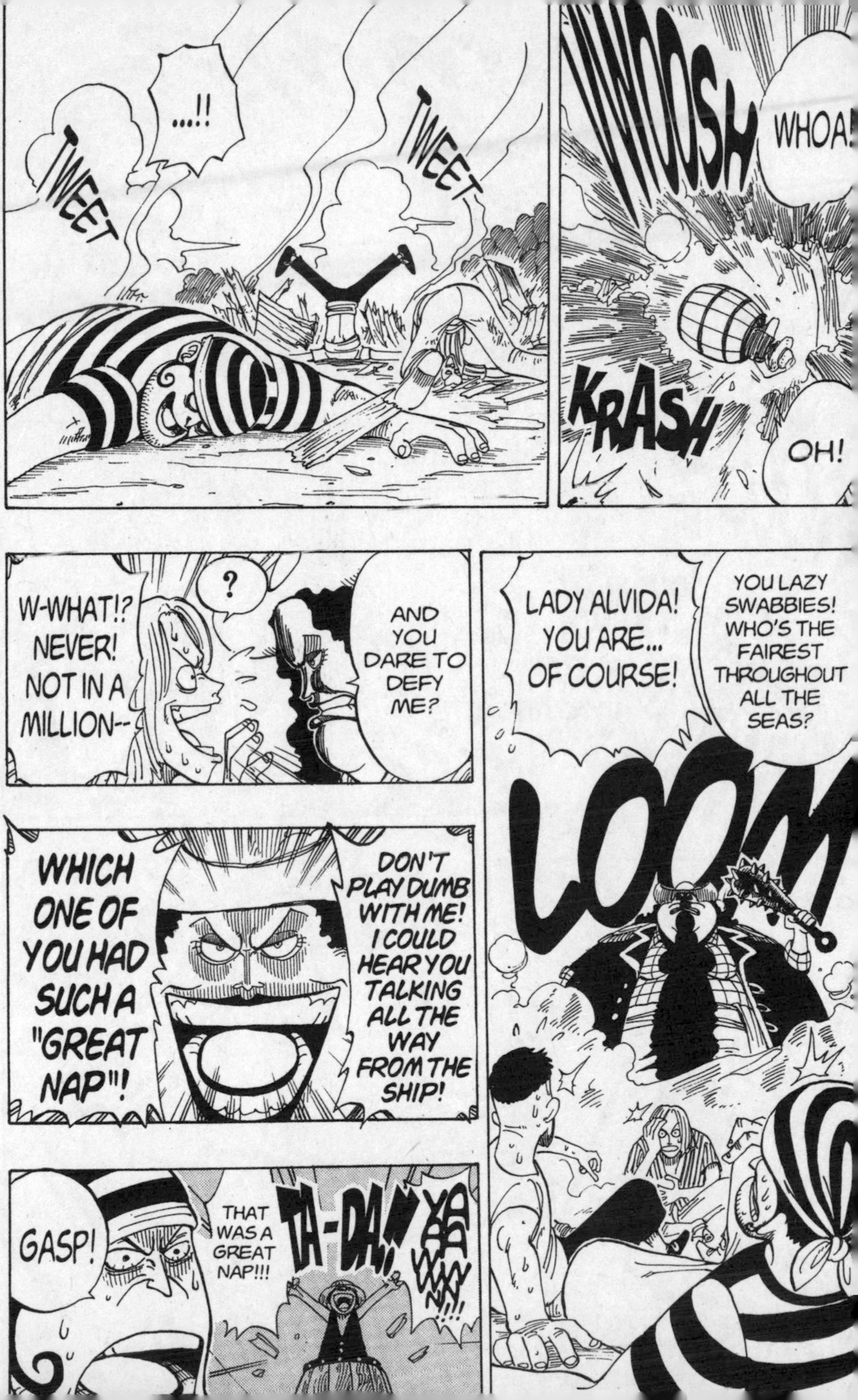
WHOOSH
WHOA!
KRASH
OH!
TWEET
...!!
TWEET
YOU LAZY SWABBIES! WHO'S THE FAIREST THROUGHOUT ALL THE SEAS?
LADY ALVIDA! YOU ARE... OF COURSE!
LOOM
AND YOU DARE TO DEFY ME?
?
W-WHAT!? NEVER! NOT IN A MILLION--
DON'T PLAY DUMB WITH ME! I COULD HEAR YOU TALKING ALL THE WAY FROM THE SHIP!
WHICH ONE OF YOU HAD SUCH A "GREAT NAP"!
TA-DA!!
THAT WAS A GREAT NAP!!!
GASP!

READ THIS WAY

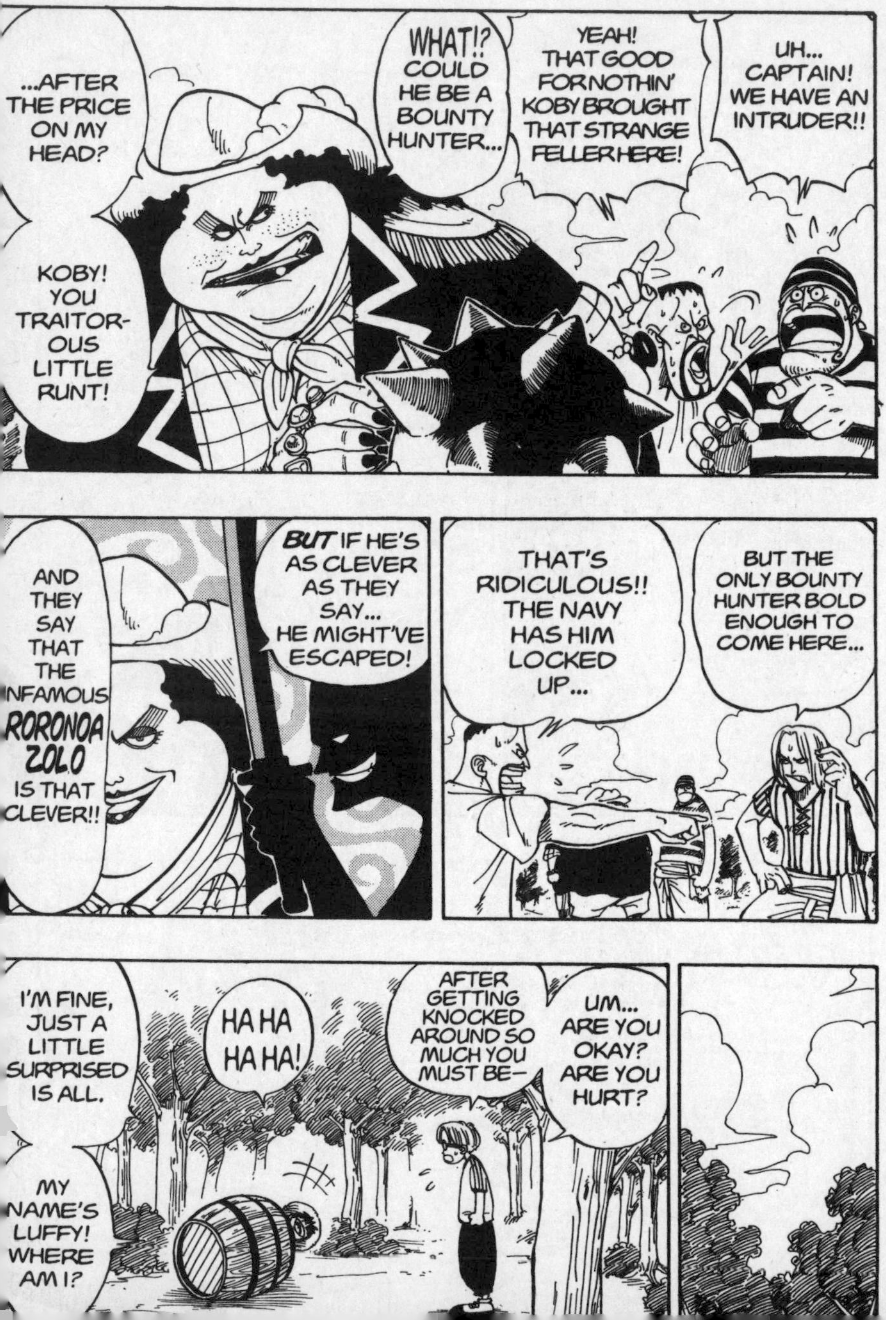
UH... CAPTAIN! WE HAVE AN INTRUDER!!
YEAH! THAT GOOD FORNOTHIN' KOBY BROUGHT THAT STRANGE FELLER HERE!
WHAT!? COULD HE BE A BOUNTY HUNTER...
...AFTER THE PRICE ON MY HEAD?
KOBY! YOU TRAITOROUS LITTLE RUNT!
BUT THE ONLY BOUNTY HUNTER BOLD ENOUGH TO COME HERE...
THAT'S RIDICULOUS!! THE NAVY HAS HIM LOCKED UP...
BUT IF HE'S AS CLEVER AS THEY SAY... HE MIGHT'VE ESCAPED!
AND THEY SAY THAT THE INFAMOUS **RORONOA ZOLO** IS THAT CLEVER!!
UM... ARE YOU OKAY? ARE YOU HURT?
AFTER GETTING KNOCKED AROUND SO MUCH YOU MUST BE–
HA HA HA HA!
I'M FINE, JUST A LITTLE SURPRISED IS ALL.
MY NAME'S LUFFY! WHERE AM I?

READ THIS WAY

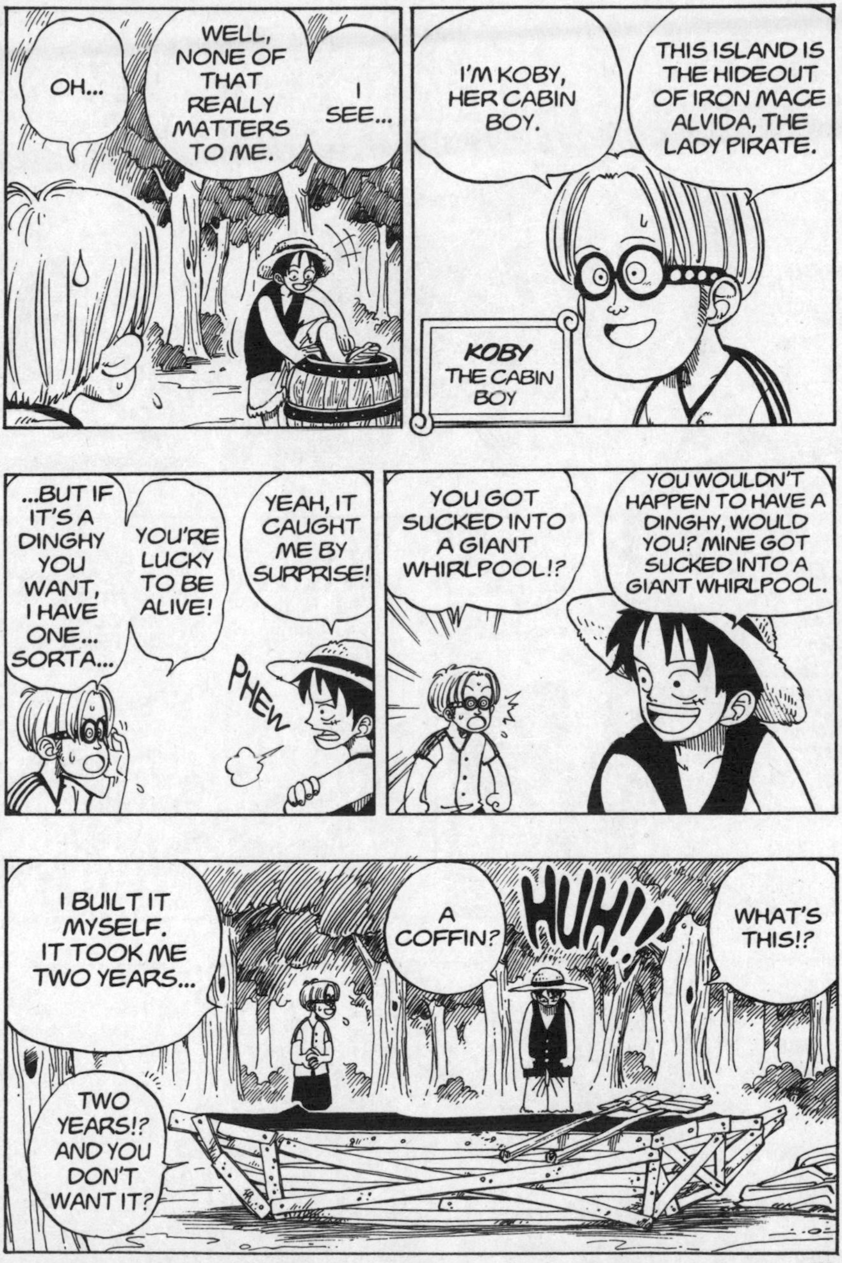
THIS ISLAND IS THE HIDEOUT OF IRON MACE ALVIDA, THE LADY PIRATE.
I'M KOBY, HER CABIN BOY.
KOBY THE CABIN BOY
WELL, NONE OF THAT REALLY MATTERS TO ME.
OH...
I SEE...
YOU WOULDN'T HAPPEN TO HAVE A DINGHY, WOULD YOU? MINE GOT SUCKED INTO A GIANT WHIRLPOOL.
YOU GOT SUCKED INTO A GIANT WHIRLPOOL!?
YEAH, IT CAUGHT ME BY SURPRISE!
PHEW
YOU'RE LUCKY TO BE ALIVE!
...BUT IF IT'S A DINGHY YOU WANT, I HAVE ONE... SORTA...
WHAT'S THIS!?
HUH!!
A COFFIN?
I BUILT IT MYSELF. IT TOOK ME TWO YEARS...
TWO YEARS!? AND YOU DON'T WANT IT?

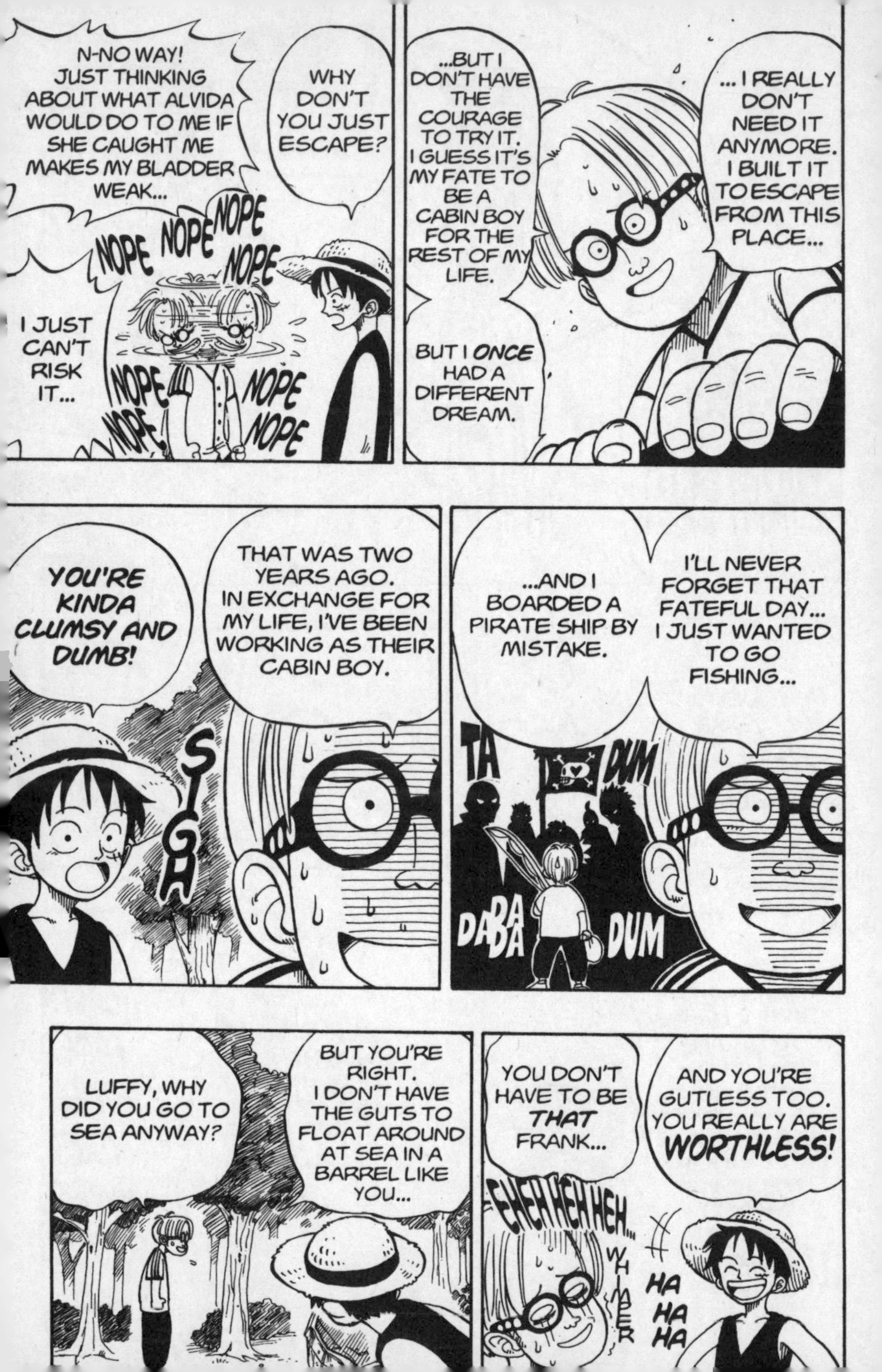
...I REALLY DON'T NEED IT ANYMORE. I BUILT IT TO ESCAPE FROM THIS PLACE...
...BUT I DON'T HAVE THE COURAGE TO TRY IT. I GUESS IT'S MY FATE TO BE A CABIN BOY FOR THE REST OF MY LIFE.
BUT I *ONCE* HAD A DIFFERENT DREAM.
WHY DON'T YOU JUST ESCAPE?
N-NO WAY! JUST THINKING ABOUT WHAT ALVIDA WOULD DO TO ME IF SHE CAUGHT ME MAKES MY BLADDER WEAK...
NOPE NOPE NOPE NOPE NOPE NOPE NOPE NOPE
I JUST CAN'T RISK IT...
I'LL NEVER FORGET THAT FATEFUL DAY... I JUST WANTED TO GO FISHING...
...AND I BOARDED A PIRATE SHIP BY MISTAKE.
TA DUM
DABADA DUM
THAT WAS TWO YEARS AGO. IN EXCHANGE FOR MY LIFE, I'VE BEEN WORKING AS THEIR CABIN BOY.
YOU'RE KINDA CLUMSY AND DUMB!
SIGH
AND YOU'RE GUTLESS TOO. YOU REALLY ARE **WORTHLESS!**
YOU DON'T HAVE TO BE *THAT* FRANK...
EHEH HEH HEH...
WHIMPER
HA HA HA
BUT YOU'RE RIGHT. I DON'T HAVE THE GUTS TO FLOAT AROUND AT SEA IN A BARREL LIKE YOU...
LUFFY, WHY DID YOU GO TO SEA ANYWAY?

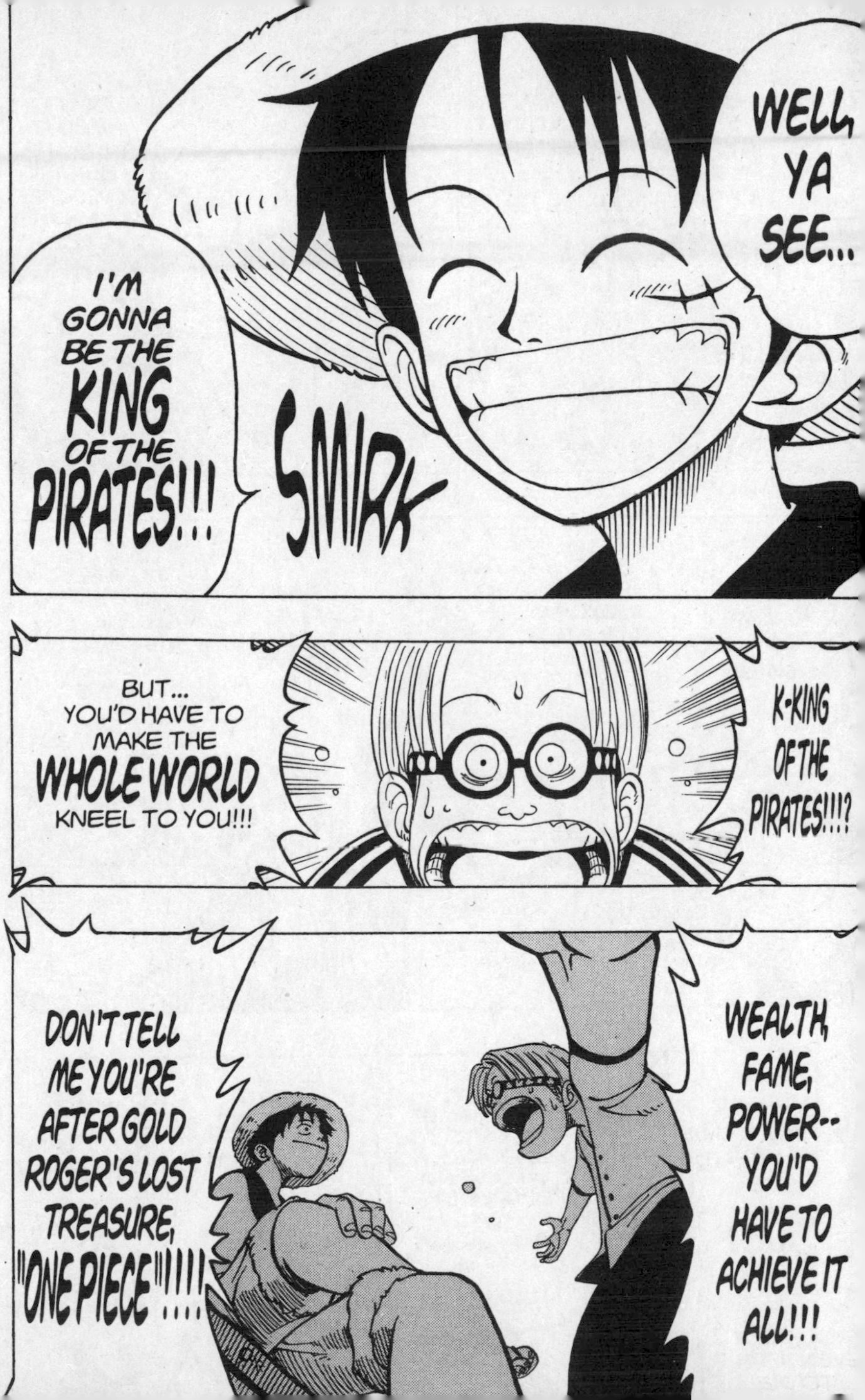

WELL, YA SEE...
I'M GONNA BE THE KING OF THE PIRATES!!!
SMIRK
K-KING OF THE PIRATES!!!?
BUT... YOU'D HAVE TO MAKE THE WHOLE WORLD KNEEL TO YOU!!!
WEALTH, FAME, POWER-- YOU'D HAVE TO ACHIEVE IT ALL!!!
DON'T TELL ME YOU'RE AFTER GOLD ROGER'S LOST TREASURE, "ONE PIECE"!!!!

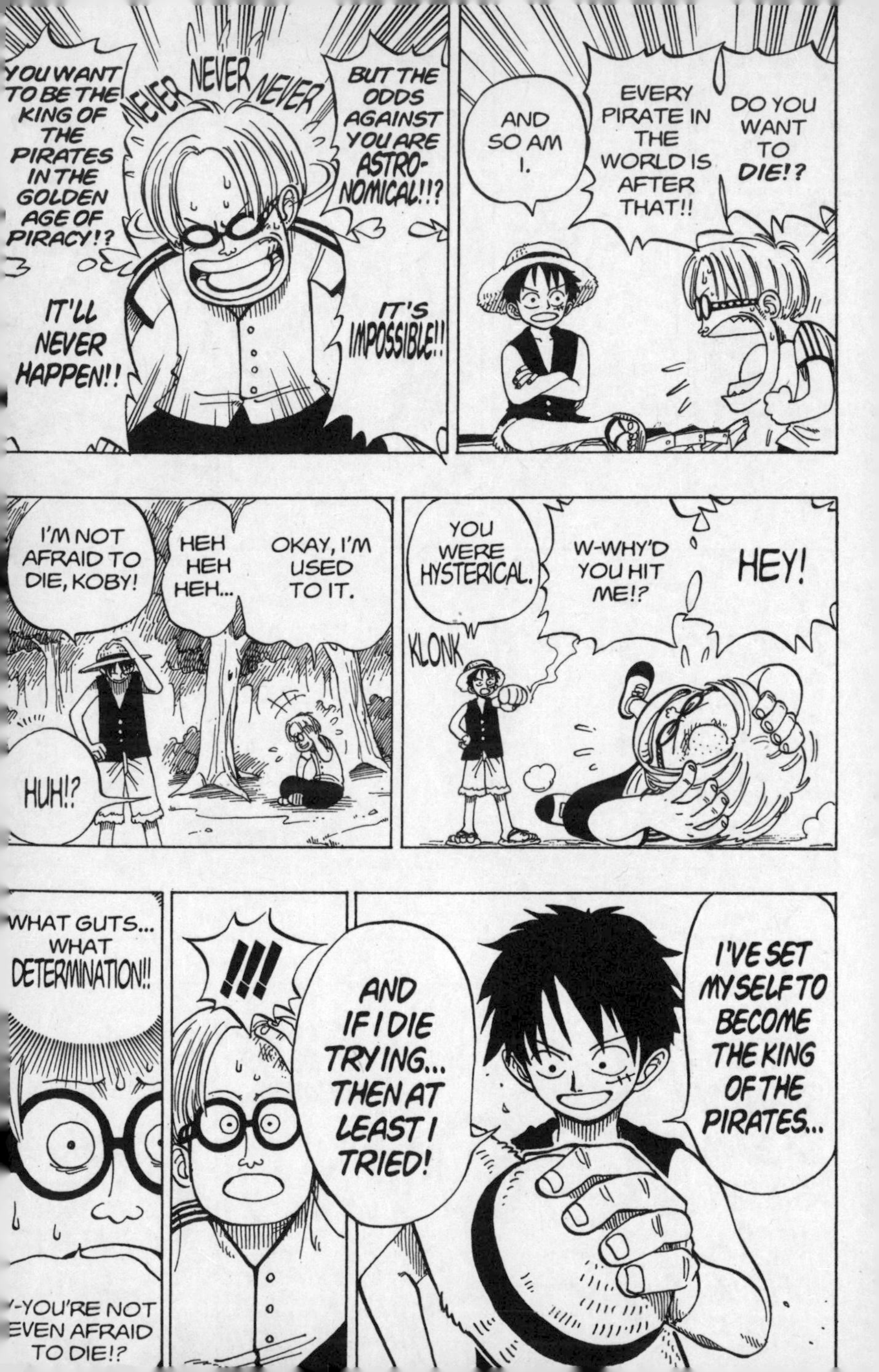
DO YOU WANT TO DIE!?
EVERY PIRATE IN THE WORLD IS AFTER THAT!!
AND SO AM I.
BUT THE ODDS AGAINST YOU ARE ASTRONOMICAL!!?
NEVER NEVER NEVER
YOU WANT TO BE THE KING OF THE PIRATES IN THE GOLDEN AGE OF PIRACY!?
IT'S IMPOSSIBLE!!
IT'LL NEVER HAPPEN!!
HEY!
W-WHY'D YOU HIT ME!?
YOU WERE HYSTERICAL.
KLONK
OKAY, I'M USED TO IT.
HEH HEH HEH...
I'M NOT AFRAID TO DIE, KOBY!
HUH!?
I'VE SET MYSELF TO BECOME THE KING OF THE PIRATES...
AND IF I DIE TRYING... THEN AT LEAST I TRIED!
!!!
WHAT GUTS... WHAT DETERMINATION!!
-YOU'RE NOT EVEN AFRAID TO DIE!?

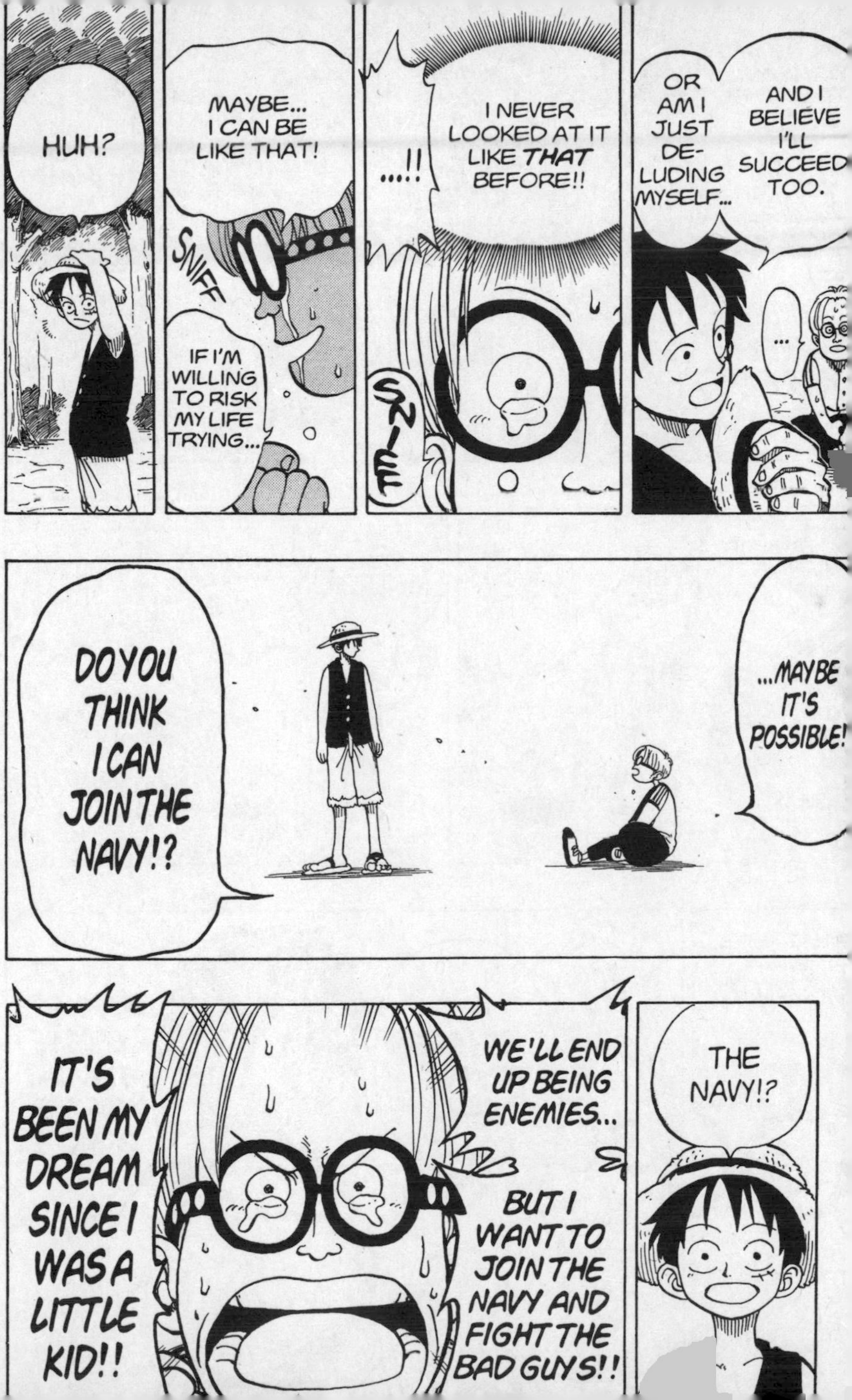
AND I BELIEVE I'LL SUCCEED TOO.
OR AM I JUST DE-LUDING MYSELF...
...
I NEVER LOOKED AT IT LIKE THAT BEFORE!!
....!!
SNIFF
MAYBE... I CAN BE LIKE THAT!
SNIFF
IF I'M WILLING TO RISK MY LIFE TRYING...
HUH?
...MAYBE IT'S POSSIBLE!
DO YOU THINK I CAN JOIN THE NAVY!?
THE NAVY!?
WE'LL END UP BEING ENEMIES...
BUT I WANT TO JOIN THE NAVY AND FIGHT THE BAD GUYS!!
IT'S BEEN MY DREAM SINCE I WAS A LITTLE KID!!

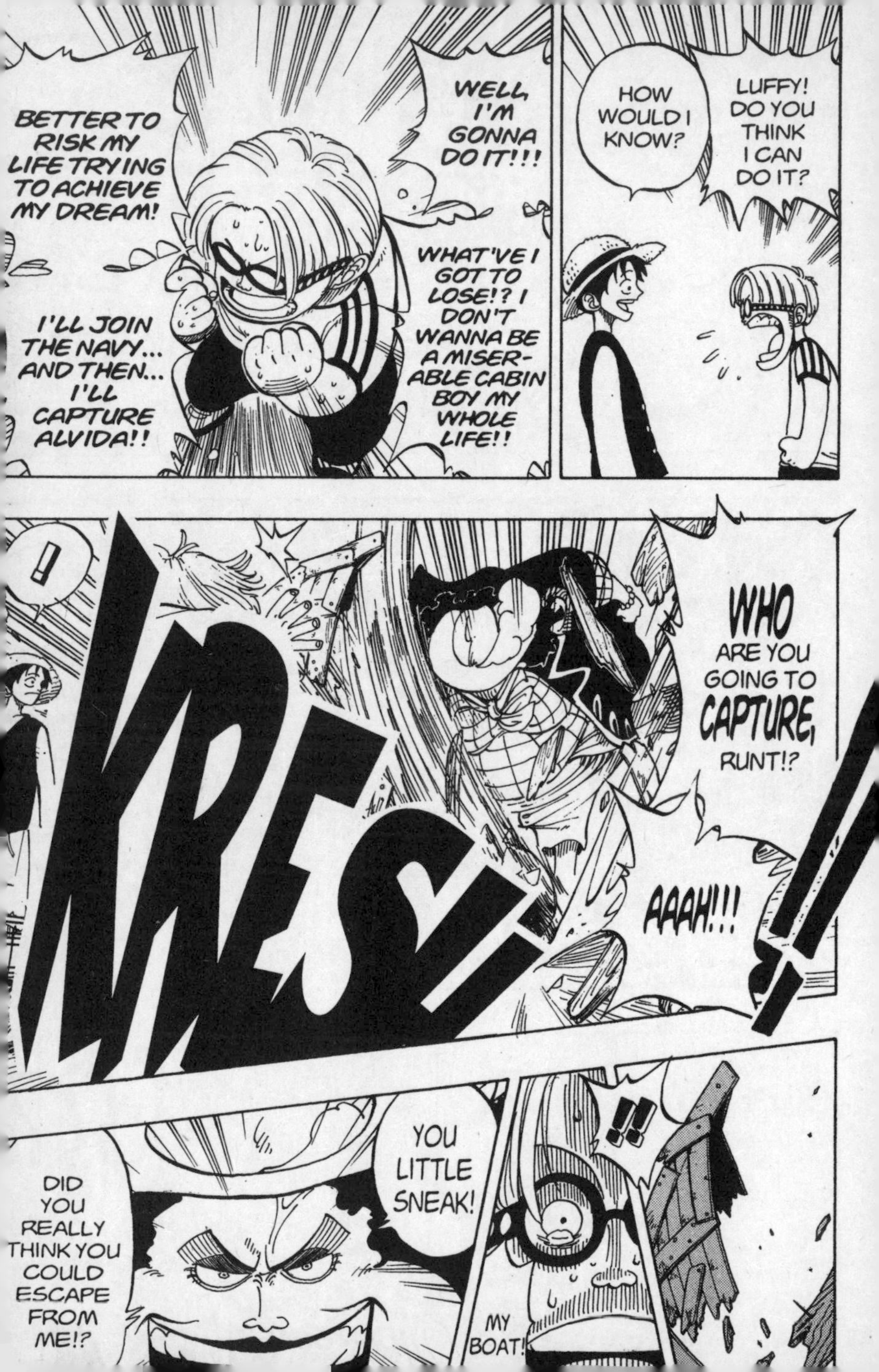
LUFFY! DO YOU THINK I CAN DO IT?
HOW WOULD I KNOW?
WELL, I'M GONNA DO IT!!!
WHAT'VE I GOT TO LOSE!? I DON'T WANNA BE A MISERABLE CABIN BOY MY WHOLE LIFE!!
BETTER TO RISK MY LIFE TRYING TO ACHIEVE MY DREAM!
I'LL JOIN THE NAVY... AND THEN... I'LL CAPTURE ALVIDA!!
WHO ARE YOU GOING TO CAPTURE, RUNT!?
AAAH!!!
KRESH!!
!
!!
YOU LITTLE SNEAK!
MY BOAT!
DID YOU REALLY THINK YOU COULD ESCAPE FROM ME!?

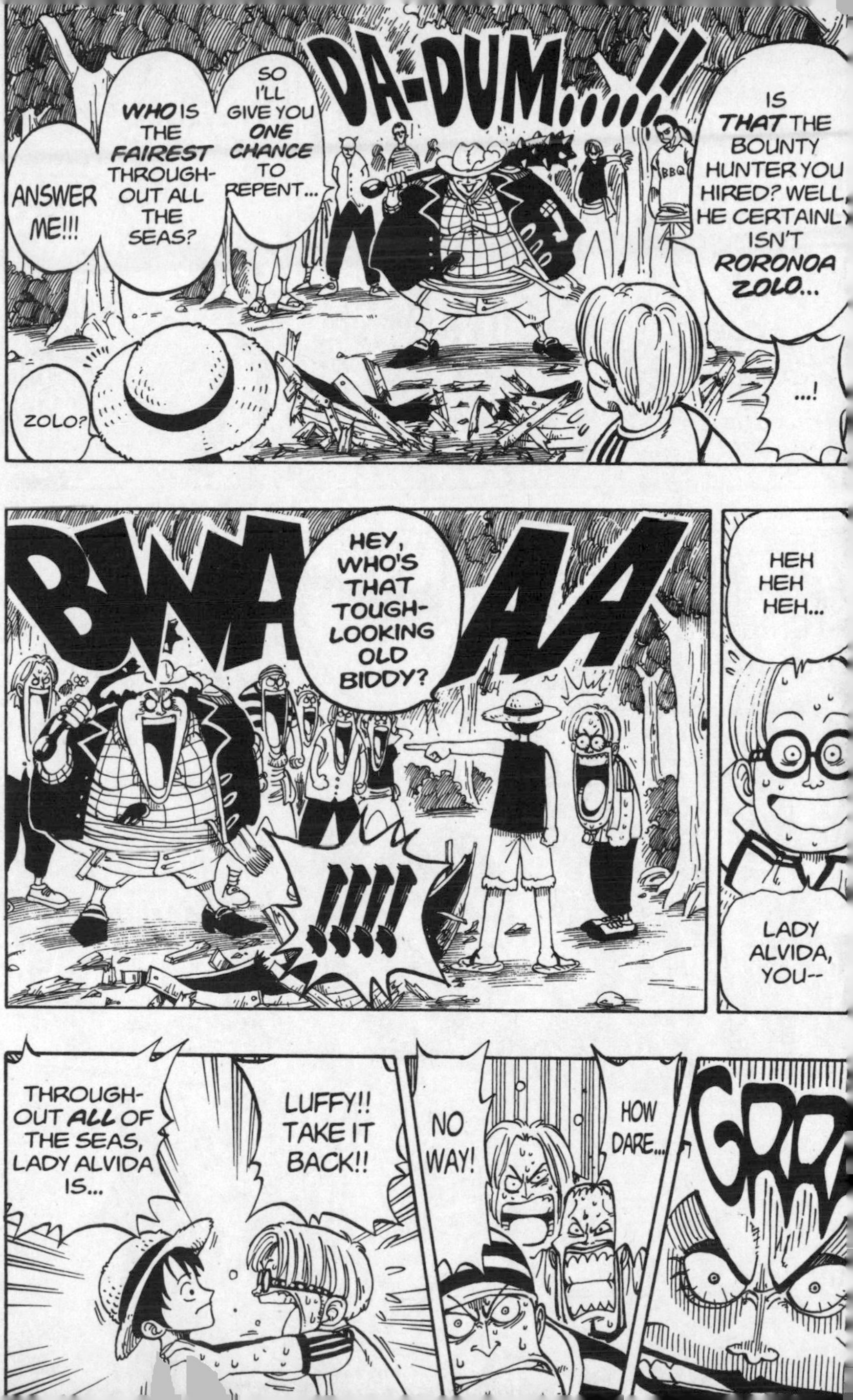
IS THAT THE BOUNTY HUNTER YOU HIRED? WELL, HE CERTAINLY ISN'T RORONOA ZOLO...
...!
DA-DUM...!!
SO I'LL GIVE YOU ONE CHANCE TO REPENT...
WHO IS THE FAIREST THROUGHOUT ALL THE SEAS?
ANSWER ME!!!
ZOLO?
HEH HEH HEH...
LADY ALVIDA, YOU--
BWA AA
HEY, WHO'S THAT TOUGH-LOOKING OLD BIDDY?
!!!!
GRR
HOW DARE...
NO WAY!
LUFFY!! TAKE IT BACK!!
THROUGHOUT ALL OF THE SEAS, LADY ALVIDA IS...

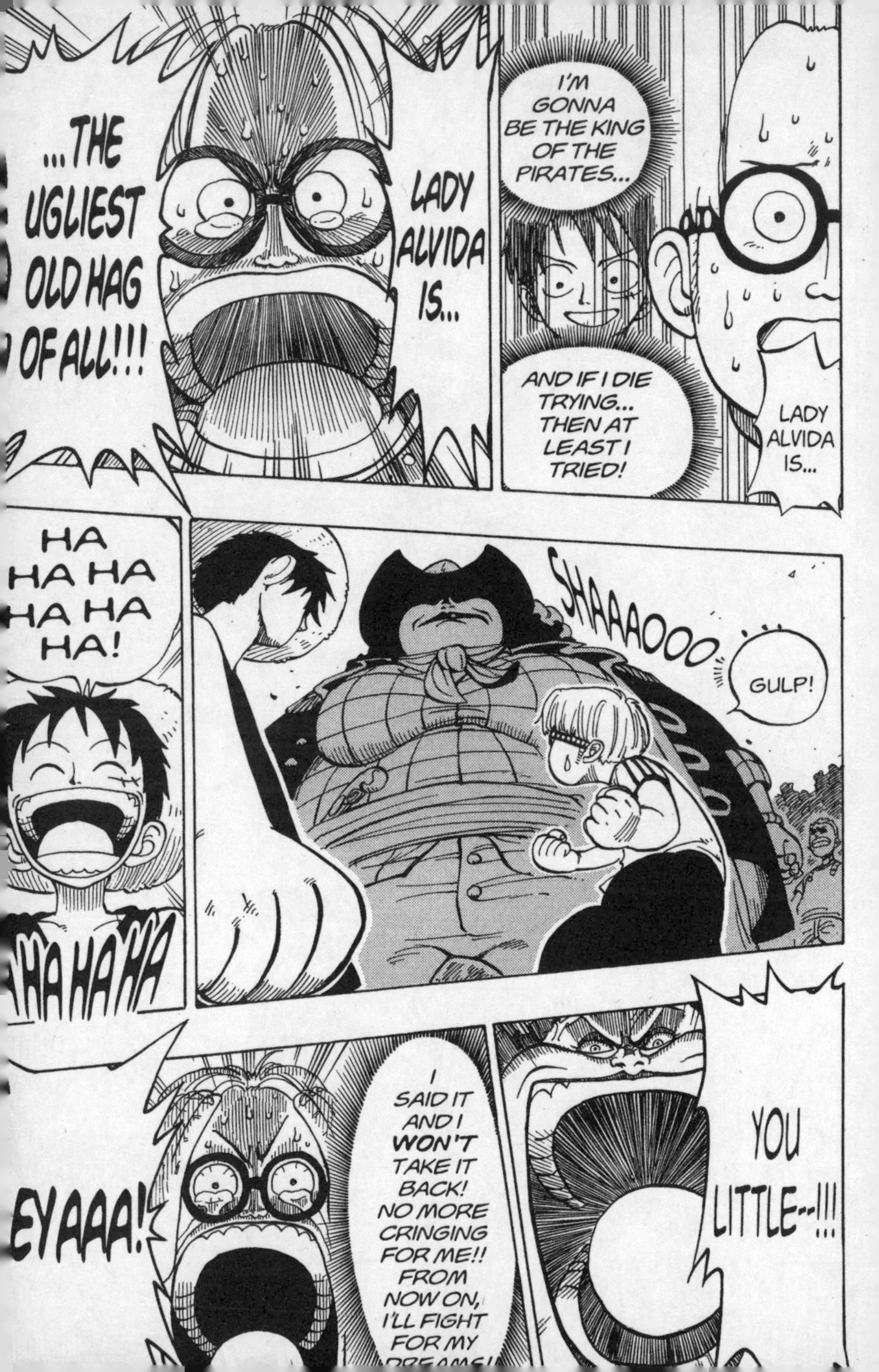
I'M GONNA BE THE KING OF THE PIRATES...
AND IF I DIE TRYING... THEN AT LEAST I TRIED!
LADY ALVIDA IS...
LADY ALVIDA IS...
...THE UGLIEST OLD HAG OF ALL!!!
SHAAAOOO
GULP!
HA HA HA HA HA HA HA!
HA HA HA
YOU LITTLE--!!!
I SAID IT AND I **WON'T** TAKE IT BACK! NO MORE CRINGING FOR ME!! FROM NOW ON, I'LL FIGHT FOR MY DREAMS!
EYAAA!!

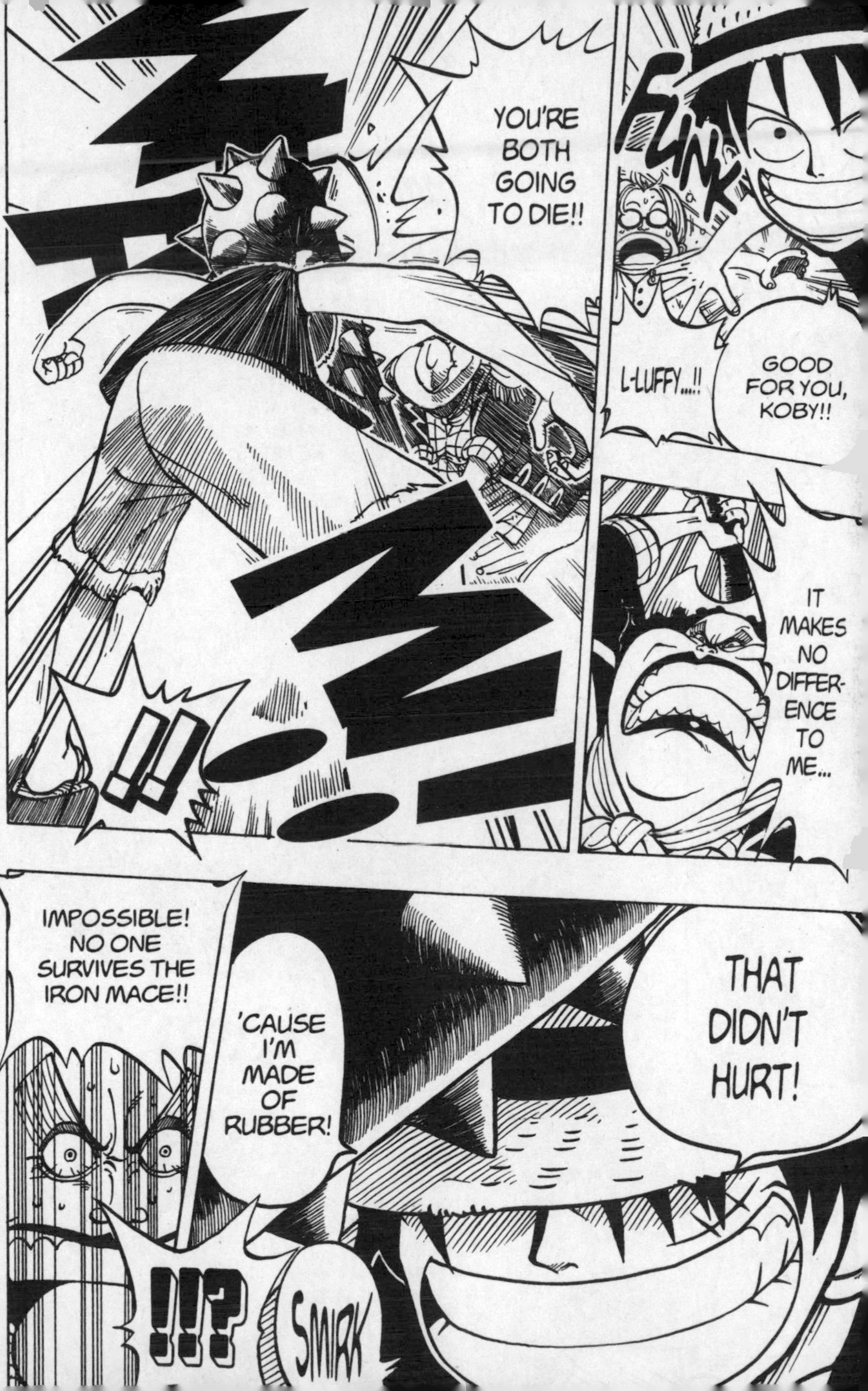
FUNK
GOOD FOR YOU, KOBY!!
L-LUFFY...!!
IT MAKES NO DIFFERENCE TO ME...
YOU'RE BOTH GOING TO DIE!!
!!
THAT DIDN'T HURT!
'CAUSE I'M MADE OF RUBBER!
SMIRK
IMPOSSIBLE! NO ONE SURVIVES THE IRON MACE!!
!!?

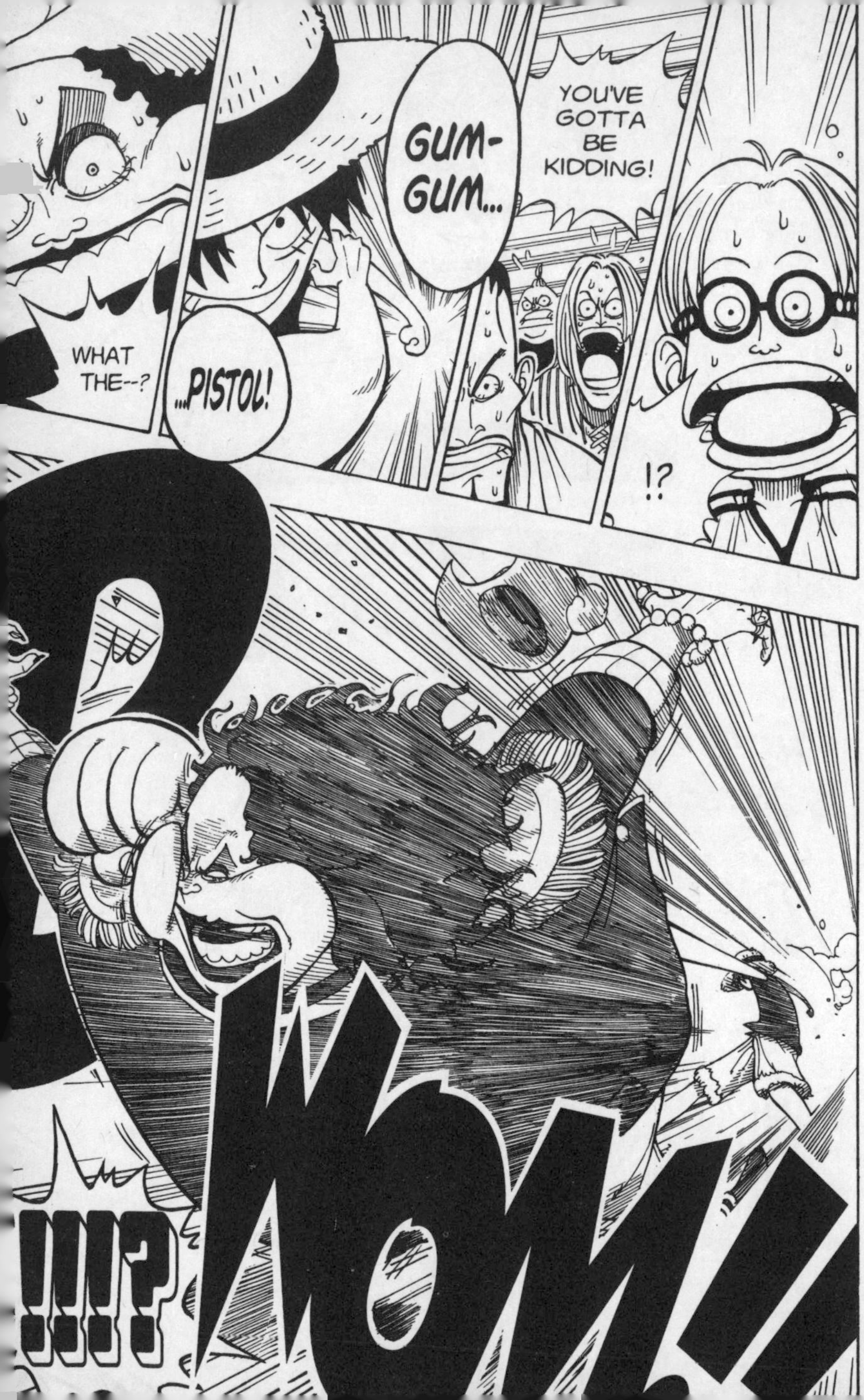
!?
YOU'VE GOTTA BE KIDDING!
GUM-GUM...
...PISTOL!
WHAT THE--?
!!!?

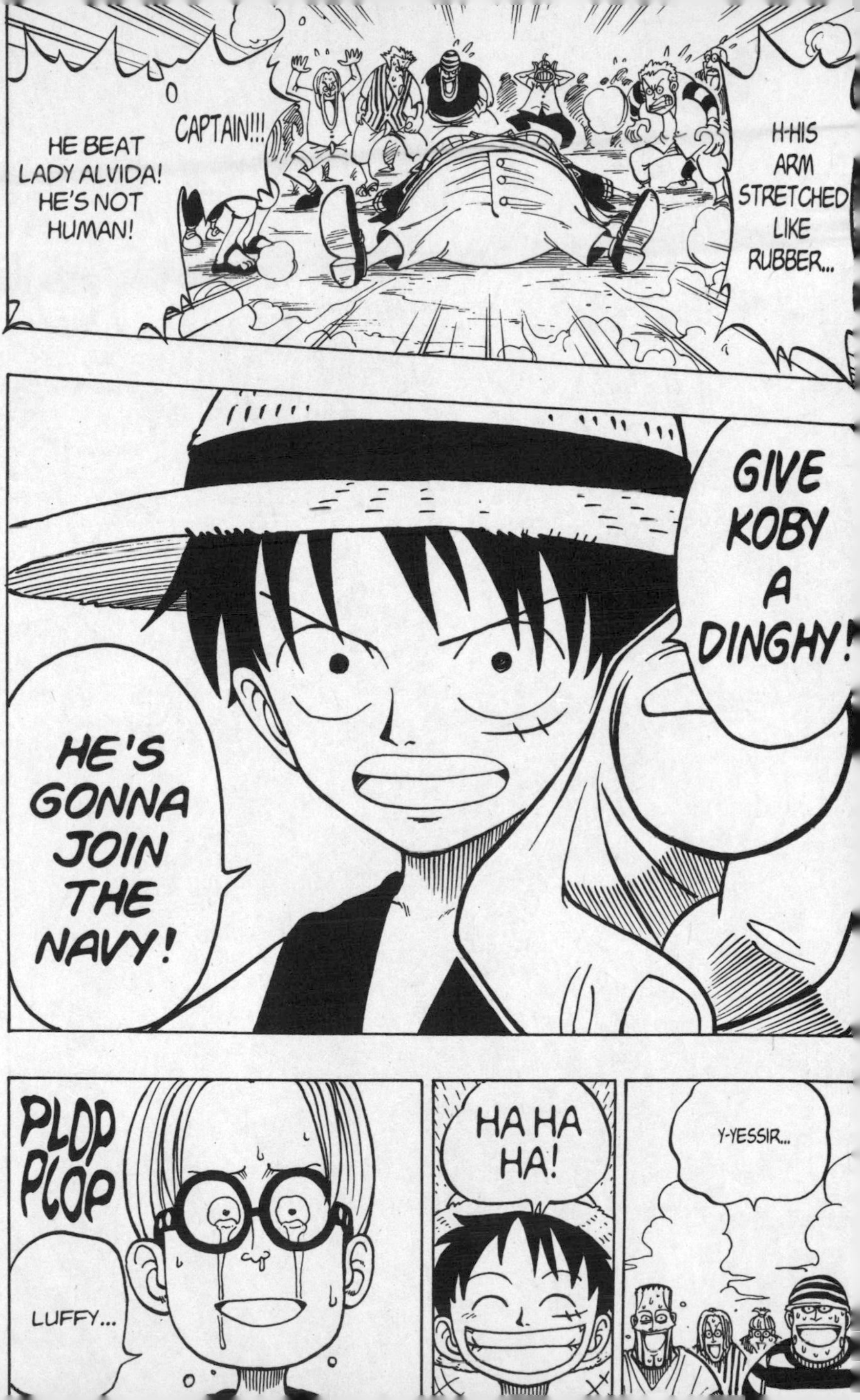
H-HIS ARM STRETCHED LIKE RUBBER...
CAPTAIN!!!
HE BEAT LADY ALVIDA! HE'S NOT HUMAN!
GIVE KOBY A DINGHY!
HE'S GONNA JOIN THE NAVY!
Y-YESSIR...
HA HA HA!
PLOP PLOP
LUFFY...

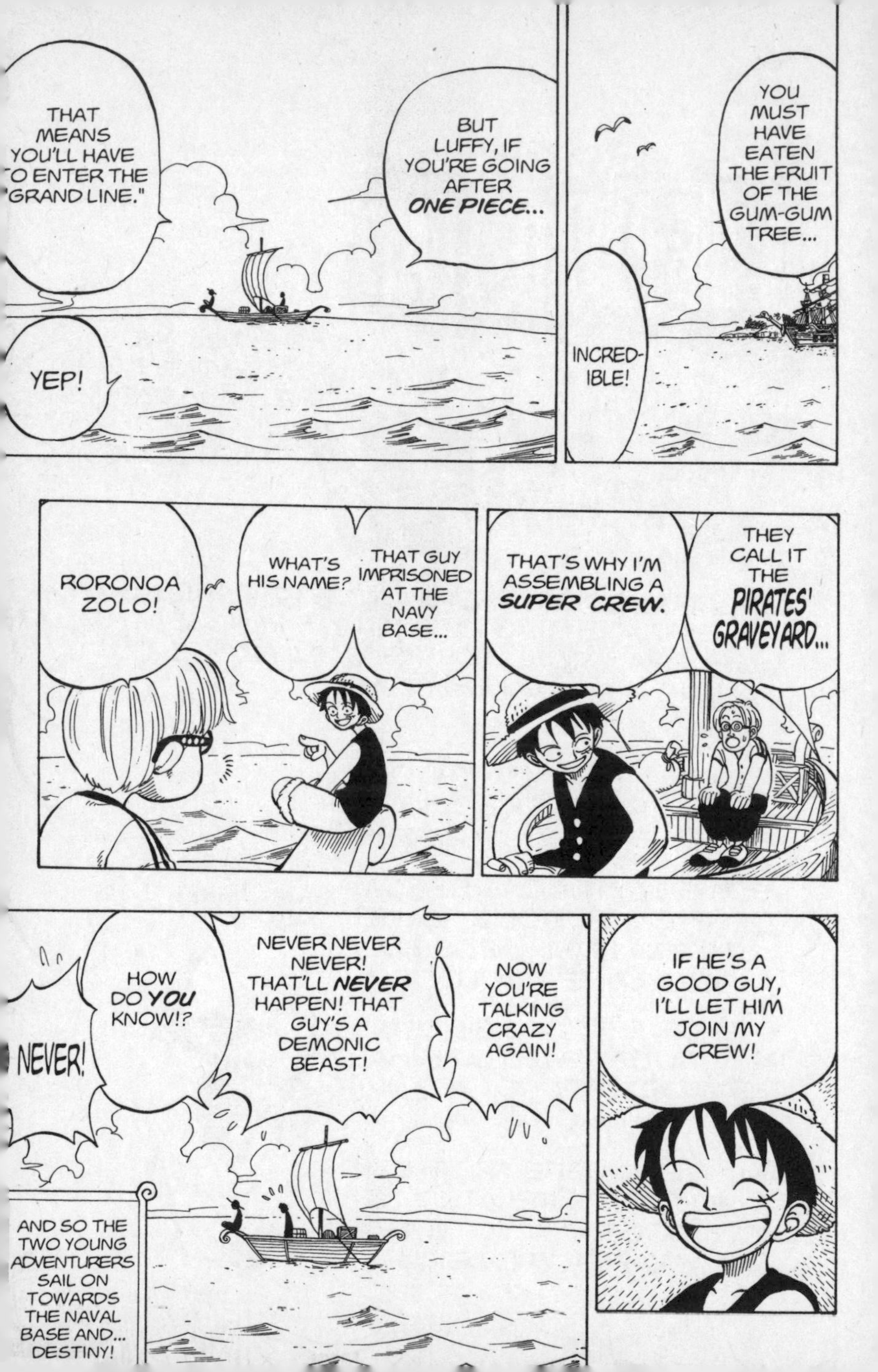
YOU MUST HAVE EATEN THE FRUIT OF THE GUM-GUM TREE...
INCREDIBLE!
BUT LUFFY, IF YOU'RE GOING AFTER *ONE PIECE*...
THAT MEANS YOU'LL HAVE TO ENTER THE "GRAND LINE."
YEP!
THEY CALL IT THE **PIRATES' GRAVEYARD...**
THAT'S WHY I'M ASSEMBLING A ***SUPER CREW.***
THAT GUY IMPRISONED AT THE NAVY BASE...
WHAT'S HIS NAME?
RORONOA ZOLO!
IF HE'S A GOOD GUY, I'LL LET HIM JOIN MY CREW!
NOW YOU'RE TALKING CRAZY AGAIN!
NEVER NEVER NEVER! THAT'LL ***NEVER*** HAPPEN! THAT GUY'S A DEMONIC BEAST!
HOW DO ***YOU*** KNOW!?
NEVER!
AND SO THE TWO YOUNG ADVENTURERS SAIL ON TOWARDS THE NAVAL BASE AND... DESTINY!

STEP 1
THE PIRATE FLAG

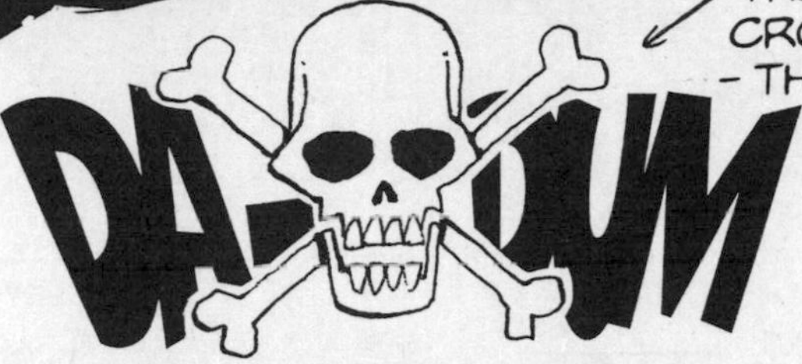
DA-DUM

"THE SKULL AND CROSSBONES" - THE CROSSBONES ARE THIGH BONES.

HERE IS SOME INFORMATION REGARDING THE PIRATE FLAG. THE PIRATE FLAG IS GENERALLY CALLED THE "JOLLY ROGER" AND IS A SYMBOL OF DEATH. SCARY, ISN'T IT?

THERE ARE MANY THEORIES CONCERNING THE ORIGIN OF THE TERM "JOLLY ROGER."

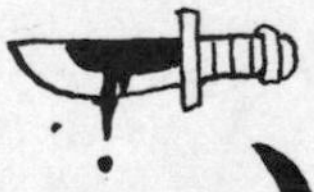

⚜ SOME SAY IT COMES FROM THE FRENCH "JOLIE ROUGE" OR "RED LOVELY," POSSIBLY REFERRING TO BLOOD.

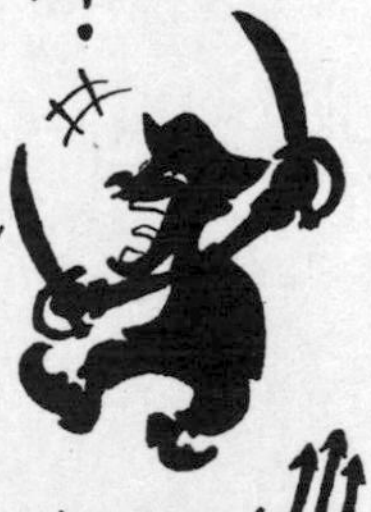

⚜ ANOTHER POSSIBILITY IS THAT "ROGER" WAS ORIGINALLY THE WORD "ROGUE," MEANING A THIEF OR VILLAIN.

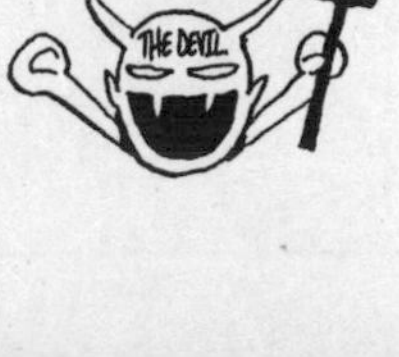
THE DEVIL

⚜ AND THEN THERE ARE THOSE WHO SAY IT'S RELATED TO "OLD ROGER," WHICH WAS A NAME FOR THE DEVIL.

CHAPTER 3: ENTER ZOLO—PIRATE HUNTER

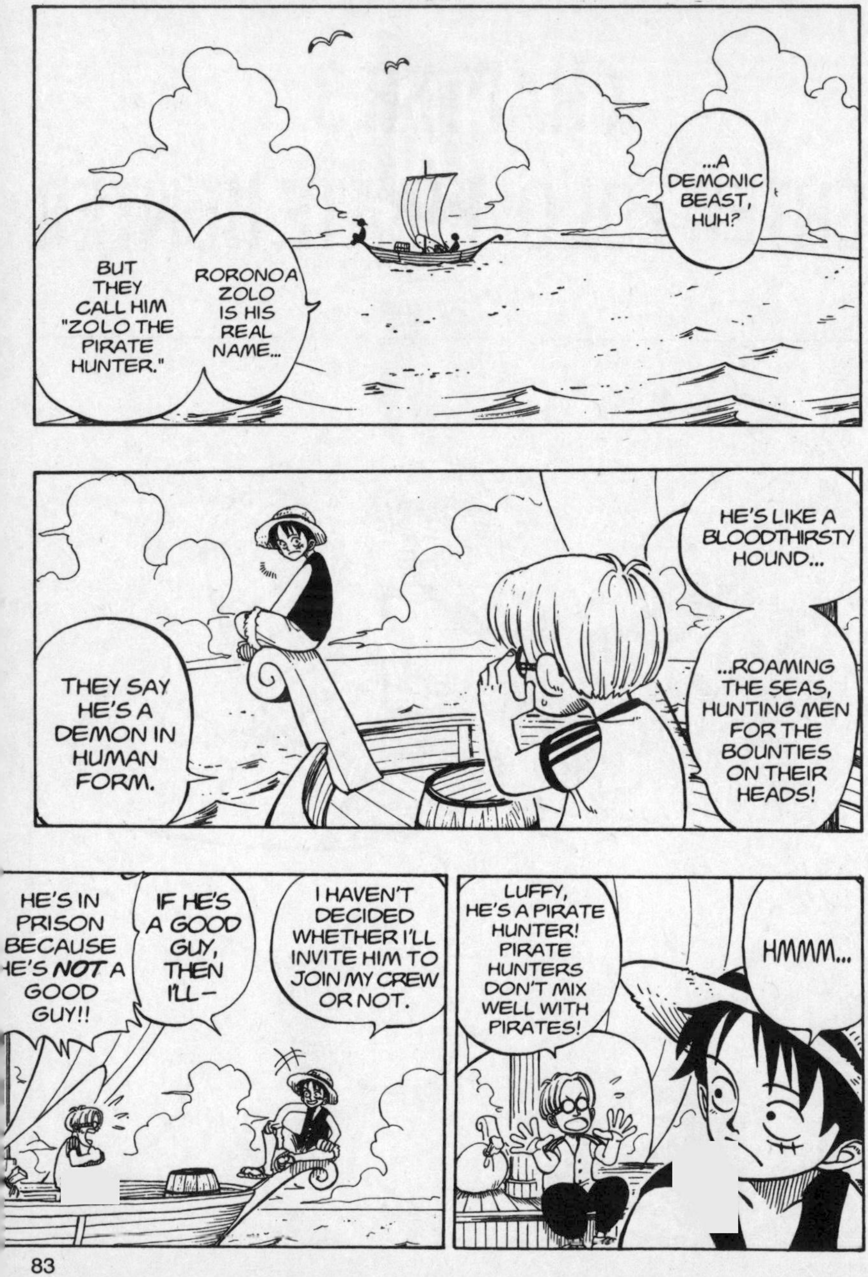
...A DEMONIC BEAST, HUH?
RORONOA ZOLO IS HIS REAL NAME...
BUT THEY CALL HIM "ZOLO THE PIRATE HUNTER."
HE'S LIKE A BLOODTHIRSTY HOUND...
...ROAMING THE SEAS, HUNTING MEN FOR THE BOUNTIES ON THEIR HEADS!
THEY SAY HE'S A DEMON IN HUMAN FORM.
HMMM...
LUFFY, HE'S A PIRATE HUNTER! PIRATE HUNTERS DON'T MIX WELL WITH PIRATES!
I HAVEN'T DECIDED WHETHER I'LL INVITE HIM TO JOIN MY CREW OR NOT.
IF HE'S A GOOD GUY, THEN I'LL—
HE'S IN PRISON BECAUSE HE'S ***NOT*** A GOOD GUY!!

CHAPTER 3 :
ENTER ZOLO: PIRATE HUNTER

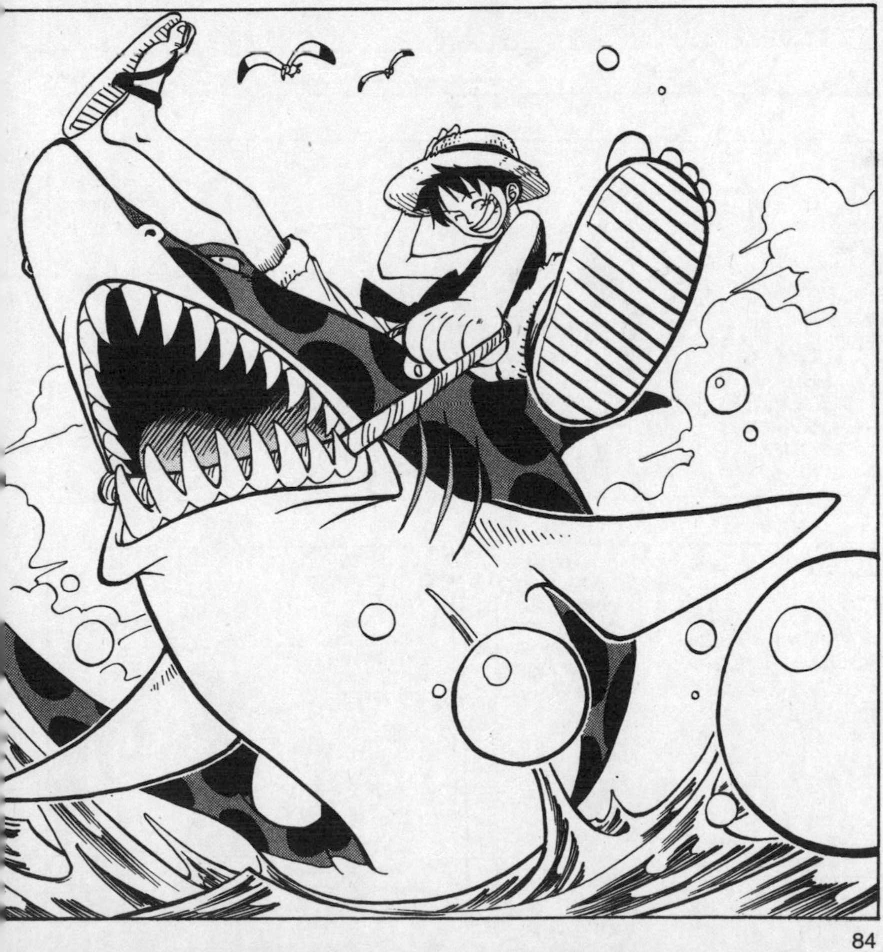

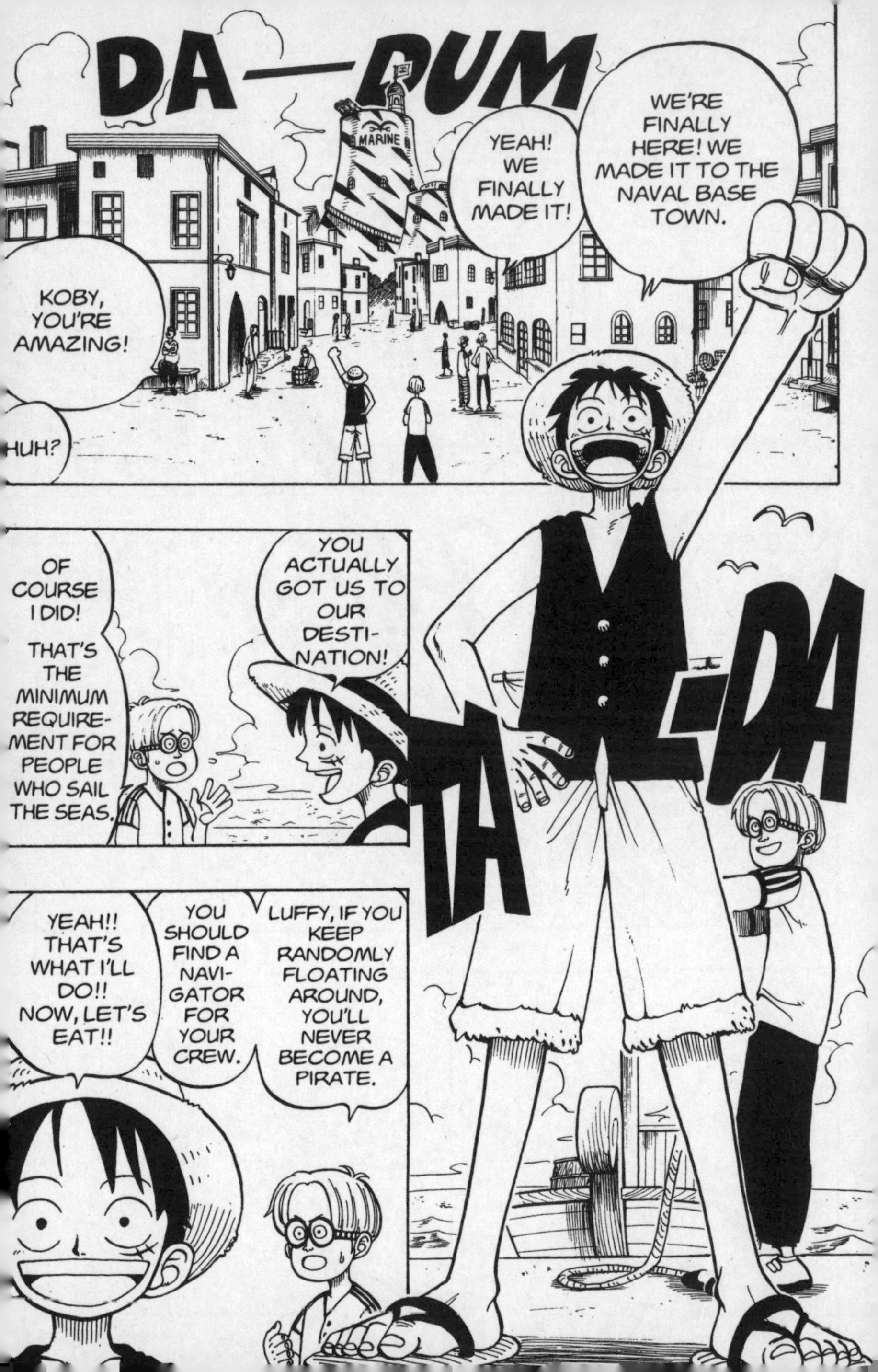

DA—DUM
WE'RE FINALLY HERE! WE MADE IT TO THE NAVAL BASE TOWN.
YEAH! WE FINALLY MADE IT!
KOBY, YOU'RE AMAZING!
HUH?
TA-DA
YOU ACTUALLY GOT US TO OUR DESTI-NATION!
OF COURSE I DID!
THAT'S THE MINIMUM REQUIRE-MENT FOR PEOPLE WHO SAIL THE SEAS.
LUFFY, IF YOU KEEP RANDOMLY FLOATING AROUND, YOU'LL NEVER BECOME A PIRATE.
YOU SHOULD FIND A NAVI-GATOR FOR YOUR CREW.
YEAH!! THAT'S WHAT I'LL DO!! NOW, LET'S EAT!!

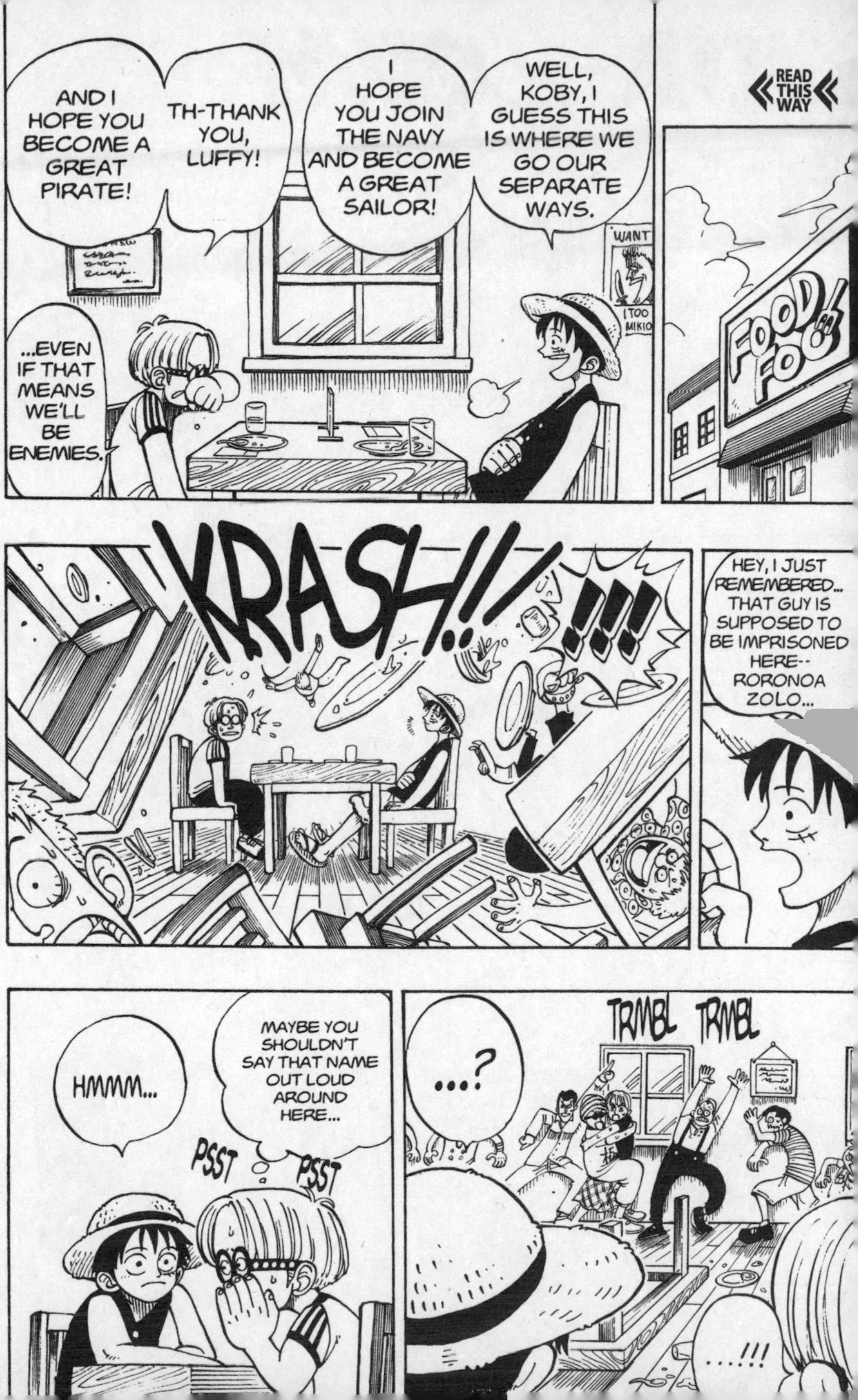
READ THIS WAY
FOOD FOO
WELL, KOBY, I GUESS THIS IS WHERE WE GO OUR SEPARATE WAYS.
I HOPE YOU JOIN THE NAVY AND BECOME A GREAT SAILOR!
WANT
I TOO MIKIO
TH-THANK YOU, LUFFY!
AND I HOPE YOU BECOME A GREAT PIRATE!
...EVEN IF THAT MEANS WE'LL BE ENEMIES.
HEY, I JUST REMEMBERED... THAT GUY IS SUPPOSED TO BE IMPRISONED HERE-- RORONOA ZOLO...
!!!
KRASH!!
TRMBL TRMBL
...?
....!!!
MAYBE YOU SHOULDN'T SAY THAT NAME OUT LOUD AROUND HERE...
PSST PSST
HMMM...

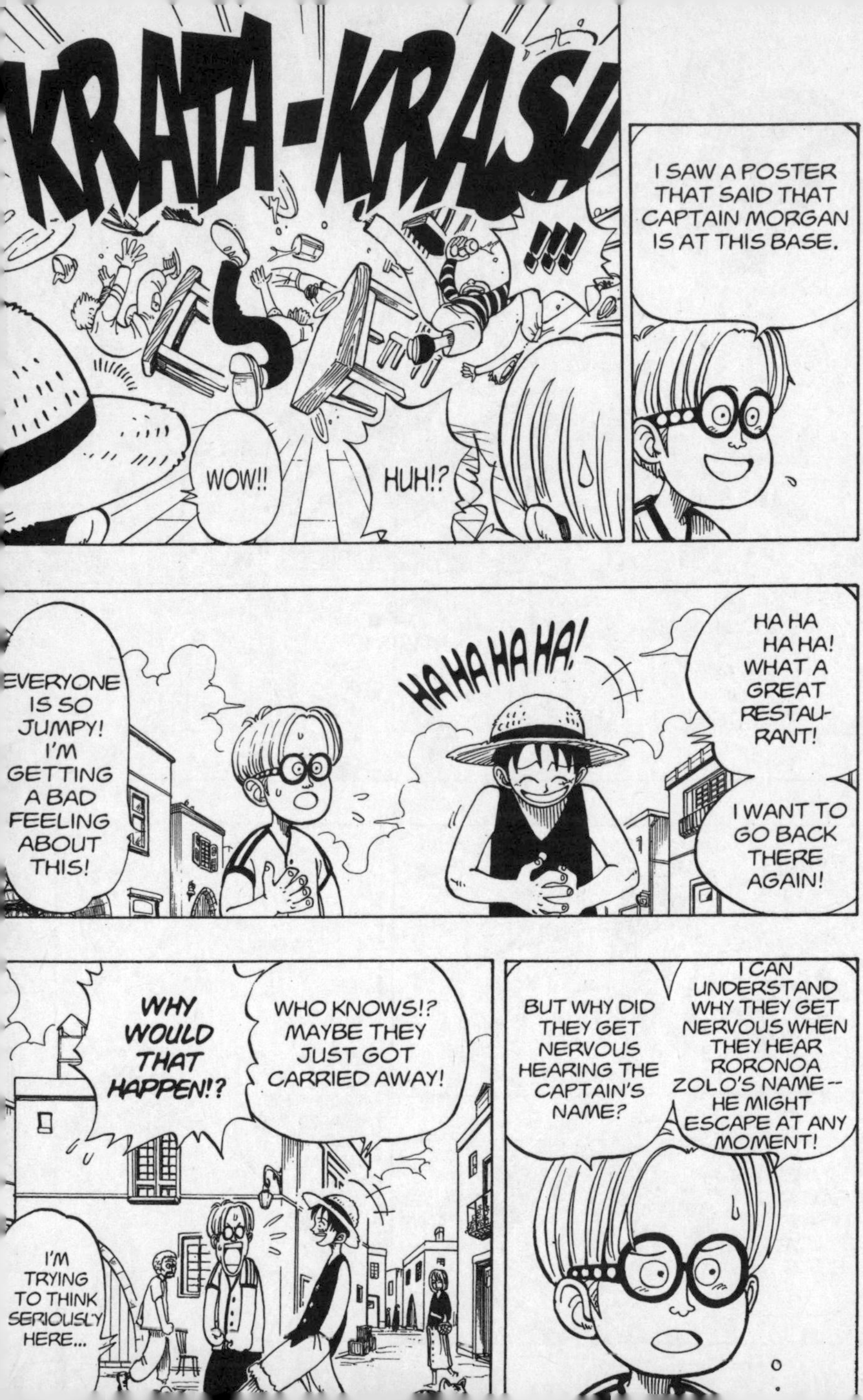
I SAW A POSTER THAT SAID THAT CAPTAIN MORGAN IS AT THIS BASE.
KRATA-KRASH!!!
HUH!?
WOW!!
HA HA HA HA! WHAT A GREAT RESTAU-RANT!
I WANT TO GO BACK THERE AGAIN!
HA HA HA HA HA!
EVERYONE IS SO JUMPY! I'M GETTING A BAD FEELING ABOUT THIS!
I CAN UNDERSTAND WHY THEY GET NERVOUS WHEN THEY HEAR RORONOA ZOLO'S NAME -- HE MIGHT ESCAPE AT ANY MOMENT!
BUT WHY DID THEY GET NERVOUS HEARING THE CAPTAIN'S NAME?
WHO KNOWS!? MAYBE THEY JUST GOT CARRIED AWAY!
WHY WOULD THAT HAPPEN!?
I'M TRYING TO THINK SERIOUSLY HERE...

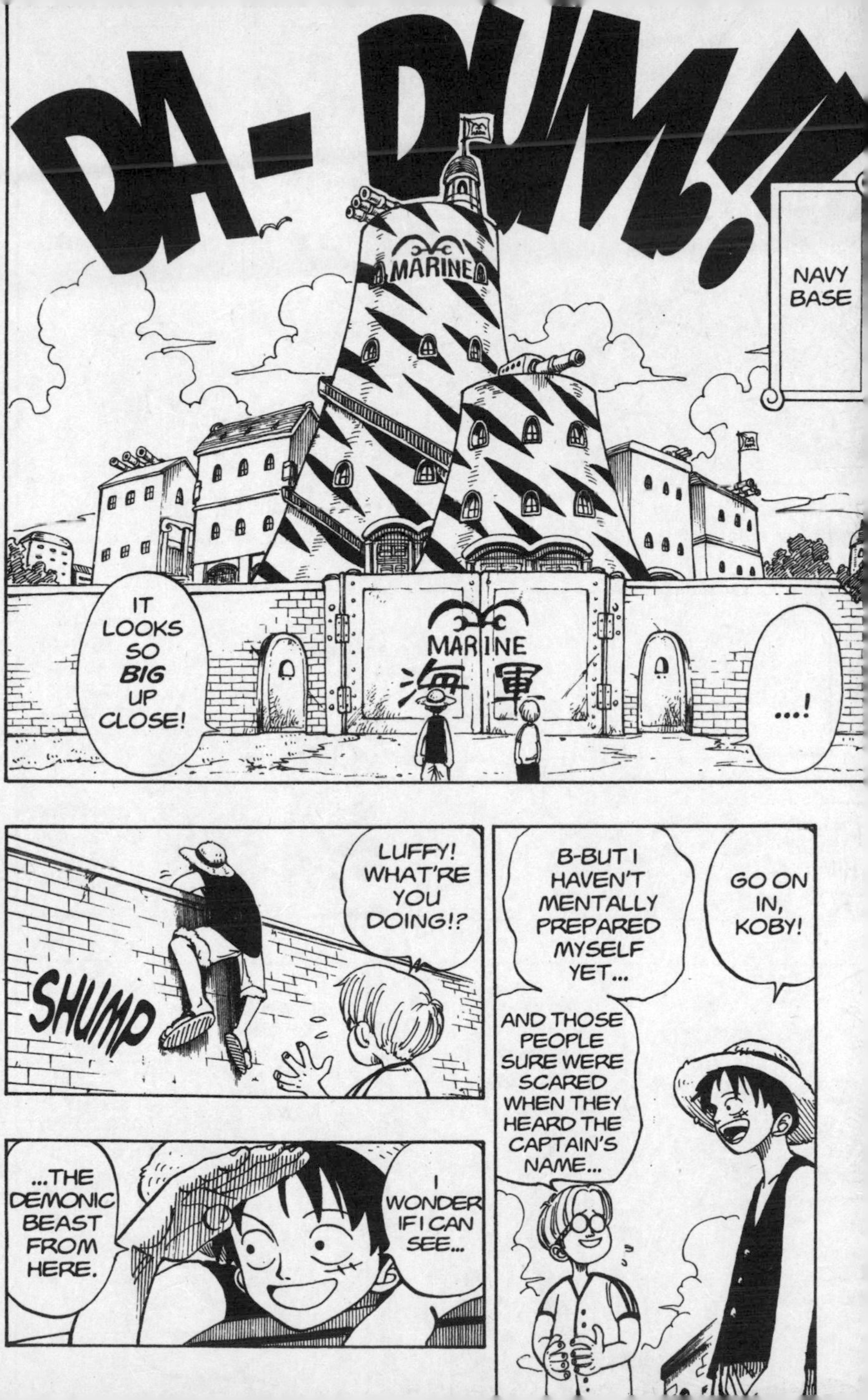
NAVY BASE
DA-DUM!!
MARINE
MARINE
海軍
...!
IT LOOKS SO BIG UP CLOSE!
GO ON IN, KOBY!
B-BUT I HAVEN'T MENTALLY PREPARED MYSELF YET...
AND THOSE PEOPLE SURE WERE SCARED WHEN THEY HEARD THE CAPTAIN'S NAME...
LUFFY! WHAT'RE YOU DOING!?
SHUMP
I WONDER IF I CAN SEE...
...THE DEMONIC BEAST FROM HERE.

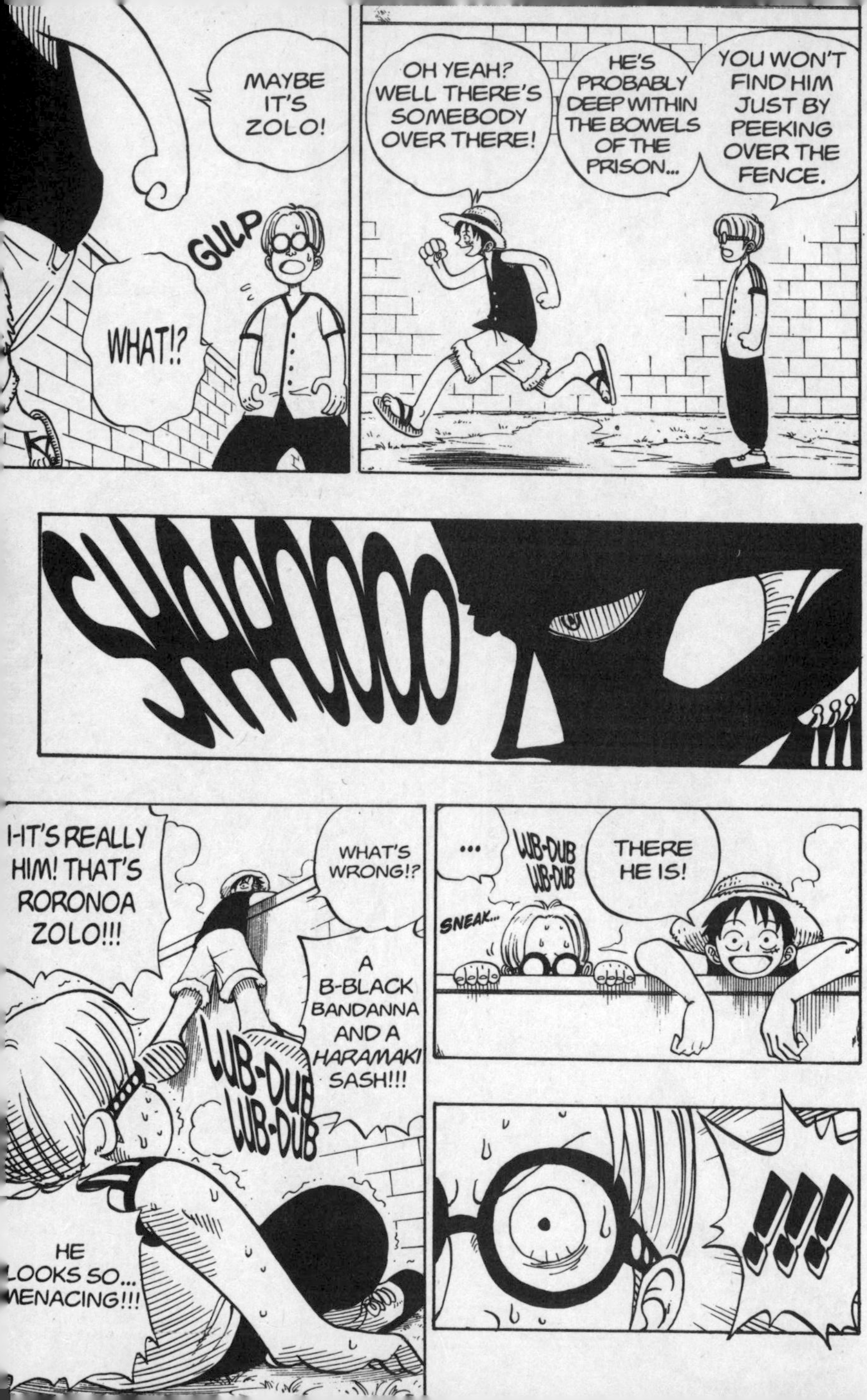
YOU WON'T FIND HIM JUST BY PEEKING OVER THE FENCE.
HE'S PROBABLY DEEP WITHIN THE BOWELS OF THE PRISON...
OH YEAH? WELL THERE'S SOMEBODY OVER THERE!
MAYBE IT'S ZOLO!
GULP
WHAT!?
SHAAOOO
THERE HE IS!
LUB-DUB LUB-DUB
...
SNEAK...
!!!
WHAT'S WRONG!?
I-IT'S REALLY HIM! THAT'S RORONOA ZOLO!!!
A B-BLACK BANDANNA AND A HARAMAKI SASH!!!
LUB-DUB LUB-DUB
HE LOOKS SO... MENACING!!!

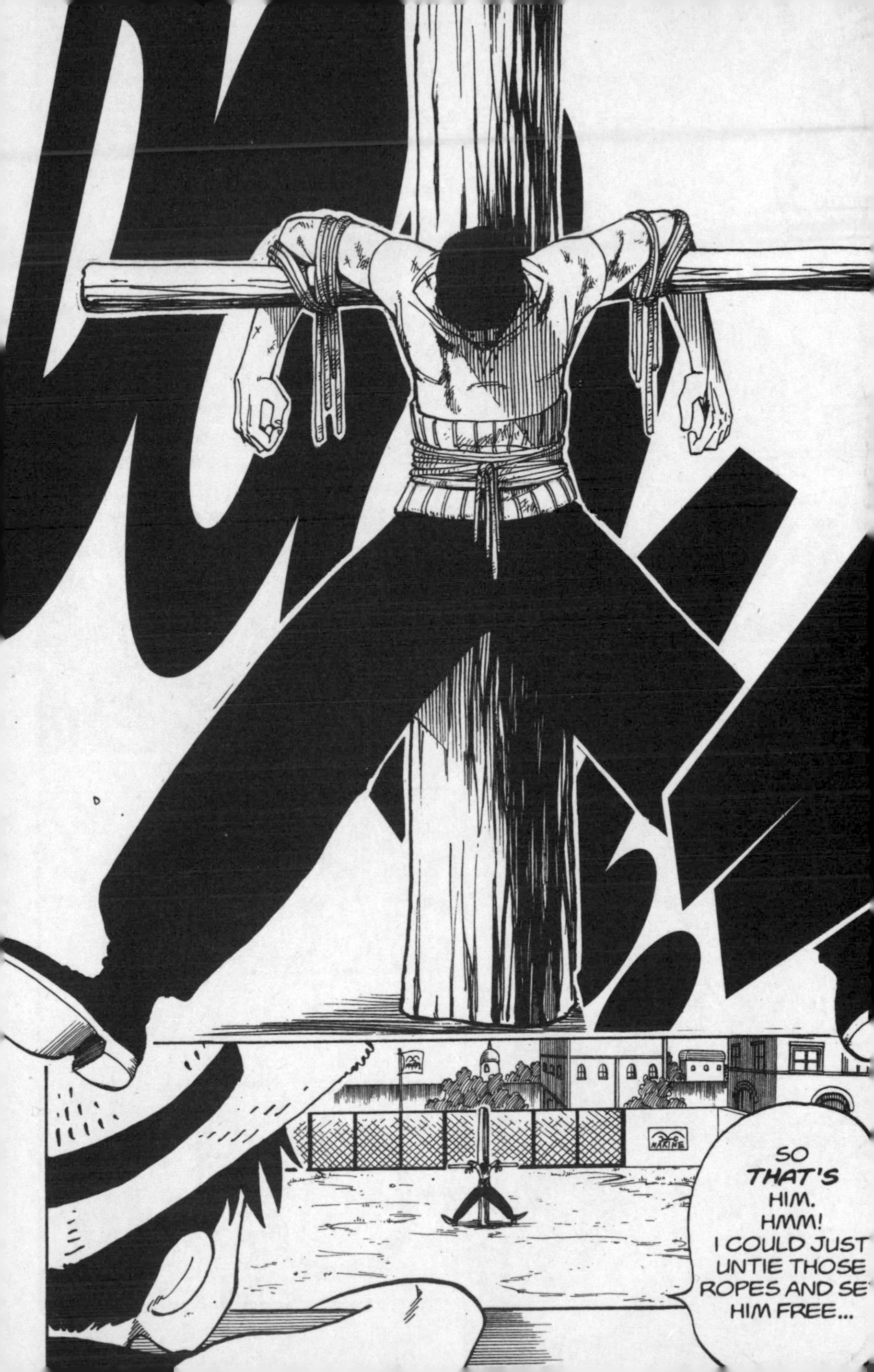
MARINE
SO THAT'S HIM. HMM! I COULD JUST UNTIE THOSE ROPES AND SET HIM FREE...

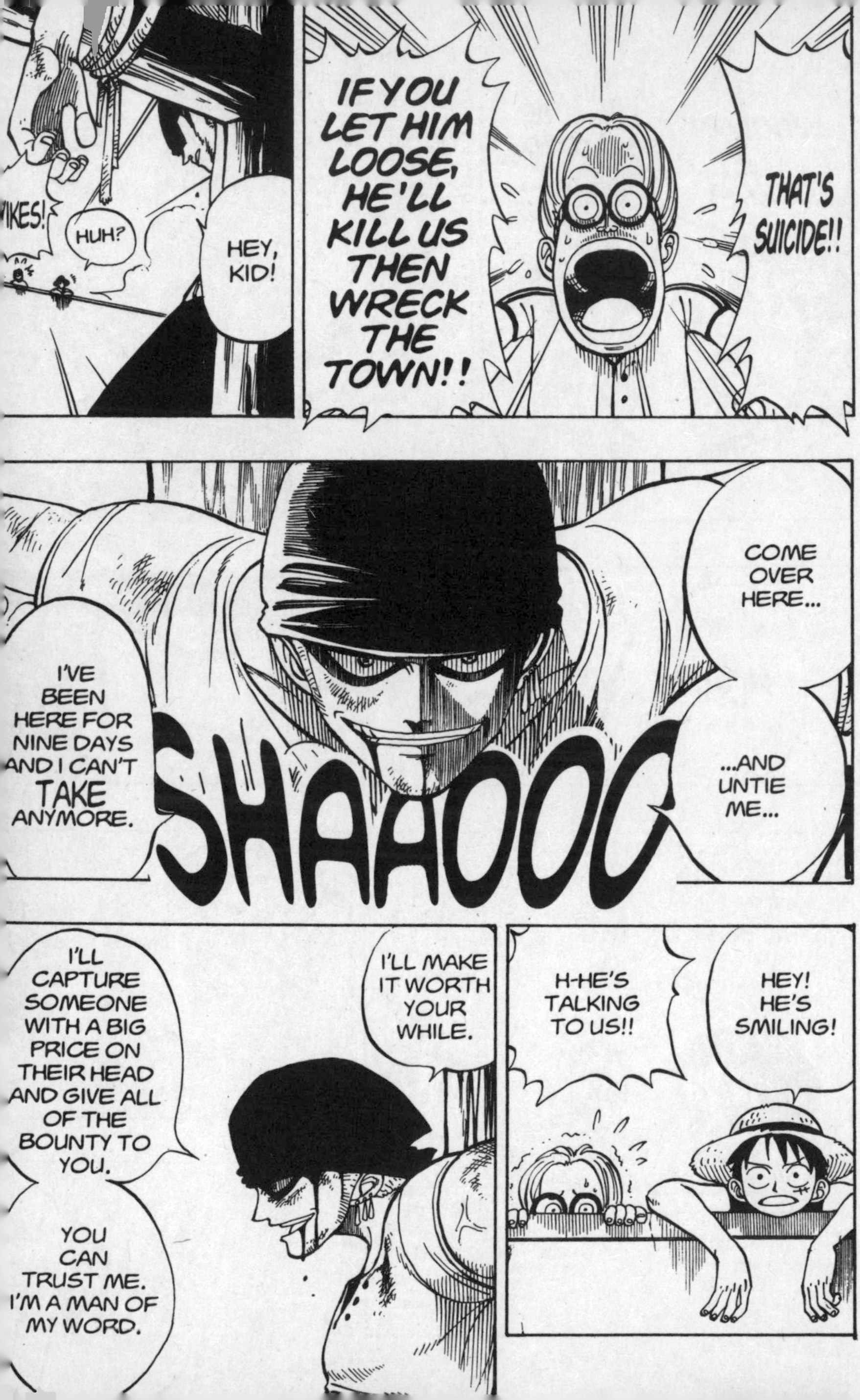
THAT'S SUICIDE!!
IF YOU LET HIM LOOSE, HE'LL KILL US THEN WRECK THE TOWN!!
HEY, KID!
HUH?
COME OVER HERE...
...AND UNTIE ME...
I'VE BEEN HERE FOR NINE DAYS AND I CAN'T TAKE ANYMORE.
SHAAOOO
HEY! HE'S SMILING!
H-HE'S TALKING TO US!!
I'LL MAKE IT WORTH YOUR WHILE.
I'LL CAPTURE SOMEONE WITH A BIG PRICE ON THEIR HEAD AND GIVE ALL OF THE BOUNTY TO YOU.
YOU CAN TRUST ME. I'M A MAN OF MY WORD.

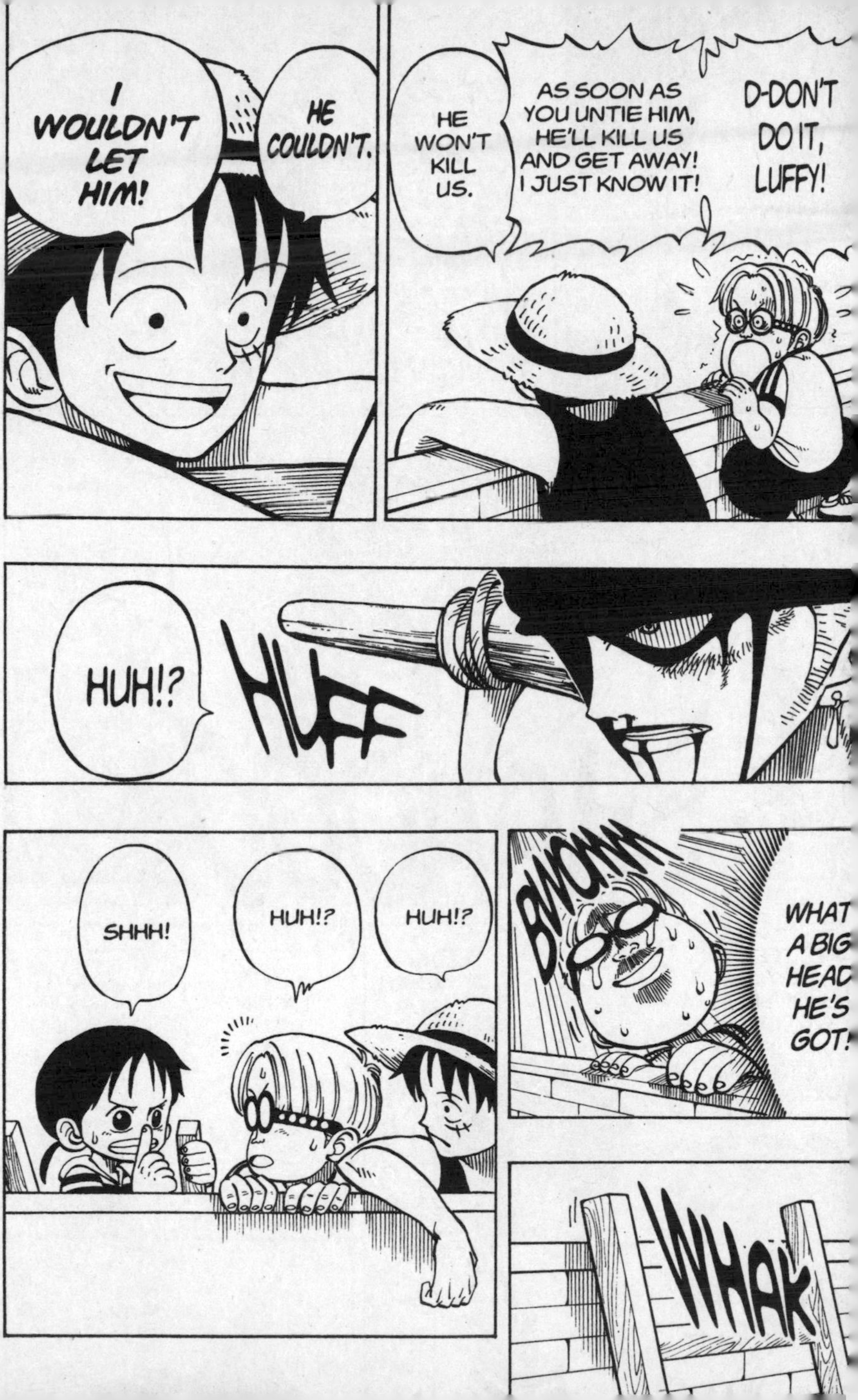
D-DON'T DO IT, LUFFY!
AS SOON AS YOU UNTIE HIM, HE'LL KILL US AND GET AWAY! I JUST KNOW IT!
HE WON'T KILL US.
HE COULDN'T.
I WOULDN'T LET HIM!
HUFF
HUH!?
WHAT A BIG HEAD HE'S GOT!
WHAK
HUH!?
HUH!?
SHHH!

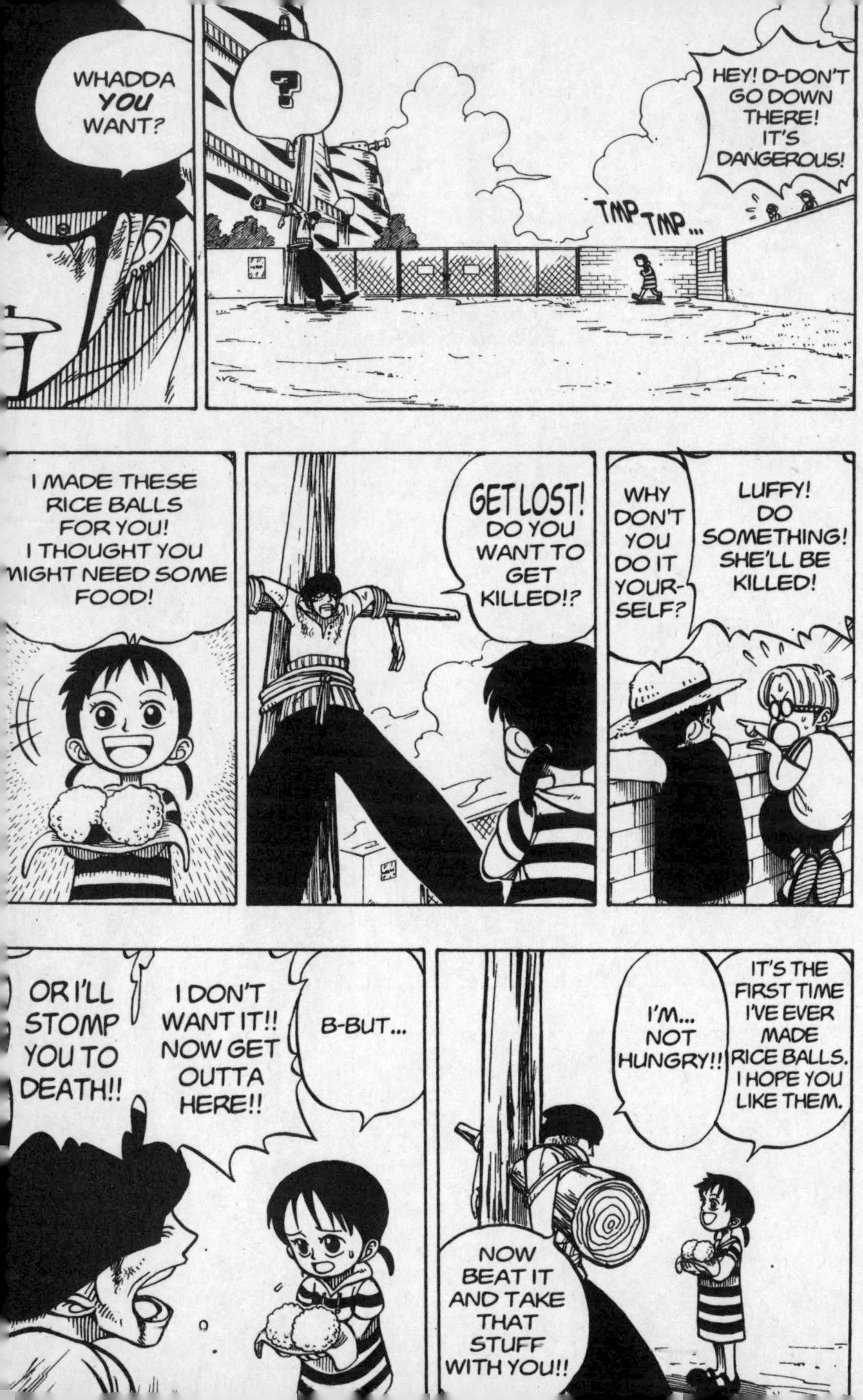
HEY! D-DON'T GO DOWN THERE! IT'S DANGEROUS!
?
TMP TMP...
WHADDA *YOU* WANT?
LUFFY! DO SOMETHING! SHE'LL BE KILLED!
WHY DON'T YOU DO IT YOUR-SELF?
GET LOST! DO YOU WANT TO GET KILLED!?
I MADE THESE RICE BALLS FOR YOU! I THOUGHT YOU MIGHT NEED SOME FOOD!
IT'S THE FIRST TIME I'VE EVER MADE RICE BALLS. I HOPE YOU LIKE THEM.
I'M... NOT HUNGRY!!
NOW BEAT IT AND TAKE THAT STUFF WITH YOU!!
B-BUT...
I DON'T WANT IT!! NOW GET OUTTA HERE!!
OR I'LL STOMP YOU TO DEATH!!

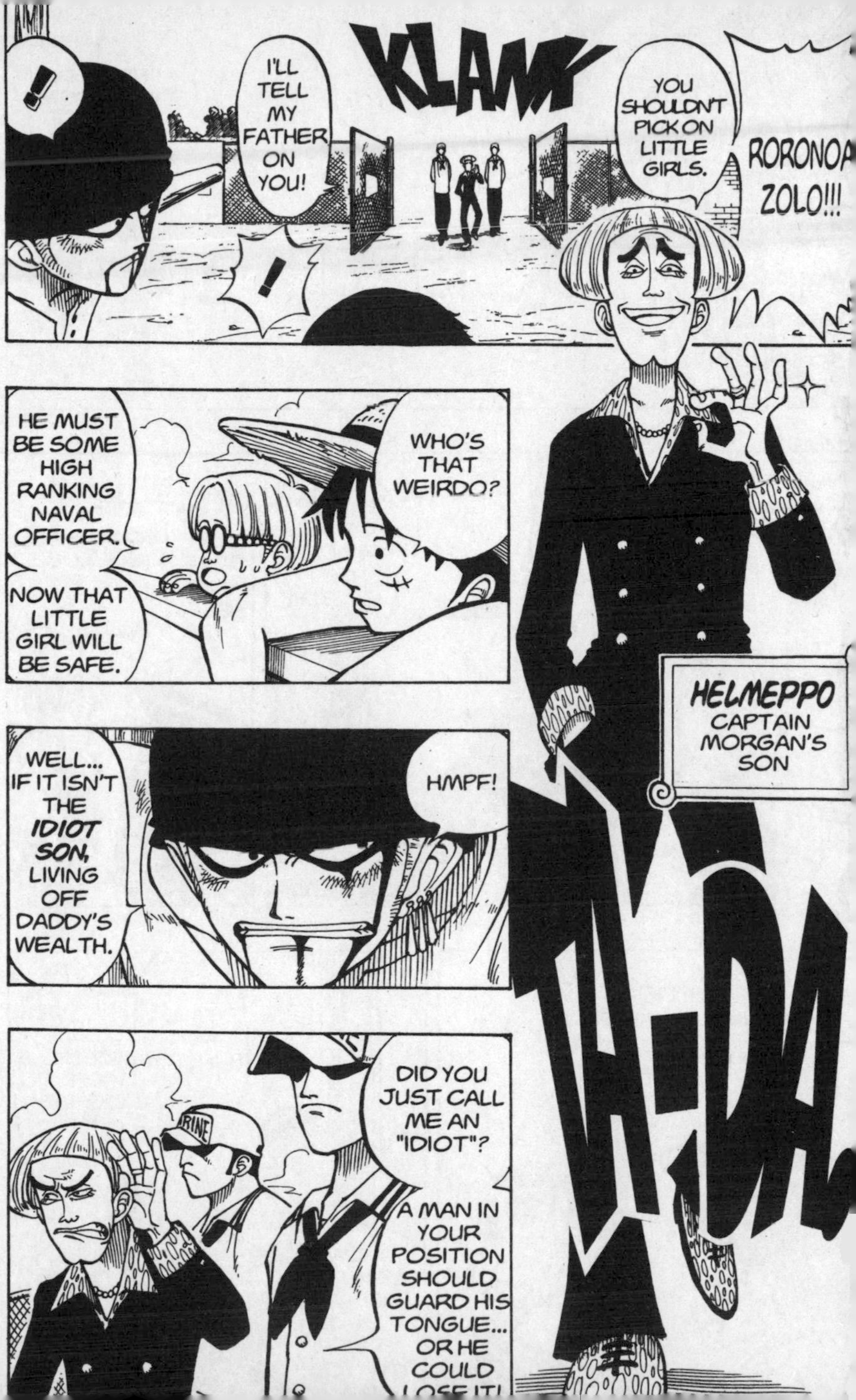
YOU SHOULDN'T PICK ON LITTLE GIRLS.
RORONOA ZOLO!!!
KLANK
I'LL TELL MY FATHER ON YOU!
!
!
HELMEPPO
CAPTAIN MORGAN'S SON
TA-DA
WHO'S THAT WEIRDO?
HE MUST BE SOME HIGH RANKING NAVAL OFFICER.
NOW THAT LITTLE GIRL WILL BE SAFE.
HMPF!
WELL... IF IT ISN'T THE *IDIOT SON*, LIVING OFF DADDY'S WEALTH.
DID YOU JUST CALL ME AN "IDIOT"?
A MAN IN YOUR POSITION SHOULD GUARD HIS TONGUE... OR HE COULD LOSE IT!

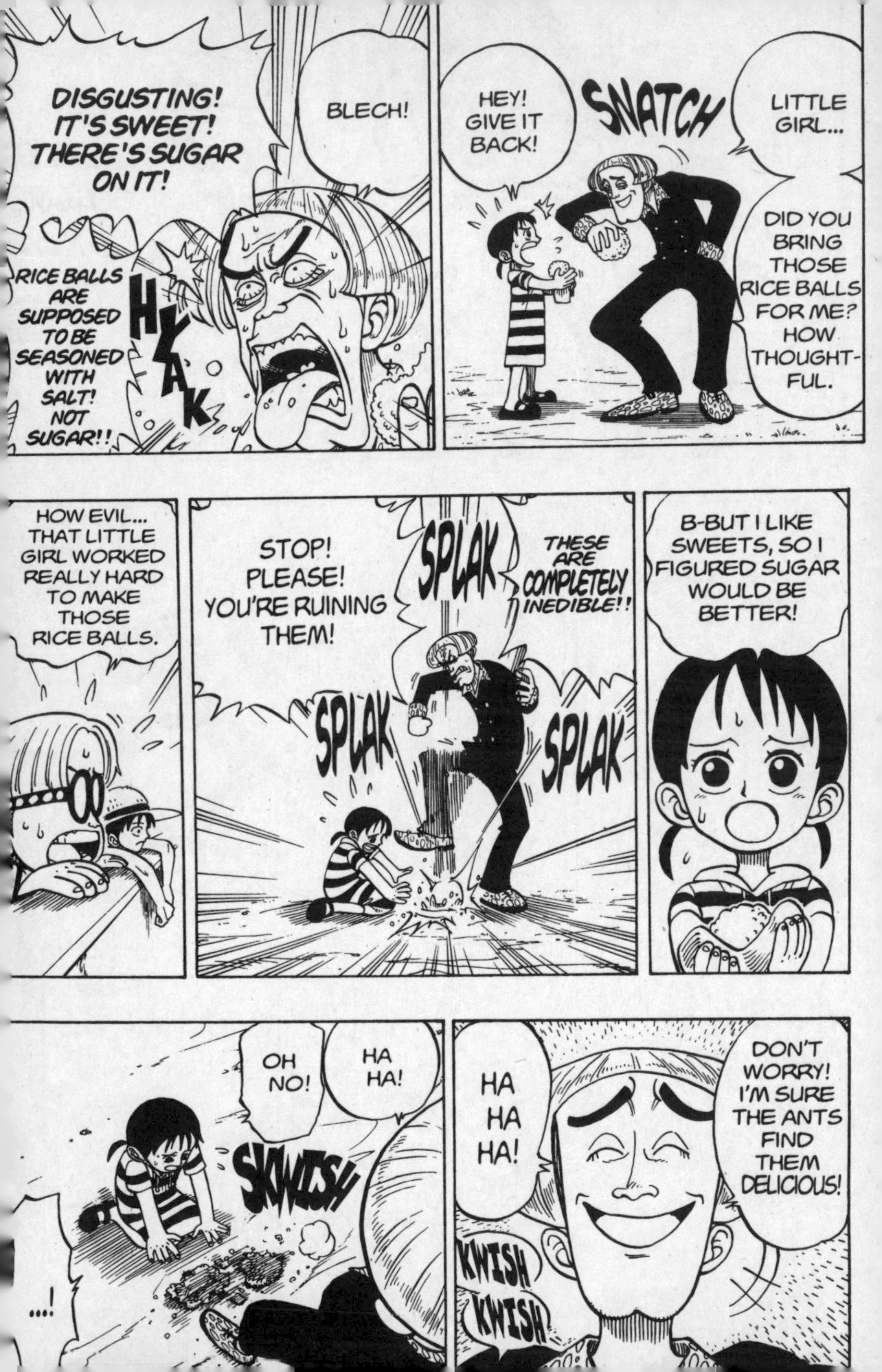
LITTLE GIRL...
DID YOU BRING THOSE RICE BALLS FOR ME? HOW THOUGHTFUL.
SNATCH
HEY! GIVE IT BACK!
BLECH!
DISGUSTING! IT'S SWEET! THERE'S SUGAR ON IT!
HYAK
RICE BALLS ARE SUPPOSED TO BE SEASONED WITH SALT! NOT SUGAR!!
B-BUT I LIKE SWEETS, SO I FIGURED SUGAR WOULD BE BETTER!
THESE ARE COMPLETELY INEDIBLE!!
SPLAK
STOP! PLEASE! YOU'RE RUINING THEM!
SPLAK
SPLAK
HOW EVIL... THAT LITTLE GIRL WORKED REALLY HARD TO MAKE THOSE RICE BALLS.
DON'T WORRY! I'M SURE THE ANTS FIND THEM DELICIOUS!
HA HA HA!
KWISH
KWISH
HA HA!
OH NO!
SKWISH
....!

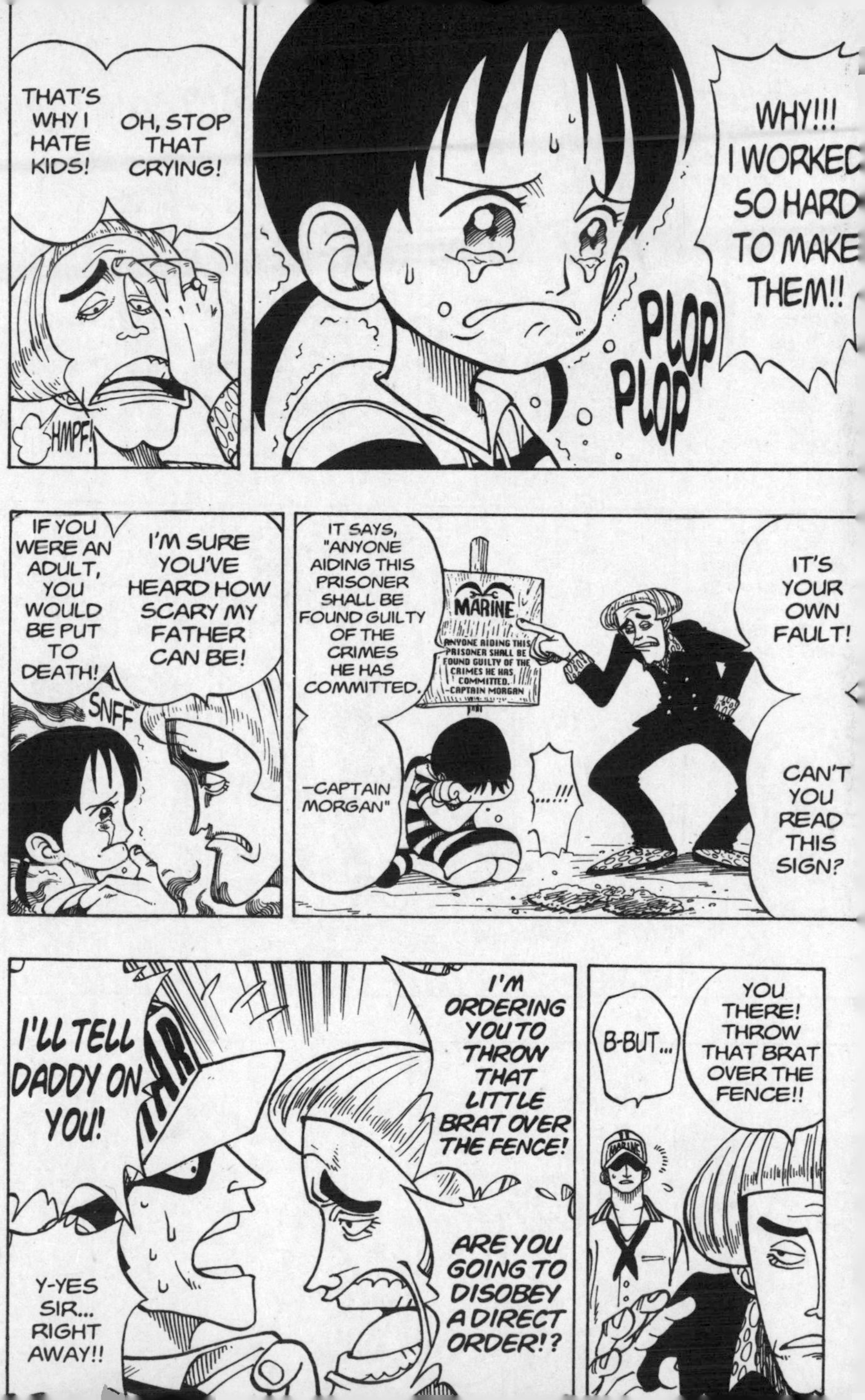
WHY!!! I WORKED SO HARD TO MAKE THEM!!
PLOP
PLOP
OH, STOP THAT CRYING!
THAT'S WHY I HATE KIDS!
HMPF!
IT'S YOUR OWN FAULT!
CAN'T YOU READ THIS SIGN?
MARINE
ANYONE AIDING THIS PRISONER SHALL BE FOUND GUILTY OF THE CRIMES HE HAS COMMITTED. —CAPTAIN MORGAN
IT SAYS, "ANYONE AIDING THIS PRISONER SHALL BE FOUND GUILTY OF THE CRIMES HE HAS COMMITTED.
—CAPTAIN MORGAN"
....!!!
I'M SURE YOU'VE HEARD HOW SCARY MY FATHER CAN BE!
IF YOU WERE AN ADULT, YOU WOULD BE PUT TO DEATH!
SNFF
YOU THERE! THROW THAT BRAT OVER THE FENCE!!
B-BUT...
MARINE
I'M ORDERING YOU TO THROW THAT LITTLE BRAT OVER THE FENCE!
I'LL TELL DADDY ON YOU!
ARE YOU GOING TO DISOBEY A DIRECT ORDER!?
Y-YES SIR... RIGHT AWAY!!

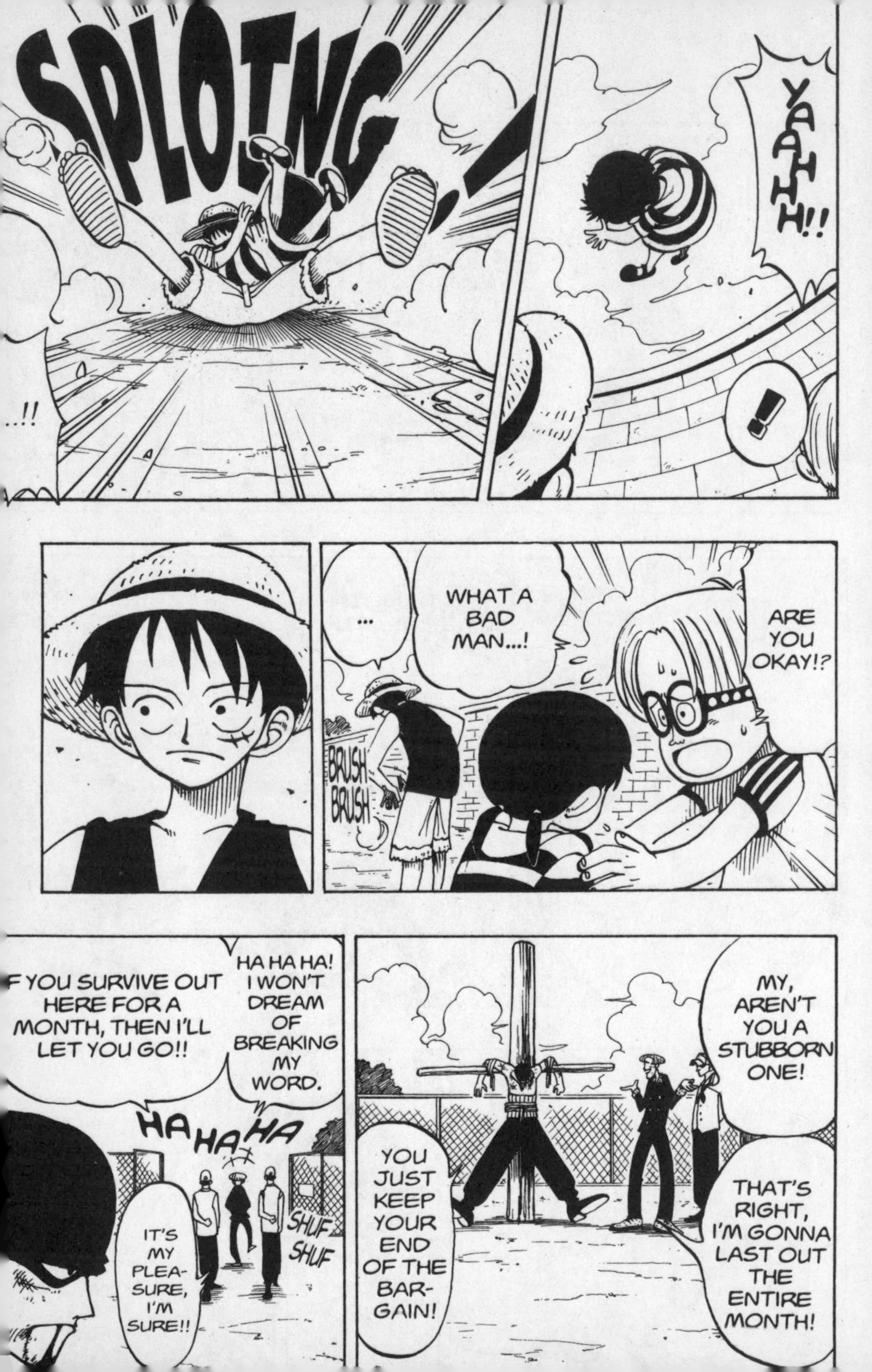
YAAHHH!!
!
SPLOING
...!!
ARE YOU OKAY!?
WHAT A BAD MAN...!
...
BRUSH BRUSH
MY, AREN'T YOU A STUBBORN ONE!
THAT'S RIGHT, I'M GONNA LAST OUT THE ENTIRE MONTH!
YOU JUST KEEP YOUR END OF THE BAR-GAIN!
HA HA HA! I WON'T DREAM OF BREAKING MY WORD.
F YOU SURVIVE OUT HERE FOR A MONTH, THEN I'LL LET YOU GO!!
HA HA HA
SHUF SHUF
IT'S MY PLEA-SURE, I'M SURE!!

READ THIS WAY

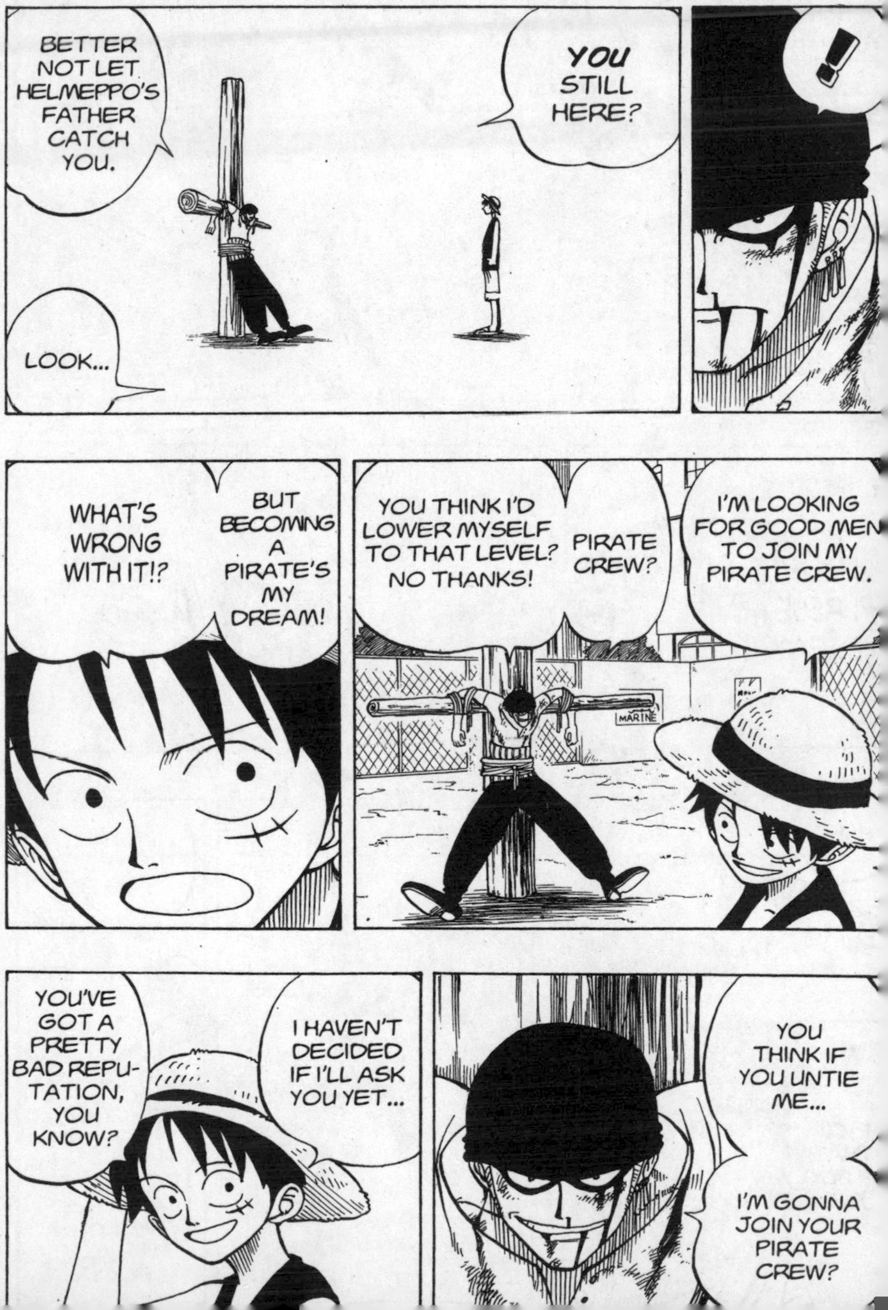
!
YOU STILL HERE?
BETTER NOT LET HELMEPPO'S FATHER CATCH YOU.
LOOK...
I'M LOOKING FOR GOOD MEN TO JOIN MY PIRATE CREW.
PIRATE CREW?
YOU THINK I'D LOWER MYSELF TO THAT LEVEL? NO THANKS!
MARINE
BUT BECOMING A PIRATE'S MY DREAM!
WHAT'S WRONG WITH IT!?
YOU THINK IF YOU UNTIE ME...
I'M GONNA JOIN YOUR PIRATE CREW?
I HAVEN'T DECIDED IF I'LL ASK YOU YET...
YOU'VE GOT A PRETTY BAD REPUTATION, YOU KNOW?

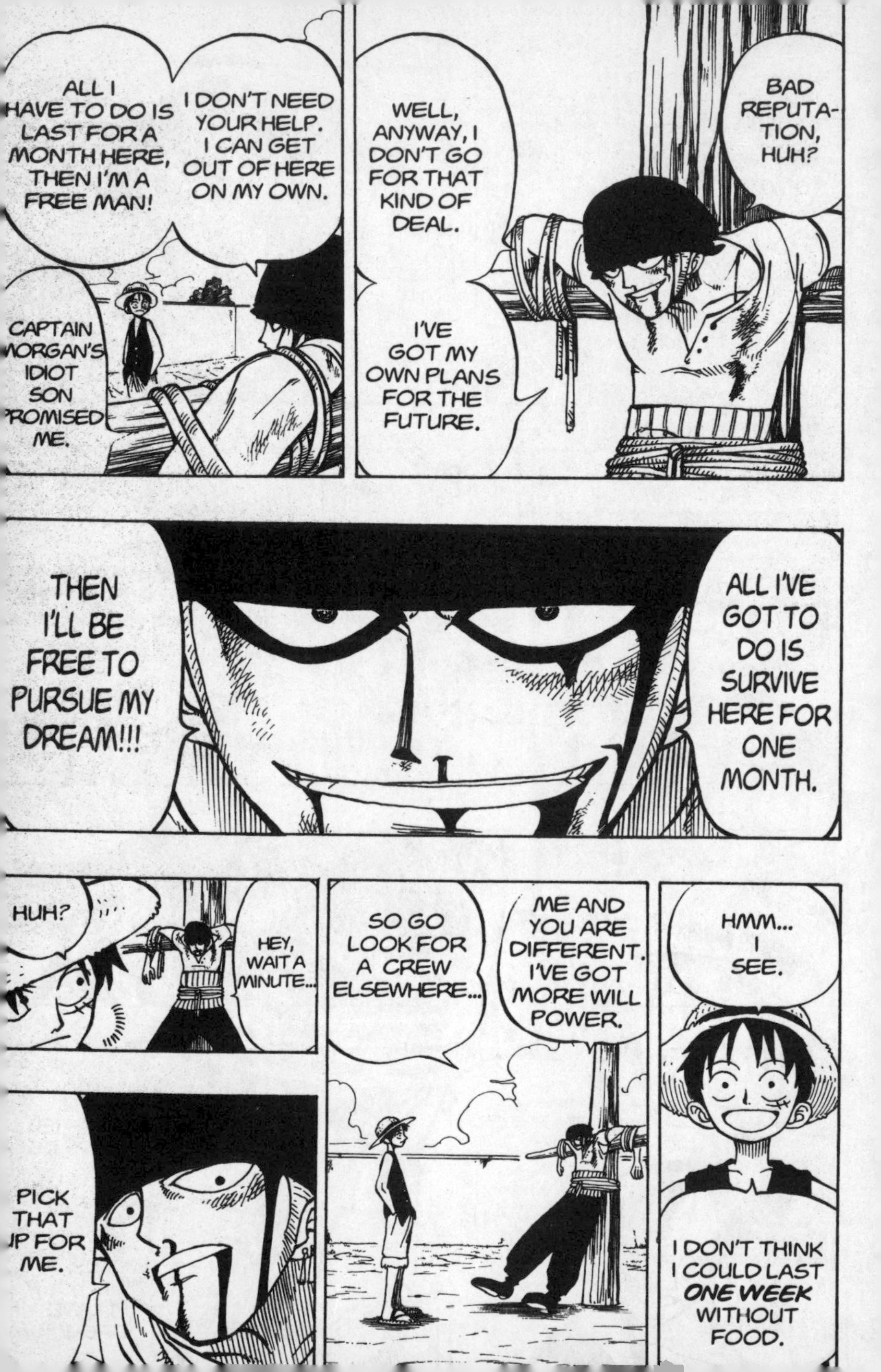
BAD REPUTATION, HUH?
WELL, ANYWAY, I DON'T GO FOR THAT KIND OF DEAL.
I'VE GOT MY OWN PLANS FOR THE FUTURE.
I DON'T NEED YOUR HELP. I CAN GET OUT OF HERE ON MY OWN.
ALL I HAVE TO DO IS LAST FOR A MONTH HERE, THEN I'M A FREE MAN!
CAPTAIN MORGAN'S IDIOT SON PROMISED ME.
ALL I'VE GOT TO DO IS SURVIVE HERE FOR ONE MONTH.
THEN I'LL BE FREE TO PURSUE MY DREAM!!!
HMM... I SEE.
I DON'T THINK I COULD LAST ONE WEEK WITHOUT FOOD.
ME AND YOU ARE DIFFERENT. I'VE GOT MORE WILL POWER.
SO GO LOOK FOR A CREW ELSEWHERE...
HEY, WAIT A MINUTE...
HUH?
PICK THAT UP FOR ME.

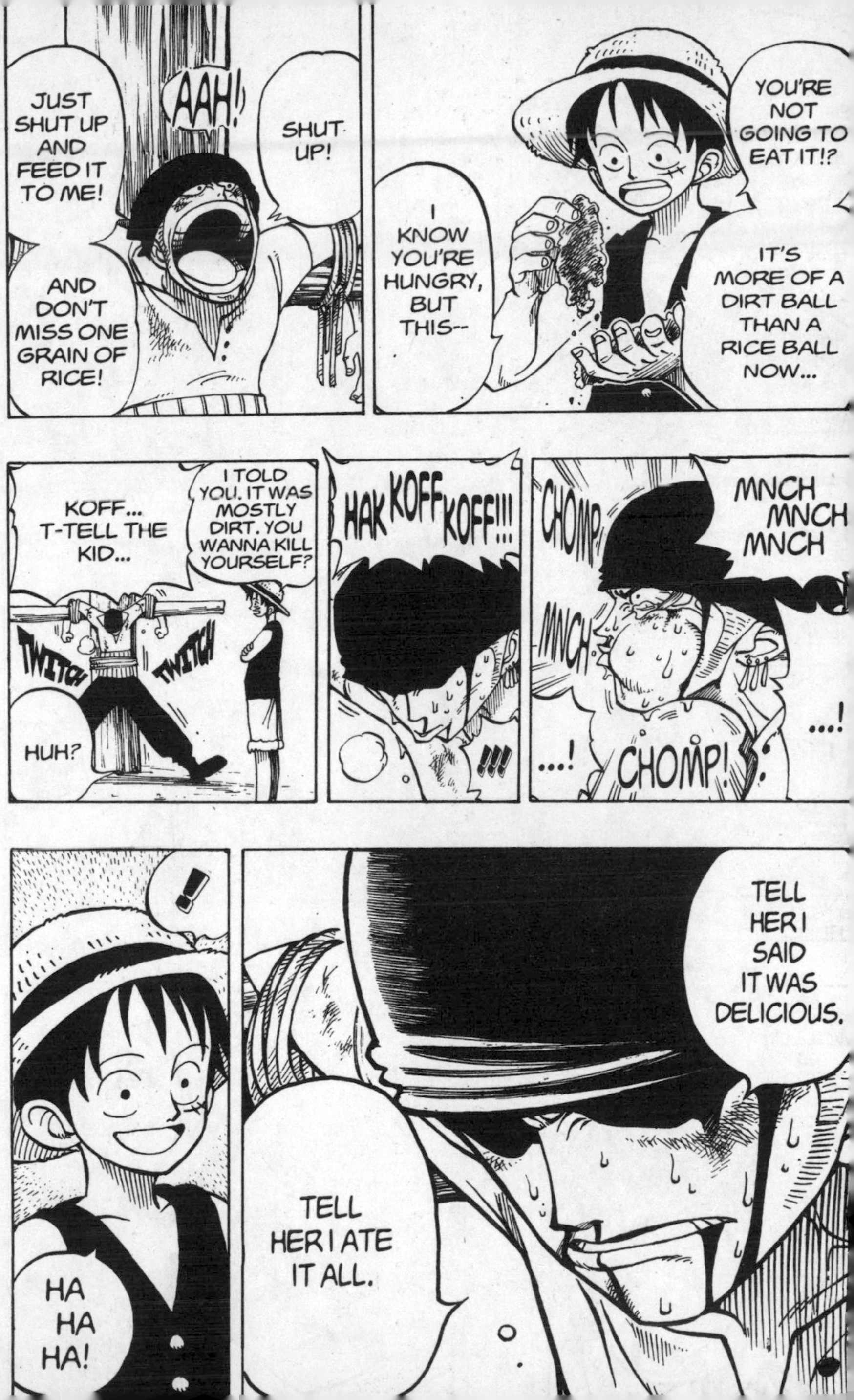
YOU'RE NOT GOING TO EAT IT!?
IT'S MORE OF A DIRT BALL THAN A RICE BALL NOW...
I KNOW YOU'RE HUNGRY, BUT THIS--
AAH!
SHUT UP!
JUST SHUT UP AND FEED IT TO ME!
AND DON'T MISS ONE GRAIN OF RICE!
MNCH MNCH MNCH
CHOMP
MNCH
...!
CHOMP!
...!
HAK KOFF KOFF!!!
!!!
I TOLD YOU. IT WAS MOSTLY DIRT. YOU WANNA KILL YOURSELF?
KOFF... T-TELL THE KID...
TWITCH
TWITCH
HUH?
TELL HER I SAID IT WAS DELICIOUS.
TELL HER I ATE IT ALL.
!
HA HA HA!

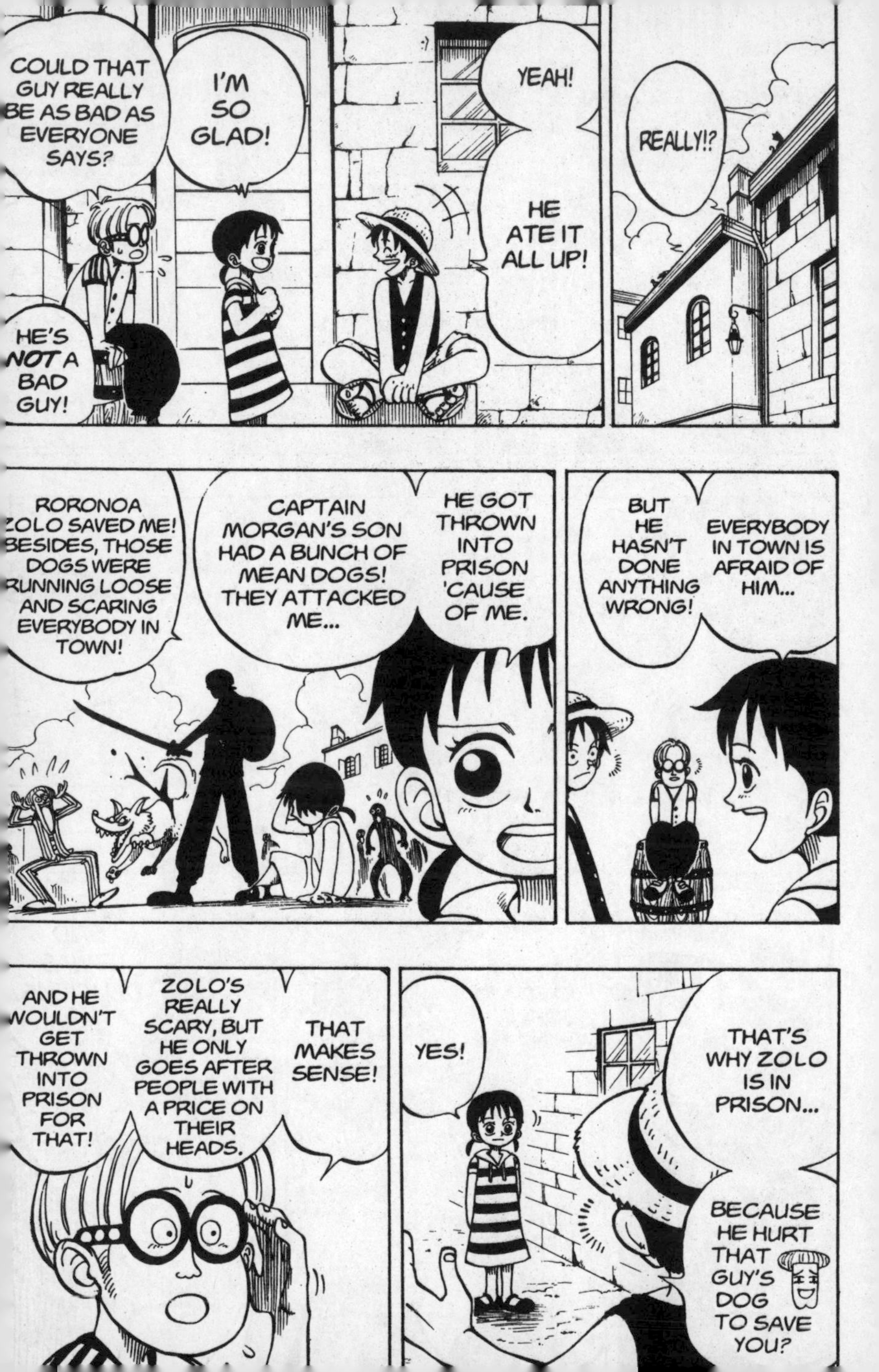
REALLY!?
YEAH!
HE ATE IT ALL UP!
I'M SO GLAD!
COULD THAT GUY REALLY BE AS BAD AS EVERYONE SAYS?
HE'S *NOT* A BAD GUY!
EVERYBODY IN TOWN IS AFRAID OF HIM...
BUT HE HASN'T DONE ANYTHING WRONG!
HE GOT THROWN INTO PRISON 'CAUSE OF ME.
CAPTAIN MORGAN'S SON HAD A BUNCH OF MEAN DOGS! THEY ATTACKED ME...
RORONOA ZOLO SAVED ME! BESIDES, THOSE DOGS WERE RUNNING LOOSE AND SCARING EVERYBODY IN TOWN!
THAT'S WHY ZOLO IS IN PRISON...
BECAUSE HE HURT THAT GUY'S DOG TO SAVE YOU?
YES!
THAT MAKES SENSE!
ZOLO'S REALLY SCARY, BUT HE ONLY GOES AFTER PEOPLE WITH A PRICE ON THEIR HEADS.
AND HE WOULDN'T GET THROWN INTO PRISON FOR THAT!

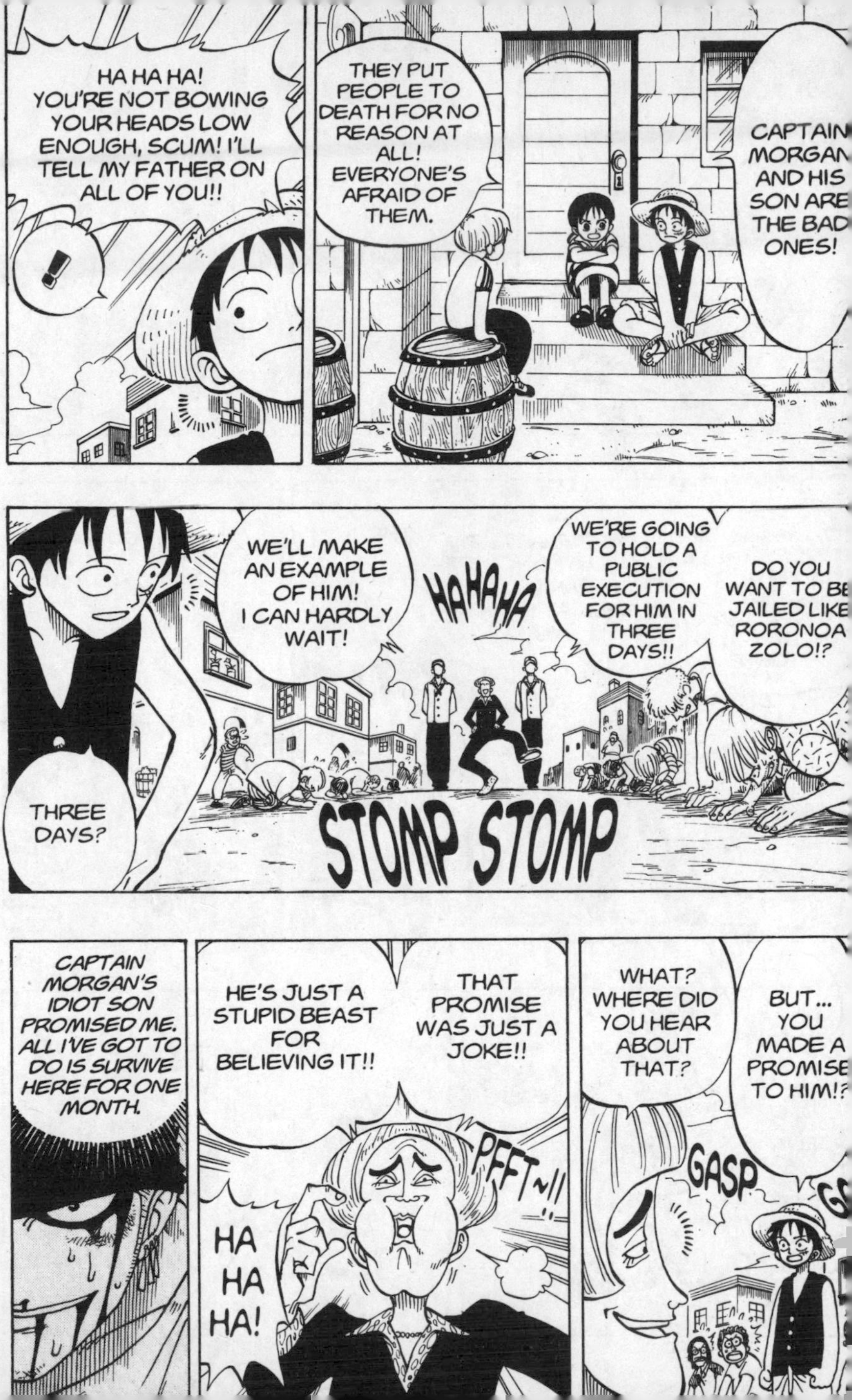
CAPTAIN MORGAN AND HIS SON ARE THE BAD ONES!
THEY PUT PEOPLE TO DEATH FOR NO REASON AT ALL! EVERYONE'S AFRAID OF THEM.
HA HA HA! YOU'RE NOT BOWING YOUR HEADS LOW ENOUGH, SCUM! I'LL TELL MY FATHER ON ALL OF YOU!!
!
DO YOU WANT TO BE JAILED LIKE RORONOA ZOLO!?
WE'RE GOING TO HOLD A PUBLIC EXECUTION FOR HIM IN THREE DAYS!!
HAHAHA
WE'LL MAKE AN EXAMPLE OF HIM! I CAN HARDLY WAIT!
STOMP STOMP
THREE DAYS?
BUT... YOU MADE A PROMISE TO HIM!?
WHAT? WHERE DID YOU HEAR ABOUT THAT?
GASP
THAT PROMISE WAS JUST A JOKE!!
HE'S JUST A STUPID BEAST FOR BELIEVING IT!!
PFFT~!!
HA HA HA!
CAPTAIN MORGAN'S IDIOT SON PROMISED ME. ALL I'VE GOT TO DO IS SURVIVE HERE FOR ONE MONTH.

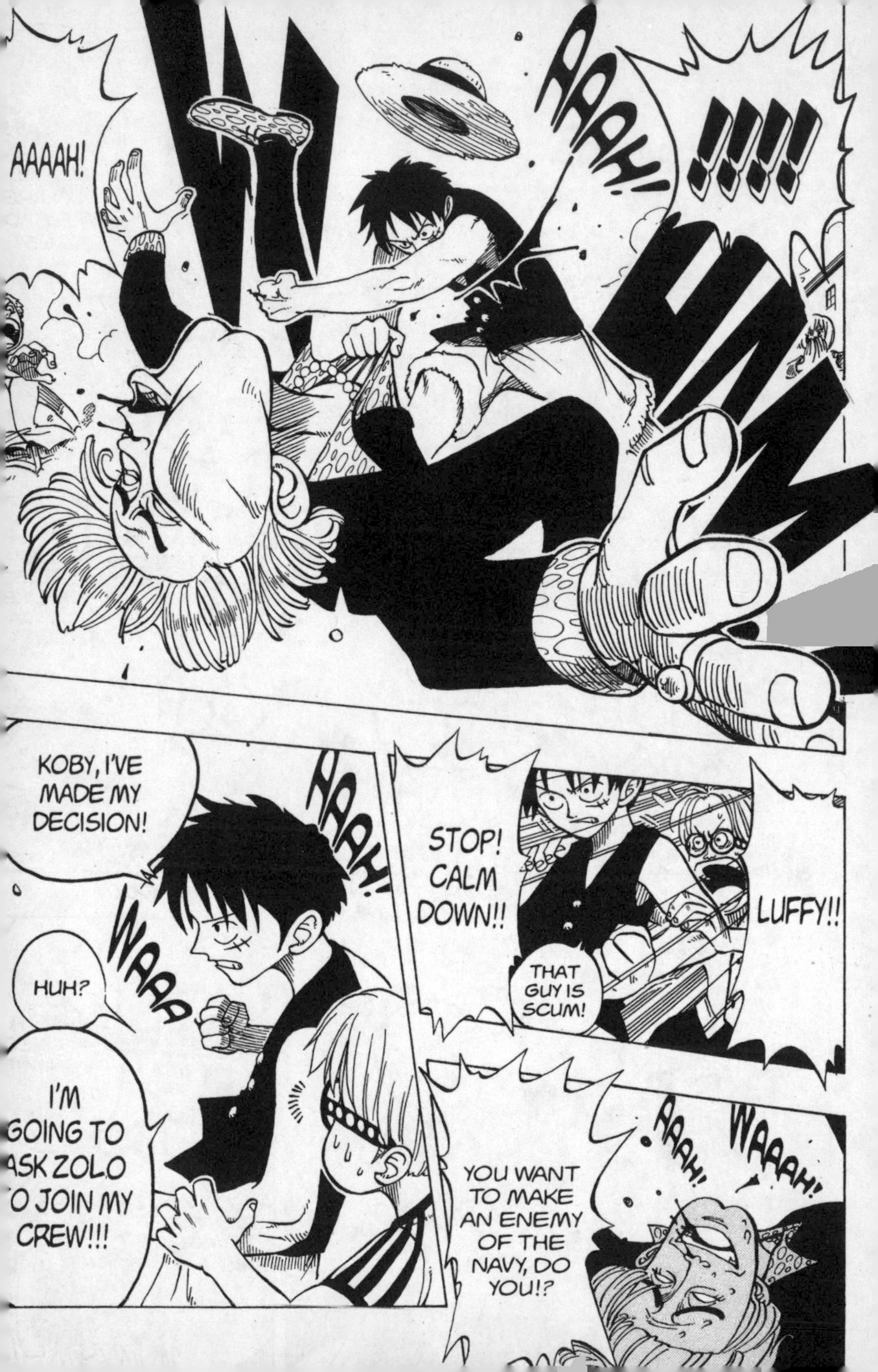
AAAH!!!!!
AAAAH!
LUFFY!!
STOP! CALM DOWN!!
THAT GUY IS SCUM!
WAAAAH!
AAAH!
YOU WANT TO MAKE AN ENEMY OF THE NAVY, DO YOU!?
KOBY, I'VE MADE MY DECISION!
AAAH!
WAAA
HUH?
I'M GOING TO ASK ZOLO TO JOIN MY CREW!!!

HOW TO DRAW THE SKULL AND CROSSBONES

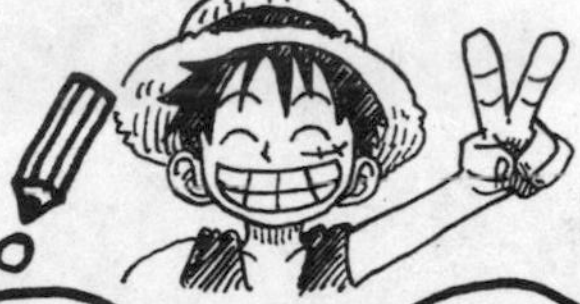

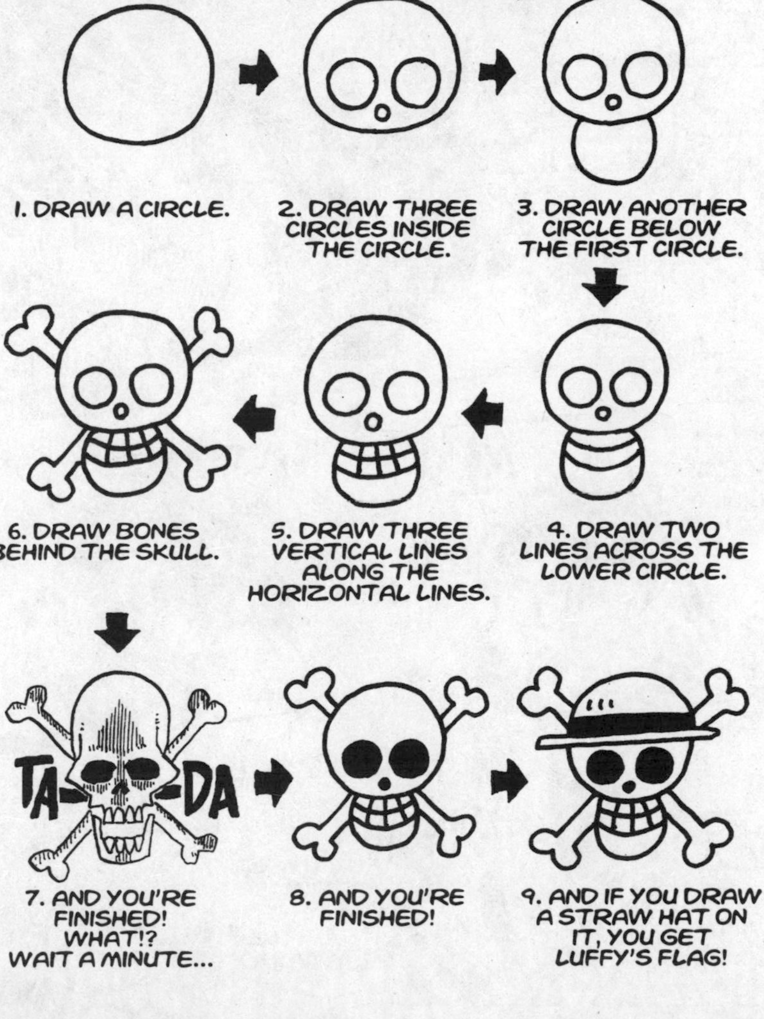
1. DRAW A CIRCLE.
2. DRAW THREE CIRCLES INSIDE THE CIRCLE.
3. DRAW ANOTHER CIRCLE BELOW THE FIRST CIRCLE.
4. DRAW TWO LINES ACROSS THE LOWER CIRCLE.
5. DRAW THREE VERTICAL LINES ALONG THE HORIZONTAL LINES.
6. DRAW BONES BEHIND THE SKULL.
TA-DA
7. AND YOU'RE FINISHED! WHAT!? WAIT A MINUTE...
8. AND YOU'RE FINISHED!
9. AND IF YOU DRAW A STRAW HAT ON IT, YOU GET LUFFY'S FLAG!

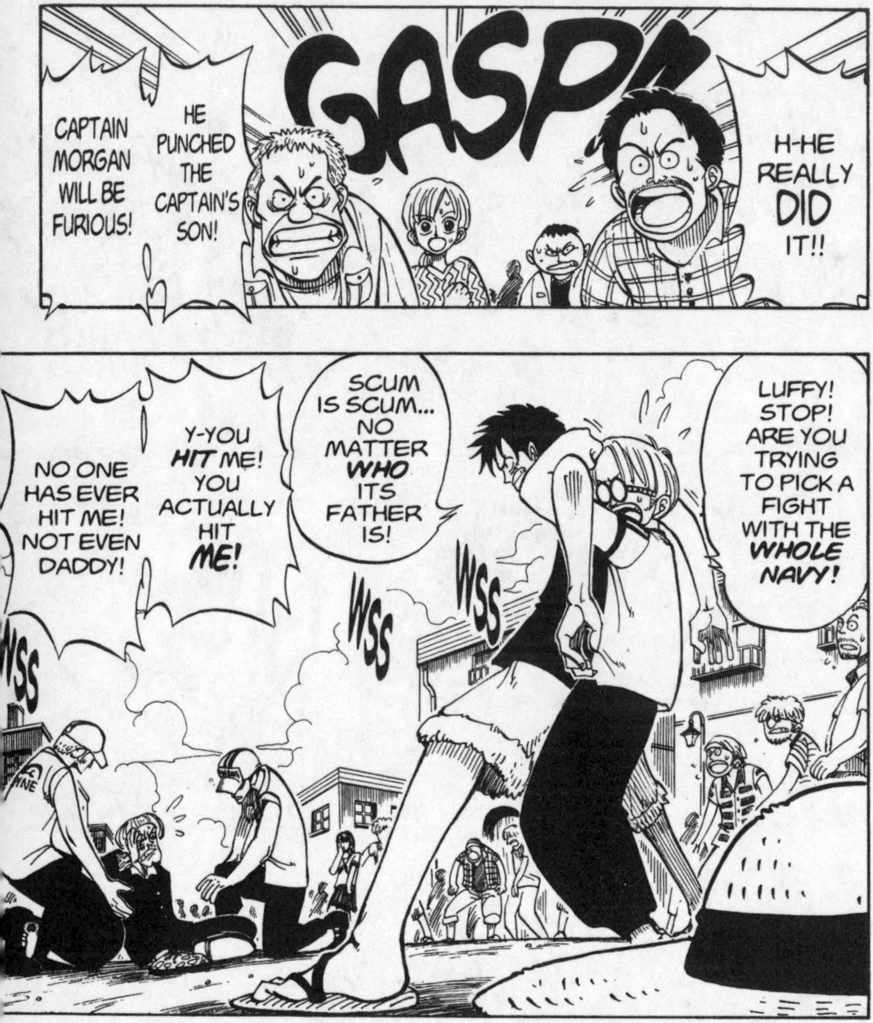
H-HE REALLY DID IT!!
GASP!
HE PUNCHED THE CAPTAIN'S SON!
CAPTAIN MORGAN WILL BE FURIOUS!
LUFFY! STOP! ARE YOU TRYING TO PICK A FIGHT WITH THE WHOLE NAVY!
SCUM IS SCUM... NO MATTER WHO ITS FATHER IS!
WSS
WSS
Y-YOU HIT ME! YOU ACTUALLY HIT ME!
NO ONE HAS EVER HIT ME! NOT EVEN DADDY!
WSS

CHAPTER 4:

THE GREAT CAPTAIN MORGAN

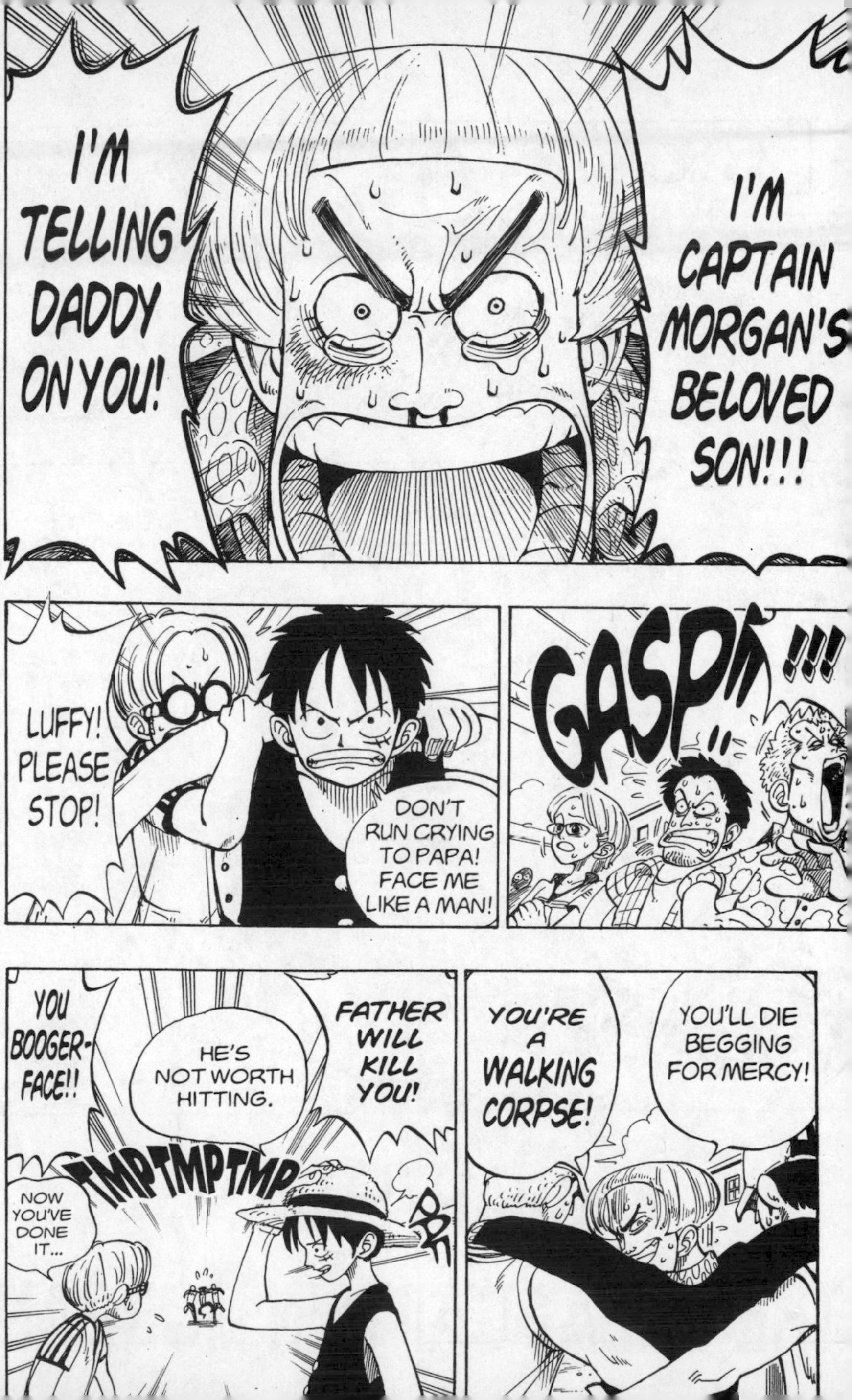
I'M CAPTAIN MORGAN'S BELOVED SON!!!
I'M TELLING DADDY ON YOU!
GASP!!!
DON'T RUN CRYING TO PAPA! FACE ME LIKE A MAN!
LUFFY! PLEASE STOP!
YOU'LL DIE BEGGING FOR MERCY!
YOU'RE A WALKING CORPSE!
FATHER WILL KILL YOU!
HE'S NOT WORTH HITTING.
YOU BOOGER-FACE!!
TMPTMPTMP
POF
NOW YOU'VE DONE IT...

READ THIS WAY

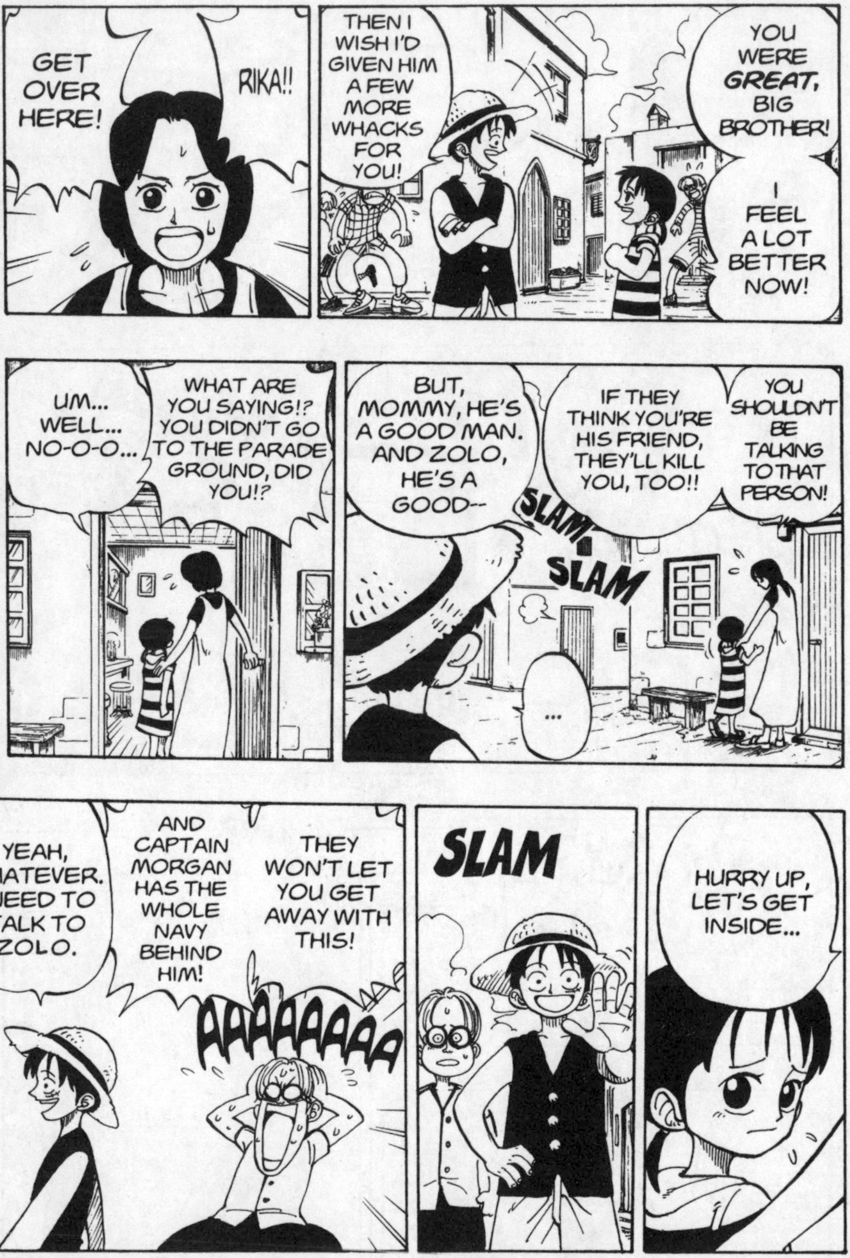
YOU WERE GREAT, BIG BROTHER!
I FEEL A LOT BETTER NOW!
THEN I WISH I'D GIVEN HIM A FEW MORE WHACKS FOR YOU!
RIKA!!
GET OVER HERE!
YOU SHOULDN'T BE TALKING TO THAT PERSON!
IF THEY THINK YOU'RE HIS FRIEND, THEY'LL KILL YOU, TOO!!
BUT, MOMMY, HE'S A GOOD MAN. AND ZOLO, HE'S A GOOD--
SLAM
SLAM
...
WHAT ARE YOU SAYING!? YOU DIDN'T GO TO THE PARADE GROUND, DID YOU!?
UM... WELL... NO-O-O...
HURRY UP, LET'S GET INSIDE...
SLAM
THEY WON'T LET YOU GET AWAY WITH THIS!
AND CAPTAIN MORGAN HAS THE WHOLE NAVY BEHIND HIM!
AAAAAAAA
YEAH, WHATEVER. I NEED TO TALK TO ZOLO.

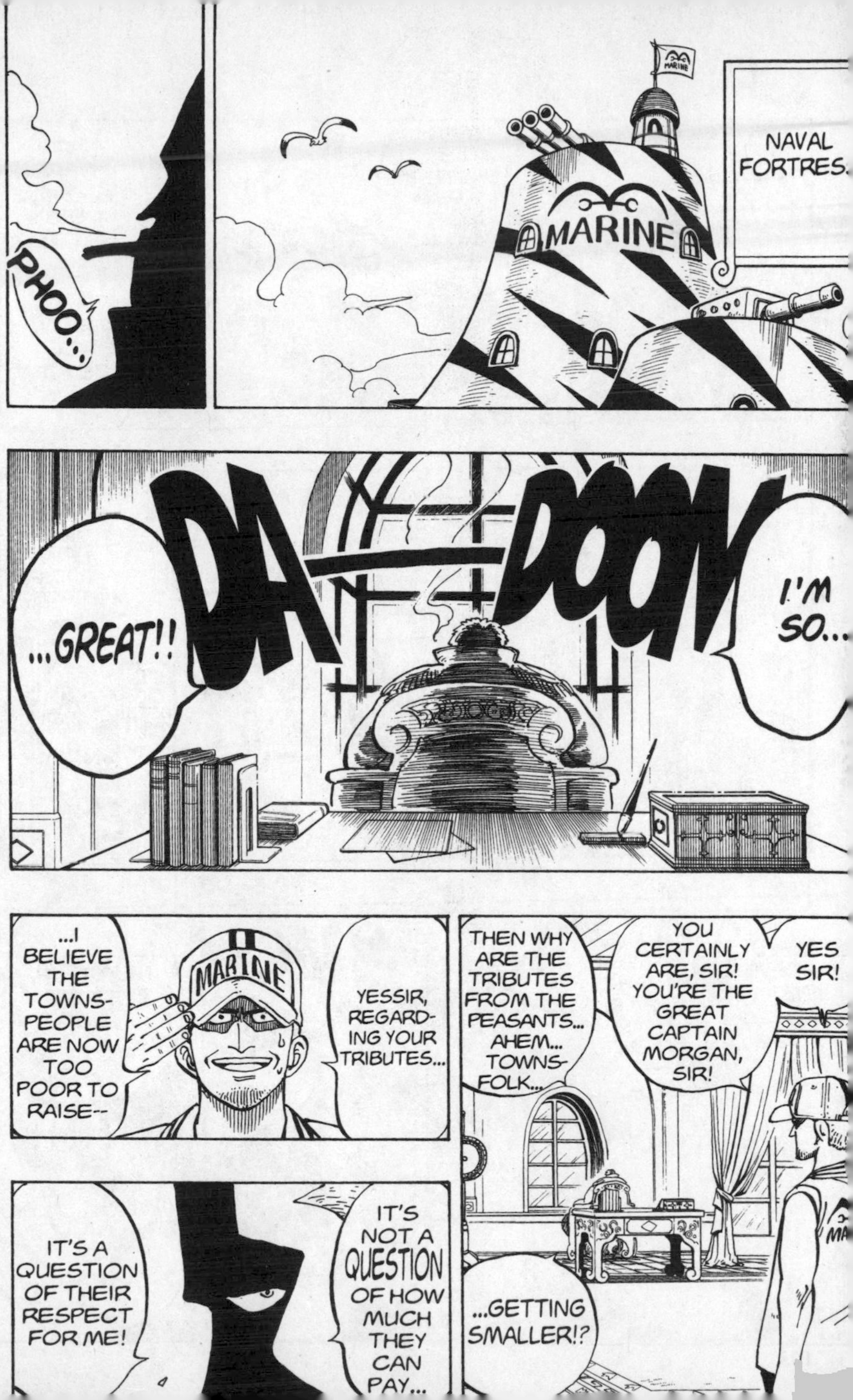
NAVAL FORTRES...
MARINE
MARINE
PHOO...
I'M SO...
DA—DOOM
...GREAT!!
YES SIR!
YOU CERTAINLY ARE, SIR! YOU'RE THE GREAT CAPTAIN MORGAN, SIR!
THEN WHY ARE THE TRIBUTES FROM THE PEASANTS... AHEM... TOWNSFOLK...
...GETTING SMALLER!?
MARINE
YESSIR, REGARDING YOUR TRIBUTES...
...I BELIEVE THE TOWNSPEOPLE ARE NOW TOO POOR TO RAISE--
IT'S NOT A QUESTION OF HOW MUCH THEY CAN PAY...
IT'S A QUESTION OF THEIR RESPECT FOR ME!

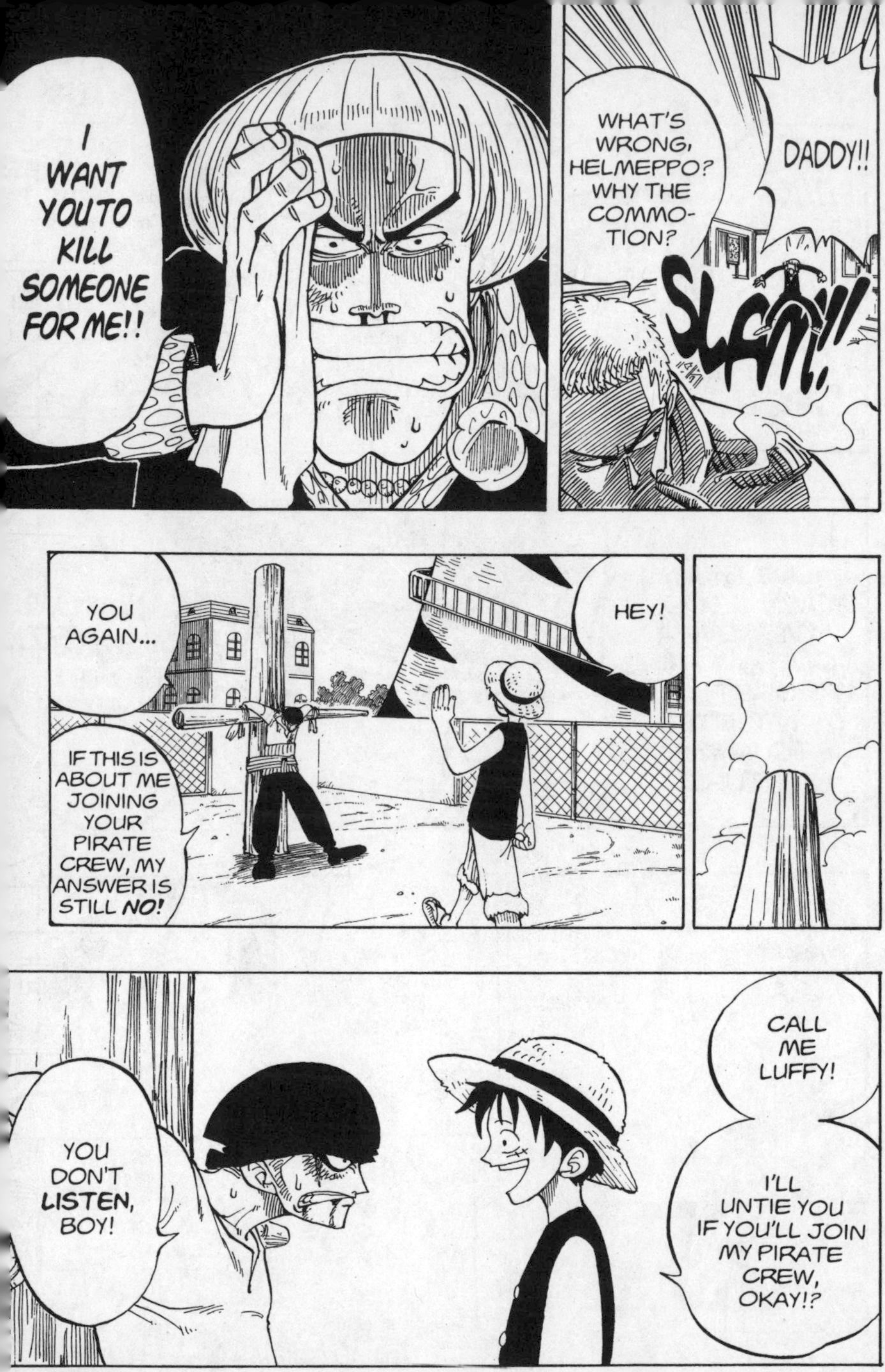
DADDY!!
WHAT'S WRONG, HELMEPPO? WHY THE COMMOTION?
SLAM!!
I WANT YOU TO KILL SOMEONE FOR ME!!
HEY!
YOU AGAIN...
IF THIS IS ABOUT ME JOINING YOUR PIRATE CREW, MY ANSWER IS STILL NO!
CALL ME LUFFY!
I'LL UNTIE YOU IF YOU'LL JOIN MY PIRATE CREW, OKAY!?
YOU DON'T LISTEN, BOY!

READ THIS WAY

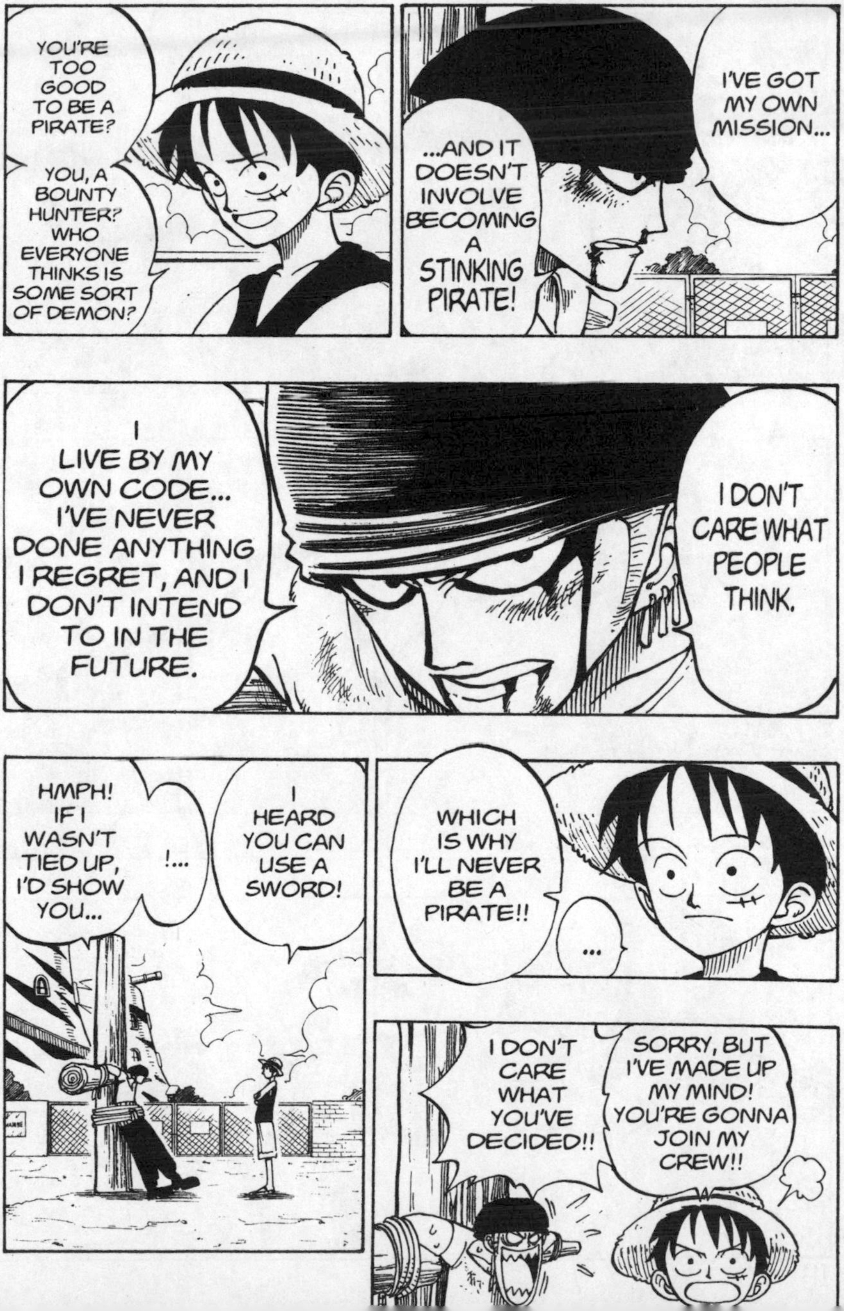
I'VE GOT MY OWN MISSION...
...AND IT DOESN'T INVOLVE BECOMING A STINKING PIRATE!
YOU'RE TOO GOOD TO BE A PIRATE?
YOU, A BOUNTY HUNTER? WHO EVERYONE THINKS IS SOME SORT OF DEMON?
I DON'T CARE WHAT PEOPLE THINK.
I LIVE BY MY OWN CODE... I'VE NEVER DONE ANYTHING I REGRET, AND I DON'T INTEND TO IN THE FUTURE.
WHICH IS WHY I'LL NEVER BE A PIRATE!!
...
SORRY, BUT I'VE MADE UP MY MIND! YOU'RE GONNA JOIN MY CREW!!
I DON'T CARE WHAT YOU'VE DECIDED!!
I HEARD YOU CAN USE A SWORD!
!...
HMPH! IF I WASN'T TIED UP, I'D SHOW YOU...

READ THIS WAY

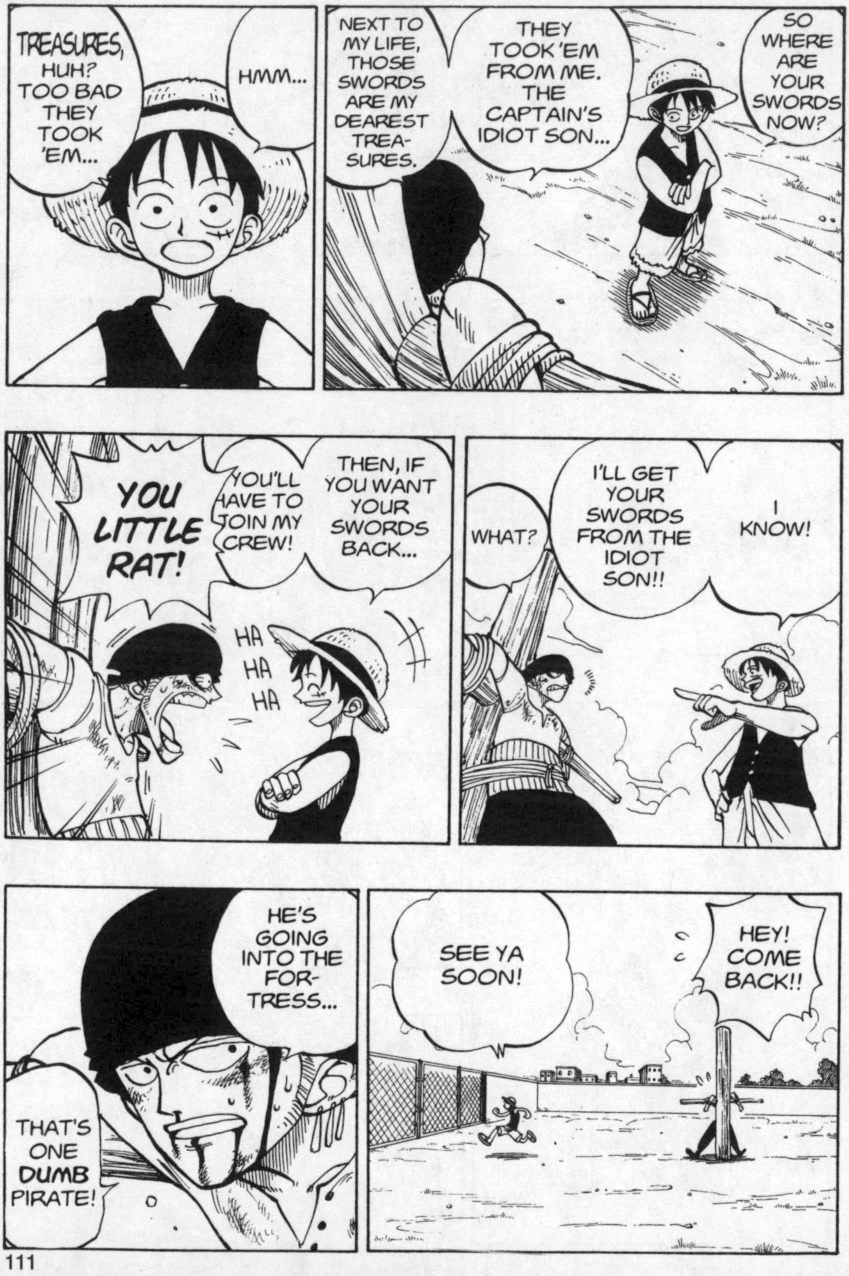
SO WHERE ARE YOUR SWORDS NOW?
THEY TOOK 'EM FROM ME. THE CAPTAIN'S IDIOT SON...
NEXT TO MY LIFE, THOSE SWORDS ARE MY DEAREST TREA-SURES.
HMM...
TREASURES, HUH? TOO BAD THEY TOOK 'EM...
I KNOW!
I'LL GET YOUR SWORDS FROM THE IDIOT SON!!
WHAT?
THEN, IF YOU WANT YOUR SWORDS BACK...
YOU'LL HAVE TO JOIN MY CREW!
HA HA HA
YOU LITTLE RAT!
HEY! COME BACK!!
SEE YA SOON!
HE'S GOING INTO THE FOR-TRESS...
THAT'S ONE DUMB PIRATE!

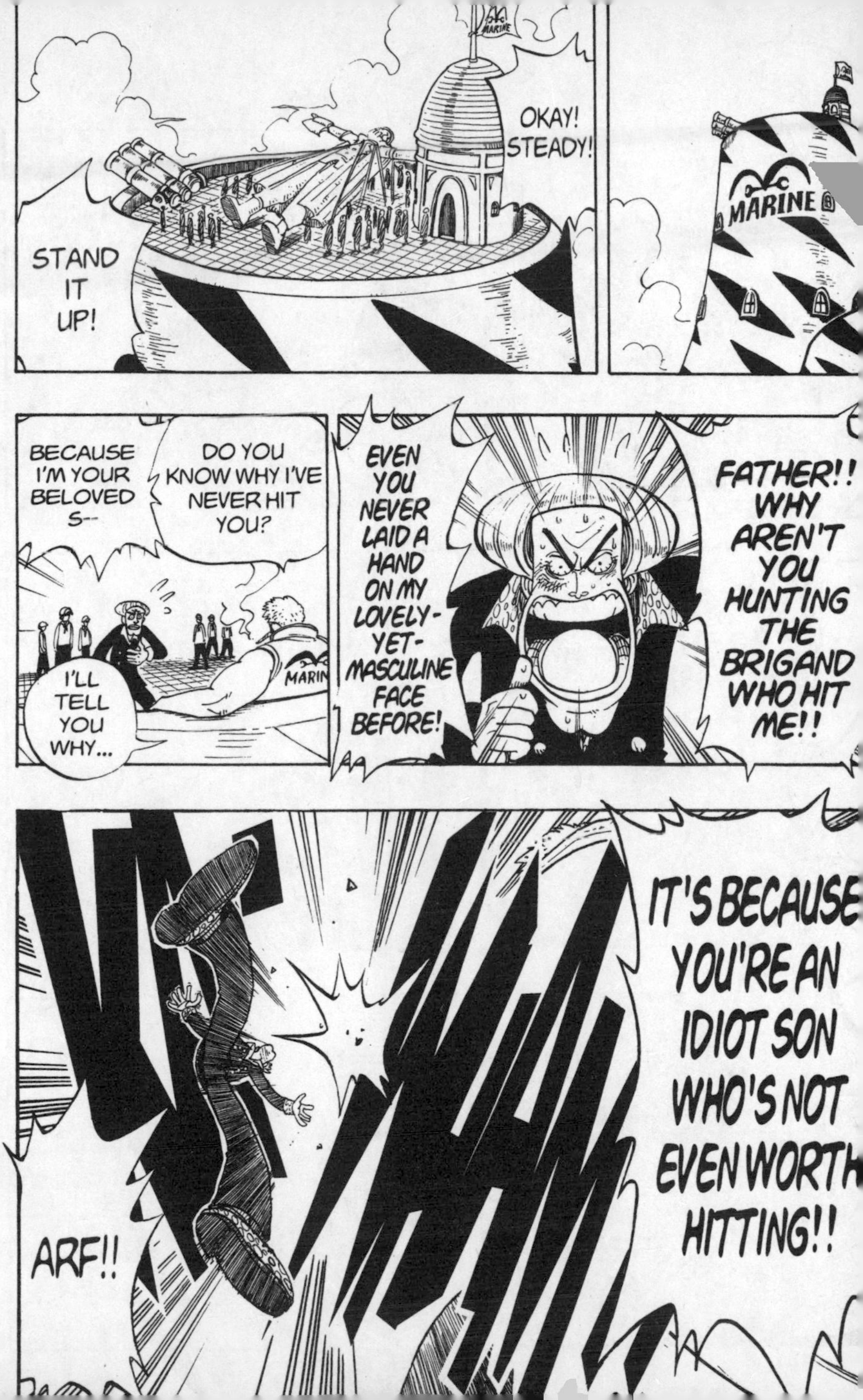
MARINE
OKAY! STEADY!
STAND IT UP!
FATHER!! WHY AREN'T YOU HUNTING THE BRIGAND WHO HIT ME!!
EVEN YOU NEVER LAID A HAND ON MY LOVELY-YET-MASCULINE FACE BEFORE!
DO YOU KNOW WHY I'VE NEVER HIT YOU?
BECAUSE I'M YOUR BELOVED S--
I'LL TELL YOU WHY...
IT'S BECAUSE YOU'RE AN IDIOT SON WHO'S NOT EVEN WORTH HITTING!!
ARF!!

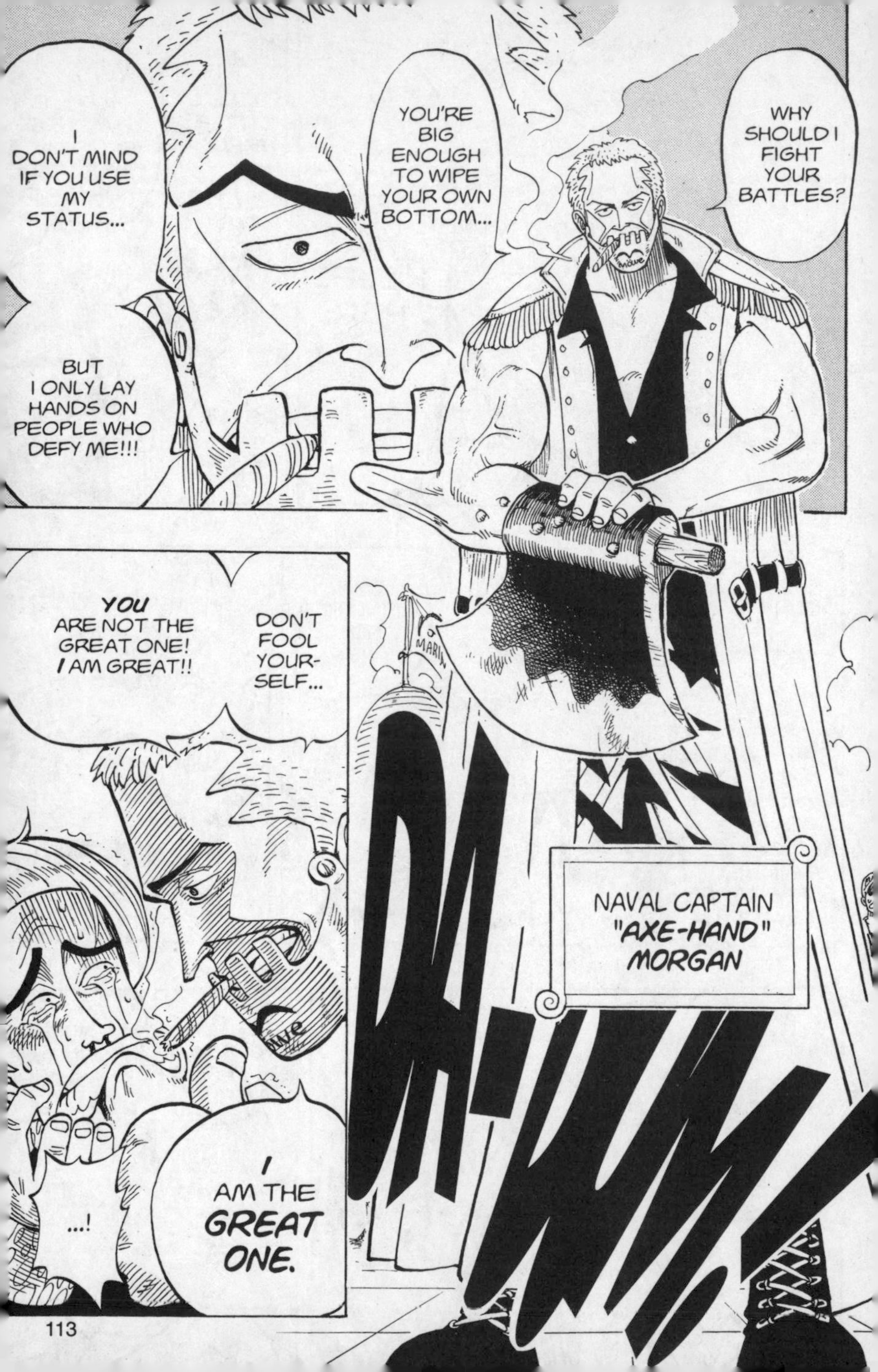
WHY SHOULD I FIGHT YOUR BATTLES?
YOU'RE BIG ENOUGH TO WIPE YOUR OWN BOTTOM...
I DON'T MIND IF YOU USE MY STATUS...
BUT I ONLY LAY HANDS ON PEOPLE WHO DEFY ME!!!
NAVAL CAPTAIN "AXE-HAND" MORGAN
DON'T FOOL YOURSELF...
YOU ARE NOT THE GREAT ONE! I AM GREAT!!
I AM THE GREAT ONE.
...!

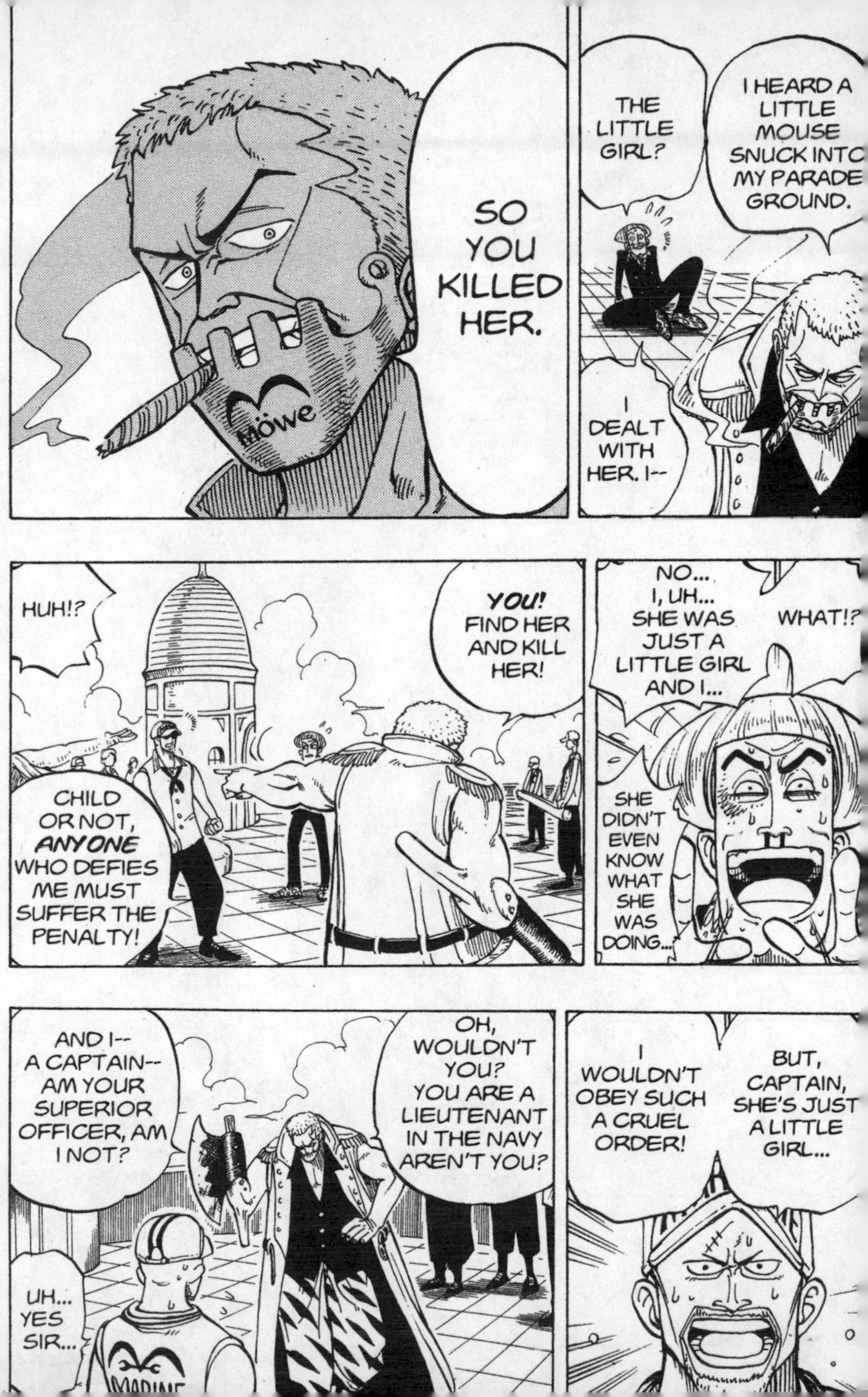
I HEARD A LITTLE MOUSE SNUCK INTO MY PARADE GROUND.
THE LITTLE GIRL?
I DEALT WITH HER. I--
SO YOU KILLED HER.
MÖWE
WHAT!?
NO... I, UH... SHE WAS JUST A LITTLE GIRL AND I...
SHE DIDN'T EVEN KNOW WHAT SHE WAS DOING...
YOU! FIND HER AND KILL HER!
HUH!?
CHILD OR NOT, *ANYONE* WHO DEFIES ME MUST SUFFER THE PENALTY!
BUT, CAPTAIN, SHE'S JUST A LITTLE GIRL...
I WOULDN'T OBEY SUCH A CRUEL ORDER!
OH, WOULDN'T YOU? YOU ARE A LIEUTENANT IN THE NAVY AREN'T YOU?
AND I-- A CAPTAIN-- AM YOUR SUPERIOR OFFICER, AM I NOT?
UH... YES SIR...

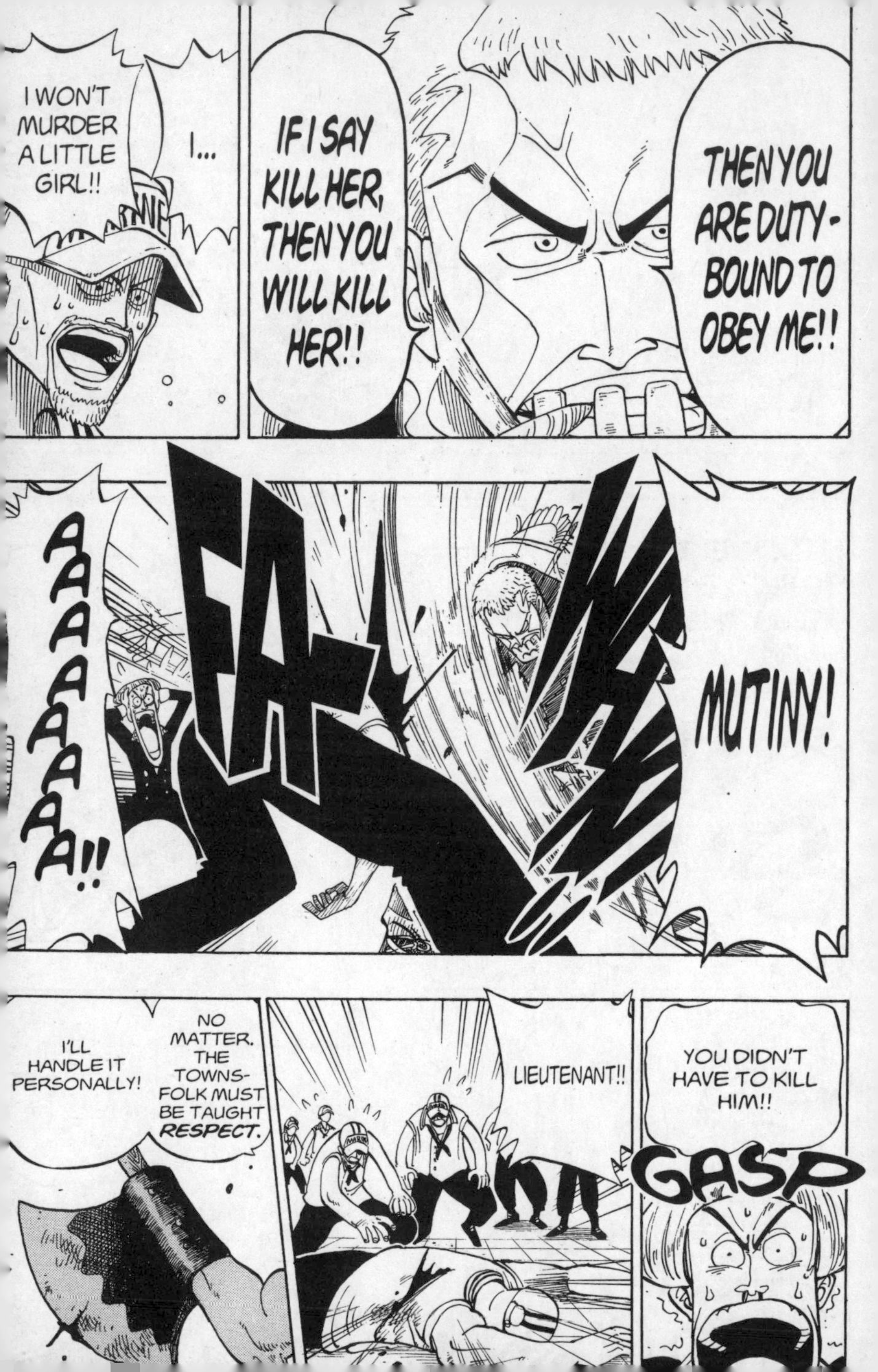
THEN YOU ARE DUTY-BOUND TO OBEY ME!!
IF I SAY KILL HER, THEN YOU WILL KILL HER!!
I...
I WON'T MURDER A LITTLE GIRL!!
MUTINY!
FA-
AAAAAAAAA!!
YOU DIDN'T HAVE TO KILL HIM!!
GASP
LIEUTENANT!!
NO MATTER. THE TOWNS-FOLK MUST BE TAUGHT *RESPECT*.
I'LL HANDLE IT PERSONALLY!

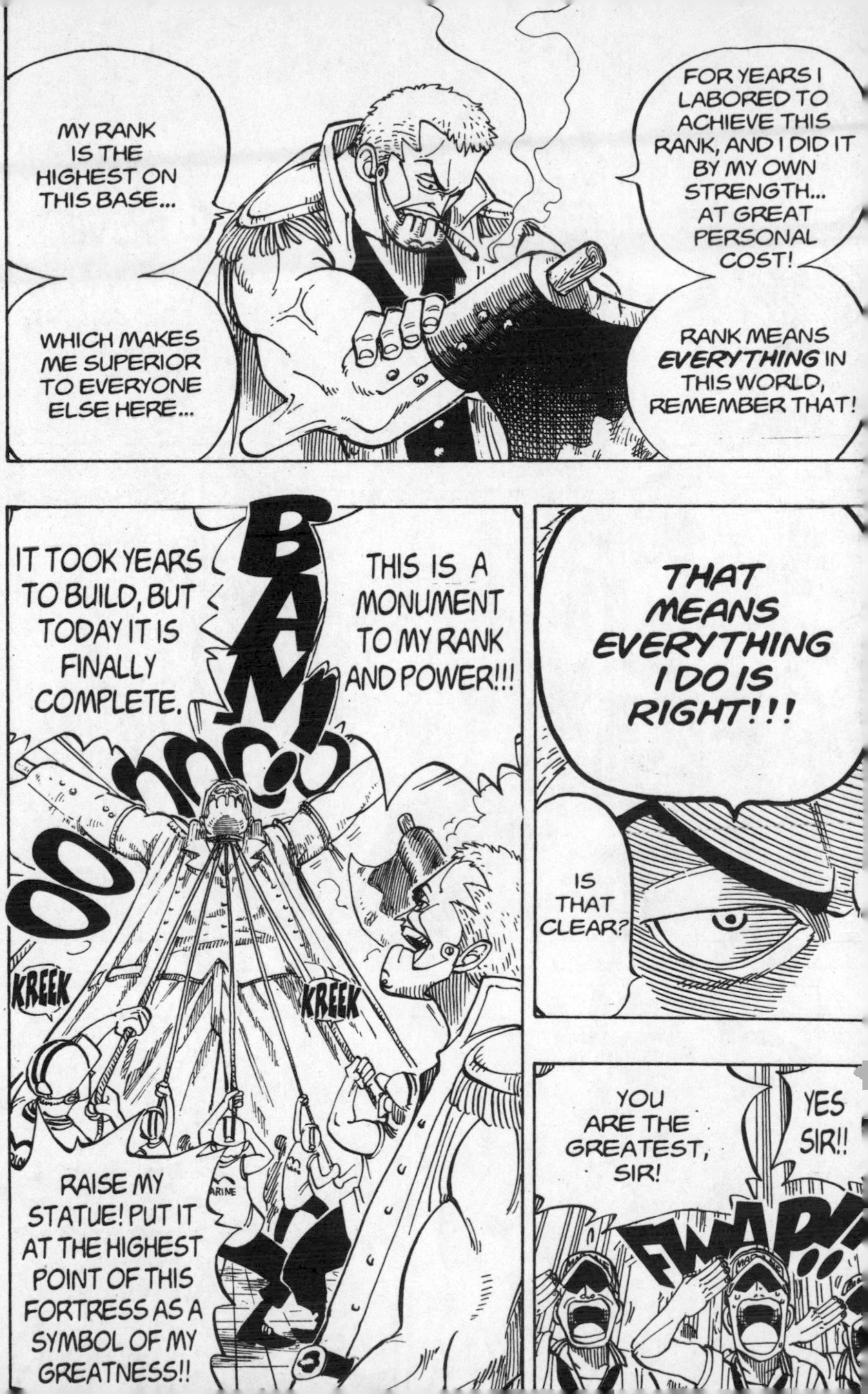
FOR YEARS I LABORED TO ACHIEVE THIS RANK, AND I DID IT BY MY OWN STRENGTH... AT GREAT PERSONAL COST!
MY RANK IS THE HIGHEST ON THIS BASE...
RANK MEANS *EVERYTHING* IN THIS WORLD, REMEMBER THAT!
WHICH MAKES ME SUPERIOR TO EVERYONE ELSE HERE...
THAT MEANS EVERYTHING I DO IS RIGHT!!!
IS THAT CLEAR?
YES SIR!!
YOU ARE THE GREATEST, SIR!
THIS IS A MONUMENT TO MY RANK AND POWER!!!
BAM!
IT TOOK YEARS TO BUILD, BUT TODAY IT IS FINALLY COMPLETE.
KREEK
KREEK
RAISE MY STATUE! PUT IT AT THE HIGHEST POINT OF THIS FORTRESS AS A SYMBOL OF MY GREATNESS!!

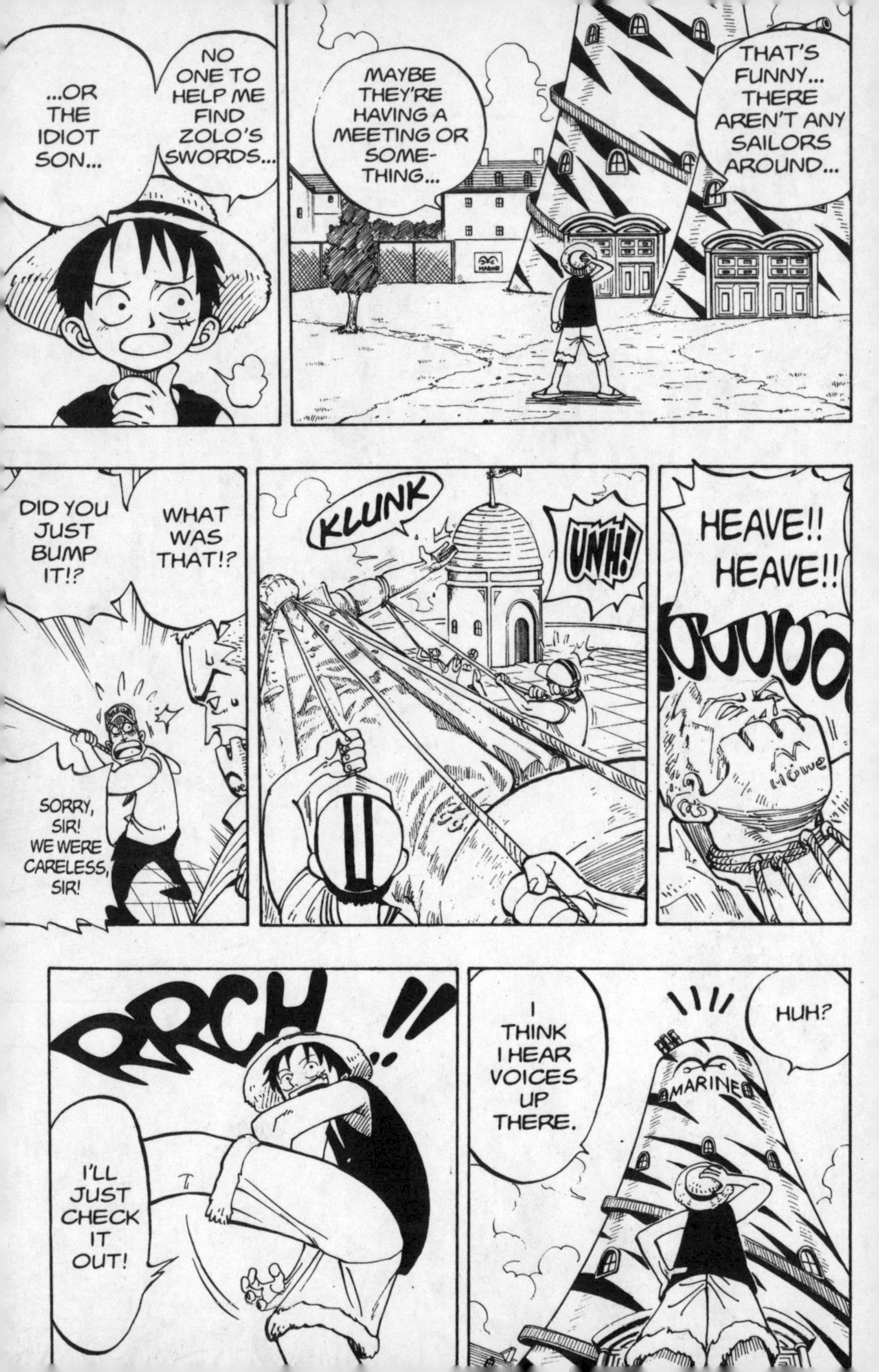

THAT'S FUNNY... THERE AREN'T ANY SAILORS AROUND...
MAYBE THEY'RE HAVING A MEETING OR SOME-THING...
NO ONE TO HELP ME FIND ZOLO'S SWORDS...
...OR THE IDIOT SON...
HEAVE!! HEAVE!!
UNH!
KLUNK
WHAT WAS THAT!?
DID YOU JUST BUMP IT!?
SORRY, SIR! WE WERE CARELESS, SIR!
HUH?
MARINE
I THINK I HEAR VOICES UP THERE.
BRRCH!!
I'LL JUST CHECK IT OUT!

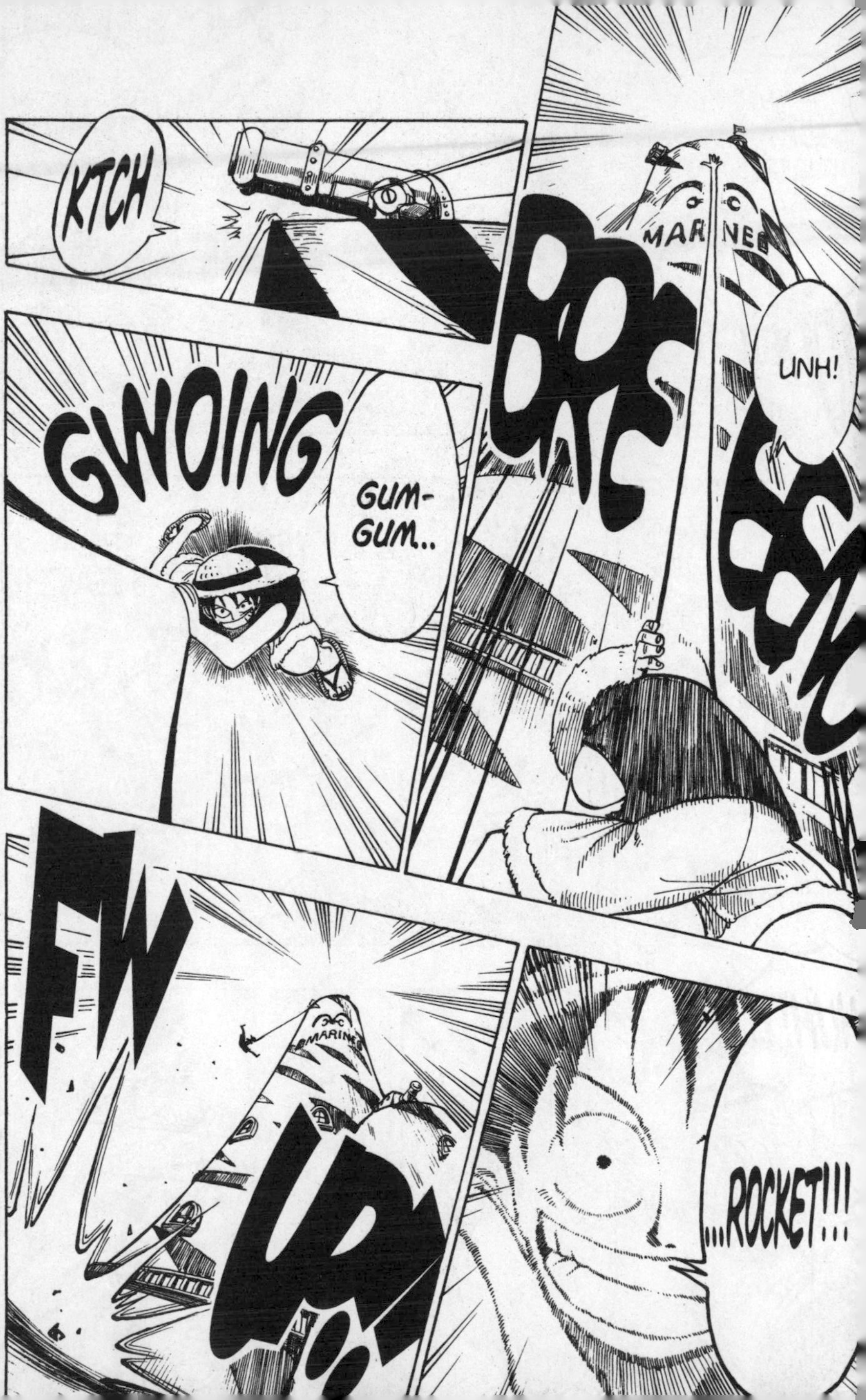
MARINE
UNH!
KTCH
GWOING
GUM-
GUM...
...ROCKET!!!
MARINE

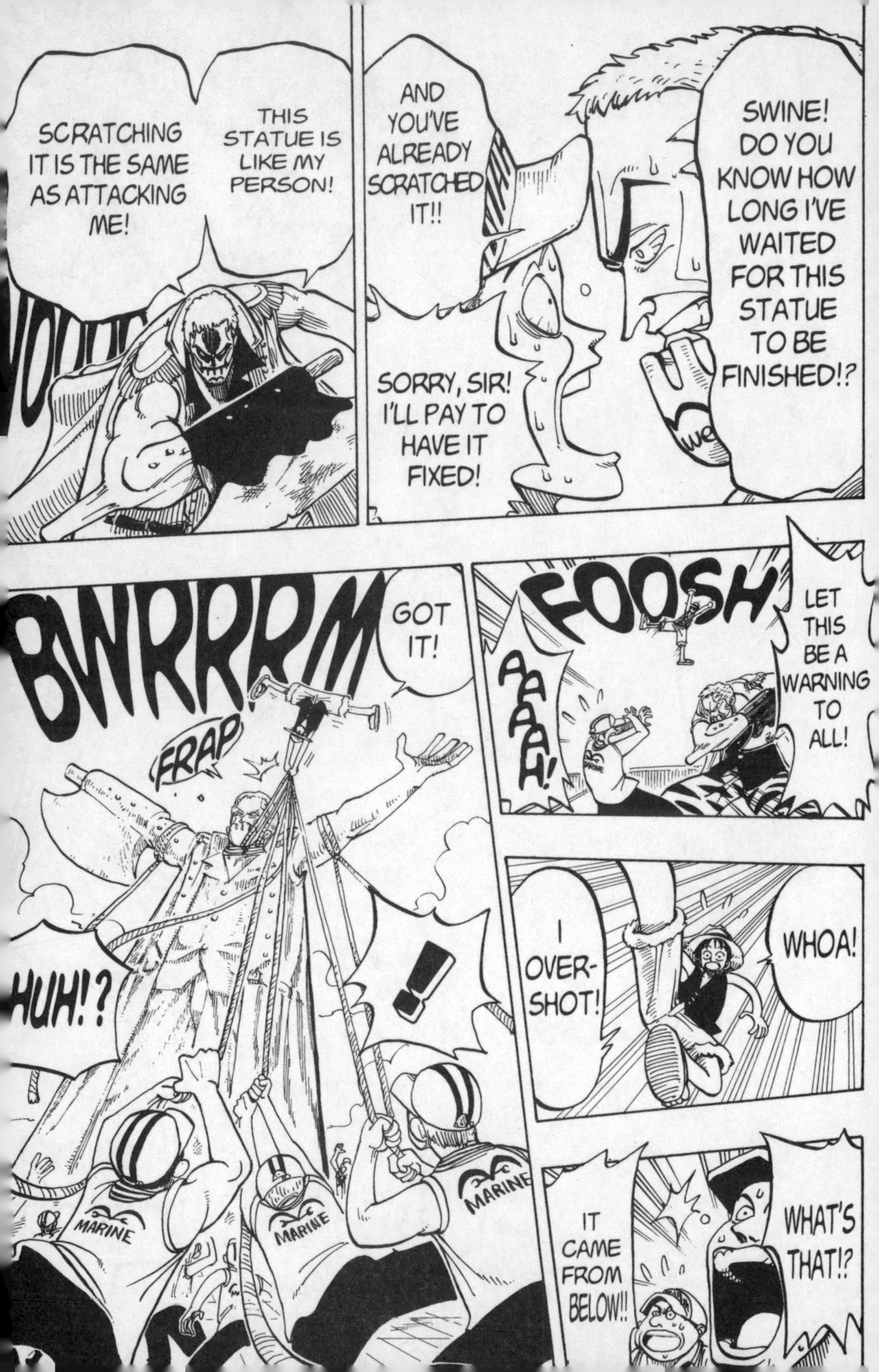
SWINE! DO YOU KNOW HOW LONG I'VE WAITED FOR THIS STATUE TO BE FINISHED!?
AND YOU'VE ALREADY SCRATCHED IT!!
SORRY, SIR! I'LL PAY TO HAVE IT FIXED!
THIS STATUE IS LIKE MY PERSON!
SCRATCHING IT IS THE SAME AS ATTACKING ME!
LET THIS BE A WARNING TO ALL!
FOOSH
AAAAH!
WHOA!
I OVER-SHOT!
WHAT'S THAT!?
IT CAME FROM BELOW!!
GOT IT!
BWRRRM
FRAP
!
HUH!?

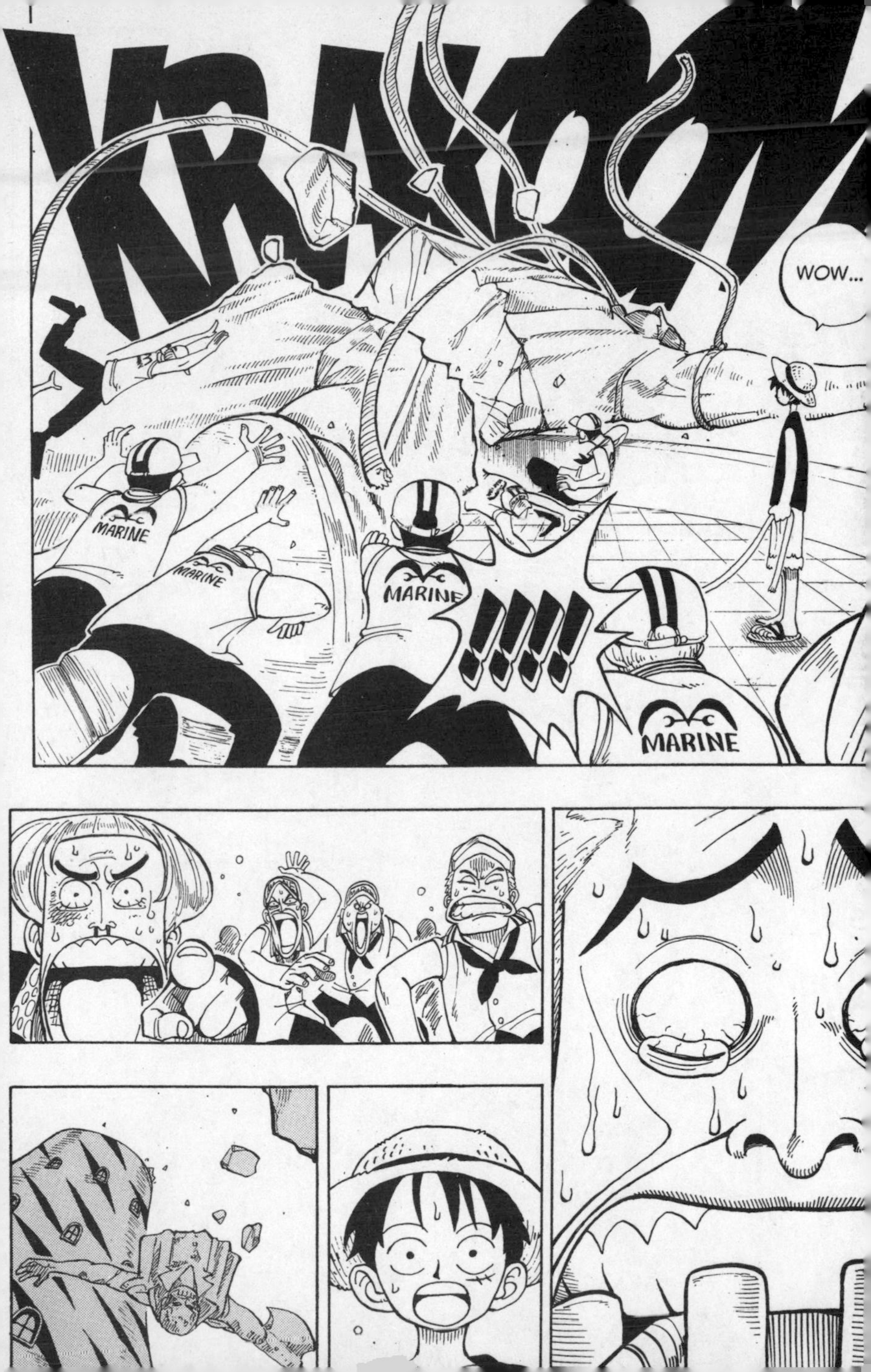
WOW...
MARINE
!!!!
MARINE
MARINE
MARINE

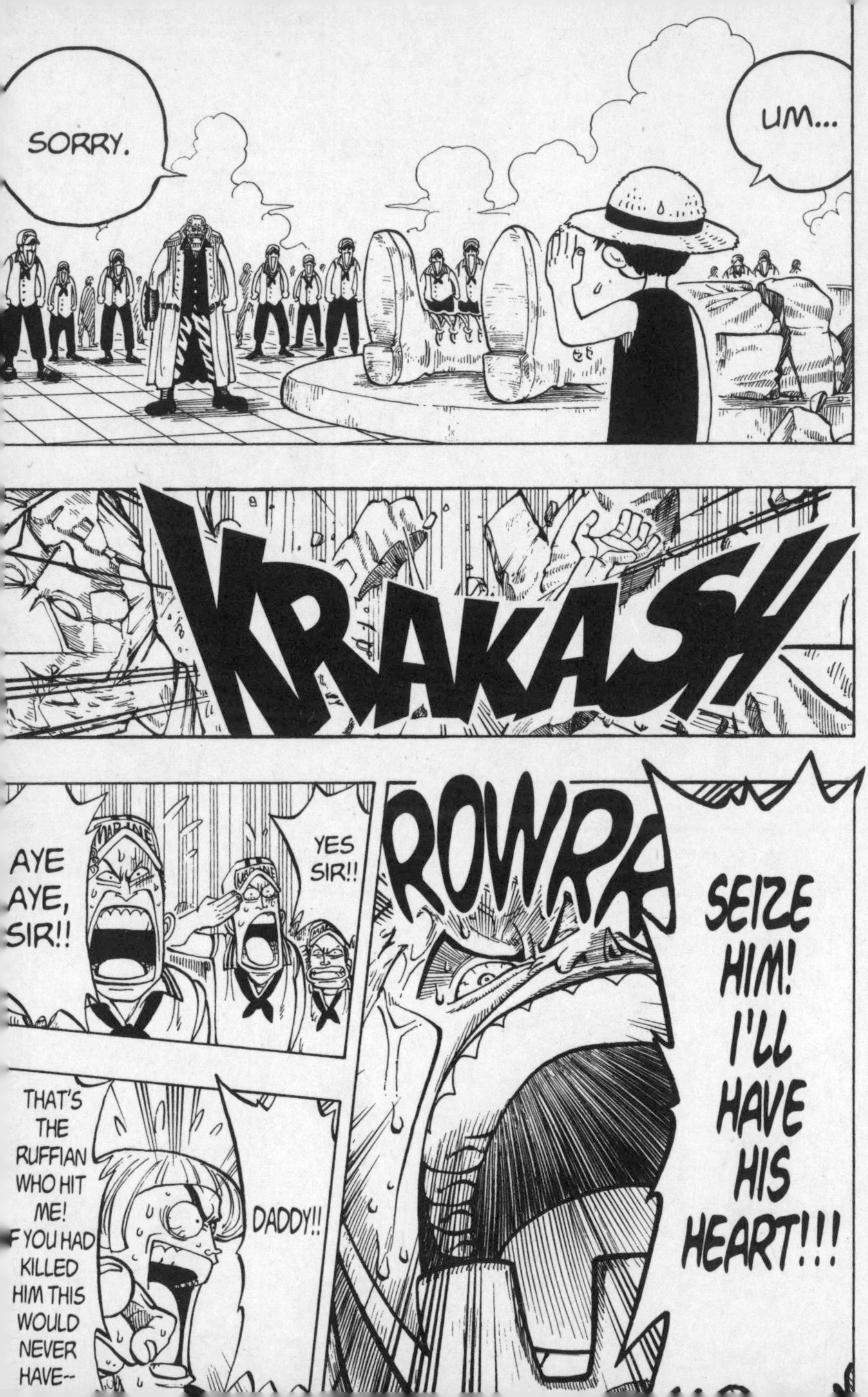
UM...
SORRY.
KRAKASH
ROWRA
SEIZE HIM! I'LL HAVE HIS HEART!!!
YES SIR!!
AYE AYE, SIR!!
DADDY!!
THAT'S THE RUFFIAN WHO HIT ME! F YOU HAD KILLED HIM THIS WOULD NEVER HAVE--

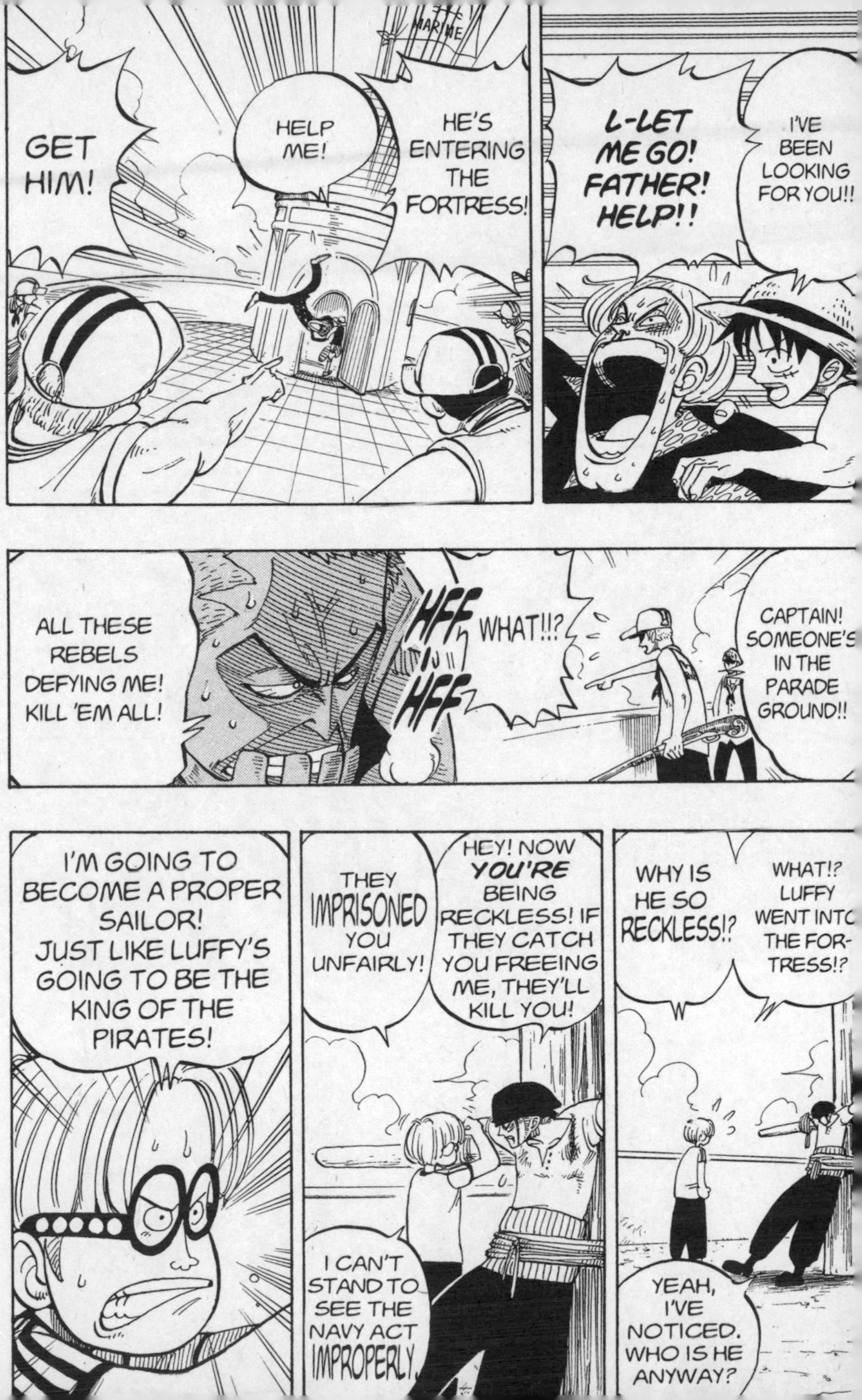
I'VE BEEN LOOKING FOR YOU!!
L-LET ME GO! FATHER! HELP!!
MARINE
HE'S ENTERING THE FORTRESS!
HELP ME!
GET HIM!
CAPTAIN! SOMEONE'S IN THE PARADE GROUND!!
WHAT!!?
HFF HFF
ALL THESE REBELS DEFYING ME! KILL 'EM ALL!
WHAT!? LUFFY WENT INTO THE FORTRESS!?
WHY IS HE SO RECKLESS!?
YEAH, I'VE NOTICED. WHO IS HE ANYWAY?
HEY! NOW YOU'RE BEING RECKLESS! IF THEY CATCH YOU FREEING ME, THEY'LL KILL YOU!
THEY IMPRISONED YOU UNFAIRLY!
I CAN'T STAND TO SEE THE NAVY ACT IMPROPERLY.
I'M GOING TO BECOME A PROPER SAILOR! JUST LIKE LUFFY'S GOING TO BE THE KING OF THE PIRATES!

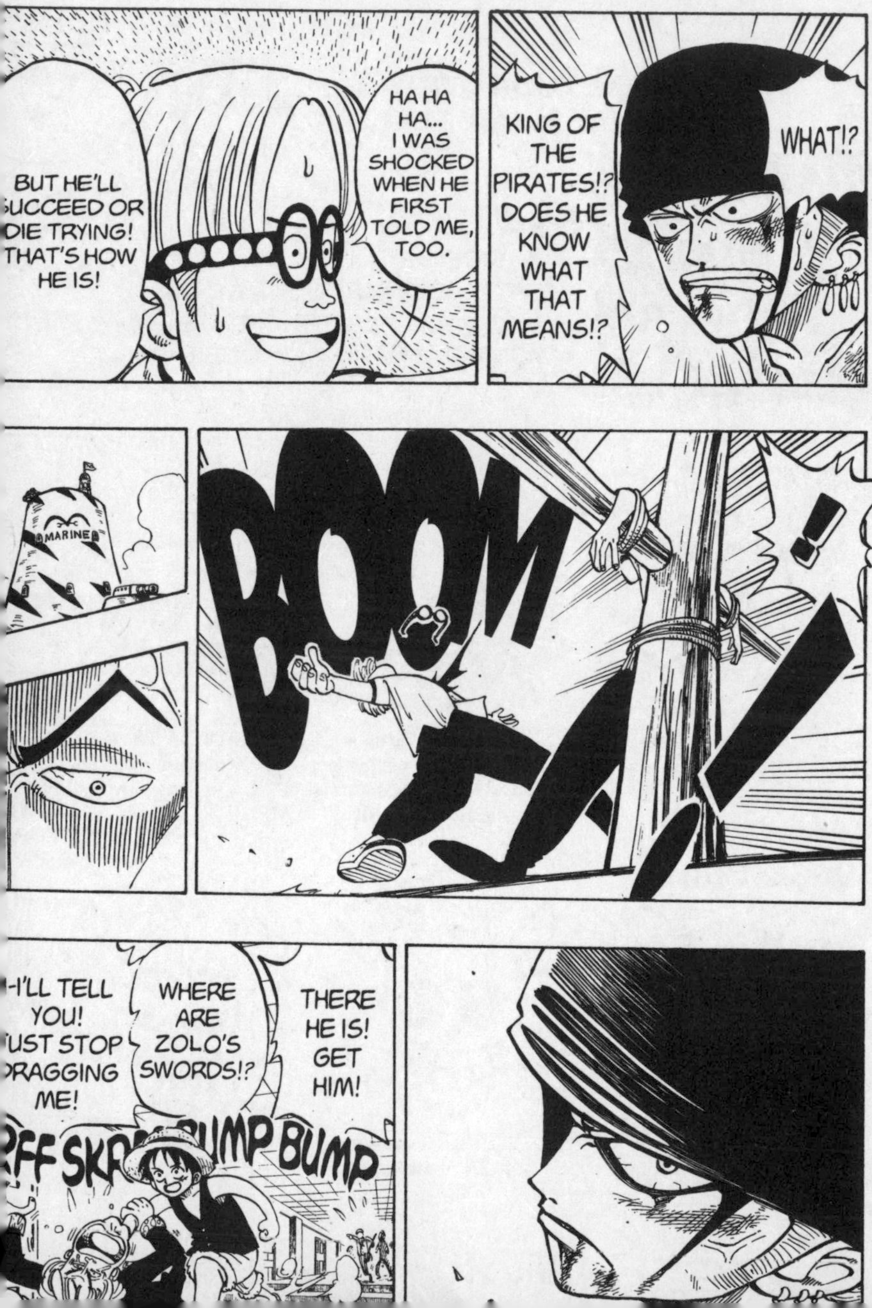
WHAT!?
KING OF THE PIRATES!? DOES HE KNOW WHAT THAT MEANS!?
HA HA HA... I WAS SHOCKED WHEN HE FIRST TOLD ME, TOO.
BUT HE'LL SUCCEED OR DIE TRYING! THAT'S HOW HE IS!
BOOM
!
THERE HE IS! GET HIM!
WHERE ARE ZOLO'S SWORDS!?
-I'LL TELL YOU! UST STOP RAGGING ME!
RFF SKR UMP BUMP

MAKE YOUR OWN ORIGINAL PIRATE FLAG!

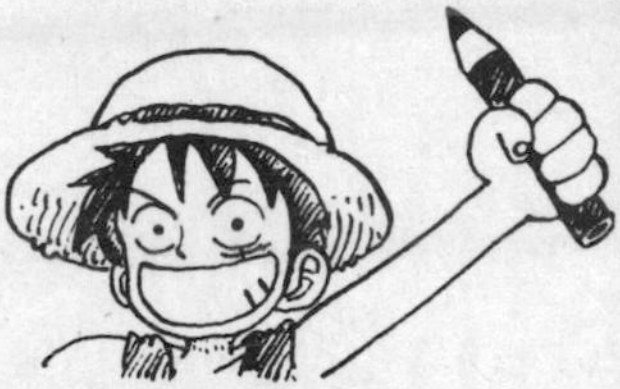

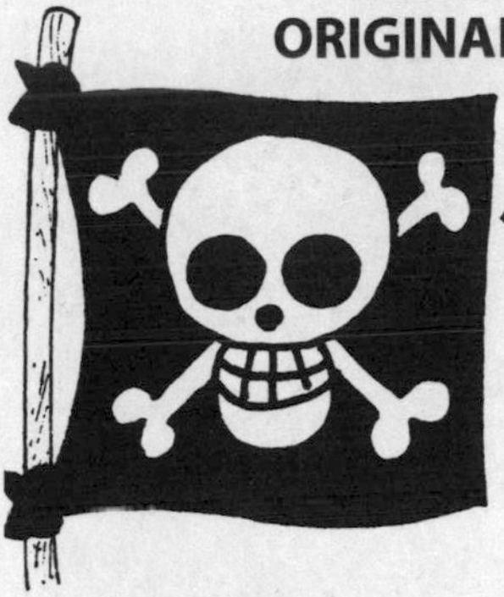

HAVE YOU MASTERED THE BASICS OF THE SKULL AND CROSSBONES? NEXT, WE'LL SHOW YOU HOW TO CREATE YOUR OWN ORIGINAL DESIGNS!

EXAMPLES

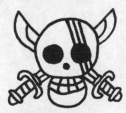

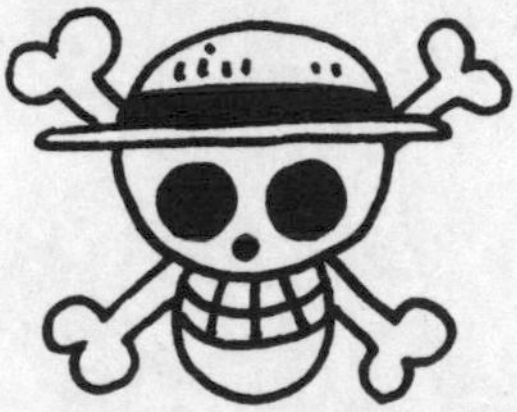

LUFFY'S FLAG
Just add a straw hat!

SHANKS' FLAG
Add three scars on the left eye and replace the cross-bones with swords.

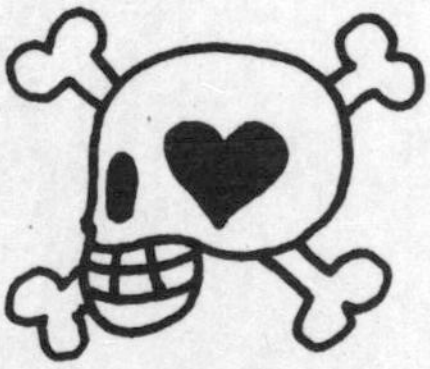

ALVIDA'S FLAG
In profile with a heart symbol.

SUGGESTIONS

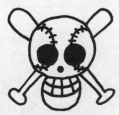

If you like baseball you can do something like this!

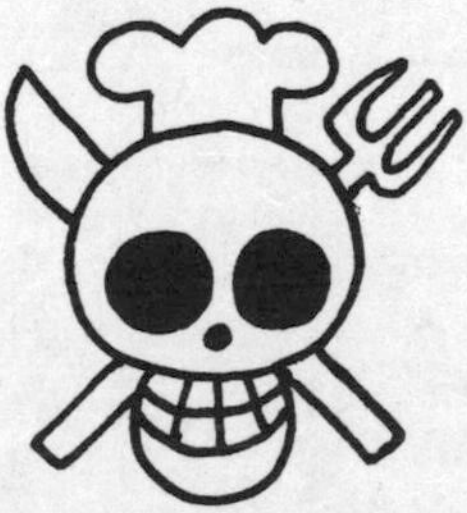

...Or like this, if you want to be a cook!

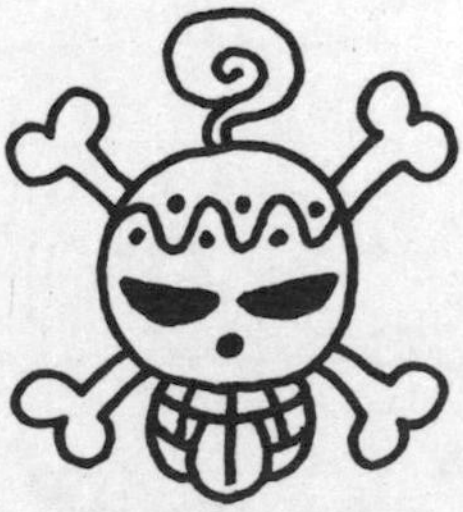

Here's another original design!

CHAPTER 5:
THE KING OF THE PIRATES AND THE MASTER SWORDSMAN

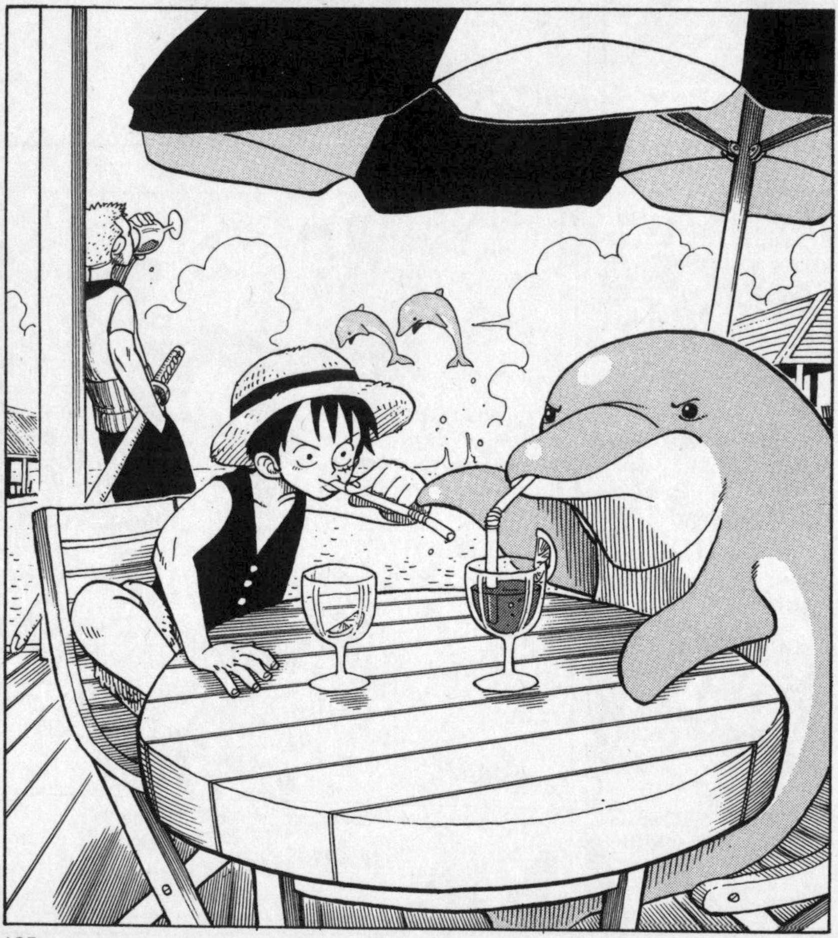

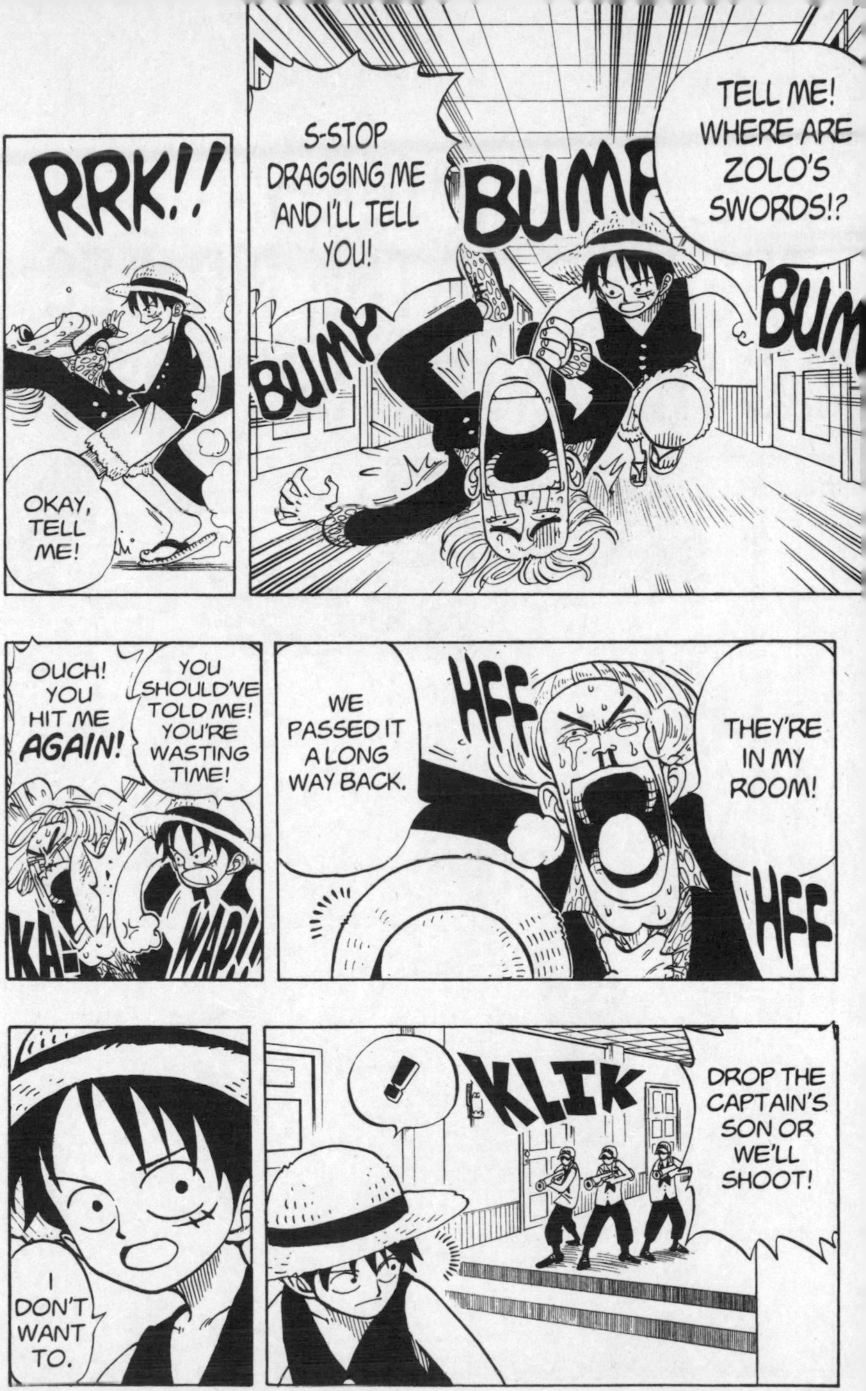
TELL ME! WHERE ARE ZOLO'S SWORDS!?
BUMP
BUM
S-STOP DRAGGING ME AND I'LL TELL YOU!
BUMP
RRK!!
OKAY, TELL ME!
THEY'RE IN MY ROOM!
HFF
HFF
WE PASSED IT A LONG WAY BACK.
YOU SHOULD'VE TOLD ME! YOU'RE WASTING TIME!
OUCH! YOU HIT ME ***AGAIN***!
WAP!!
KA-
DROP THE CAPTAIN'S SON OR WE'LL SHOOT!
KLIK
!
I DON'T WANT TO.

READ THIS WAY

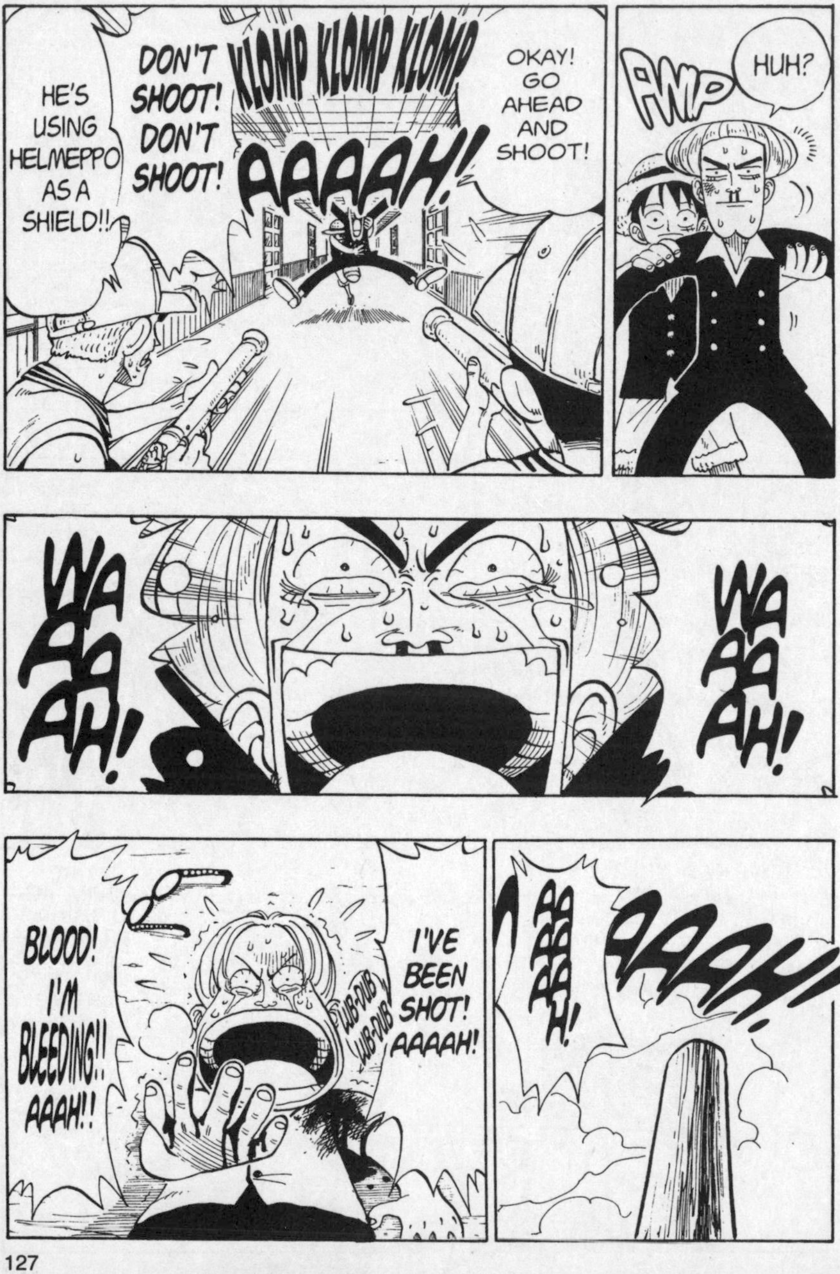
AMP
HUH?
OKAY! GO AHEAD AND SHOOT!
KLOMP KLOMP KLOMP
AAAAH!
DON'T SHOOT! DON'T SHOOT!
HE'S USING HELMEPPO AS A SHIELD!!
WAAAAH!
WAAAAH!
AAAH!!
AAAAAH!
I'VE BEEN SHOT! AAAAH!
WUB-DUB WUB-DUB
BLOOD! I'M BLEEDING!! AAAH!!

READ THIS WAY

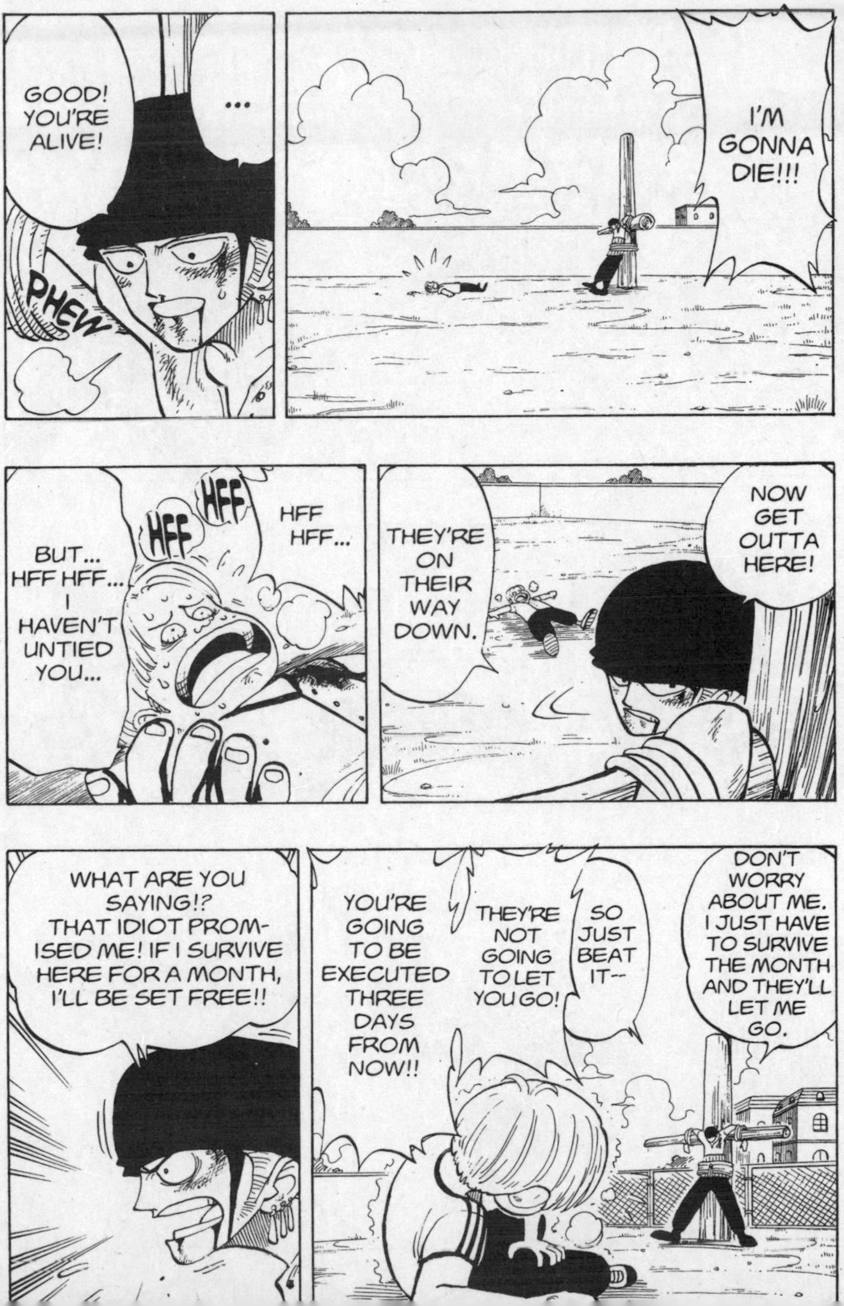
I'M GONNA DIE!!!
...
GOOD! YOU'RE ALIVE!
PHEW
NOW GET OUTTA HERE!
THEY'RE ON THEIR WAY DOWN.
HFF HFF...
HFF
HFF
BUT... HFF HFF... I HAVEN'T UNTIED YOU...
DON'T WORRY ABOUT ME. I JUST HAVE TO SURVIVE THE MONTH AND THEY'LL LET ME GO.
SO JUST BEAT IT--
THEY'RE NOT GOING TO LET YOU GO!
YOU'RE GOING TO BE EXECUTED THREE DAYS FROM NOW!!
WHAT ARE YOU SAYING!? THAT IDIOT PROMISED ME! IF I SURVIVE HERE FOR A MONTH, I'LL BE SET FREE!!

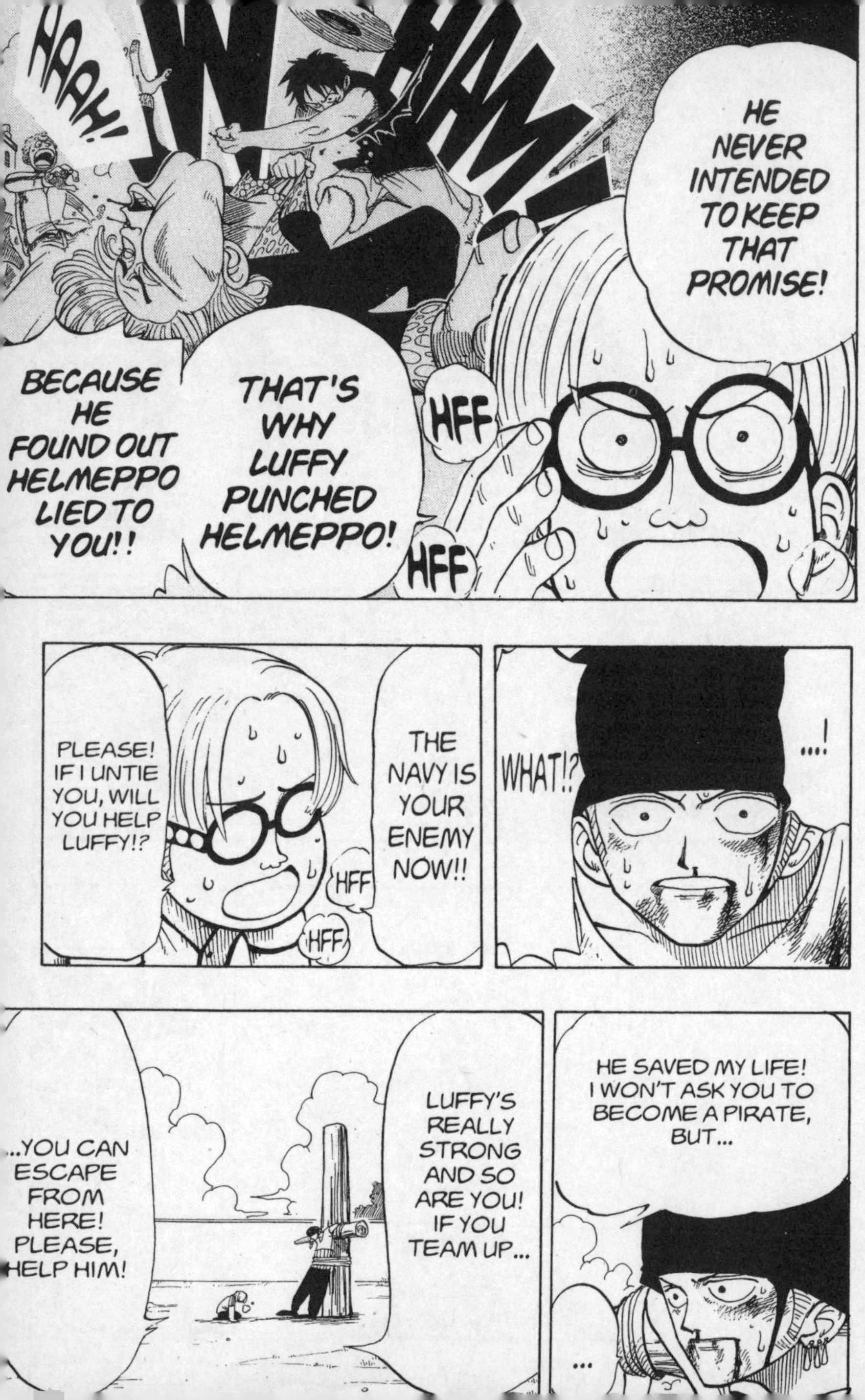
WHAM!
HAAH!
HE NEVER INTENDED TO KEEP THAT PROMISE!
HFF
HFF
THAT'S WHY LUFFY PUNCHED HELMEPPO!
BECAUSE HE FOUND OUT HELMEPPO LIED TO YOU!!
...!
WHAT!?
THE NAVY IS YOUR ENEMY NOW!!
HFF
HFF
PLEASE! IF I UNTIE YOU, WILL YOU HELP LUFFY!?
HE SAVED MY LIFE! I WON'T ASK YOU TO BECOME A PIRATE, BUT...
...
LUFFY'S REALLY STRONG AND SO ARE YOU! IF YOU TEAM UP...
...YOU CAN ESCAPE FROM HERE! PLEASE, HELP HIM!

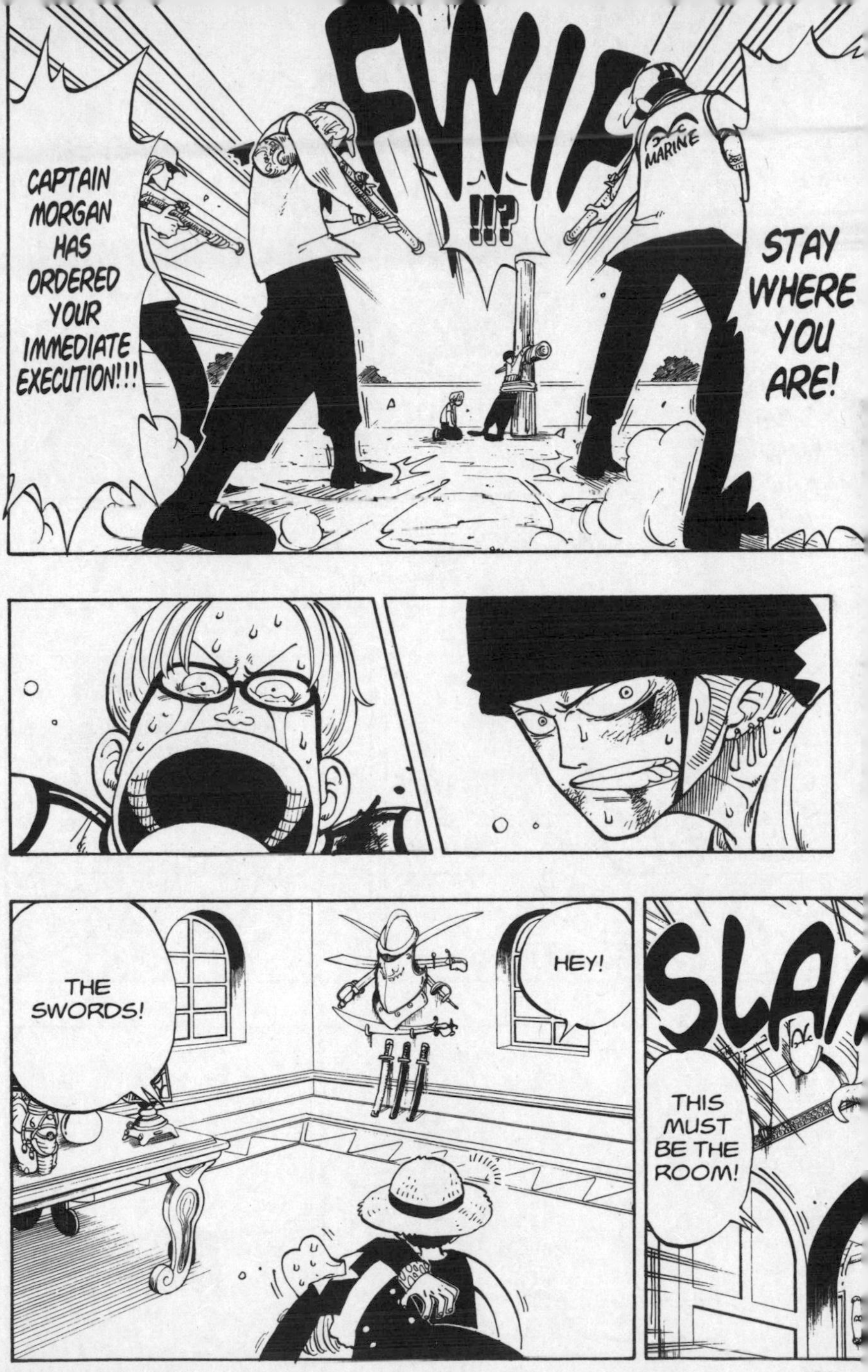
FWIP
!!?
STAY WHERE YOU ARE!
CAPTAIN MORGAN HAS ORDERED YOUR IMMEDIATE EXECUTION!!!
SLA
THIS MUST BE THE ROOM!
HEY!
THE SWORDS!

READ THIS WAY

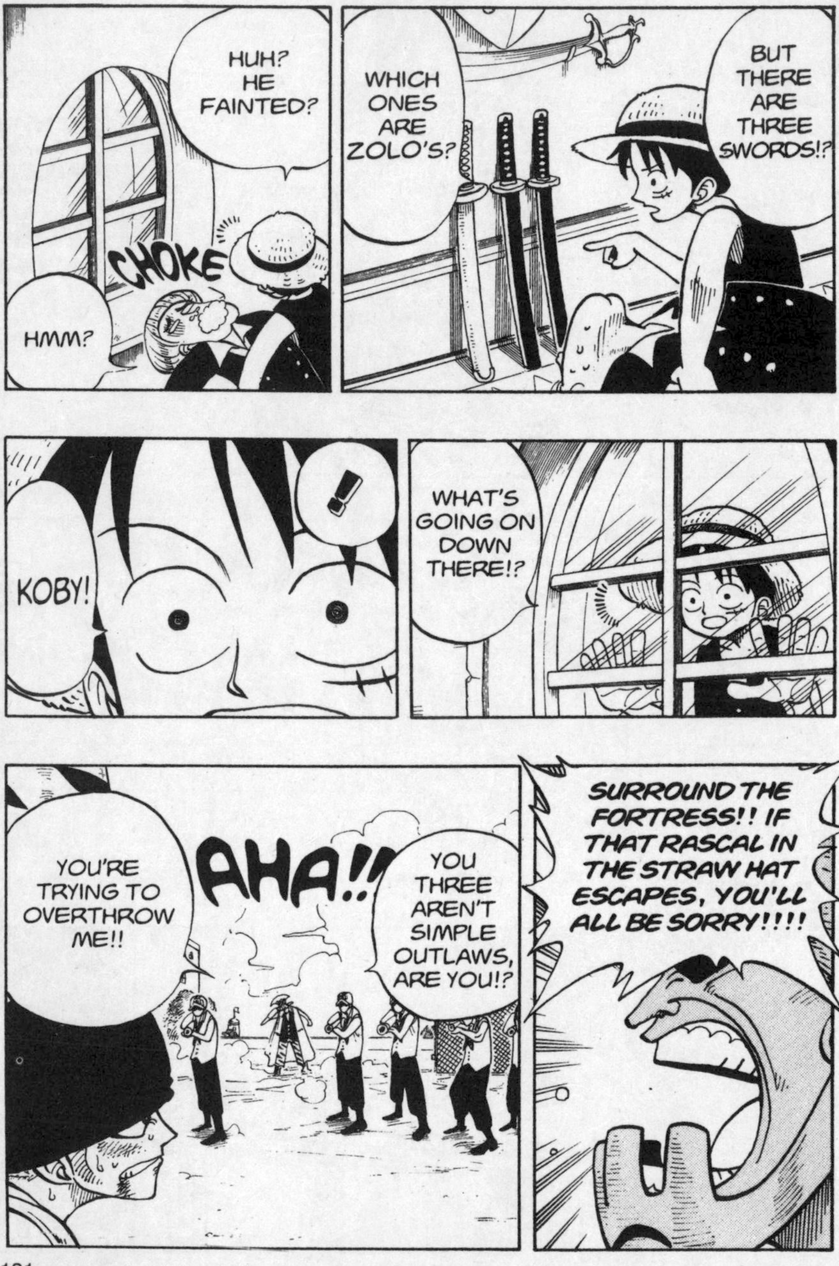
BUT THERE ARE THREE SWORDS!?
WHICH ONES ARE ZOLO'S?
HUH? HE FAINTED?
CHOKE
HMM?
WHAT'S GOING ON DOWN THERE!?
!
KOBY!
SURROUND THE FORTRESS!! IF THAT RASCAL IN THE STRAW HAT ESCAPES, YOU'LL ALL BE SORRY!!!!
YOU THREE AREN'T SIMPLE OUTLAWS, ARE YOU!?
AHA!!
YOU'RE TRYING TO OVERTHROW ME!!

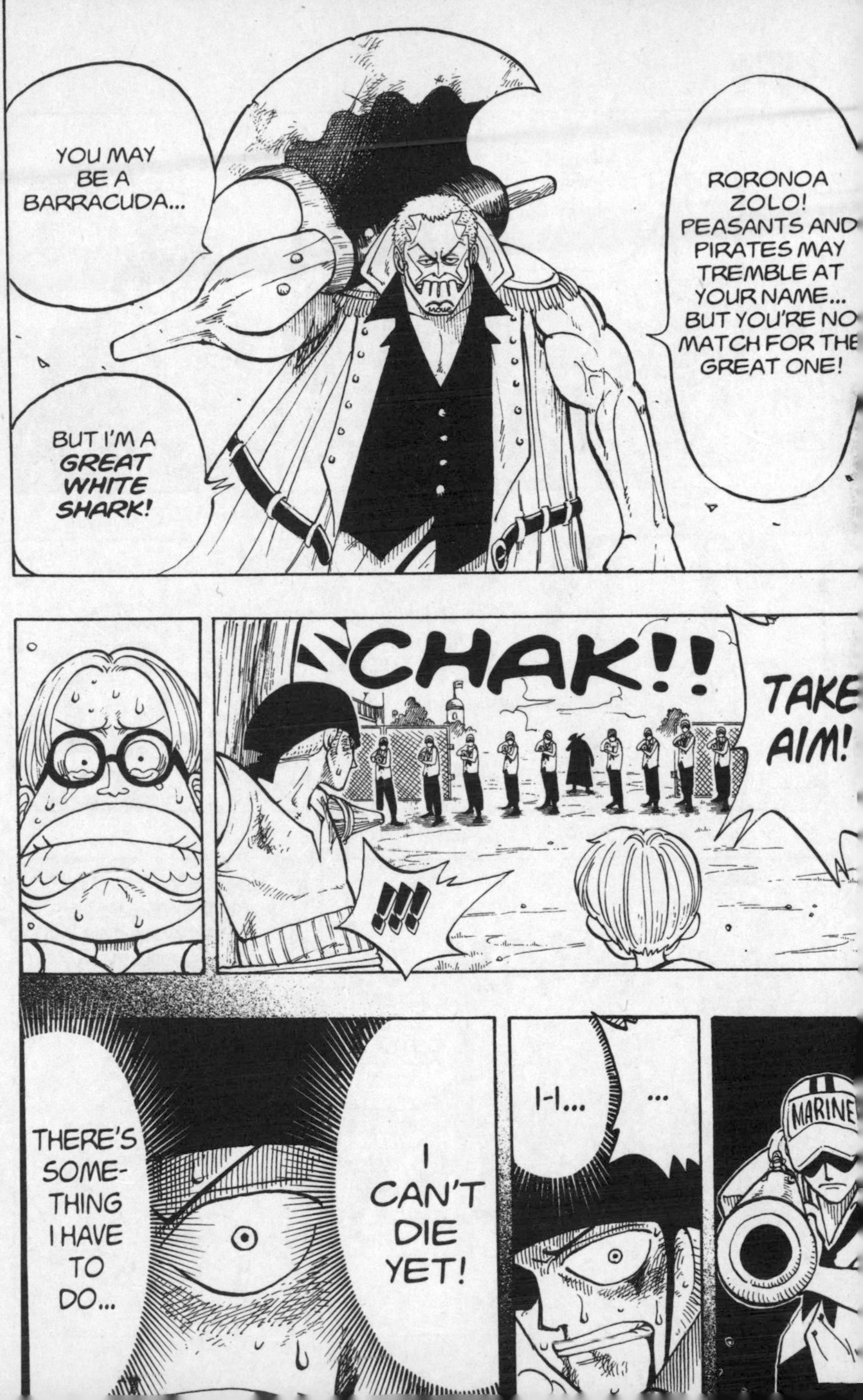
RORONOA ZOLO! PEASANTS AND PIRATES MAY TREMBLE AT YOUR NAME... BUT YOU'RE NO MATCH FOR THE GREAT ONE!
YOU MAY BE A BARRACUDA...
BUT I'M A *GREAT WHITE SHARK!*
TAKE AIM!
CHAK!!
!!!
I-I... ...
I CAN'T DIE YET!
THERE'S SOME-THING I HAVE TO DO...

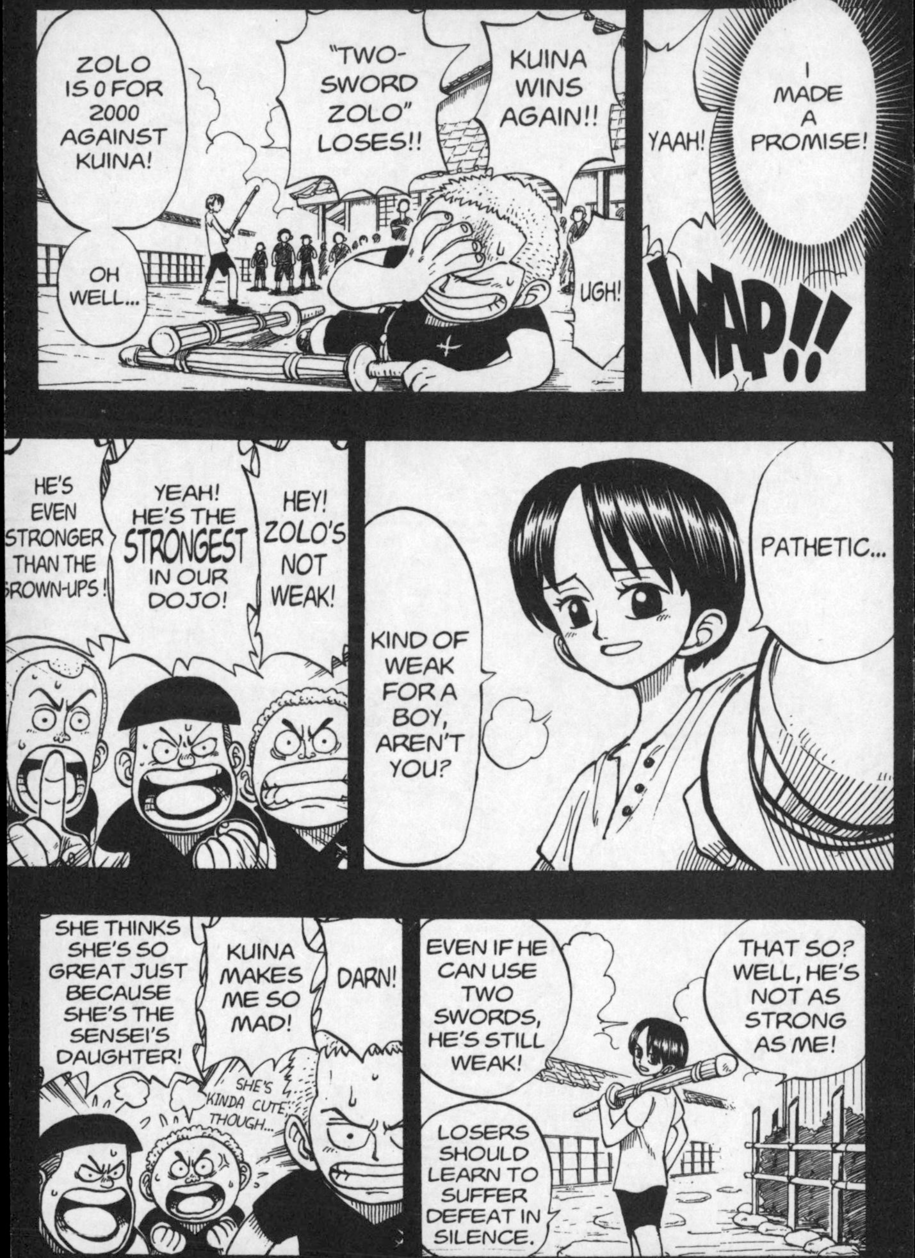
I MADE A PROMISE!
YAAH!
WAP!!
KUINA WINS AGAIN!!
"TWO-SWORD ZOLO" LOSES!!
ZOLO IS 0 FOR 2000 AGAINST KUINA!
UGH!
OH WELL...
PATHETIC...
KIND OF WEAK FOR A BOY, AREN'T YOU?
HEY! ZOLO'S NOT WEAK!
YEAH! HE'S THE STRONGEST IN OUR DOJO!
HE'S EVEN STRONGER THAN THE GROWN-UPS!
THAT SO? WELL, HE'S NOT AS STRONG AS ME!
EVEN IF HE CAN USE TWO SWORDS, HE'S STILL WEAK!
LOSERS SHOULD LEARN TO SUFFER DEFEAT IN SILENCE.
DARN!
KUINA MAKES ME SO MAD!
SHE THINKS SHE'S SO GREAT JUST BECAUSE SHE'S THE SENSEI'S DAUGHTER!
SHE'S KINDA CUTE, THOUGH...

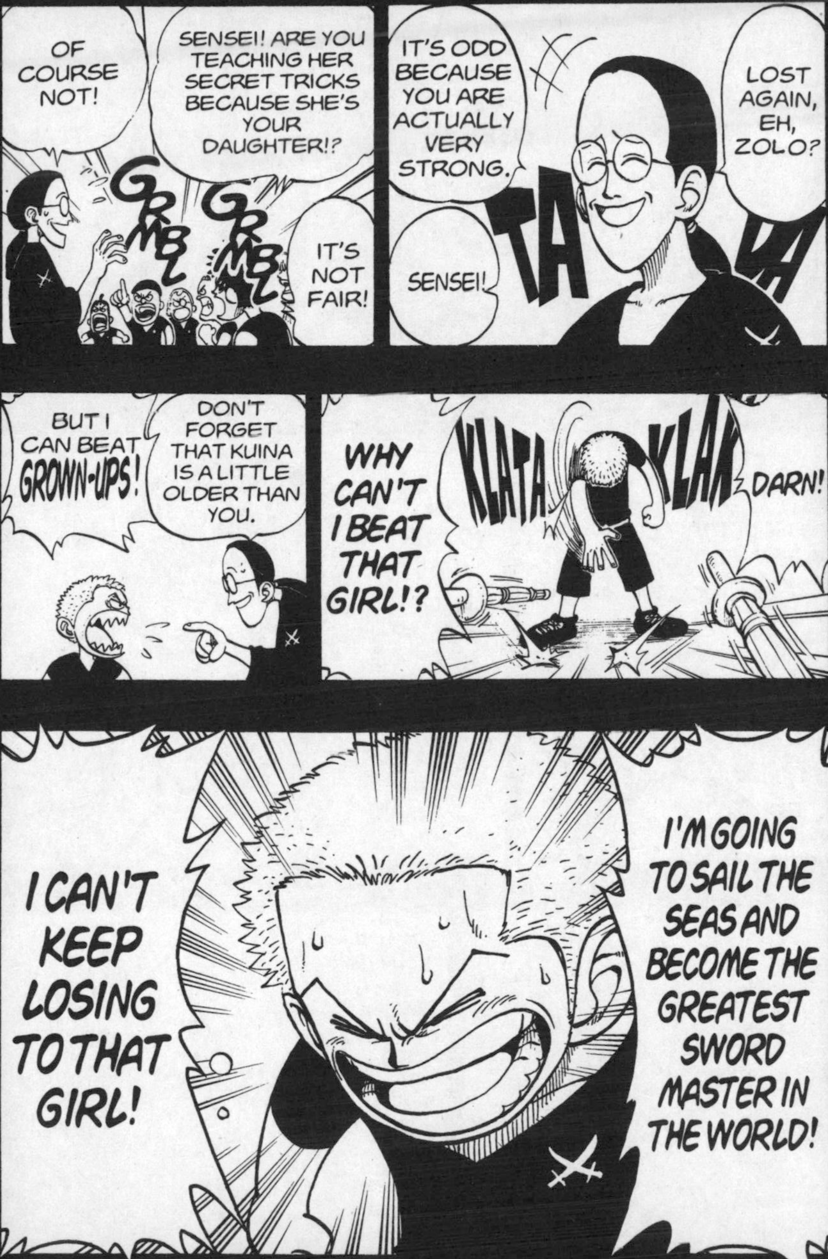
LOST AGAIN, EH, ZOLO?
IT'S ODD BECAUSE YOU ARE ACTUALLY VERY STRONG.
TA
DA
SENSEI!
SENSEI! ARE YOU TEACHING HER SECRET TRICKS BECAUSE SHE'S YOUR DAUGHTER!?
OF COURSE NOT!
IT'S NOT FAIR!
GRMBL
GRMBL
KLATA
KLAK
DARN!
WHY CAN'T I BEAT THAT GIRL!?
DON'T FORGET THAT KUINA IS A LITTLE OLDER THAN YOU.
BUT I CAN BEAT GROWN-UPS!
I'M GOING TO SAIL THE SEAS AND BECOME THE GREATEST SWORD MASTER IN THE WORLD!
I CAN'T KEEP LOSING TO THAT GIRL!

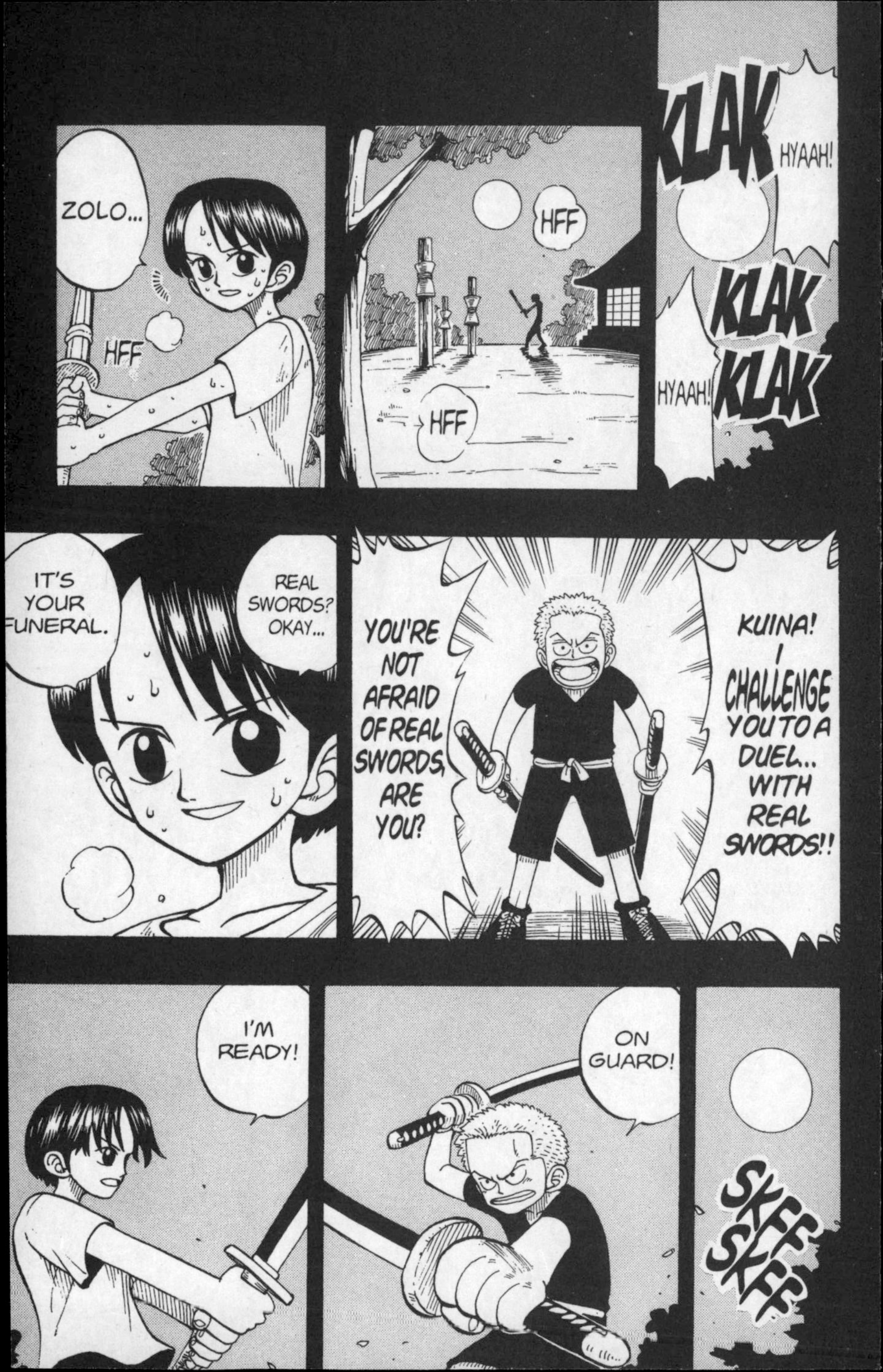
KLAK
HYAAH!
KLAK KLAK
HYAAH!
HFF
HFF
ZOLO...
HFF
KUINA! I CHALLENGE YOU TO A DUEL... WITH REAL SWORDS!!
YOU'RE NOT AFRAID OF REAL SWORDS, ARE YOU?
REAL SWORDS? OKAY...
IT'S YOUR FUNERAL.
SKFF SKFF
ON GUARD!
I'M READY!

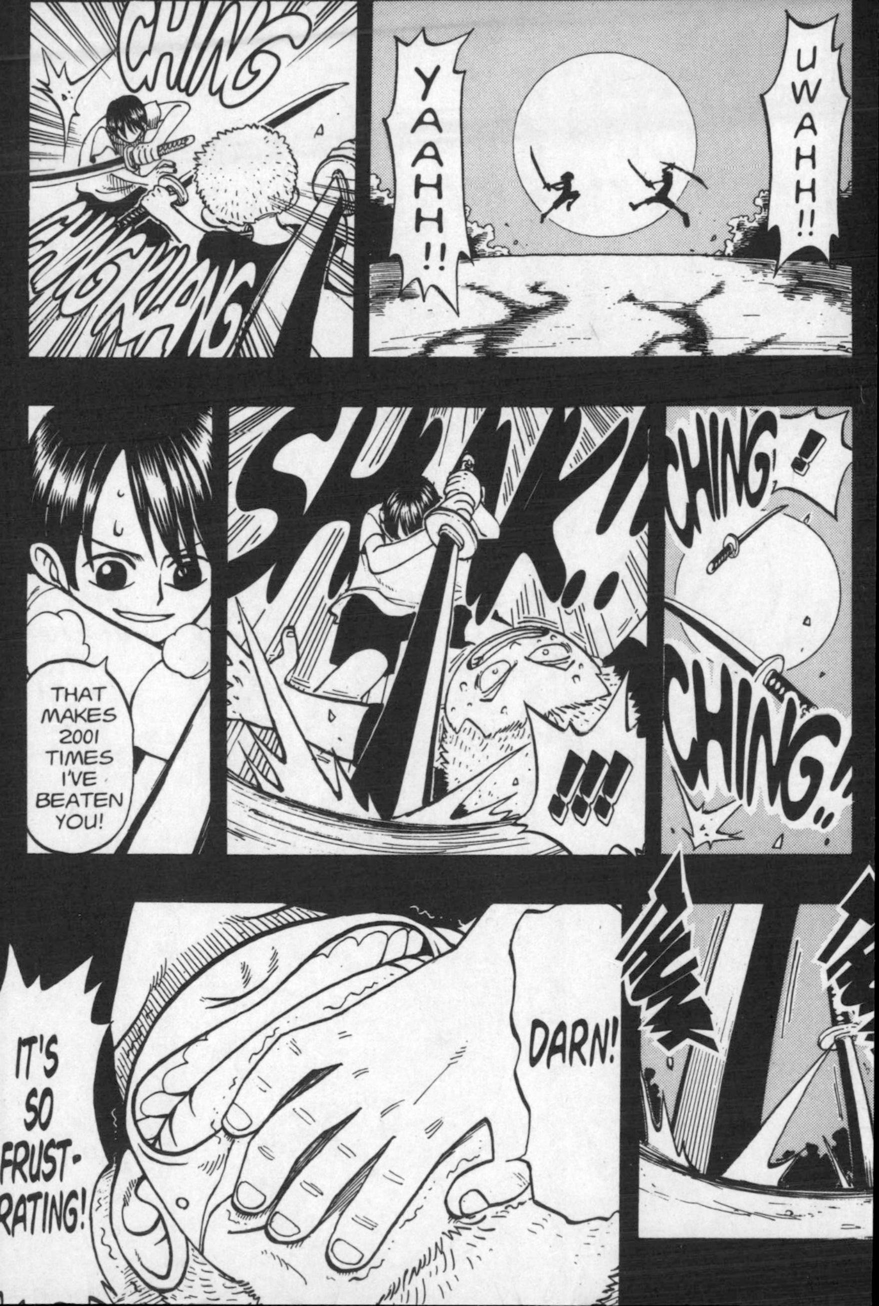
UWAHH!!
YAAHH!!
CHING
CHING!
CHING CHING!!
!!!
THAT MAKES 2001 TIMES I'VE BEATEN YOU!
THUNK
DARN!
IT'S SO FRUST-RATING!

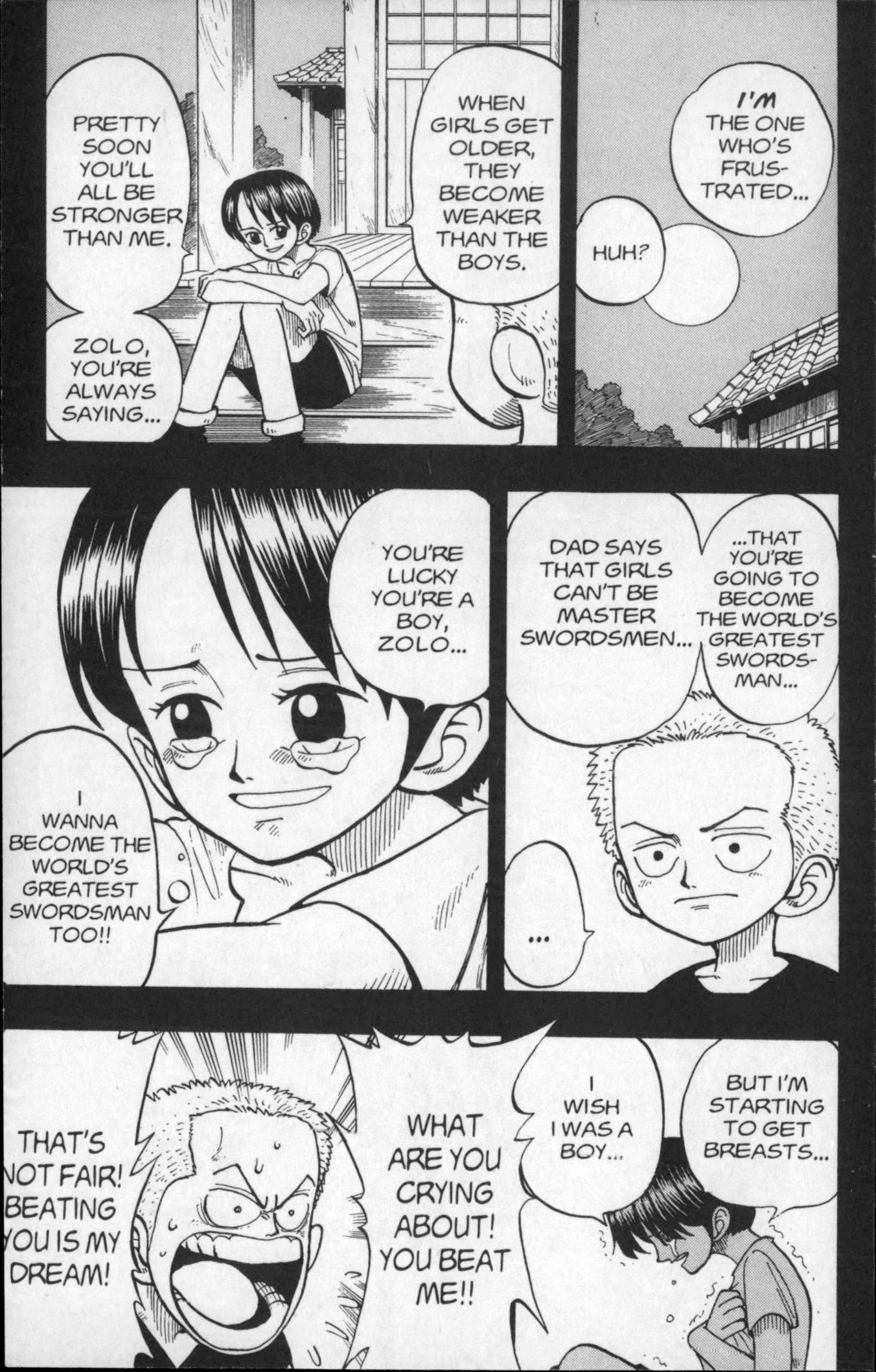
I'M THE ONE WHO'S FRUSTRATED...
HUH?
WHEN GIRLS GET OLDER, THEY BECOME WEAKER THAN THE BOYS.
PRETTY SOON YOU'LL ALL BE STRONGER THAN ME.
ZOLO, YOU'RE ALWAYS SAYING...
...THAT YOU'RE GOING TO BECOME THE WORLD'S GREATEST SWORDSMAN...
DAD SAYS THAT GIRLS CAN'T BE MASTER SWORDSMEN...
...
YOU'RE LUCKY YOU'RE A BOY, ZOLO...
I WANNA BECOME THE WORLD'S GREATEST SWORDSMAN TOO!!
BUT I'M STARTING TO GET BREASTS...
I WISH I WAS A BOY...
WHAT ARE YOU CRYING ABOUT! YOU BEAT ME!!
THAT'S NOT FAIR! BEATING YOU IS MY DREAM!

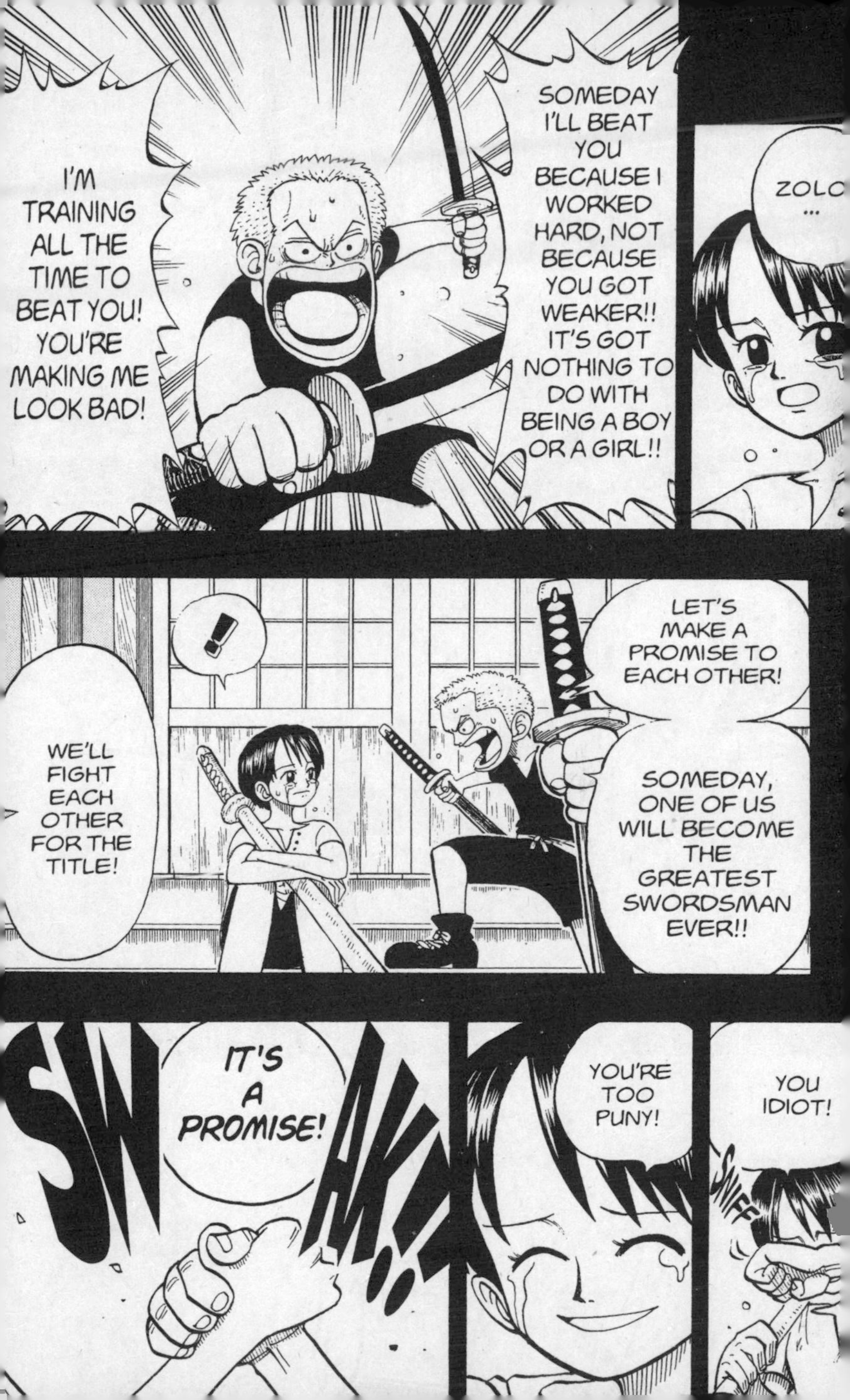
ZOLO ...
SOMEDAY I'LL BEAT YOU BECAUSE I WORKED HARD, NOT BECAUSE YOU GOT WEAKER!! IT'S GOT NOTHING TO DO WITH BEING A BOY OR A GIRL!!
I'M TRAINING ALL THE TIME TO BEAT YOU! YOU'RE MAKING ME LOOK BAD!
LET'S MAKE A PROMISE TO EACH OTHER!
SOMEDAY, ONE OF US WILL BECOME THE GREATEST SWORDSMAN EVER!!
!
WE'LL FIGHT EACH OTHER FOR THE TITLE!
YOU IDIOT!
SNIFF
YOU'RE TOO PUNY!
IT'S A PROMISE!
SWAK!!

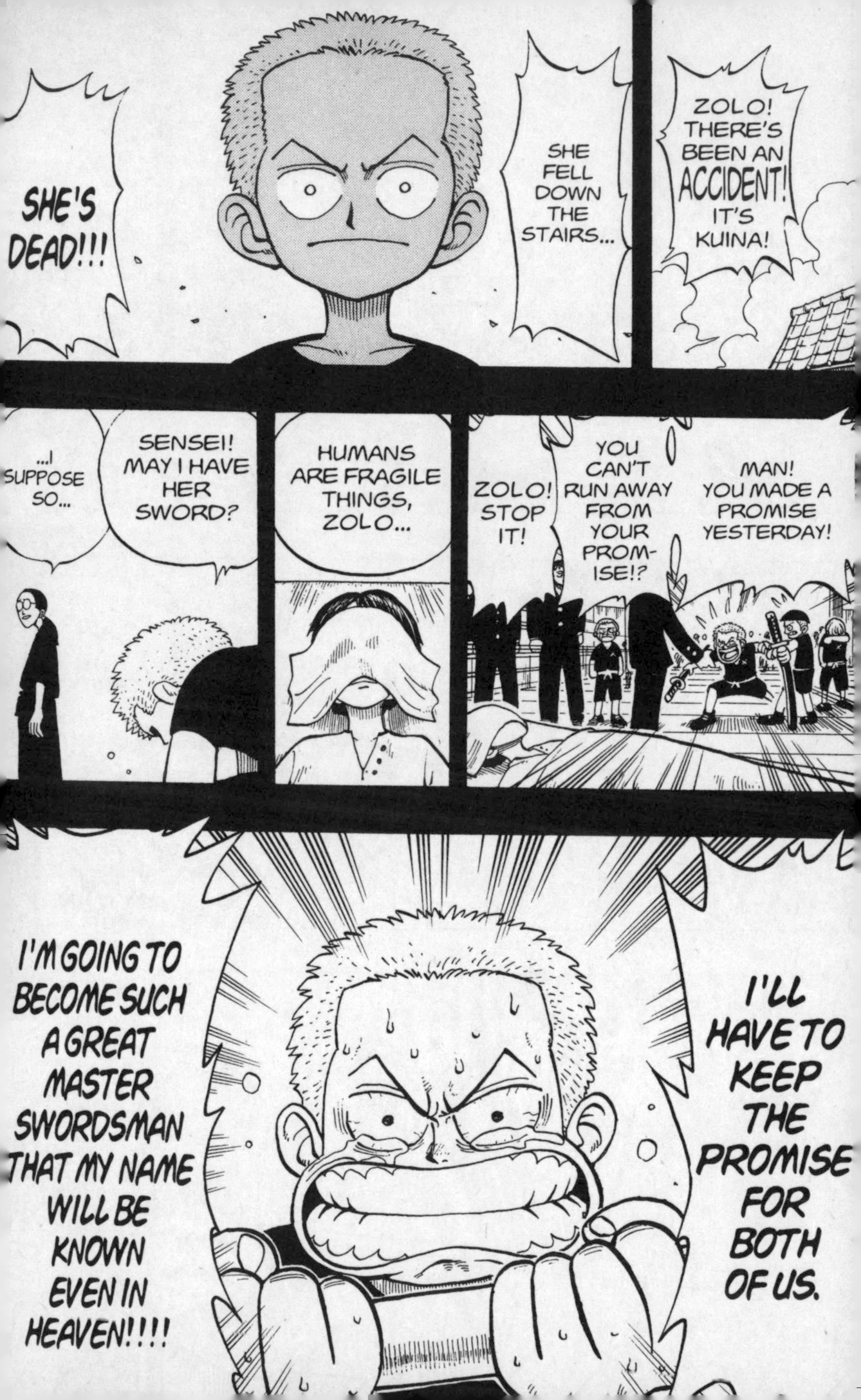
ZOLO! THERE'S BEEN AN ACCIDENT!! IT'S KUINA!
SHE FELL DOWN THE STAIRS...
SHE'S DEAD!!!
MAN! YOU MADE A PROMISE YESTERDAY!
YOU CAN'T RUN AWAY FROM YOUR PROM-ISE!?
ZOLO! STOP IT!
HUMANS ARE FRAGILE THINGS, ZOLO...
SENSEI! MAY I HAVE HER SWORD?
...I SUPPOSE SO...
I'LL HAVE TO KEEP THE PROMISE FOR BOTH OF US.
I'M GOING TO BECOME SUCH A GREAT MASTER SWORDSMAN THAT MY NAME WILL BE KNOWN EVEN IN HEAVEN!!!!

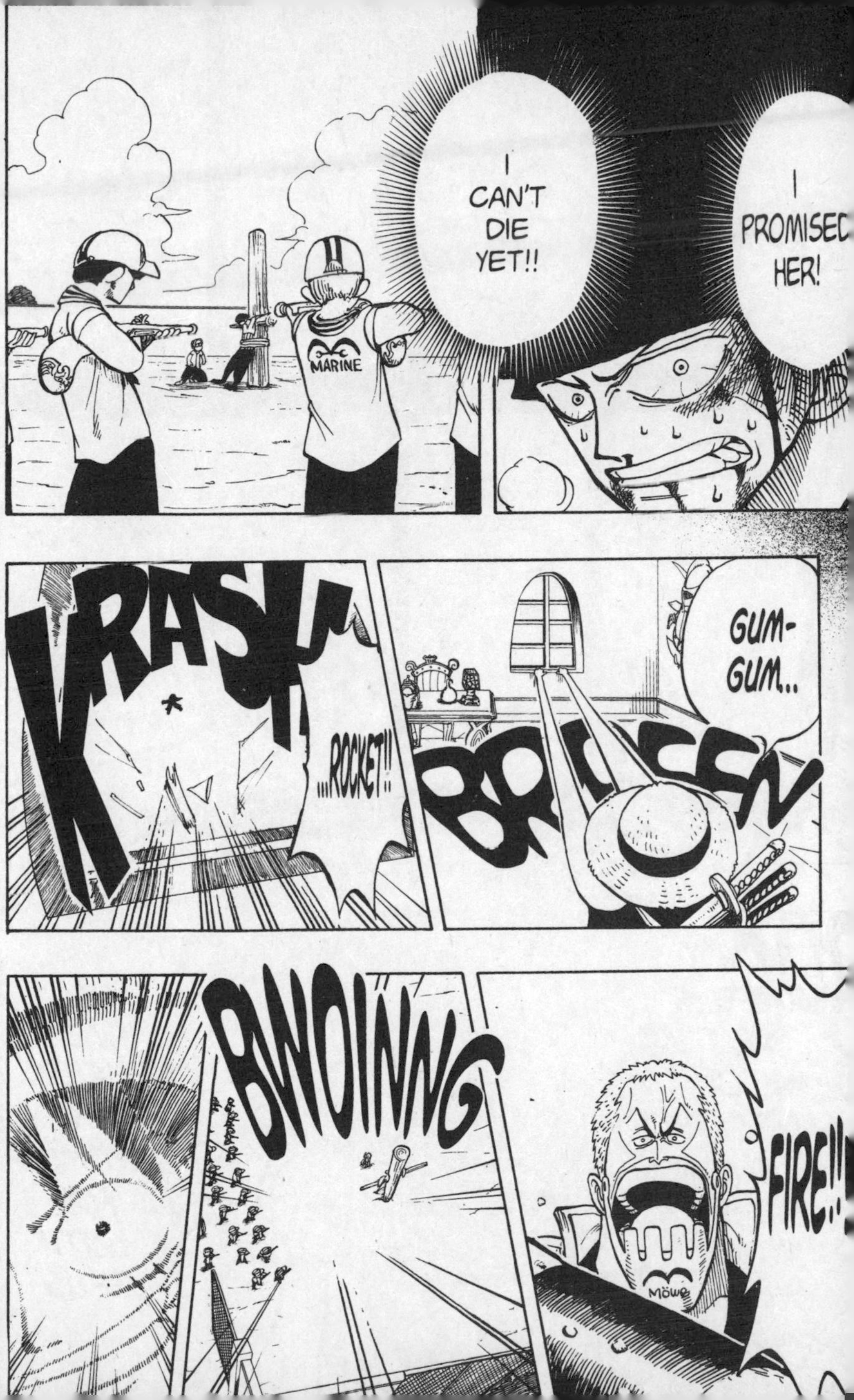
I PROMISED HER!
I CAN'T DIE YET!!
MARINE
GUM-GUM...
...ROCKET!!
KRASH
FIRE!!
MÖWE
BWOING

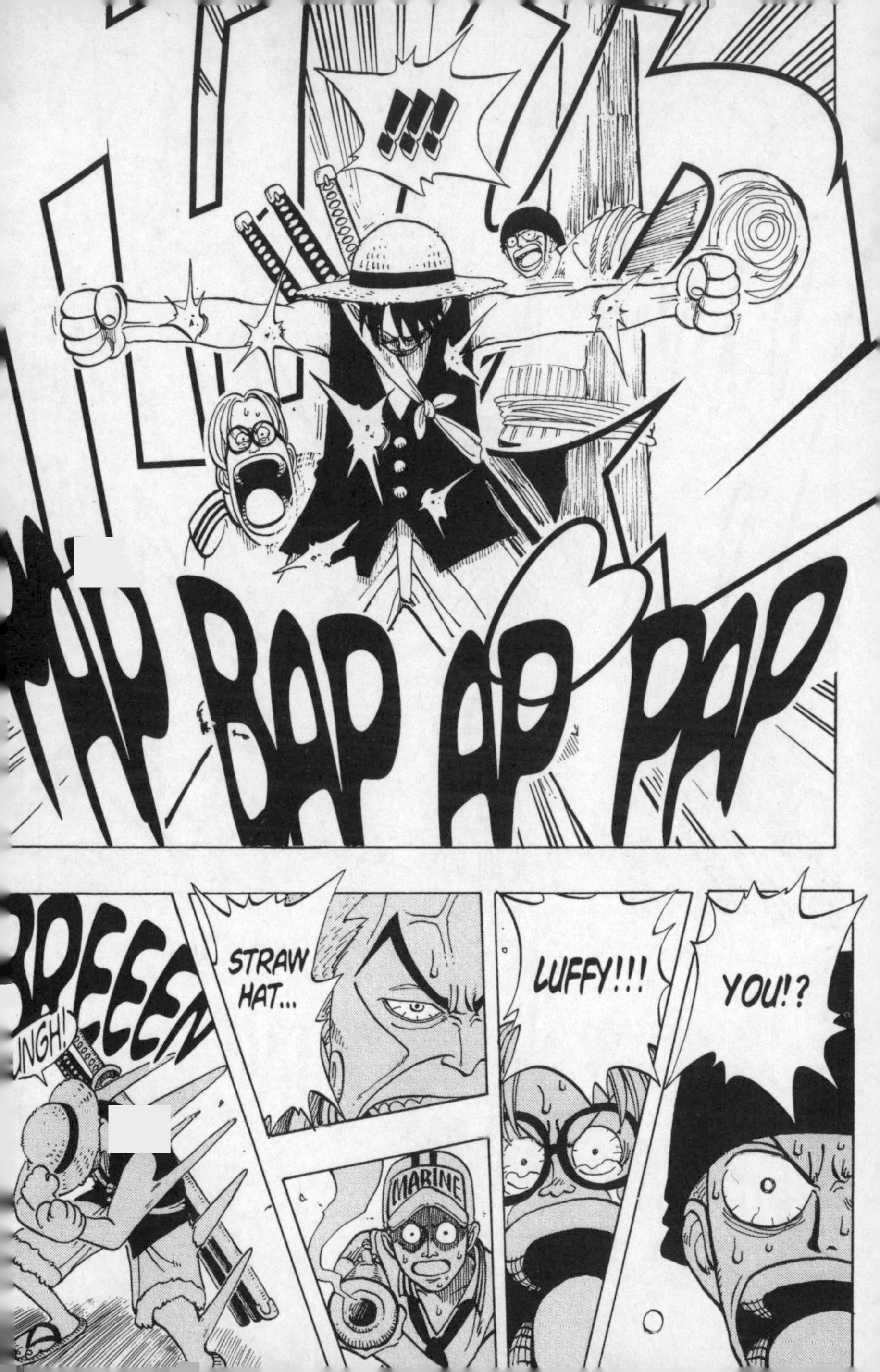
!!!
BAP BAP
YOU!?
LUFFY!!!
STRAW HAT...
UNGH!

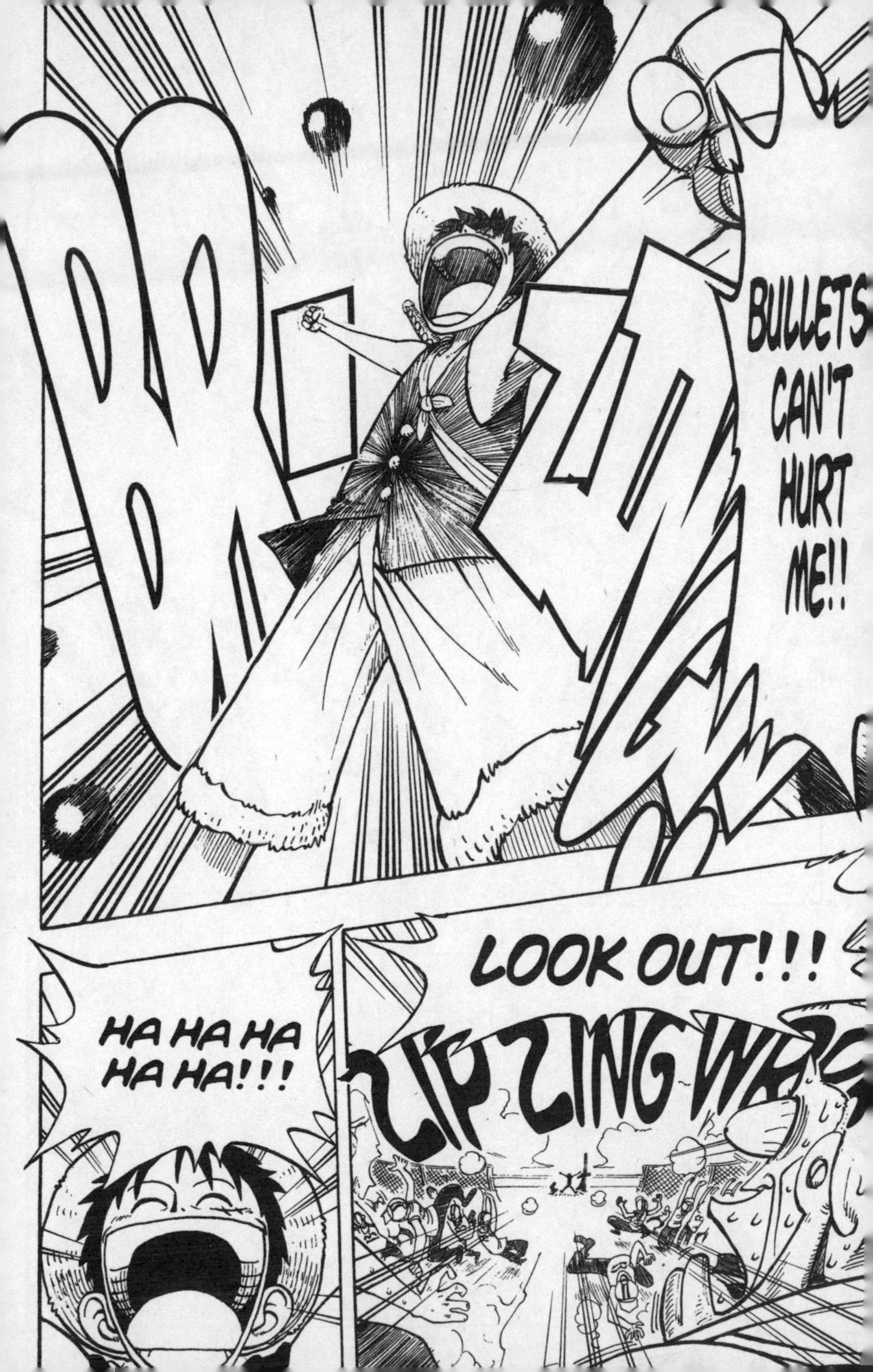
BULLETS CAN'T HURT ME!!
LOOK OUT!!!
ZIP ZING
HA HA HA HA HA!!!

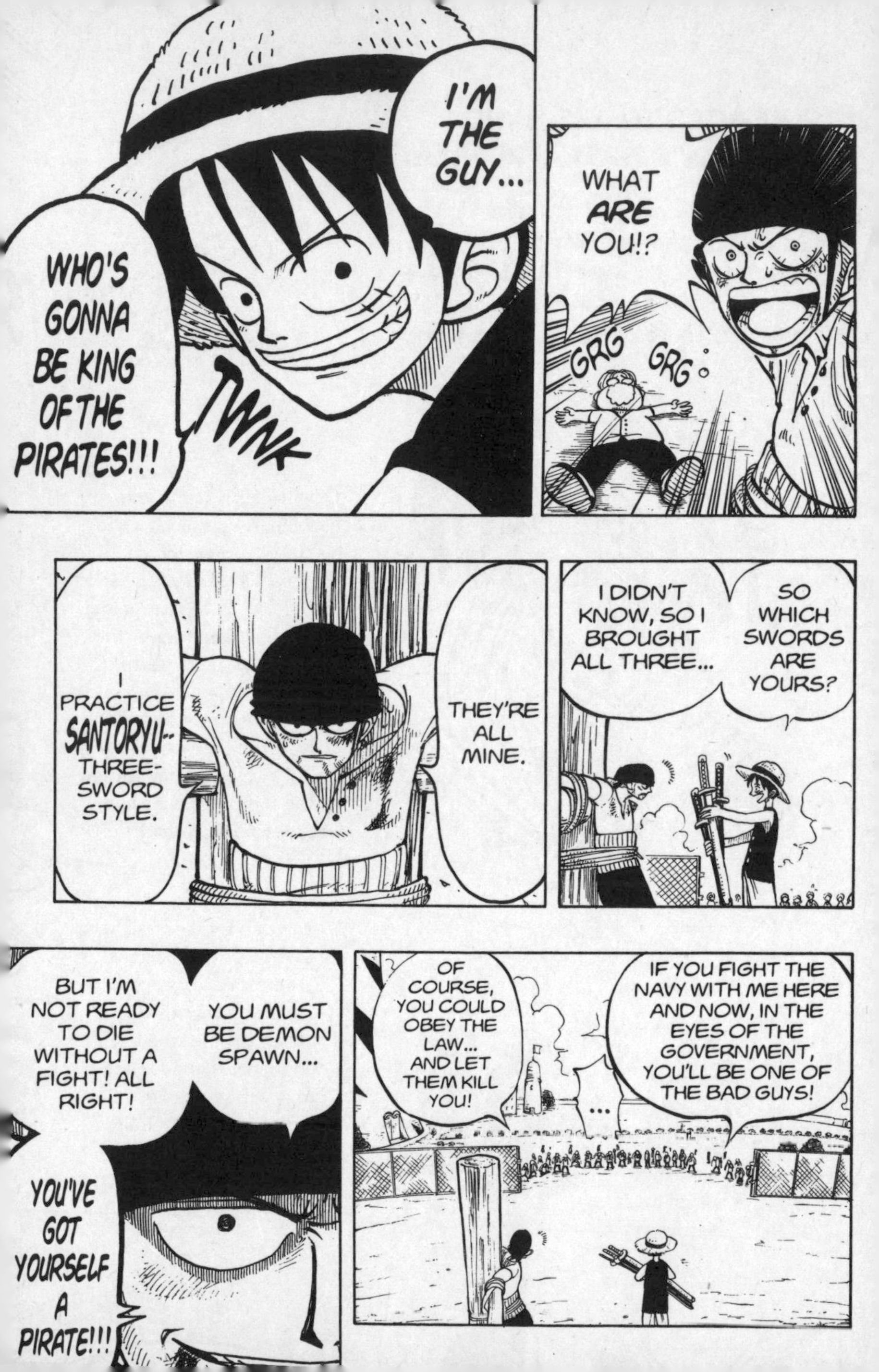
WHAT ARE YOU!?
GRG GRG
I'M THE GUY...
WHO'S GONNA BE KING OF THE PIRATES!!!
TWNK
SO WHICH SWORDS ARE YOURS?
I DIDN'T KNOW, SO I BROUGHT ALL THREE...
THEY'RE ALL MINE.
I PRACTICE SANTORYU-- THREE-SWORD STYLE.
IF YOU FIGHT THE NAVY WITH ME HERE AND NOW, IN THE EYES OF THE GOVERNMENT, YOU'LL BE ONE OF THE BAD GUYS!
OF COURSE, YOU COULD OBEY THE LAW... AND LET THEM KILL YOU!
...
YOU MUST BE DEMON SPAWN...
BUT I'M NOT READY TO DIE WITHOUT A FIGHT! ALL RIGHT!
YOU'VE GOT YOURSELF A PIRATE!!!

THE ROAD TO AXE-HAND MORGAN'S FIRST APPEARANCE

I created Helmeppo's character first, so my first thoughts when creating Captain Morgan were "He has to have a cleft chin and hair like Helmeppo's, only crazier—after all, he is the father."

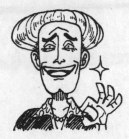

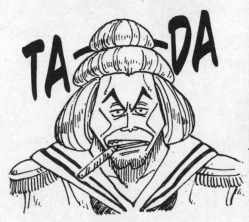

This is what I came up with. Originally his name wasn't Morgan, it was "Chop." So his full title was "Naval Captain Chop" or "Sailor Chop." What a great name! But even I didn't have the nerve to use this name. [Editor's Note: "Sailor" in Japanese is *suihei*, and *Suihei Chop* is the name of a signature fighting technique used by the famous Japanese pro wrestler Giant Baba.]

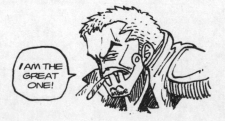

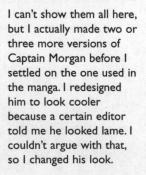

I AM THE GREAT ONE!

I can't show them all here, but I actually made two or three more versions of Captain Morgan before I settled on the one used in the manga. I redesigned him to look cooler because a certain editor told me he looked lame. I couldn't argue with that, so I changed his look.

READ THIS WAY

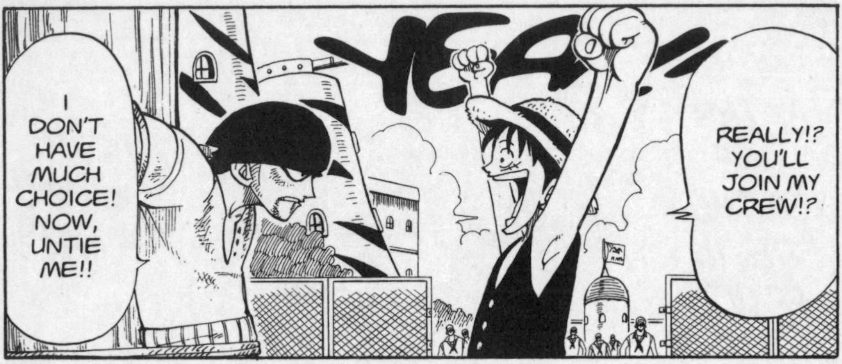
REALLY!? YOU'LL JOIN MY CREW!?
YEA!!
I DON'T HAVE MUCH CHOICE! NOW, UNTIE ME!!

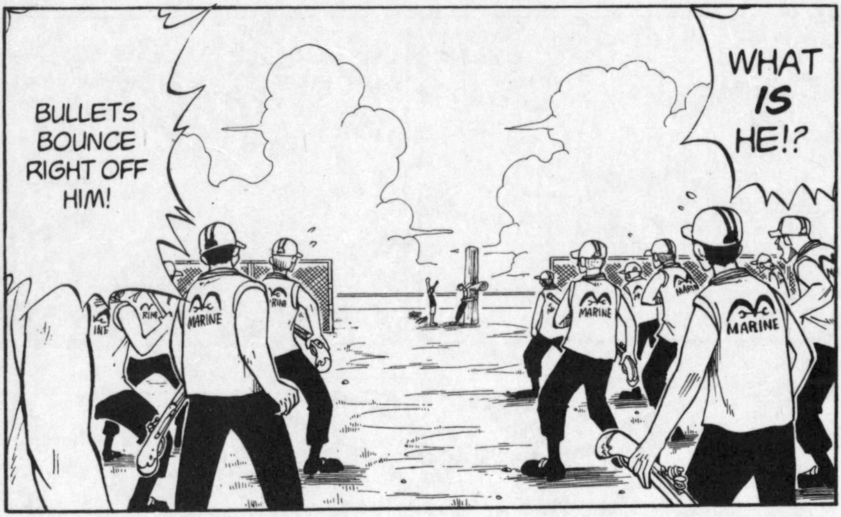
WHAT IS HE!?
BULLETS BOUNCE RIGHT OFF HIM!

CHAPTER 6 :

NUMBER ONE

READ THIS WAY

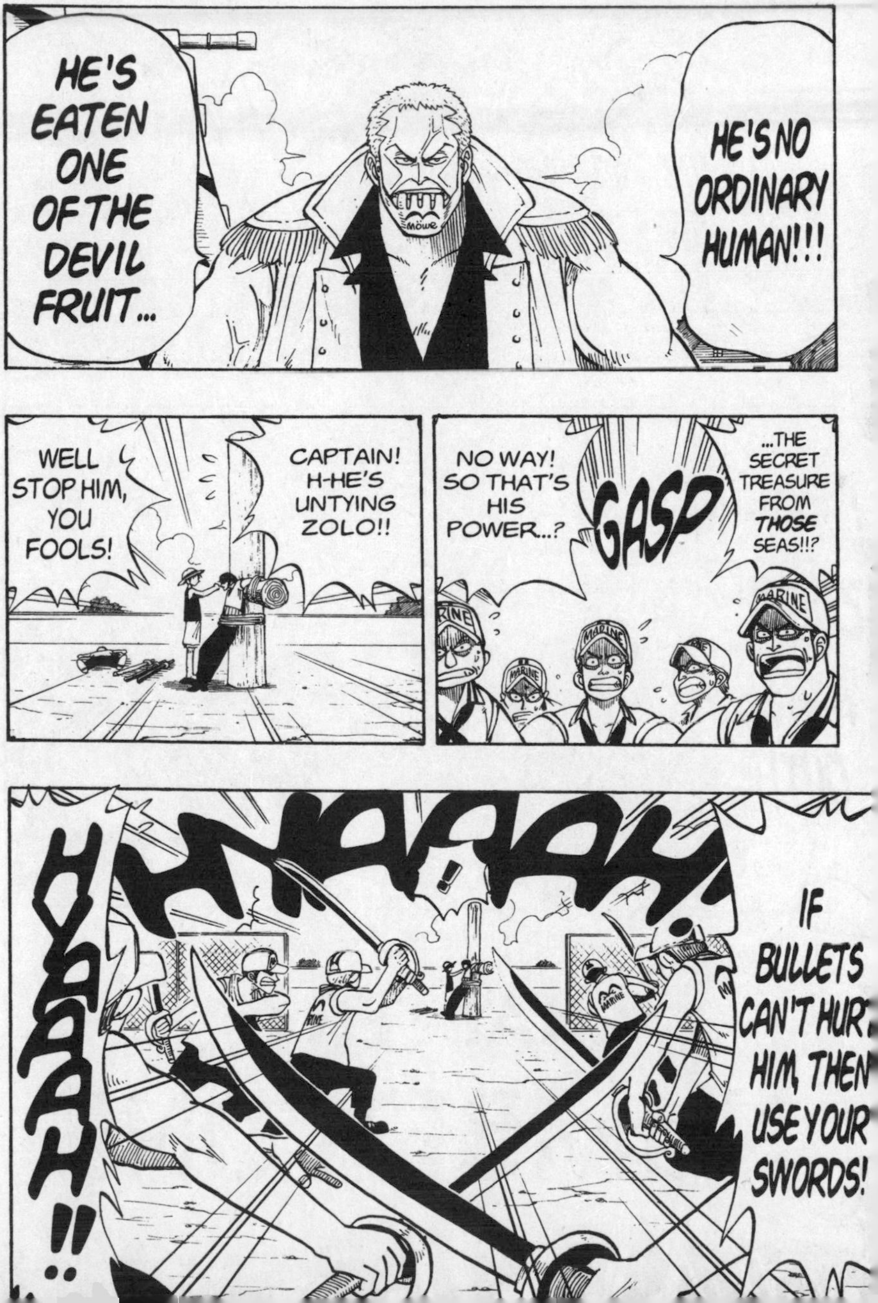
HE'S NO ORDINARY HUMAN!!!
HE'S EATEN ONE OF THE DEVIL FRUIT...
...THE SECRET TREASURE FROM THOSE SEAS!!?
GASP
NO WAY! SO THAT'S HIS POWER...?
CAPTAIN! H-HE'S UNTYING ZOLO!!
WELL STOP HIM, YOU FOOLS!
IF BULLETS CAN'T HUR
HIM, THEN USE YOUR SWORDS!

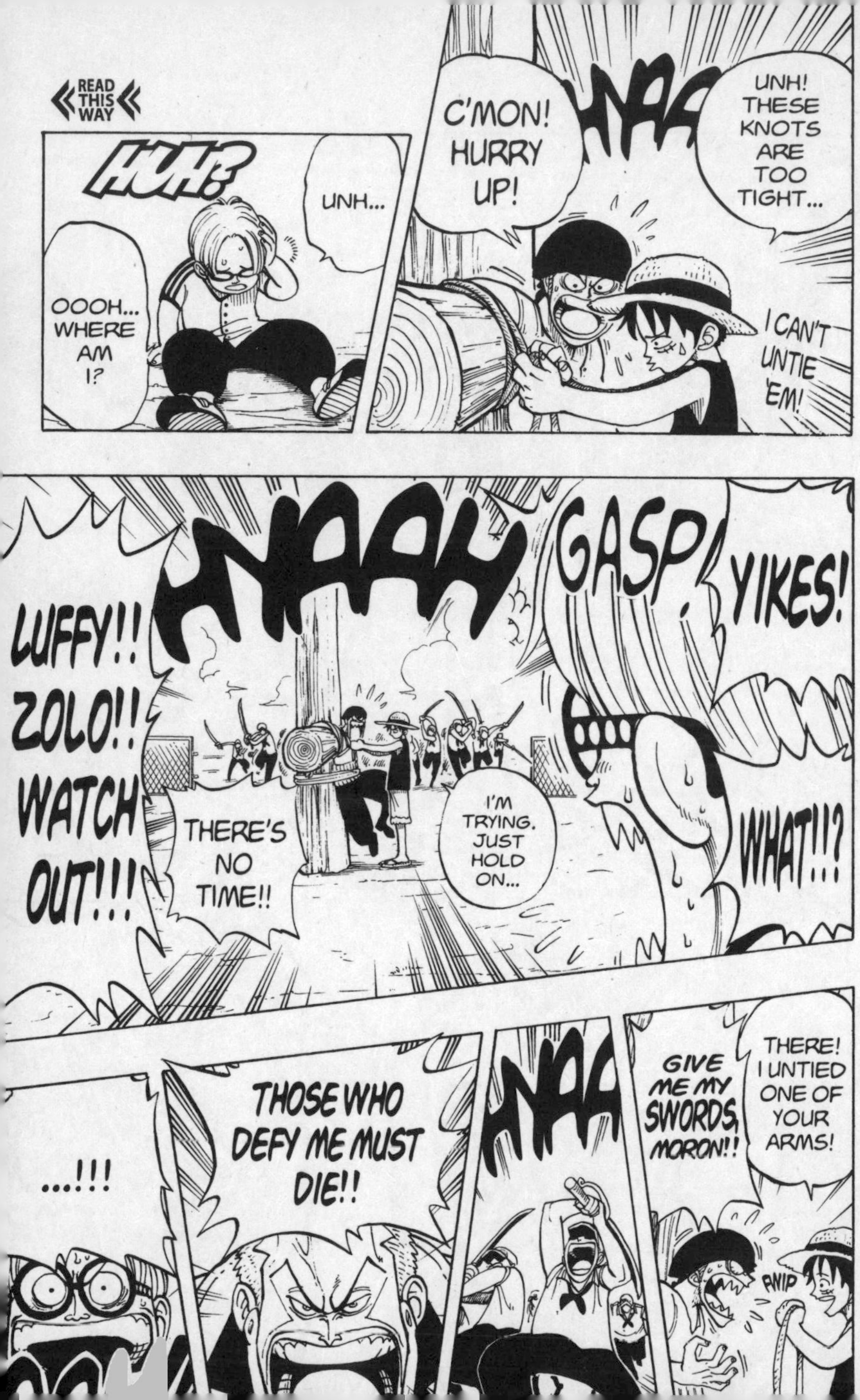
READ THIS WAY
UNH! THESE KNOTS ARE TOO TIGHT...
NAA
C'MON! HURRY UP!
I CAN'T UNTIE 'EM!
UNH...
HUH?
OOOH... WHERE AM I?
YIKES!
GASP!
WHAT!!?
NAAH
I'M TRYING. JUST HOLD ON...
THERE'S NO TIME!!
LUFFY!! ZOLO!! WATCH OUT!!!
THERE! I UNTIED ONE OF YOUR ARMS!
GIVE ME MY SWORDS, MORON!!
SNIP
NAA
THOSE WHO DEFY ME MUST DIE!!
...!!!

READ THIS WAY

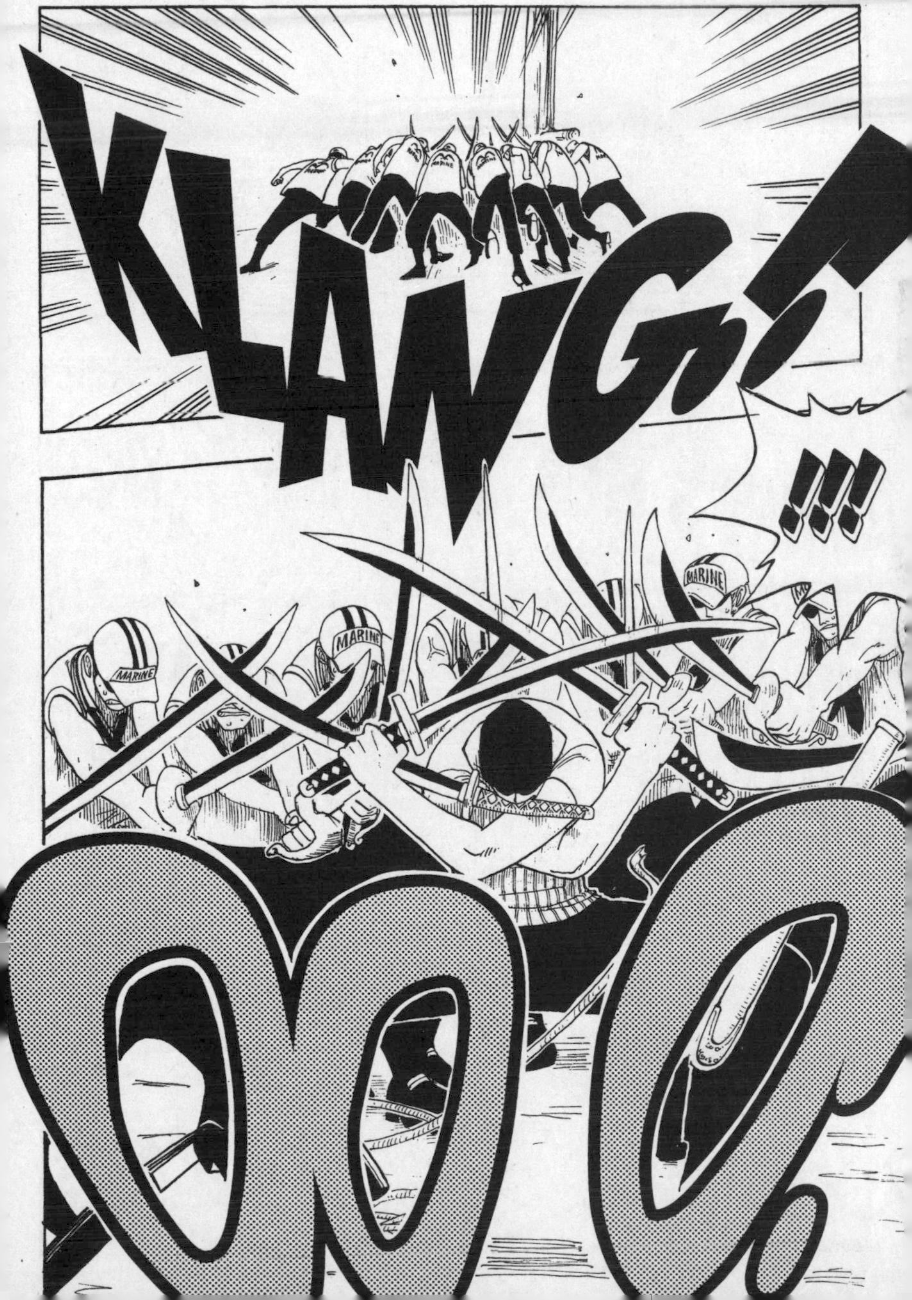
KLAWG!!!!
MARINE
MARINE
MARINE

READ THIS WAY

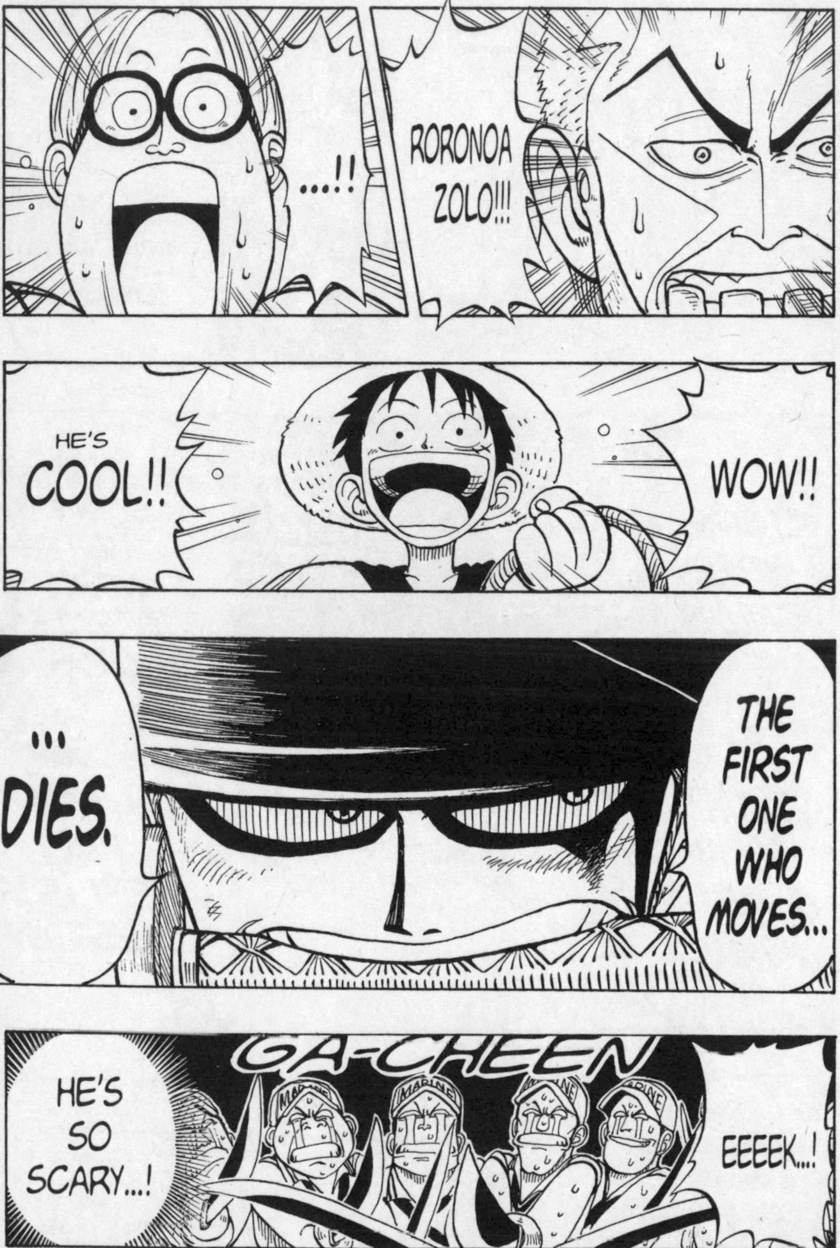
RORONOA ZOLO!!!
...!!
WOW!!
HE'S COOL!!
THE FIRST ONE WHO MOVES...
... DIES.
GA-CHEEN
EEEEK...!
HE'S SO SCARY...!

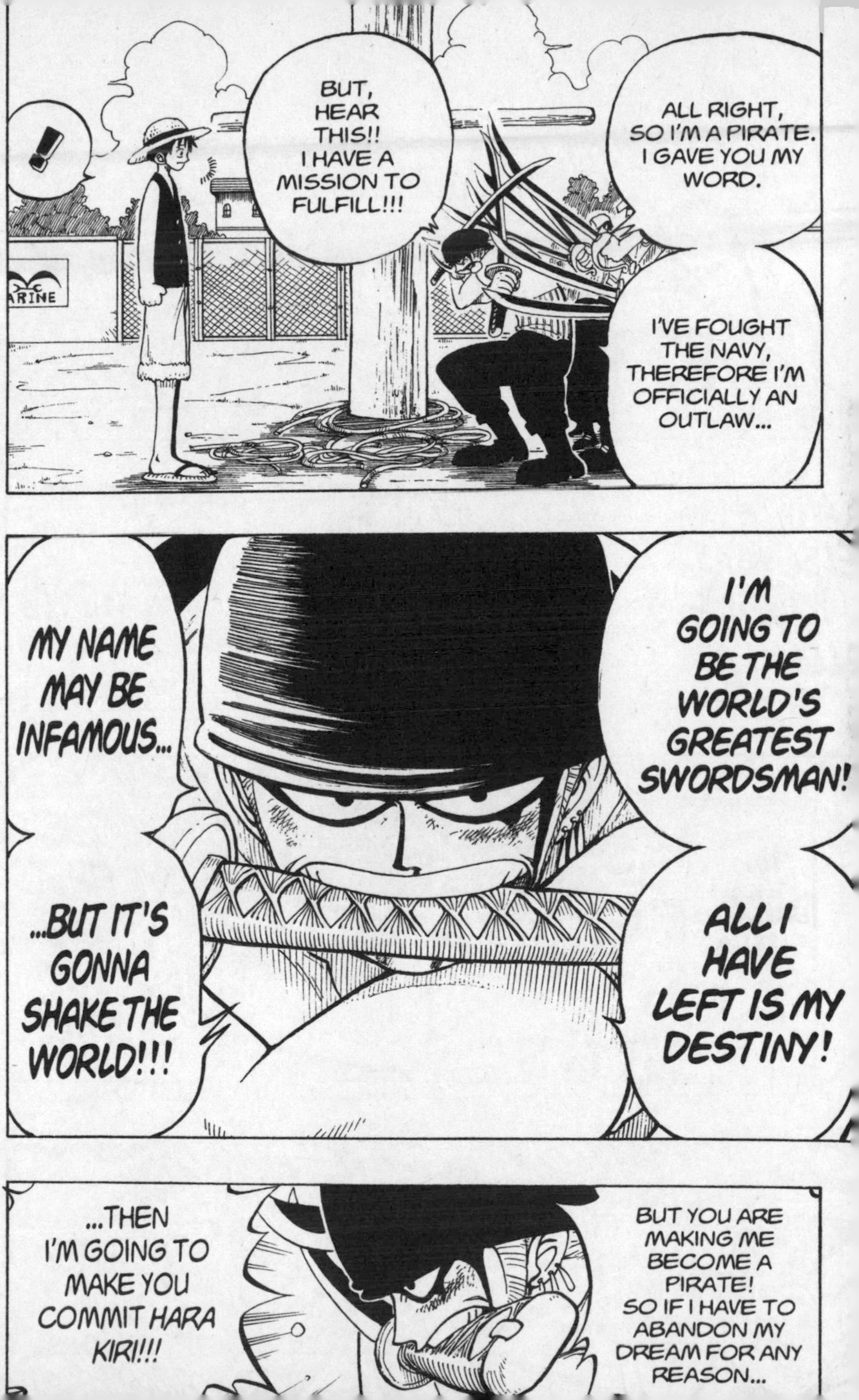
ALL RIGHT, SO I'M A PIRATE. I GAVE YOU MY WORD.
I'VE FOUGHT THE NAVY, THEREFORE I'M OFFICIALLY AN OUTLAW...
BUT, HEAR THIS!! I HAVE A MISSION TO FULFILL!!!
!
I'M GOING TO BE THE WORLD'S GREATEST SWORDSMAN!
ALL I HAVE LEFT IS MY DESTINY!
MY NAME MAY BE INFAMOUS...
...BUT IT'S GONNA SHAKE THE WORLD!!!
BUT YOU ARE MAKING ME BECOME A PIRATE! SO IF I HAVE TO ABANDON MY DREAM FOR ANY REASON...
...THEN I'M GOING TO MAKE YOU COMMIT HARA KIRI!!!

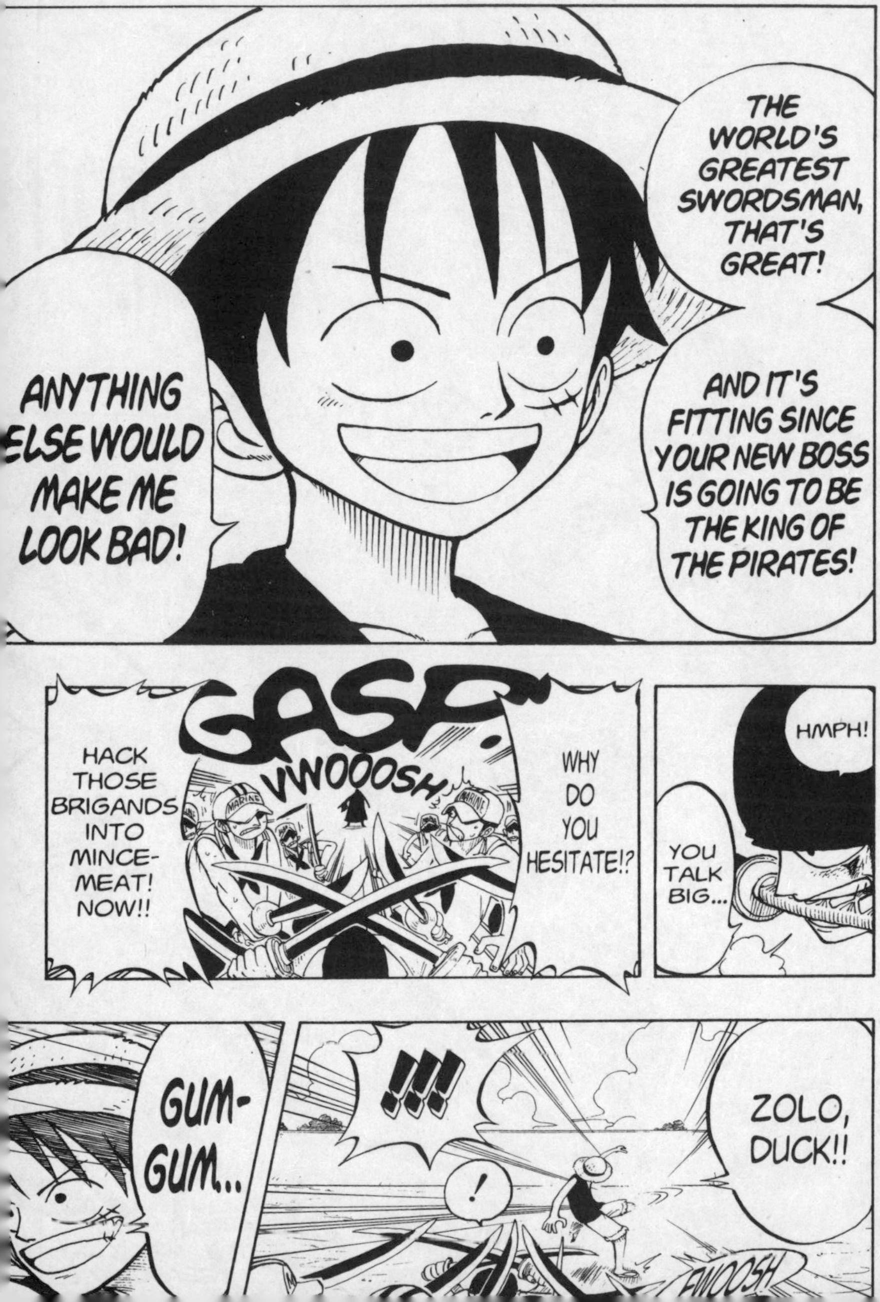
THE WORLD'S GREATEST SWORDSMAN, THAT'S GREAT!
AND IT'S FITTING SINCE YOUR NEW BOSS IS GOING TO BE THE KING OF THE PIRATES!
ANYTHING ELSE WOULD MAKE ME LOOK BAD!
HMPH!
YOU TALK BIG...
GASP
WHY DO YOU HESITATE!?
VWOOOSH
HACK THOSE BRIGANDS INTO MINCE-MEAT! NOW!!
ZOLO, DUCK!!
!!!
!
FWOOSH
GUM-GUM...

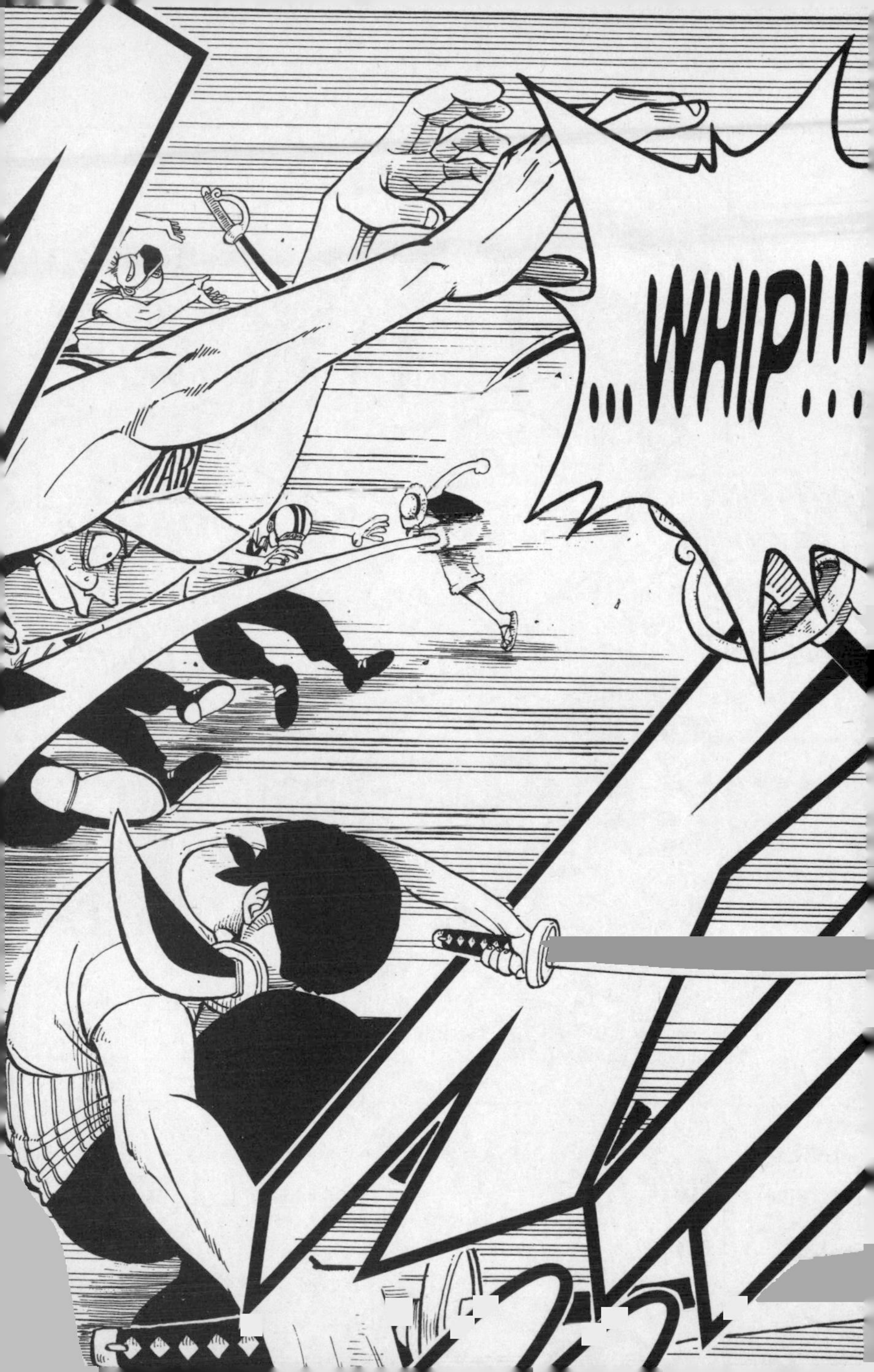
...WHIP!!!

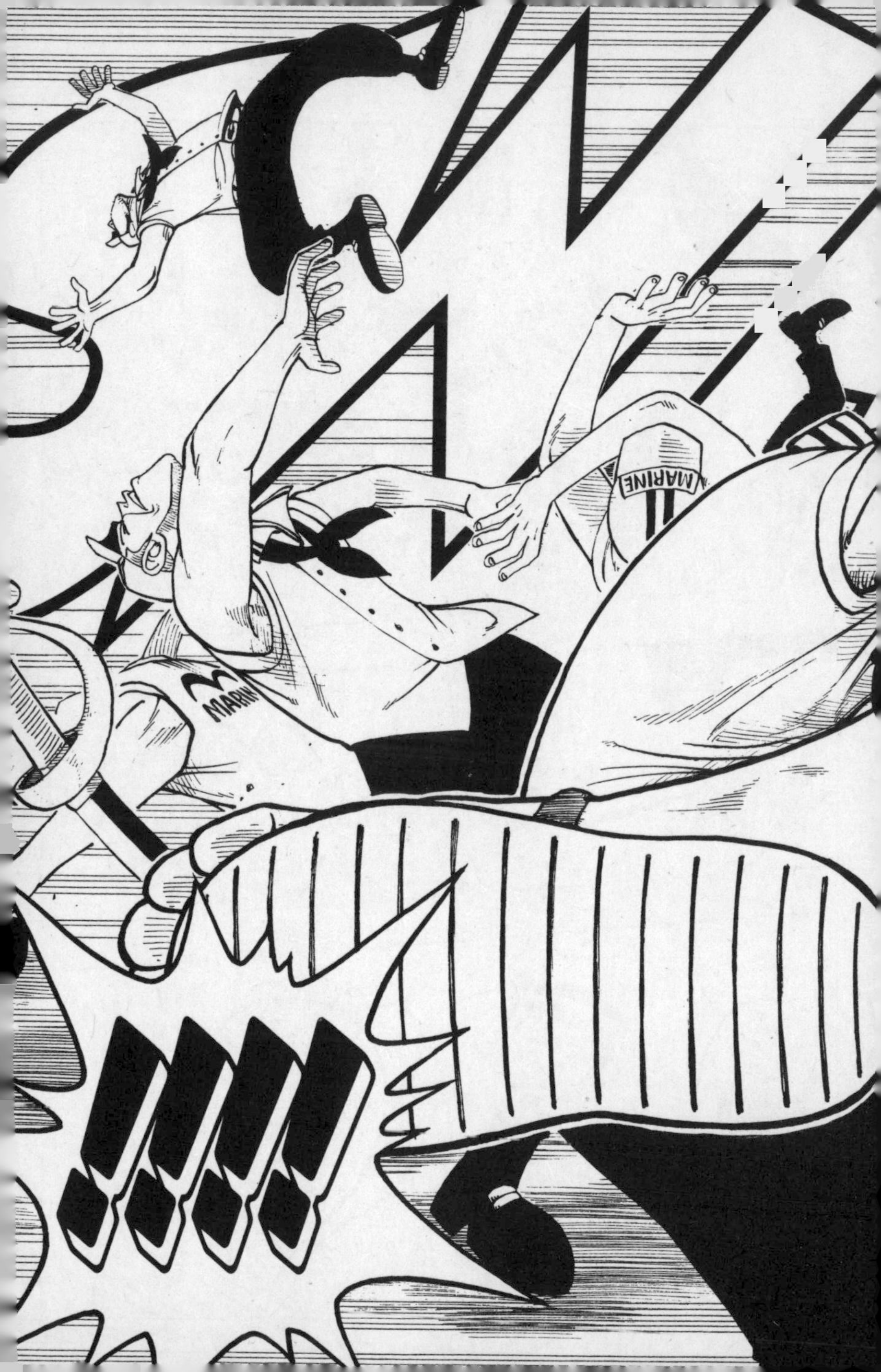
MARINE

READ THIS WAY

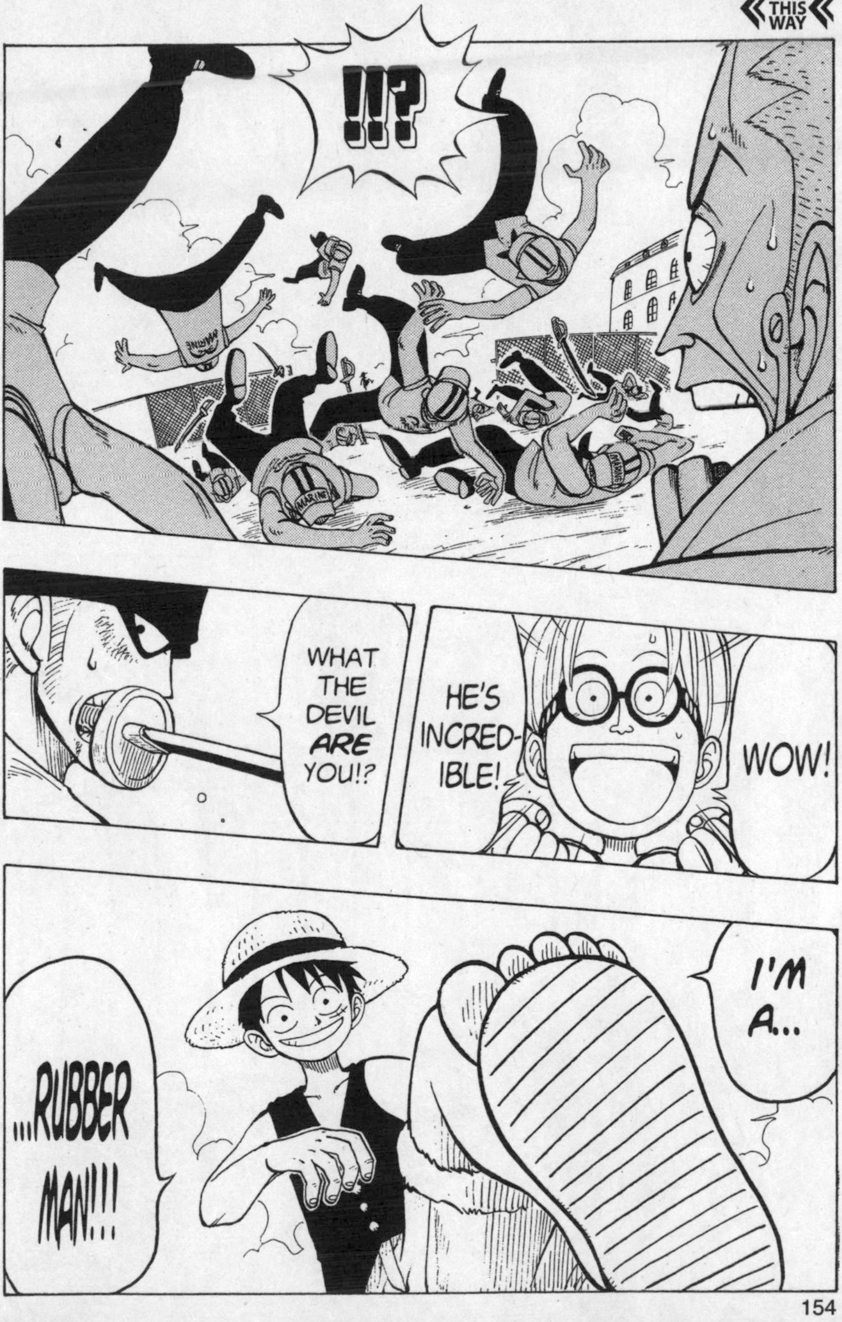
!!?
WOW!
HE'S INCRED-IBLE!
WHAT THE DEVIL *ARE* YOU!?
I'M A...
...RUBBER MAN!!!

READ THIS WAY

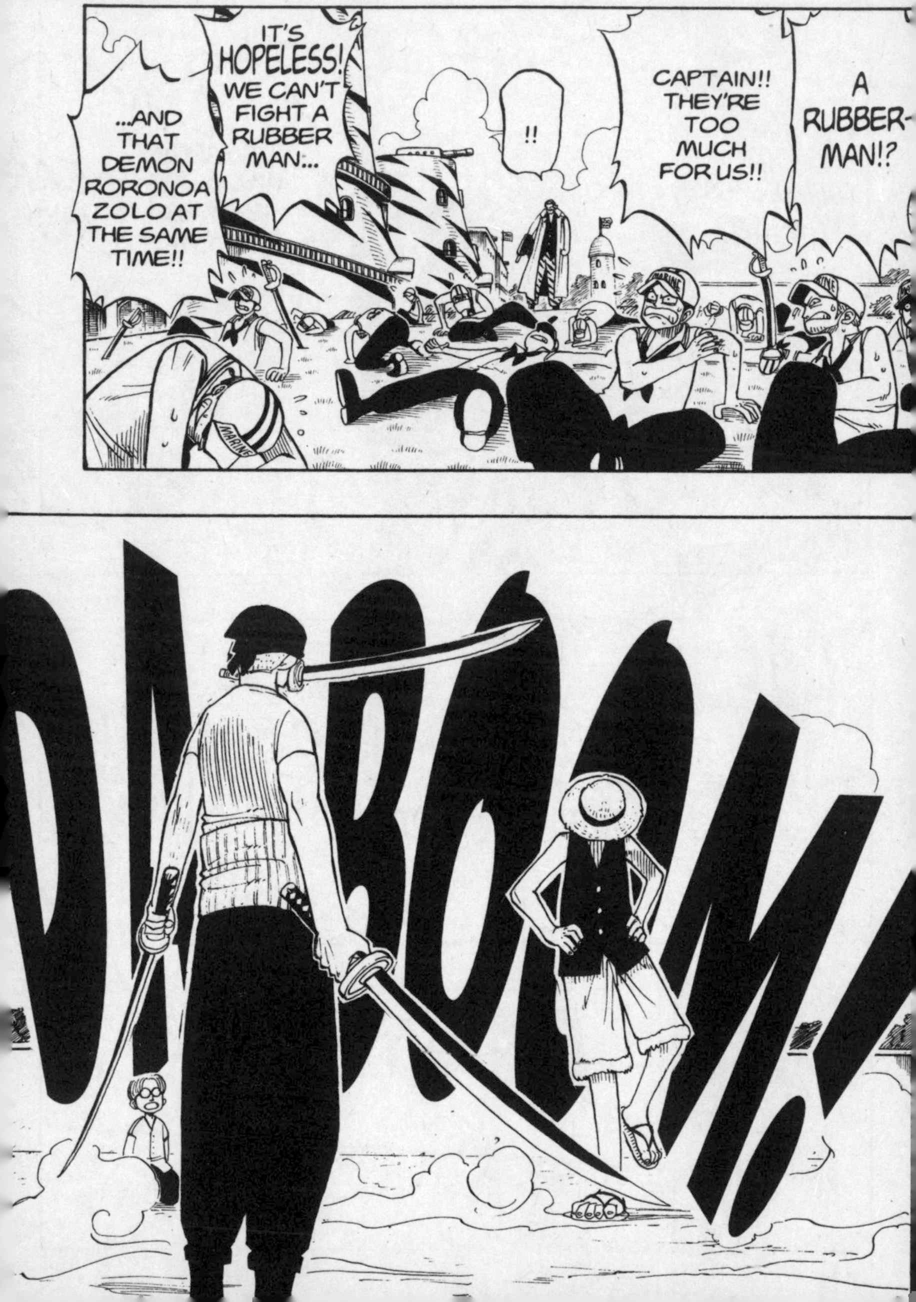
A RUBBER-MAN!?
CAPTAIN!! THEY'RE TOO MUCH FOR US!!
!!
IT'S HOPELESS! WE CAN'T FIGHT A RUBBER MAN...
...AND THAT DEMON RORONOA ZOLO AT THE SAME TIME!!

READ THIS WAY

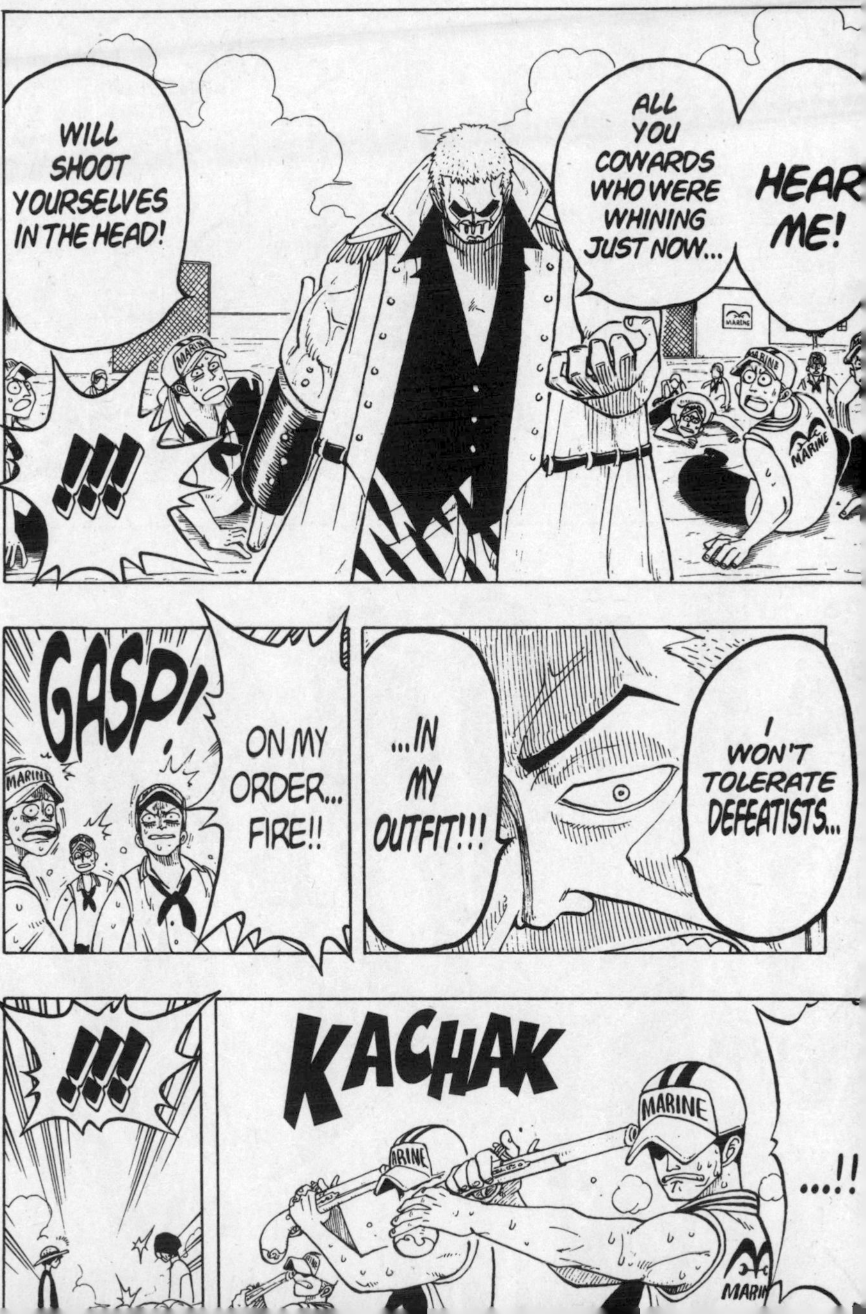
HEAR ME!
ALL YOU COWARDS WHO WERE WHINING JUST NOW...
WILL SHOOT YOURSELVES IN THE HEAD!
!!!
I WON'T TOLERATE DEFEATISTS...
...IN MY OUTFIT!!!
ON MY ORDER... FIRE!!
GASP!
MARINE
...!!
KACHAK
MARINE
!!!

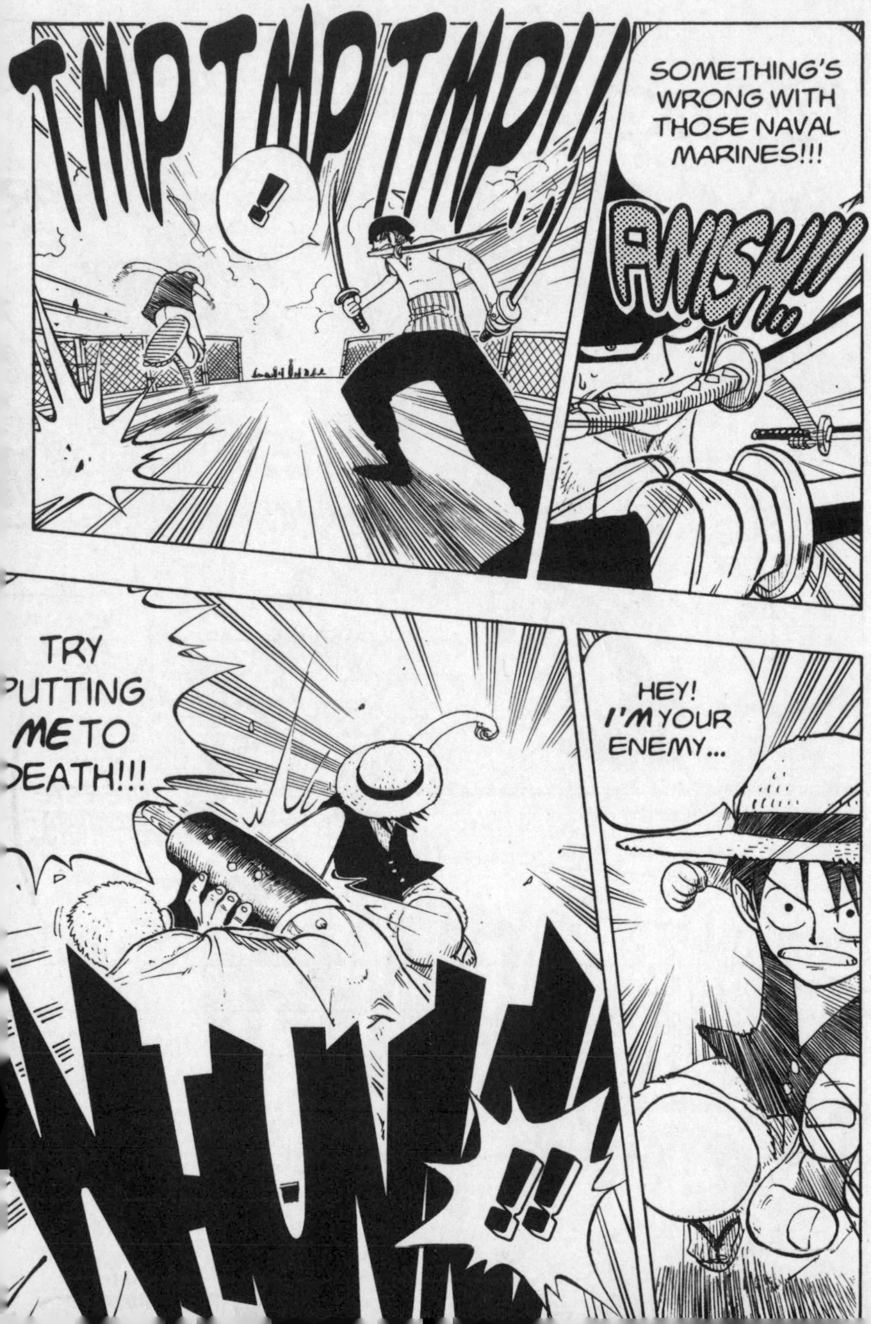
SOMETHING'S WRONG WITH THOSE NAVAL MARINES!!!
FWISH!!
TMP TMP TMP!!
!
HEY! I'M YOUR ENEMY...
TRY PUTTING ME TO DEATH!!!
THUNK!!

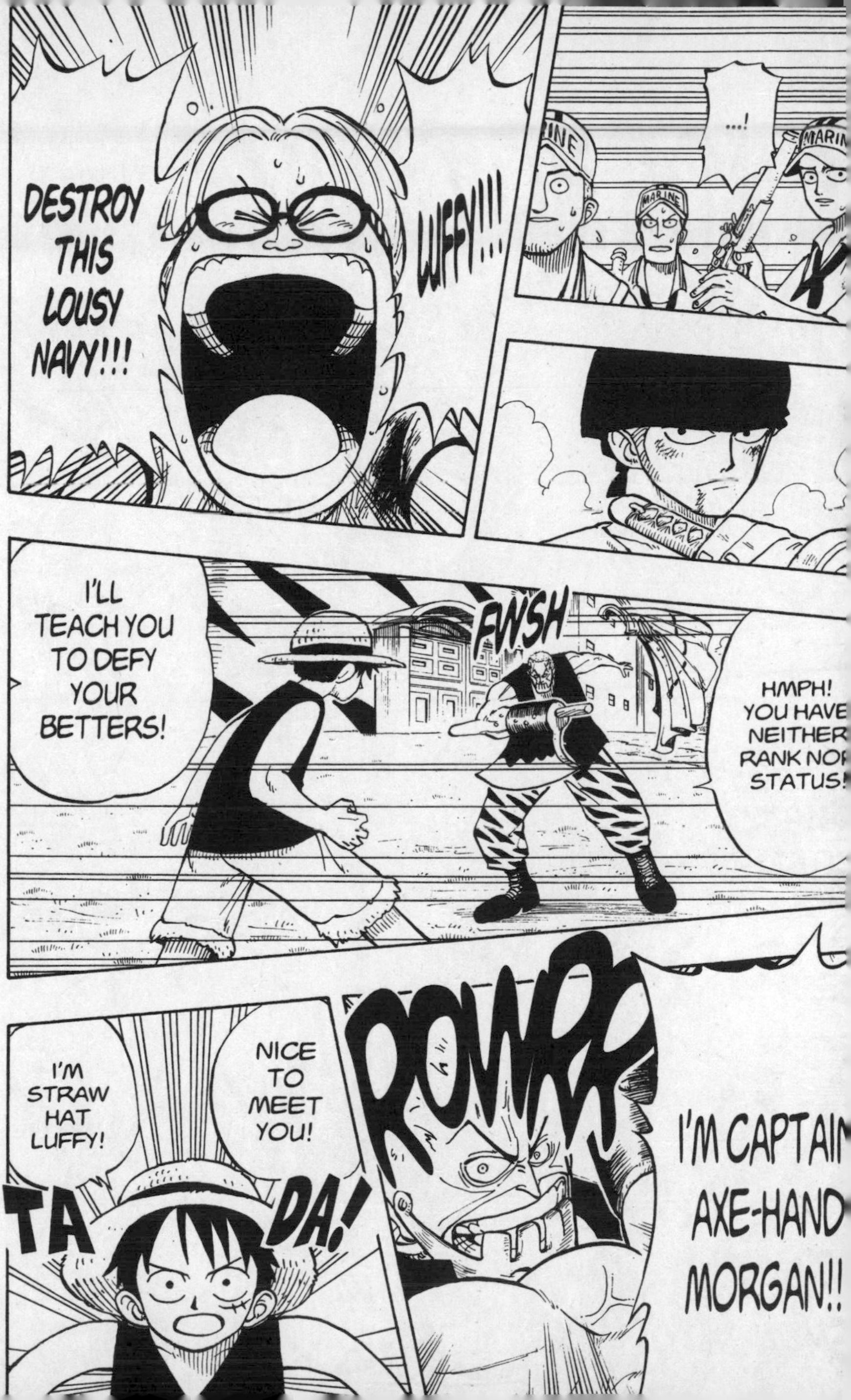
...!
LUFFY!!!!
DESTROY THIS LOUSY NAVY!!!
HMPH! YOU HAVE NEITHER RANK NOR STATUS!
FWSH
I'LL TEACH YOU TO DEFY YOUR BETTERS!
ROWR
I'M CAPTAIN AXE-HAND MORGAN!!
NICE TO MEET YOU!
I'M STRAW HAT LUFFY!
TA DA!

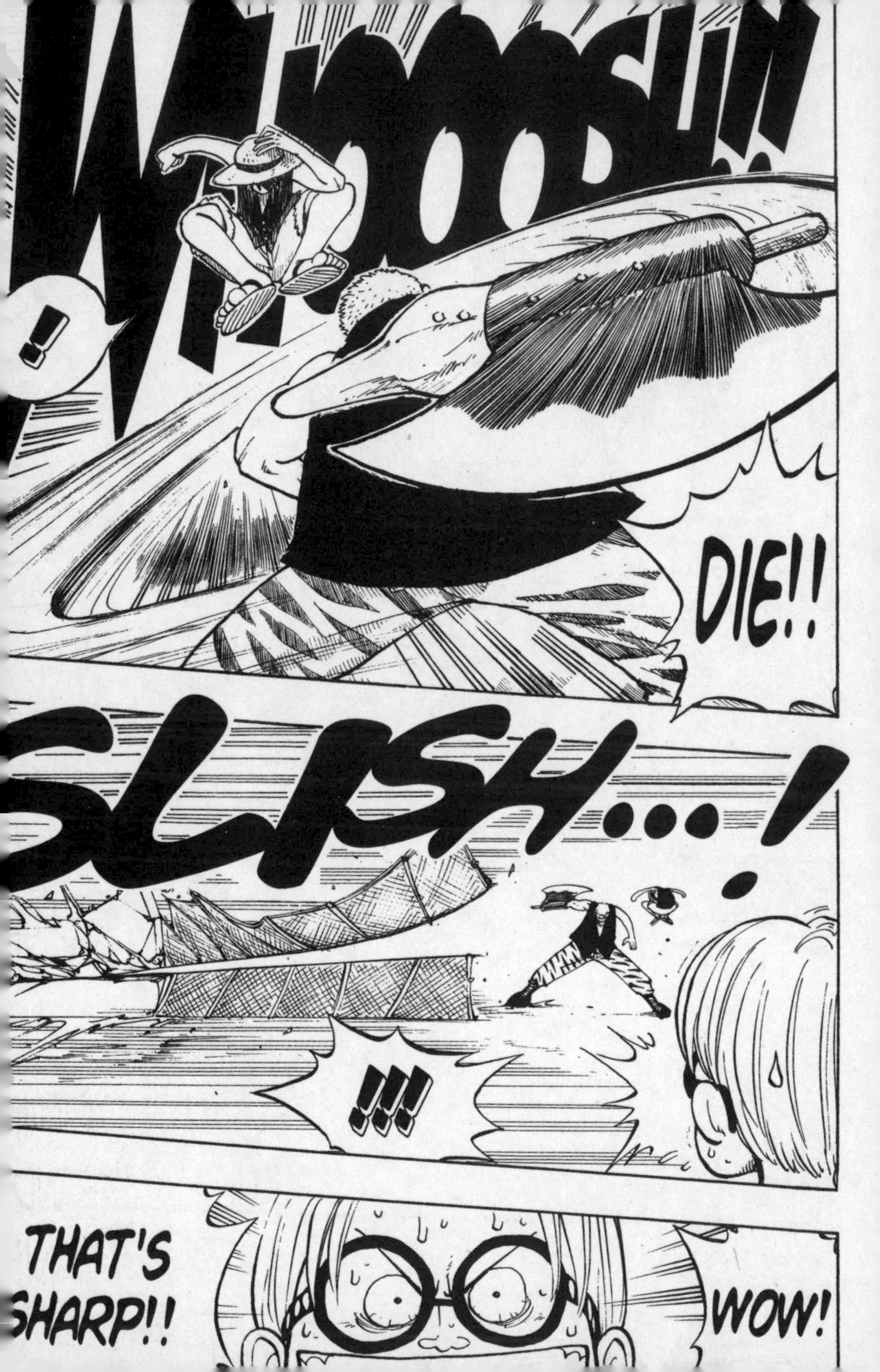
WHOOSH!!
DIE!!
!
SLASH...!
!!!
WOW!
THAT'S SHARP!!

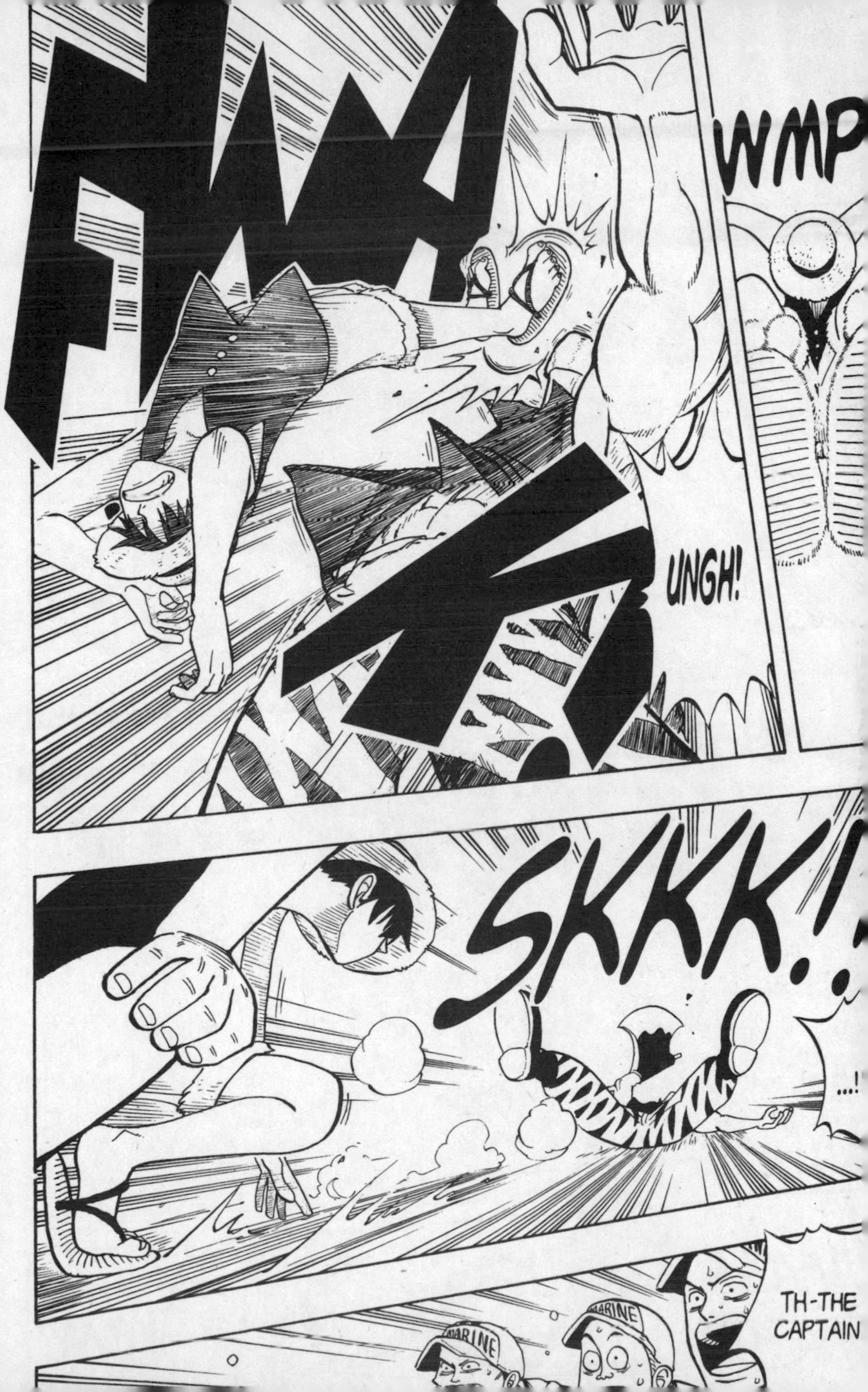
WMP
FWA
UNGH!
SKKK!!
...!
TH-THE CAPTAIN

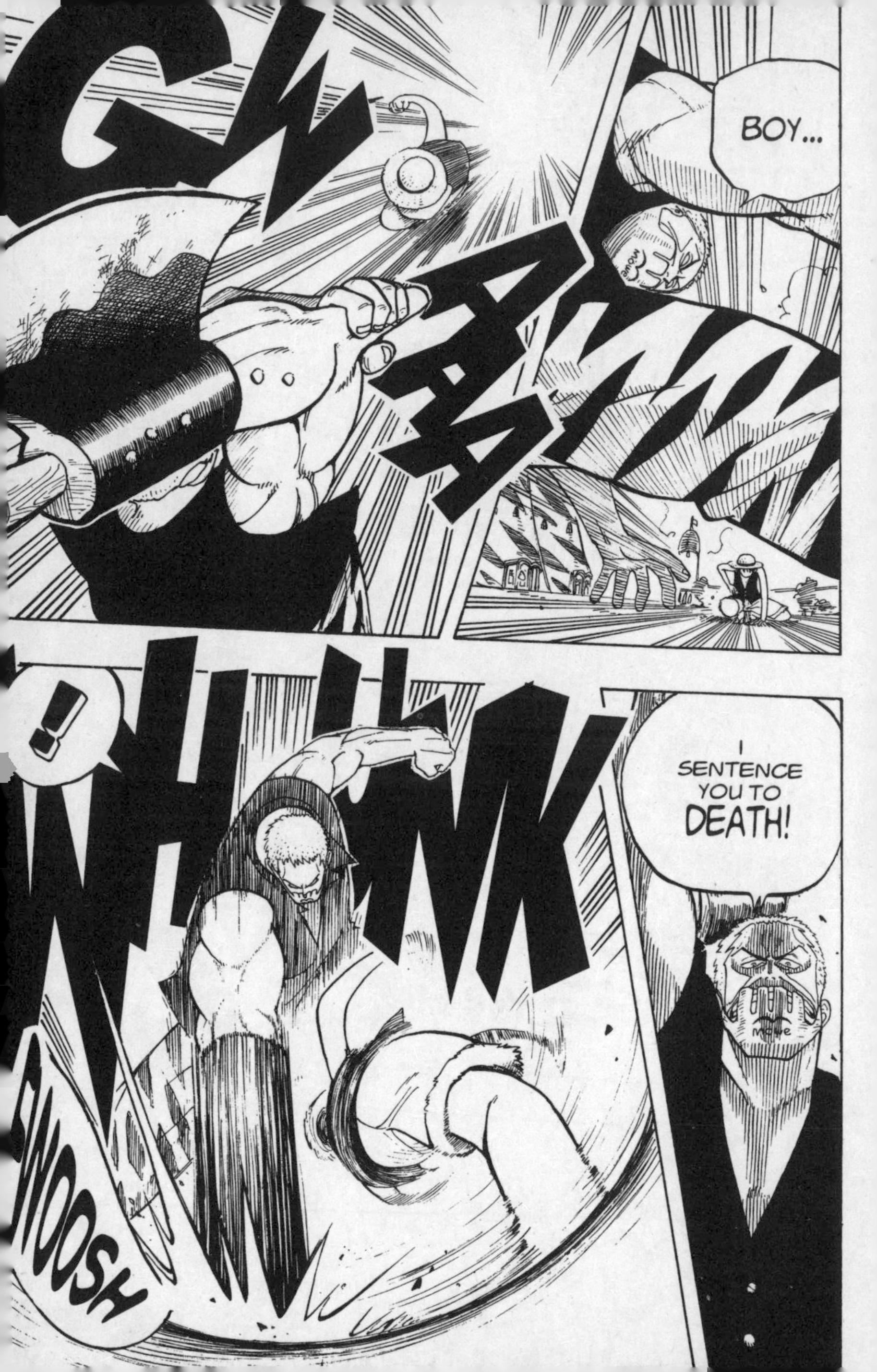
BOY...
!
I SENTENCE YOU TO DEATH!

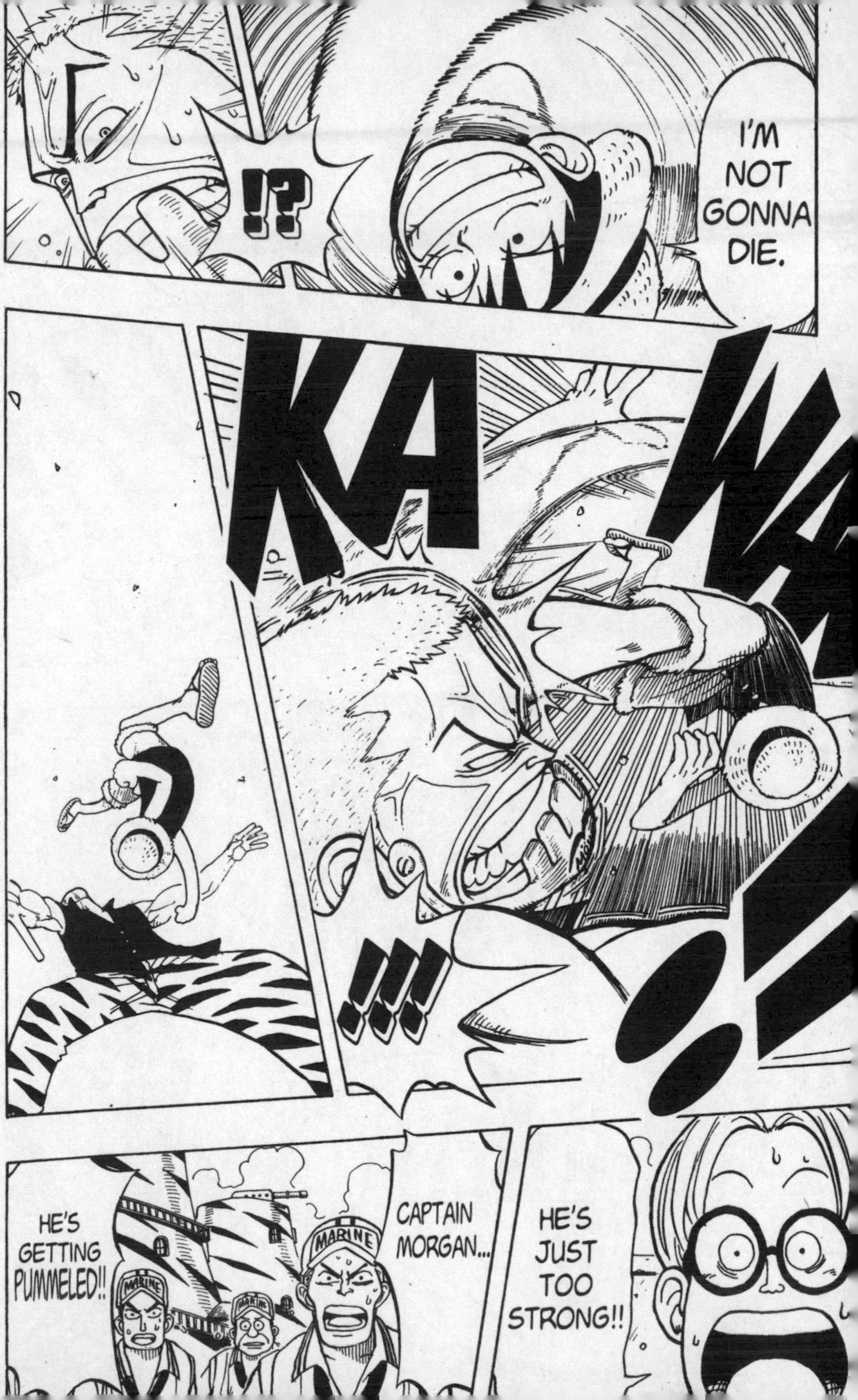
I'M NOT GONNA DIE.
!?
KA
WA
!!!
HE'S JUST TOO STRONG!!
CAPTAIN MORGAN...
HE'S GETTING PUMMELED!!

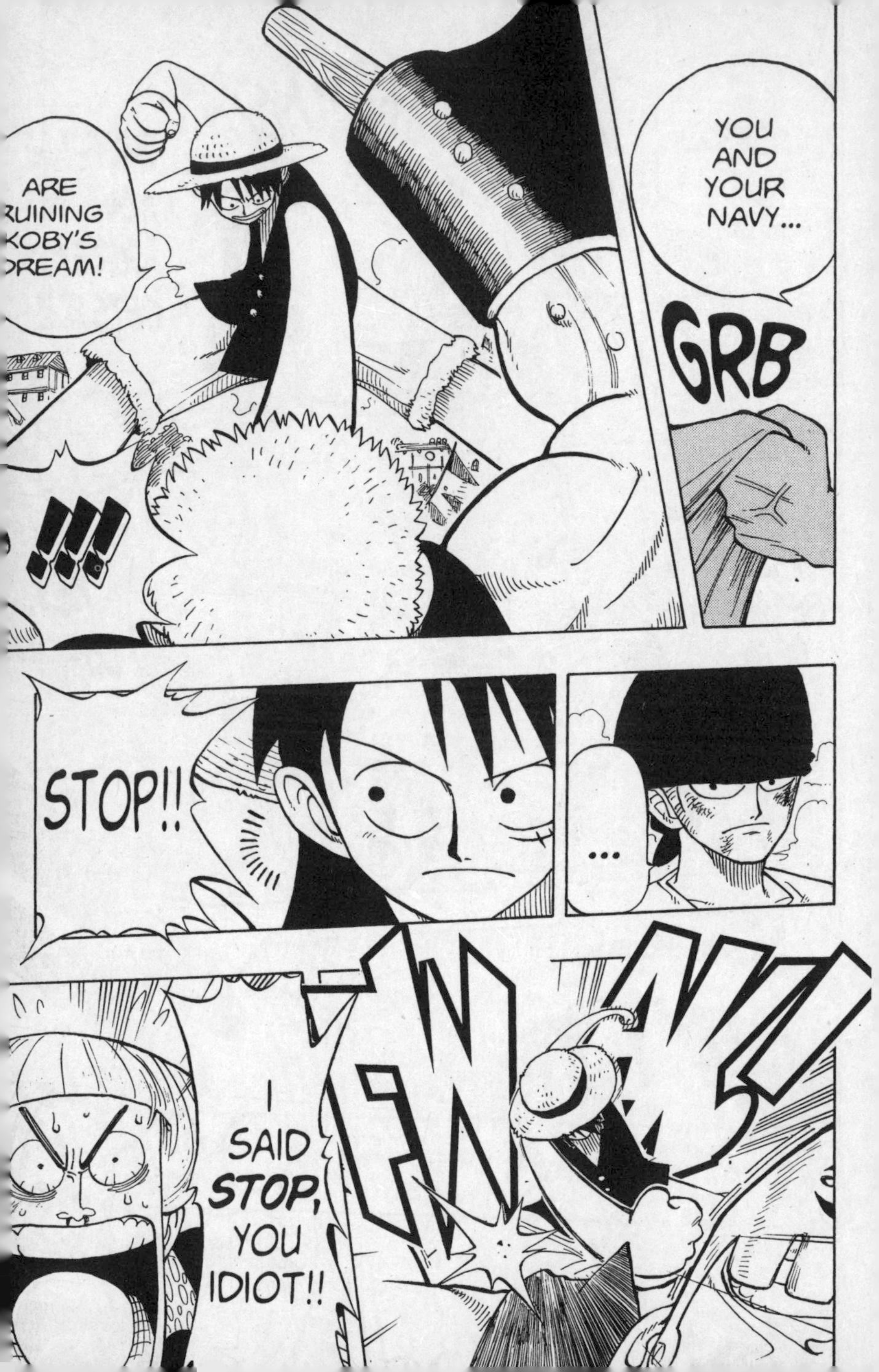
YOU AND YOUR NAVY...
GRB
ARE RUINING KOBY'S DREAM!
!!!
...
STOP!!
I SAID **STOP**, YOU IDIOT!!

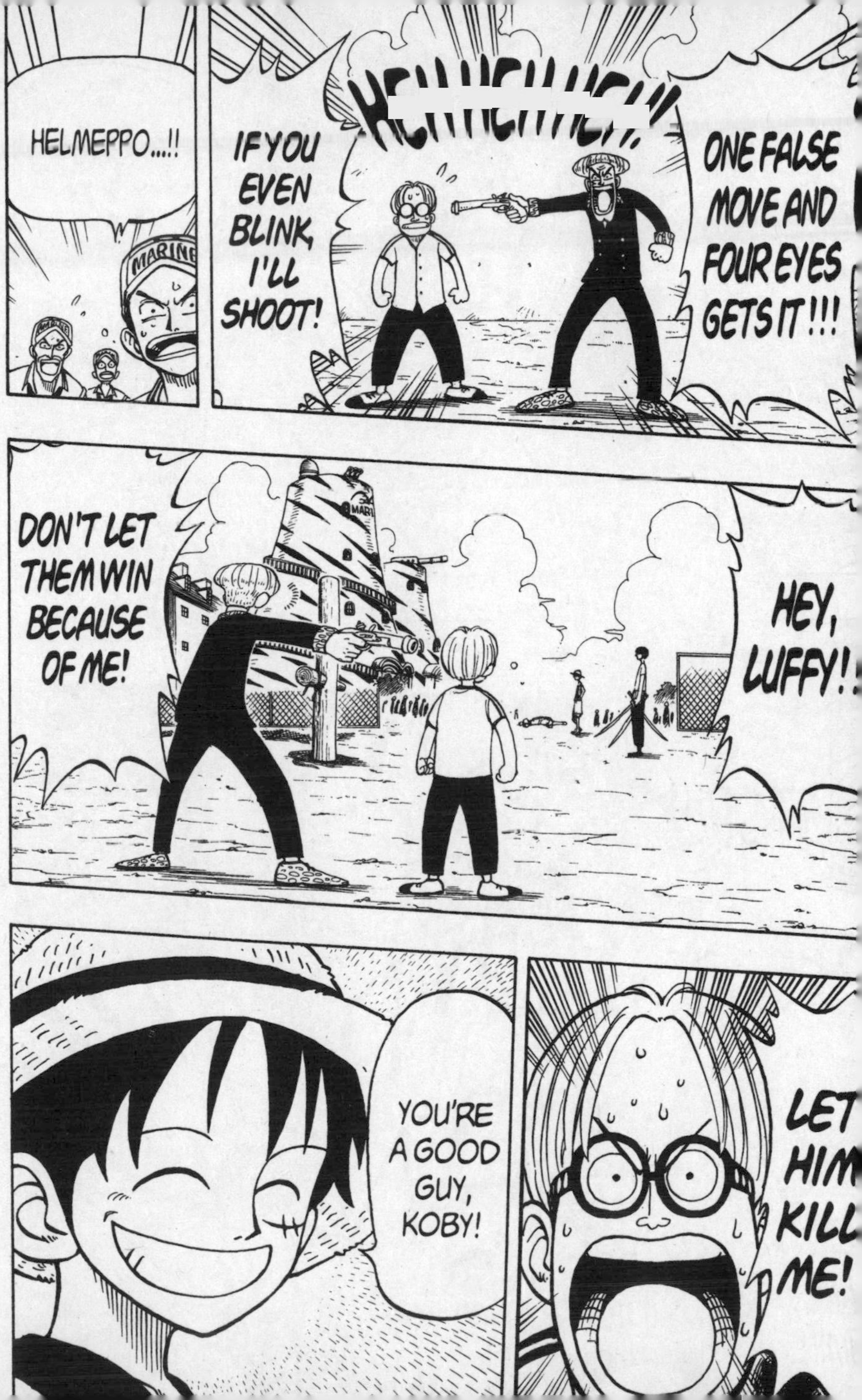
ONE FALSE MOVE AND FOUR EYES GETS IT!!!
IF YOU EVEN BLINK, I'LL SHOOT!
HELMEPPO...!!
HEY, LUFFY!!
DON'T LET THEM WIN BECAUSE OF ME!
LET HIM KILL ME!
YOU'RE A GOOD GUY, KOBY!

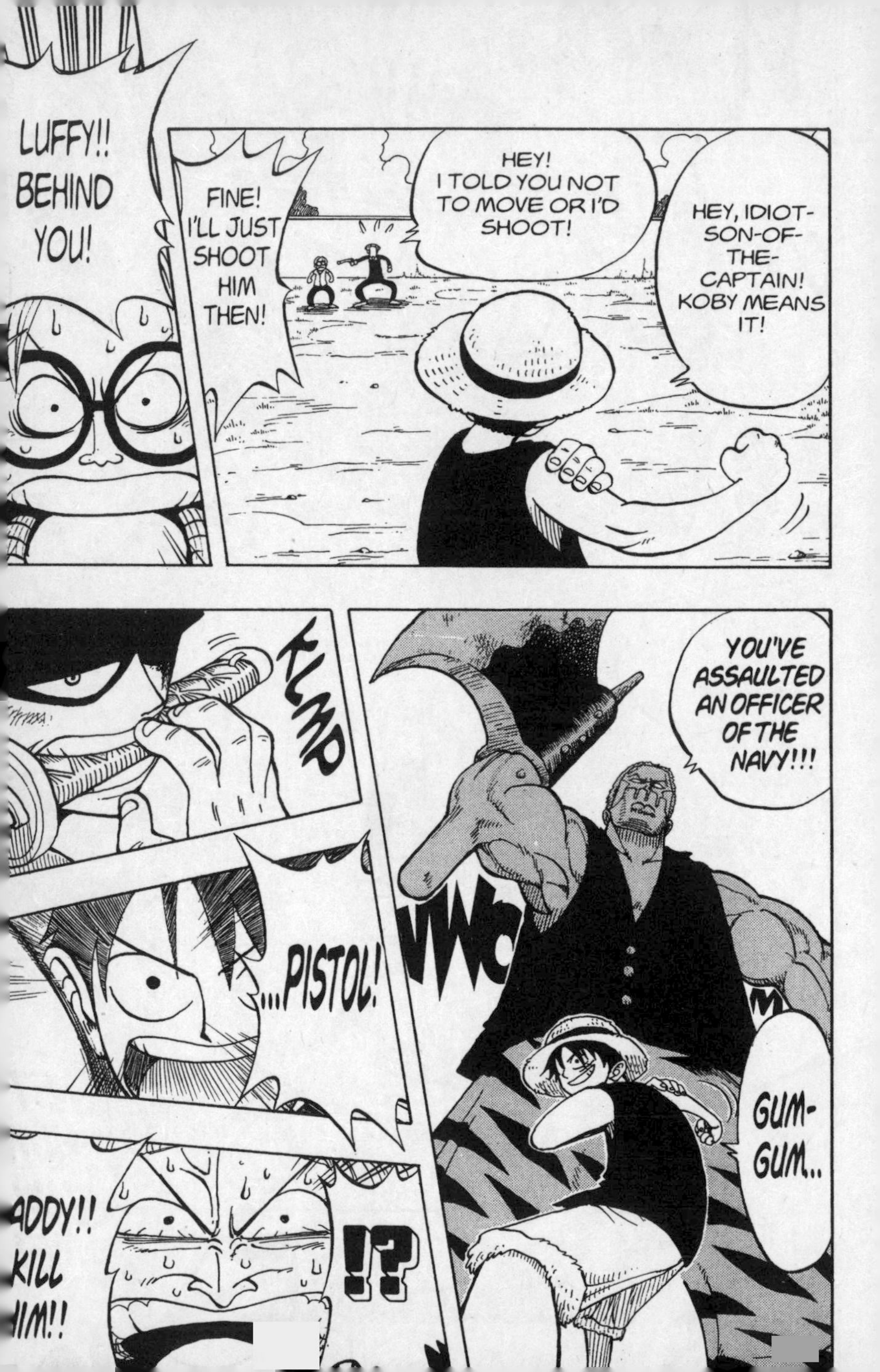
HEY, IDIOT-SON-OF-THE-CAPTAIN! KOBY MEANS IT!
HEY! I TOLD YOU NOT TO MOVE OR I'D SHOOT!
FINE! I'LL JUST SHOOT HIM THEN!
LUFFY!! BEHIND YOU!
YOU'VE ASSAULTED AN OFFICER OF THE NAVY!!!
GUM-GUM...
KLMP
...PISTOL!
ADDY!! KILL HIM!!
!?

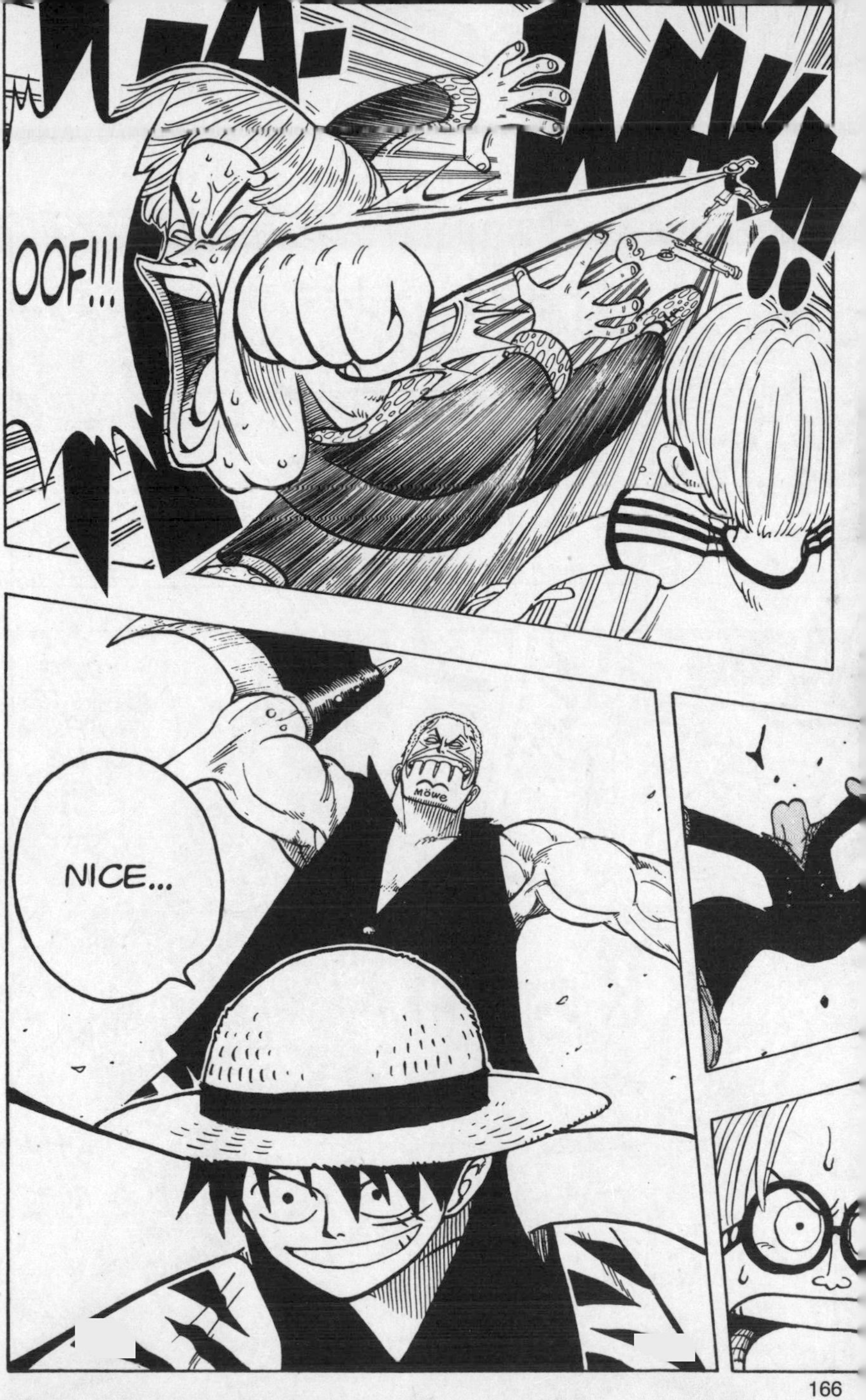
OOF!!!
NICE...
Möwe

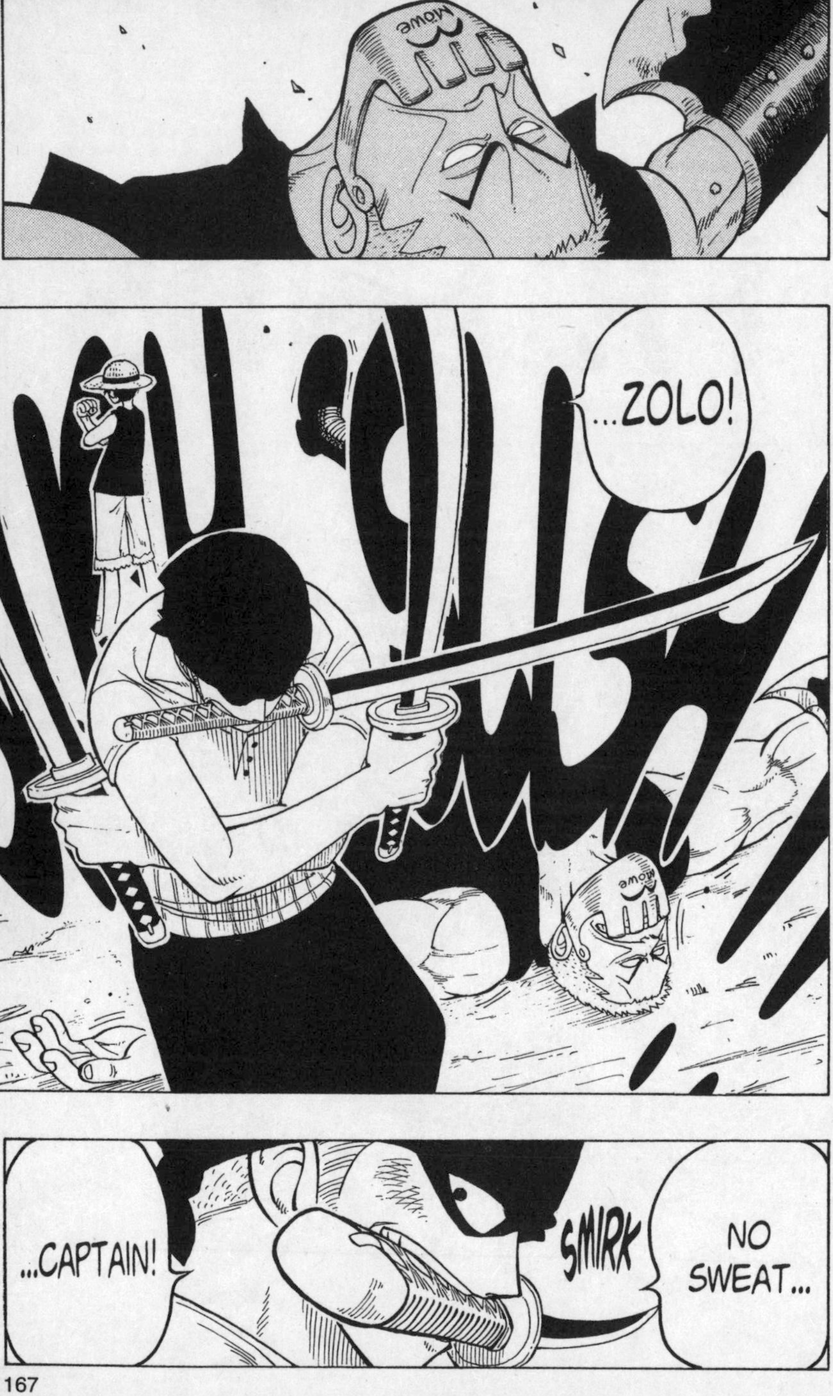
...ZOLO!
NO SWEAT...
SMIRK
...CAPTAIN!

CHAPTER 7 :
FRIENDS

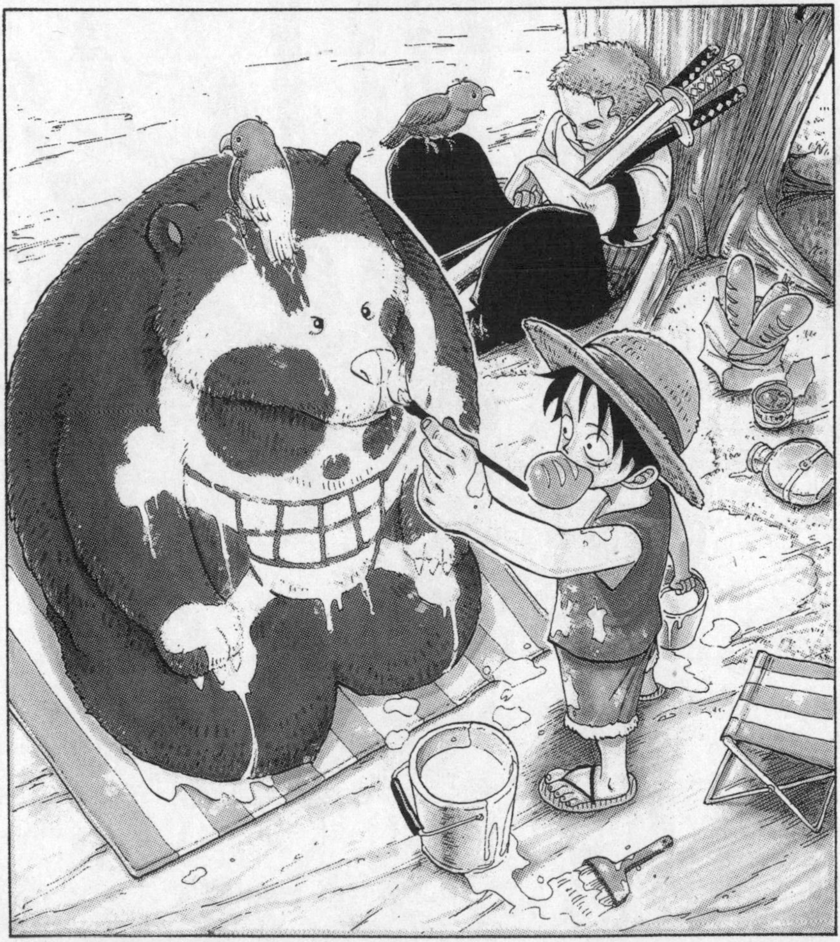

READ THIS WAY

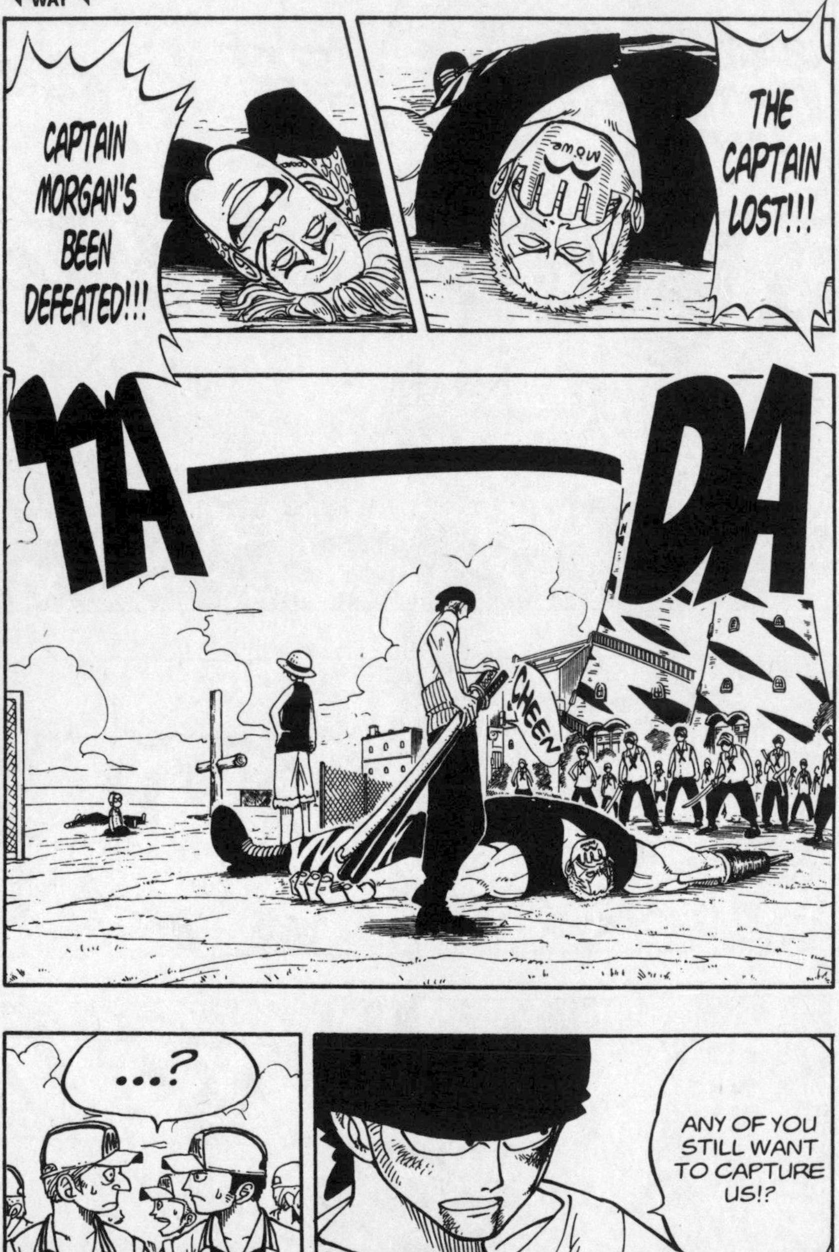
THE CAPTAIN LOST!!!
CAPTAIN MORGAN'S BEEN DEFEATED!!!
TA—DA
CHEEN
ANY OF YOU STILL WANT TO CAPTURE US!?
...?

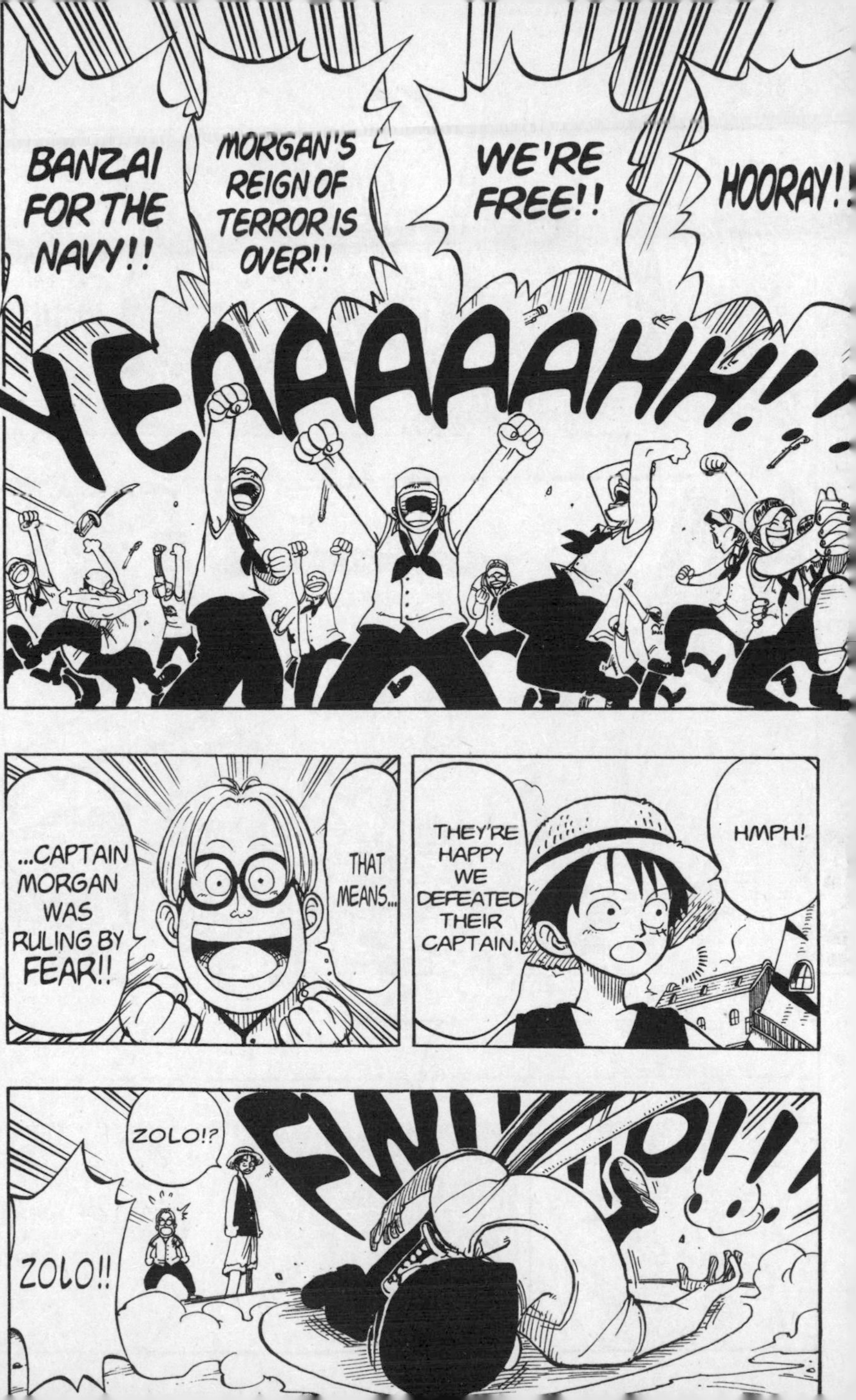
HOORAY!!
WE'RE FREE!!
MORGAN'S REIGN OF TERROR IS OVER!!
BANZAI FOR THE NAVY!!
YEAAAAAHH!!!
HMPH!
THEY'RE HAPPY WE DEFEATED THEIR CAPTAIN.
THAT MEANS...
...CAPTAIN MORGAN WAS RULING BY FEAR!!
ZOLO!?
ZOLO!!

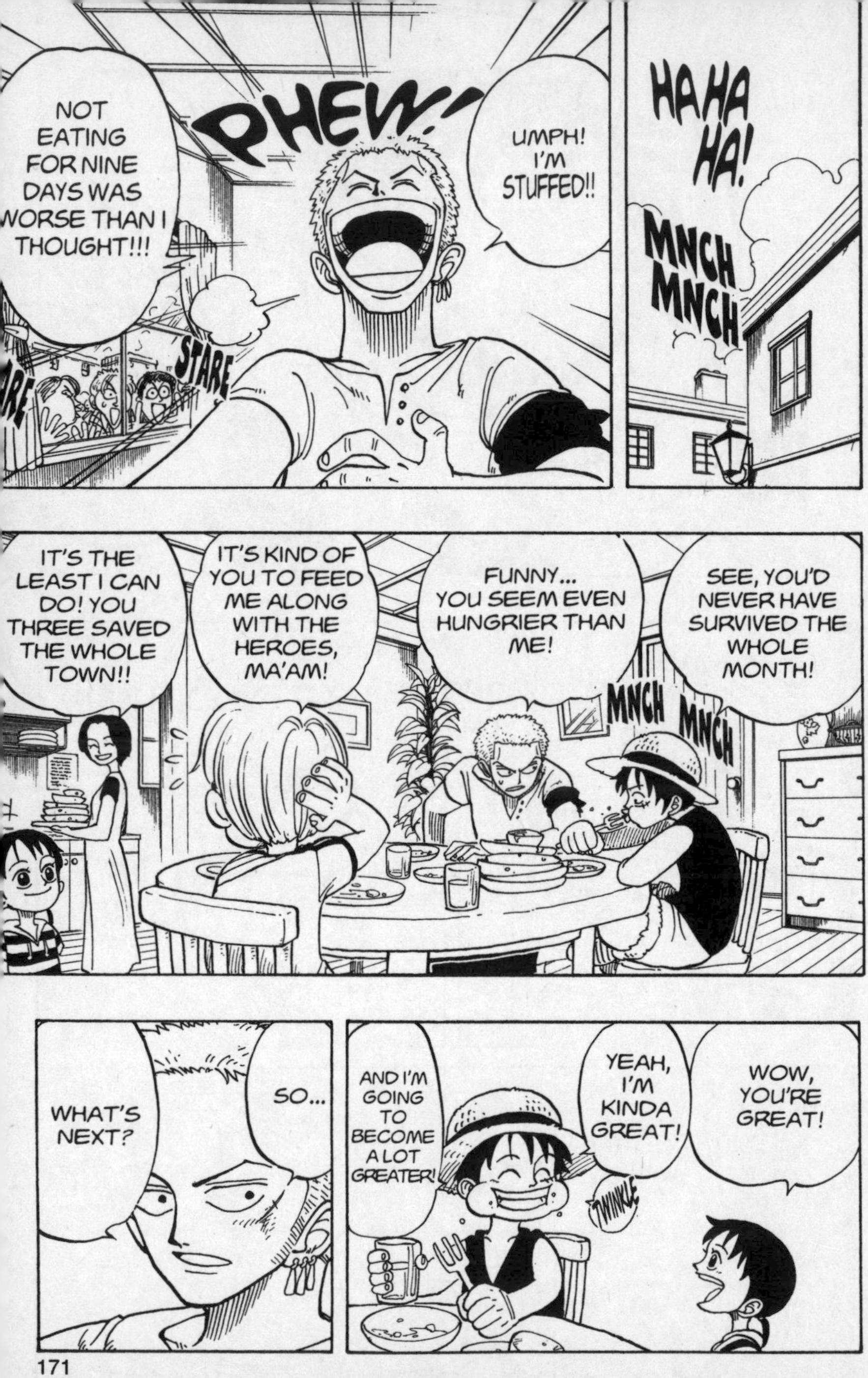
HAHA HA!
MNCH MNCH
UMPH! I'M STUFFED!!
PHEW!
NOT EATING FOR NINE DAYS WAS WORSE THAN I THOUGHT!!!
STARE
SEE, YOU'D NEVER HAVE SURVIVED THE WHOLE MONTH!
MNCH MNCH
FUNNY... YOU SEEM EVEN HUNGRIER THAN ME!
IT'S KIND OF YOU TO FEED ME ALONG WITH THE HEROES, MA'AM!
IT'S THE LEAST I CAN DO! YOU THREE SAVED THE WHOLE TOWN!!
WOW, YOU'RE GREAT!
YEAH, I'M KINDA GREAT!
TWINKLE
AND I'M GOING TO BECOME A LOT GREATER!
SO...
WHAT'S NEXT?

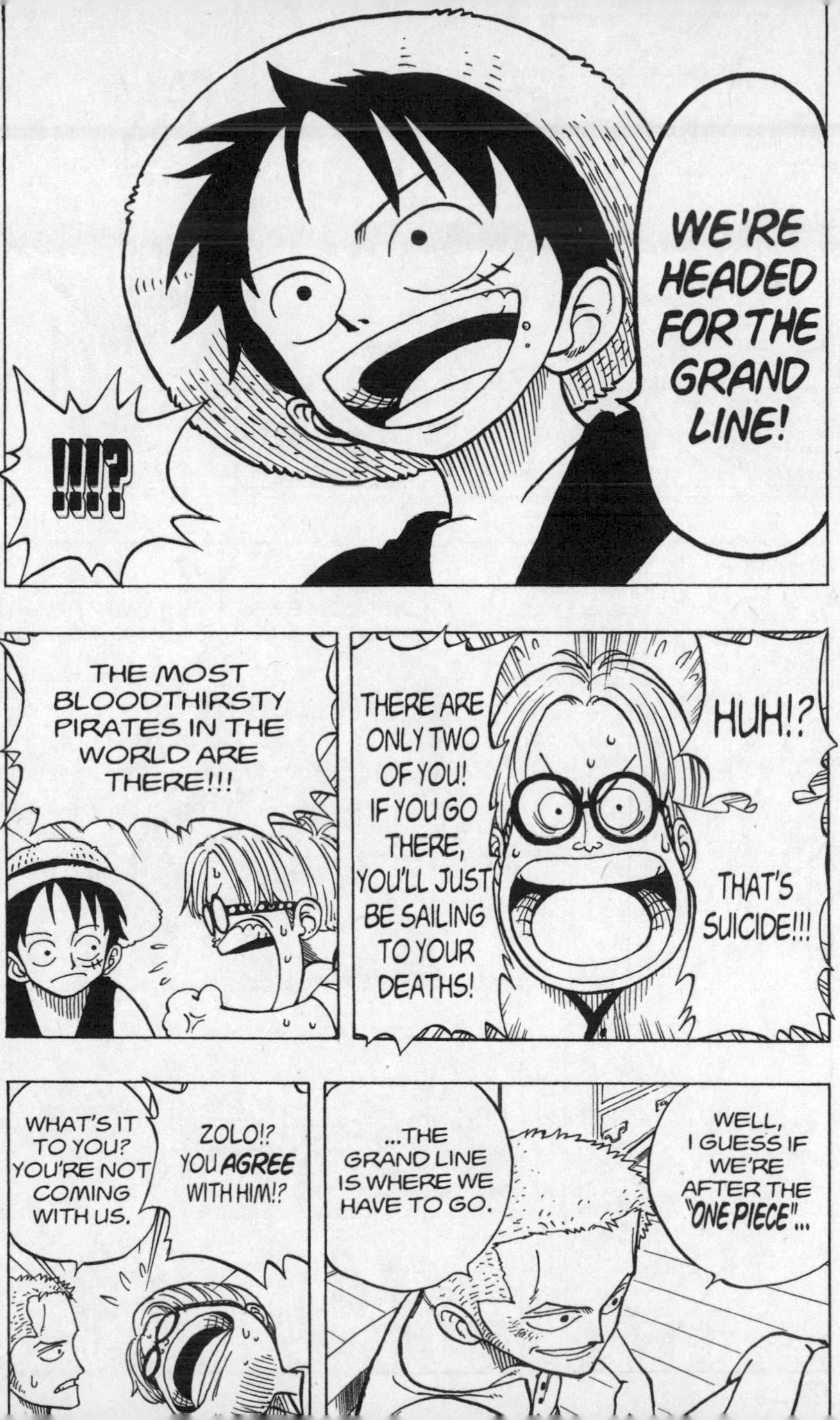
WE'RE HEADED FOR THE GRAND LINE!
!!!?
HUH!?
THAT'S SUICIDE!!!
THERE ARE ONLY TWO OF YOU! IF YOU GO THERE, YOU'LL JUST BE SAILING TO YOUR DEATHS!
THE MOST BLOODTHIRSTY PIRATES IN THE WORLD ARE THERE!!!
WELL, I GUESS IF WE'RE AFTER THE "ONE PIECE"...
...THE GRAND LINE IS WHERE WE HAVE TO GO.
ZOLO!? YOU AGREE WITH HIM!?
WHAT'S IT TO YOU? YOU'RE NOT COMING WITH US.

READ THIS WAY

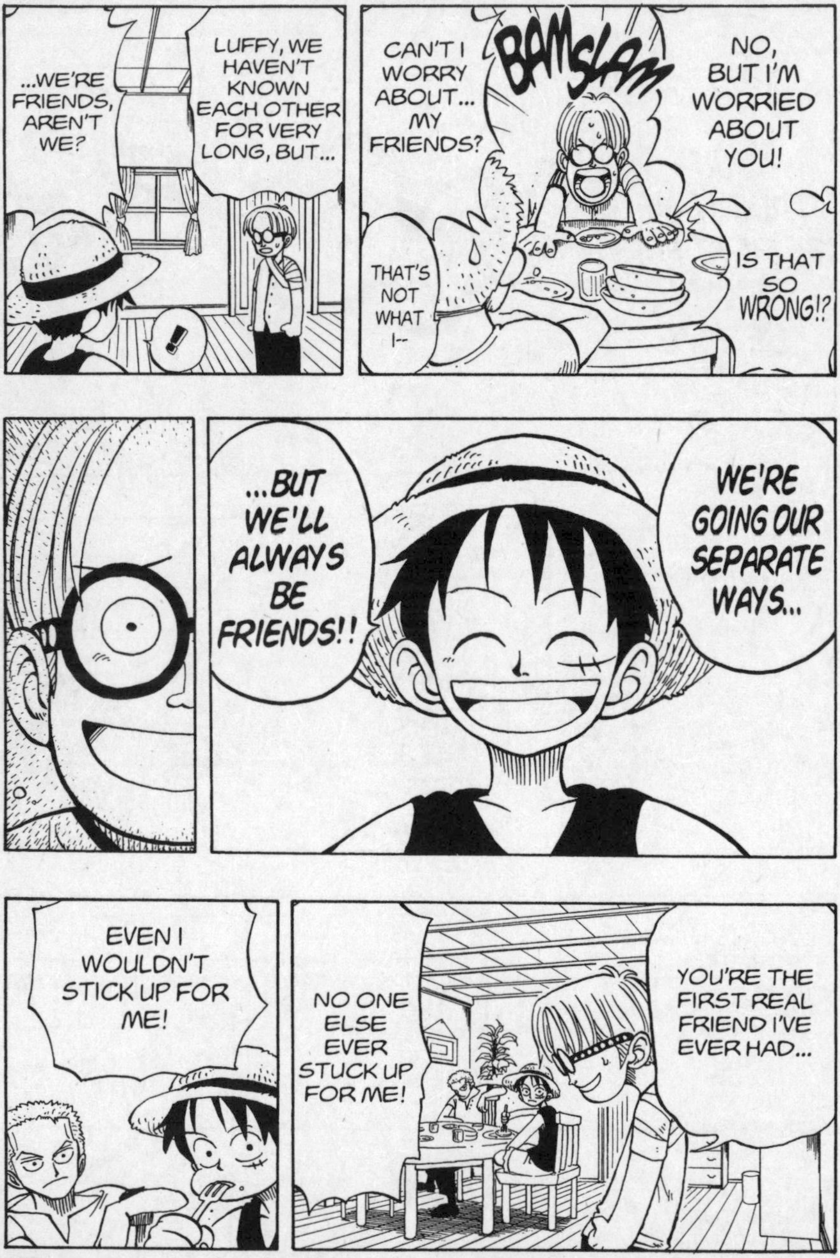
NO, BUT I'M WORRIED ABOUT YOU!
BAMSLAM
CAN'T I WORRY ABOUT... MY FRIENDS?
IS THAT SO WRONG!?
THAT'S NOT WHAT I--
LUFFY, WE HAVEN'T KNOWN EACH OTHER FOR VERY LONG, BUT...
...WE'RE FRIENDS, AREN'T WE?
!
WE'RE GOING OUR SEPARATE WAYS...
...BUT WE'LL ALWAYS BE FRIENDS!!
YOU'RE THE FIRST REAL FRIEND I'VE EVER HAD...
NO ONE ELSE EVER STUCK UP FOR ME!
EVEN I WOULDN'T STICK UP FOR ME!

READ THIS WAY

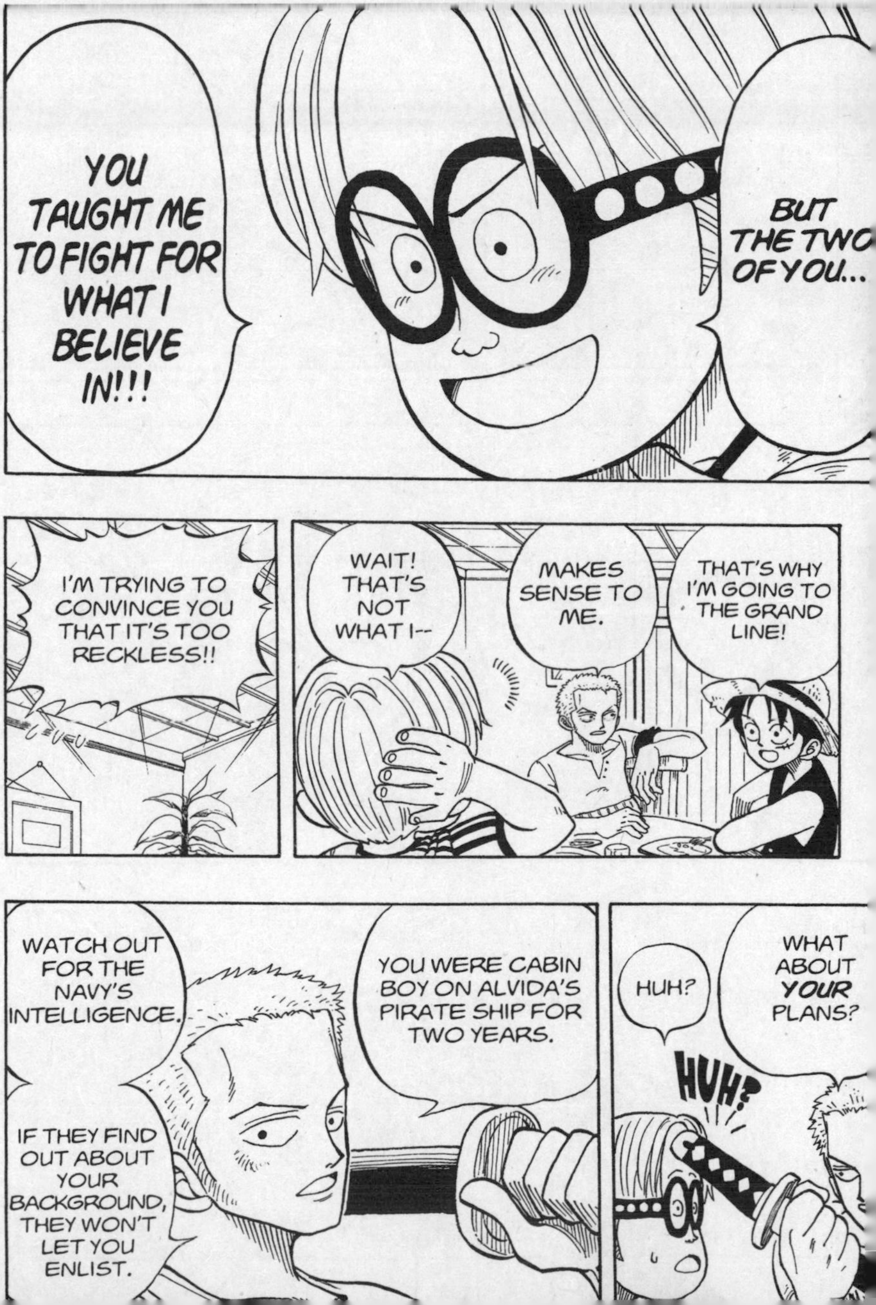
BUT THE TWO OF YOU...
YOU TAUGHT ME TO FIGHT FOR WHAT I BELIEVE IN!!!
THAT'S WHY I'M GOING TO THE GRAND LINE!
MAKES SENSE TO ME.
WAIT! THAT'S NOT WHAT I--
I'M TRYING TO CONVINCE YOU THAT IT'S TOO RECKLESS!!
WHAT ABOUT YOUR PLANS?
HUH?
HUH?
YOU WERE CABIN BOY ON ALVIDA'S PIRATE SHIP FOR TWO YEARS.
WATCH OUT FOR THE NAVY'S INTELLIGENCE.
IF THEY FIND OUT ABOUT YOUR BACKGROUND, THEY WON'T LET YOU ENLIST.

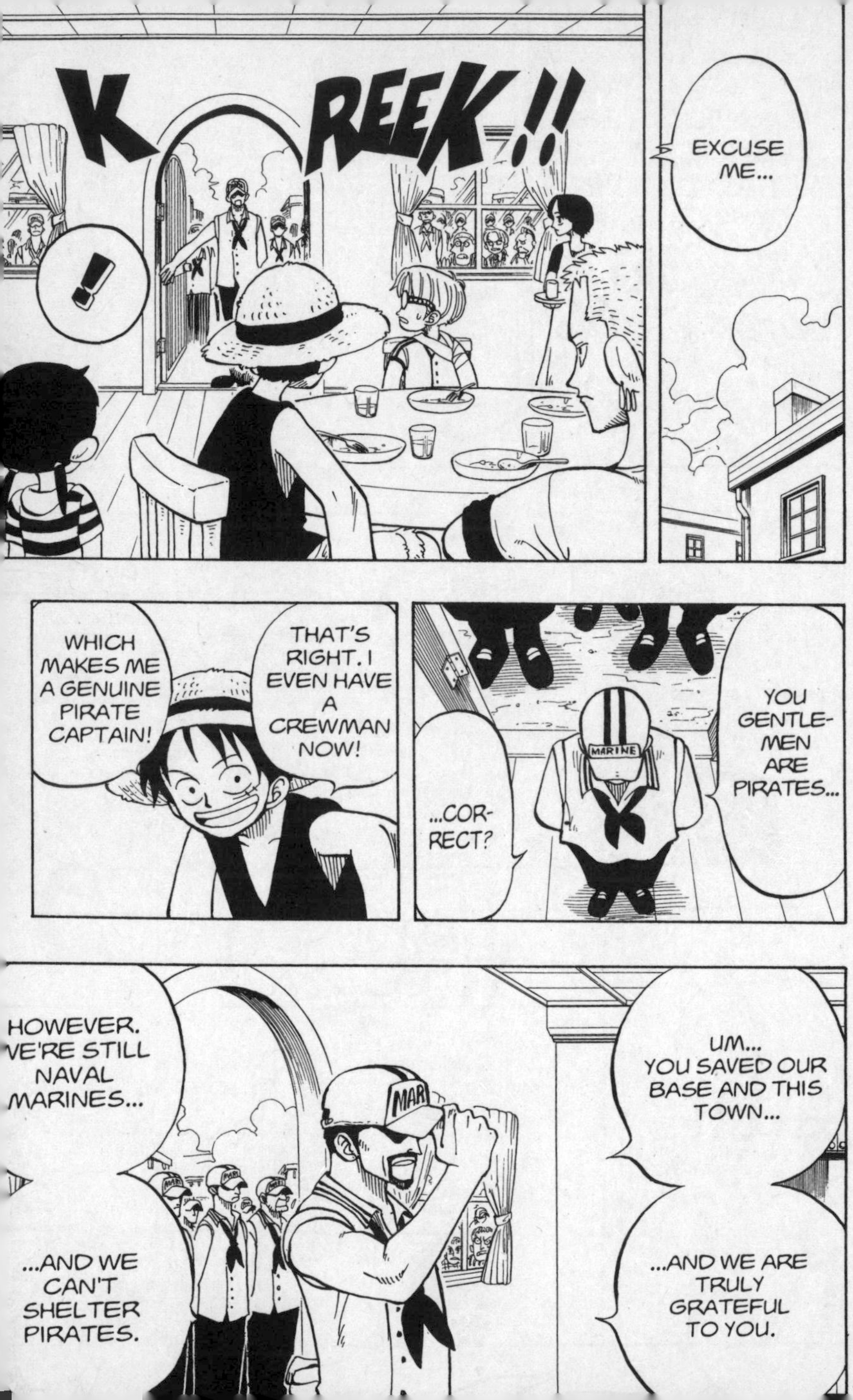
EXCUSE ME...
KREEK!!
!
YOU GENTLEMEN ARE PIRATES...
...CORRECT?
THAT'S RIGHT. I EVEN HAVE A CREWMAN NOW!
WHICH MAKES ME A GENUINE PIRATE CAPTAIN!
MARINE
UM... YOU SAVED OUR BASE AND THIS TOWN...
...AND WE ARE TRULY GRATEFUL TO YOU.
HOWEVER. WE'RE STILL NAVAL MARINES...
...AND WE CAN'T SHELTER PIRATES.

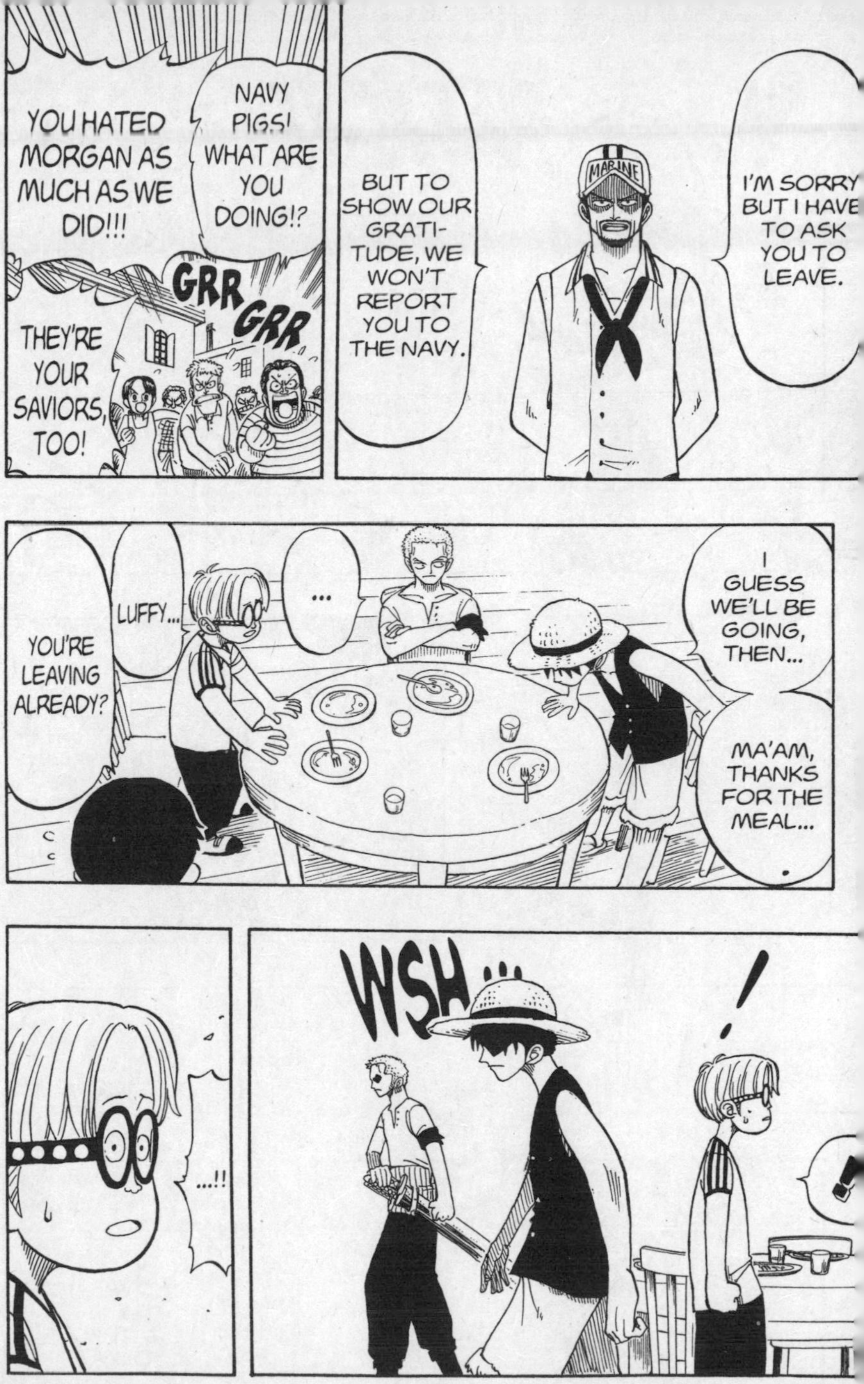
I'M SORRY BUT I HAVE TO ASK YOU TO LEAVE.
BUT TO SHOW OUR GRATITUDE, WE WON'T REPORT YOU TO THE NAVY.
NAVY PIGS! WHAT ARE YOU DOING!?
YOU HATED MORGAN AS MUCH AS WE DID!!!
GRR GRR
THEY'RE YOUR SAVIORS, TOO!
I GUESS WE'LL BE GOING, THEN...
MA'AM, THANKS FOR THE MEAL...
...
LUFFY...
YOU'RE LEAVING ALREADY?
WSH...
!
...!!

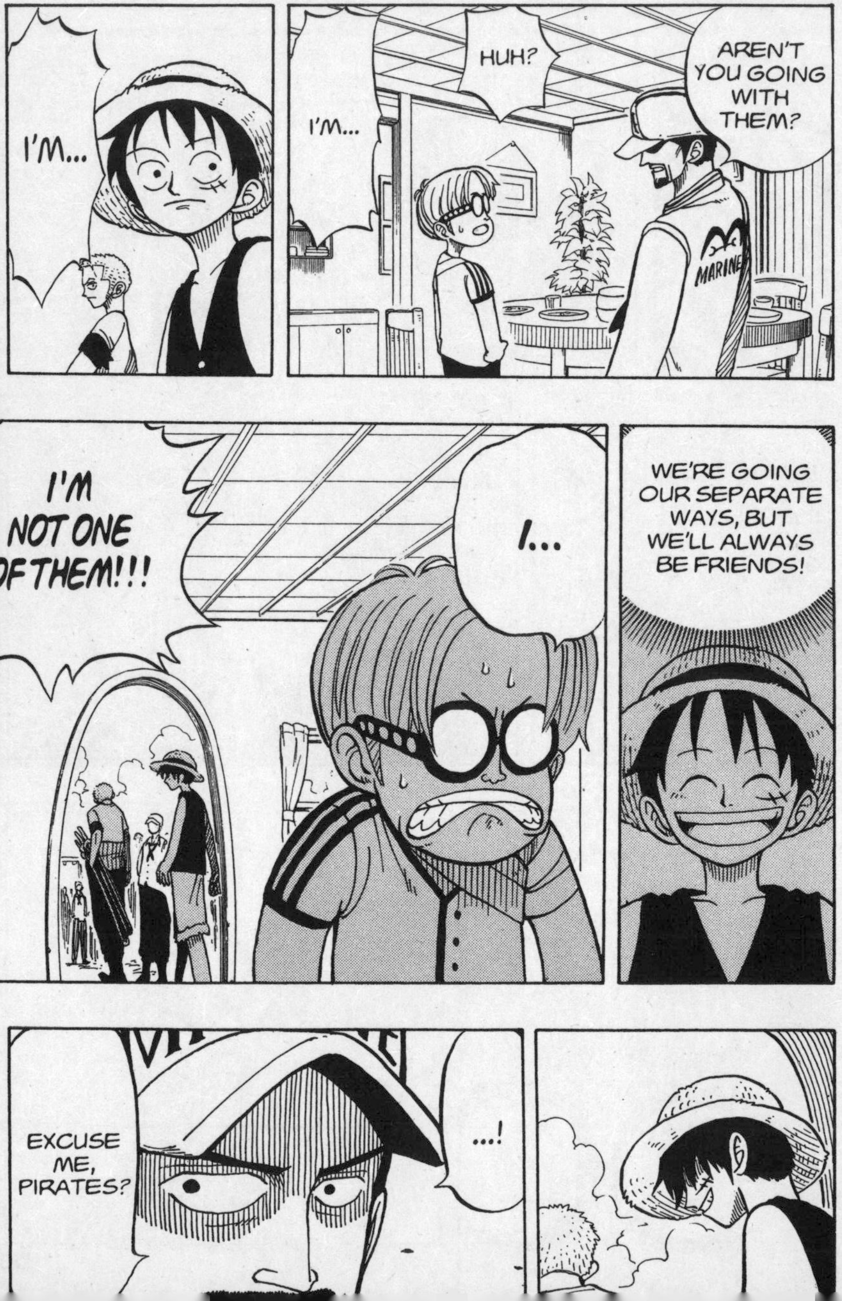
AREN'T YOU GOING WITH THEM?
HUH?
I'M...
I'M...
WE'RE GOING OUR SEPARATE WAYS, BUT WE'LL ALWAYS BE FRIENDS!
I...
I'M NOT ONE OF THEM!!!
...!
EXCUSE ME, PIRATES?

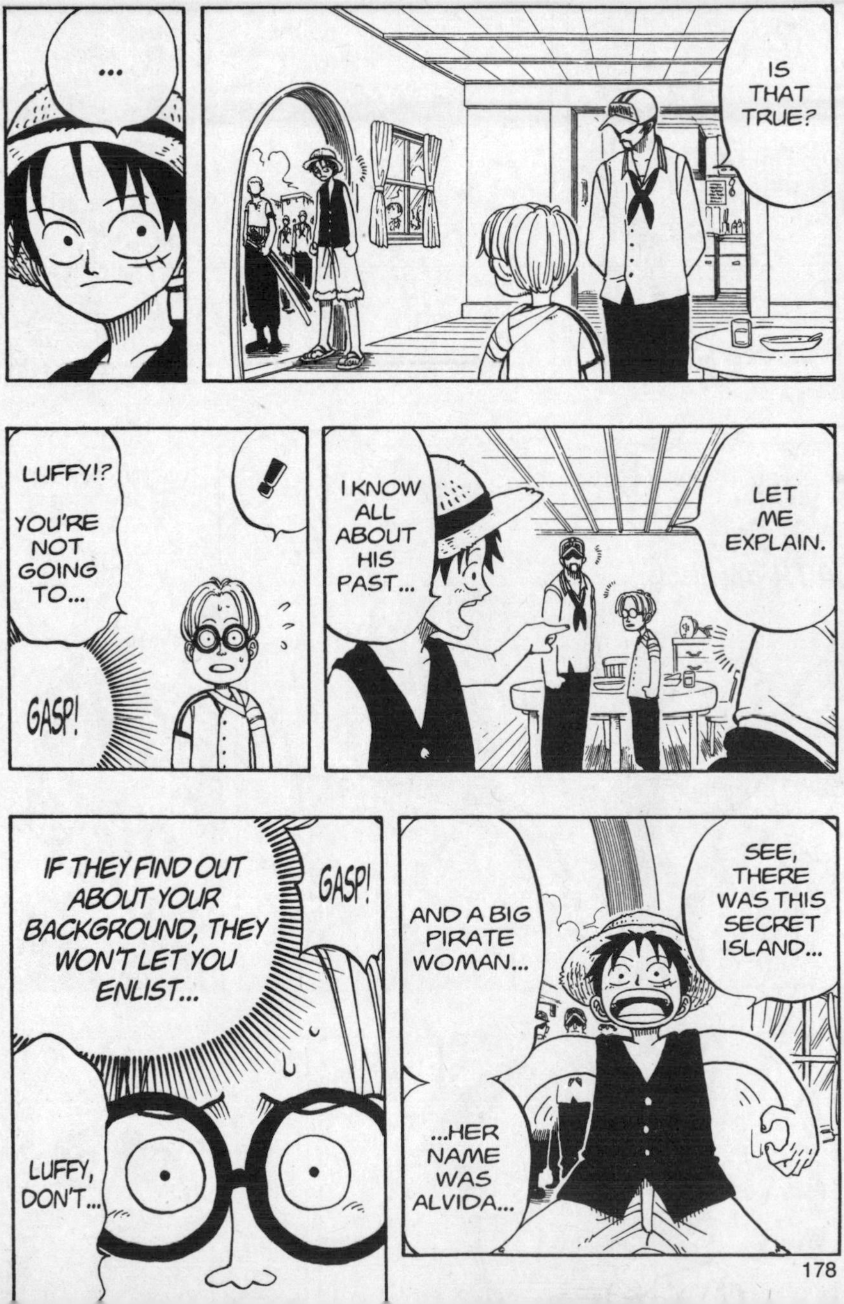
IS THAT TRUE?
...
LET ME EXPLAIN.
I KNOW ALL ABOUT HIS PAST...
!
LUFFY!? YOU'RE NOT GOING TO...
GASP!
SEE, THERE WAS THIS SECRET ISLAND...
AND A BIG PIRATE WOMAN...
...HER NAME WAS ALVIDA...
GASP!
IF THEY FIND OUT ABOUT YOUR BACKGROUND, THEY WON'T LET YOU ENLIST...
LUFFY, DON'T...

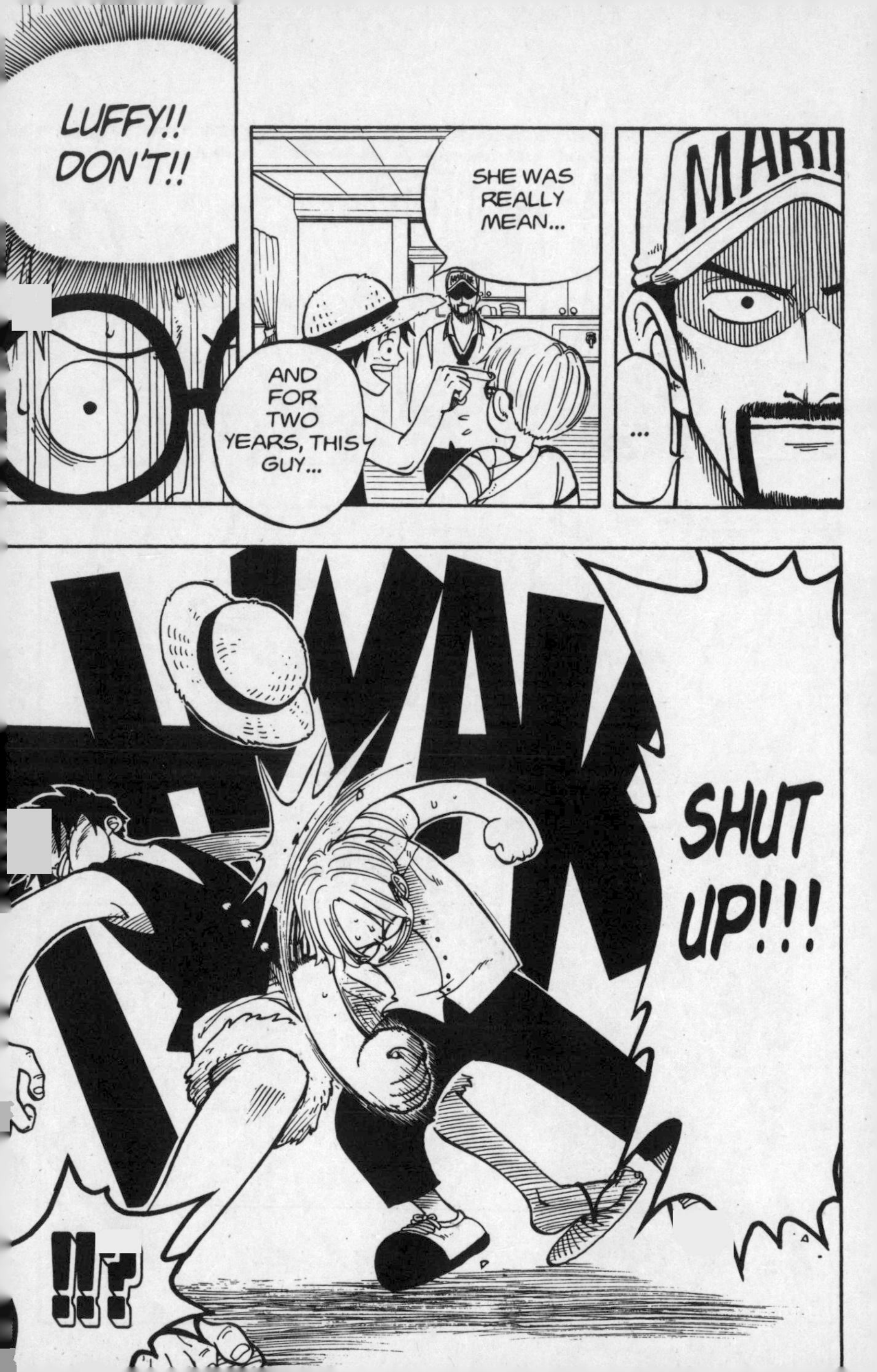
...
SHE WAS REALLY MEAN...
AND FOR TWO YEARS, THIS GUY...
LUFFY!! DON'T!!
SHUT UP!!!
!!?

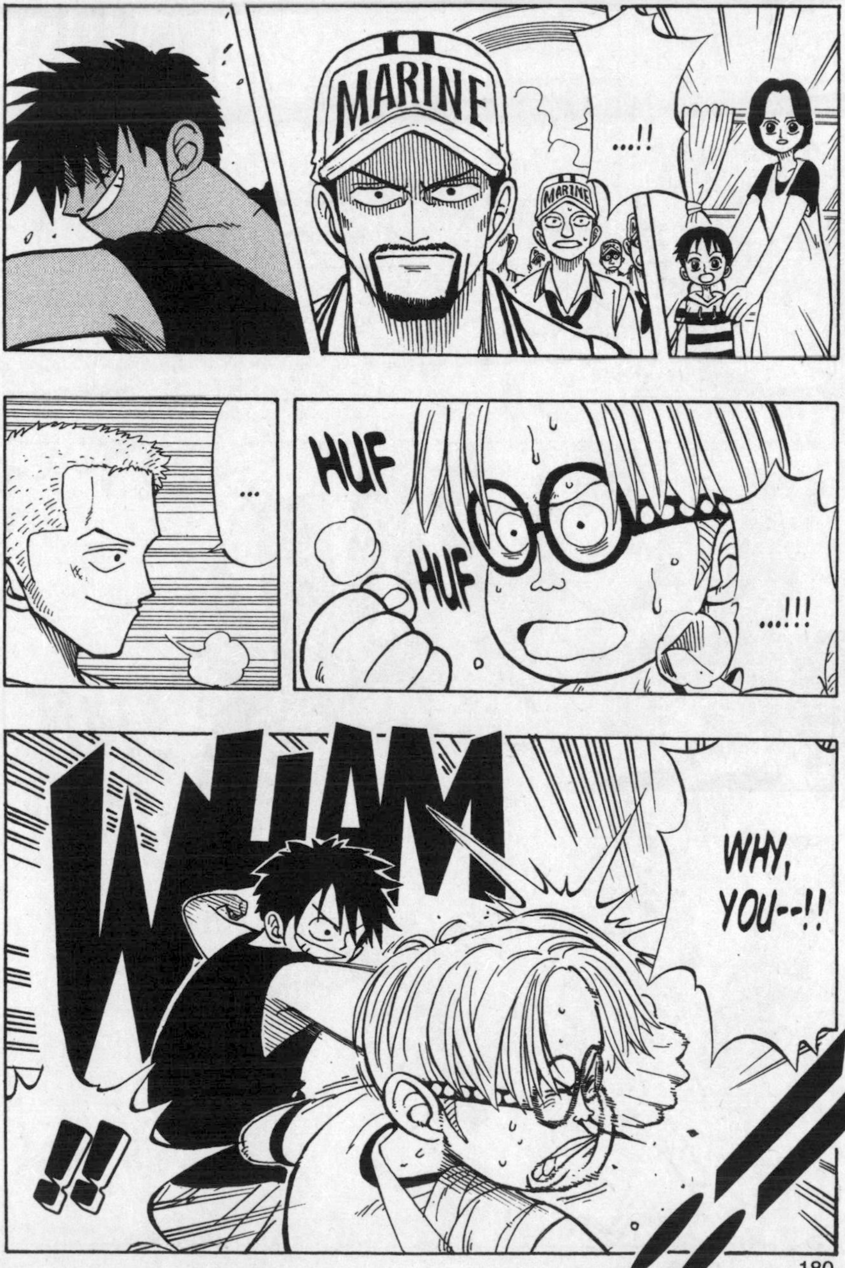
MARINE
MARINE
...!!
HUF
HUF
...!!!
...
WHAM
!!
WHY, YOU--!!

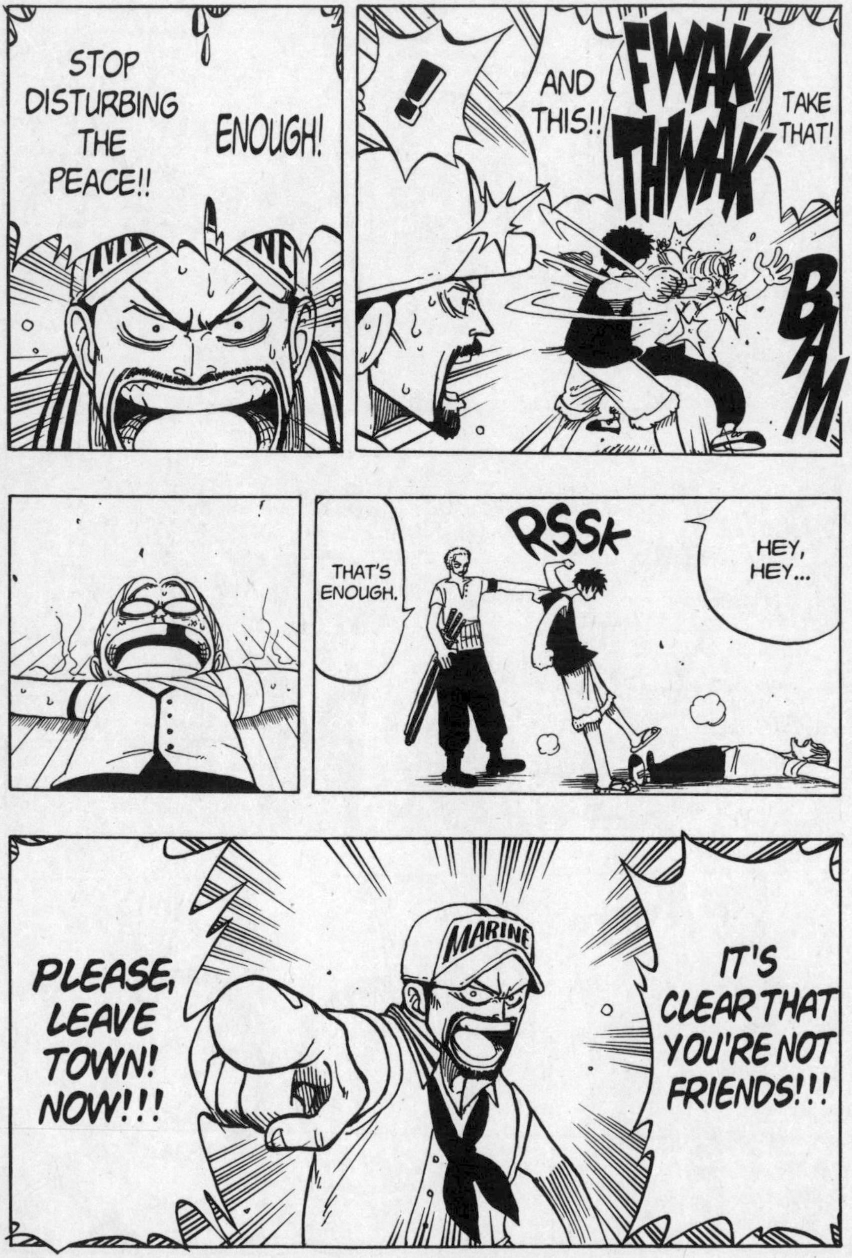

TAKE THAT!
FWAK THWAK
AND THIS!!
!
BAM
ENOUGH!
STOP DISTURBING THE PEACE!!
HEY, HEY...
RSSK
THAT'S ENOUGH.
IT'S CLEAR THAT YOU'RE NOT FRIENDS!!!
PLEASE, LEAVE TOWN! NOW!!!

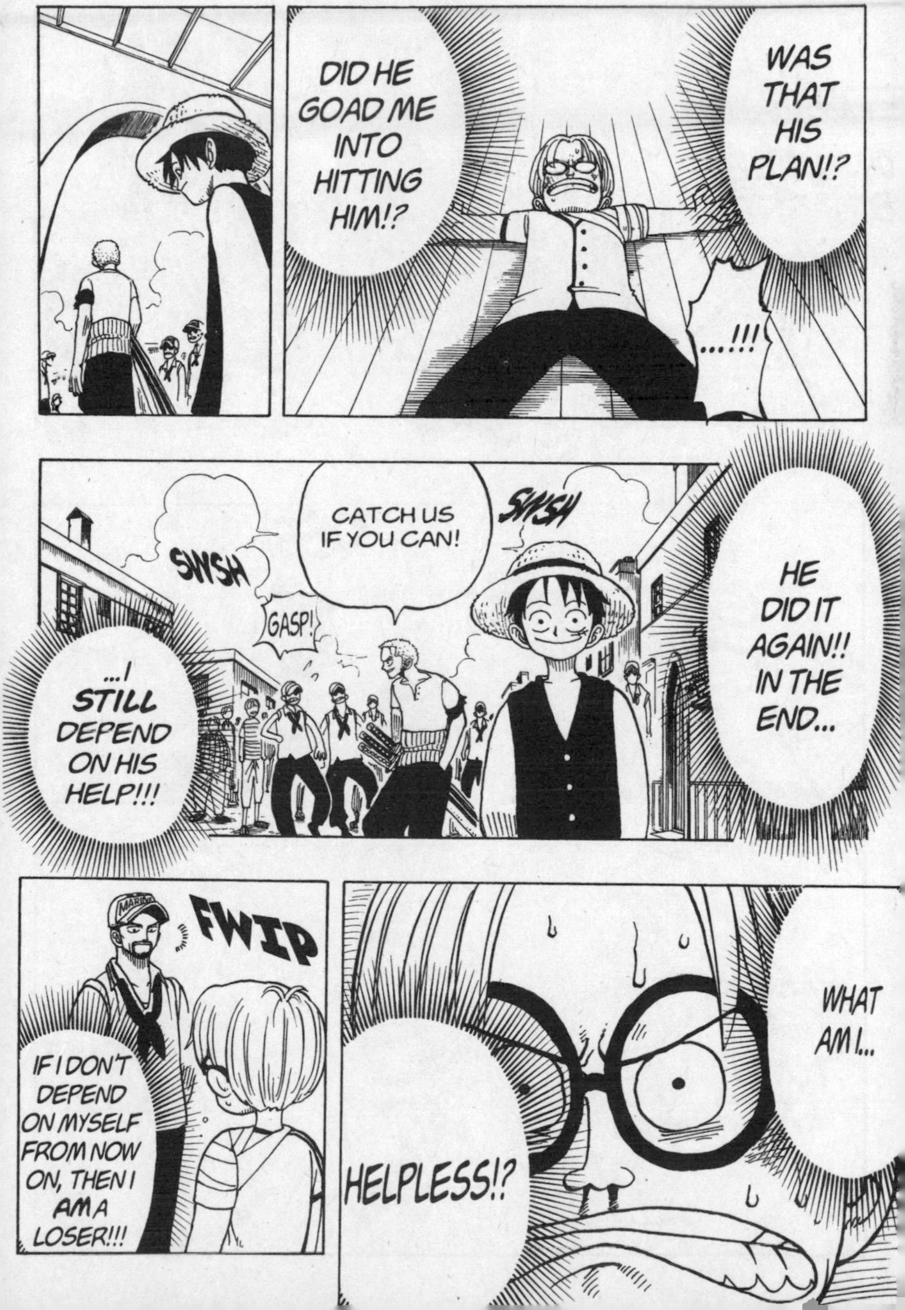
WAS THAT HIS PLAN!?
DID HE GOAD ME INTO HITTING HIM!?
...!!!
HE DID IT AGAIN!! IN THE END...
SWSH
CATCH US IF YOU CAN!
SWSH
GASP!
...I STILL DEPEND ON HIS HELP!!!
WHAT AM I...
HELPLESS!?
FWIP
MARINE
IF I DON'T DEPEND ON MYSELF FROM NOW ON, THEN I AM A LOSER!!!

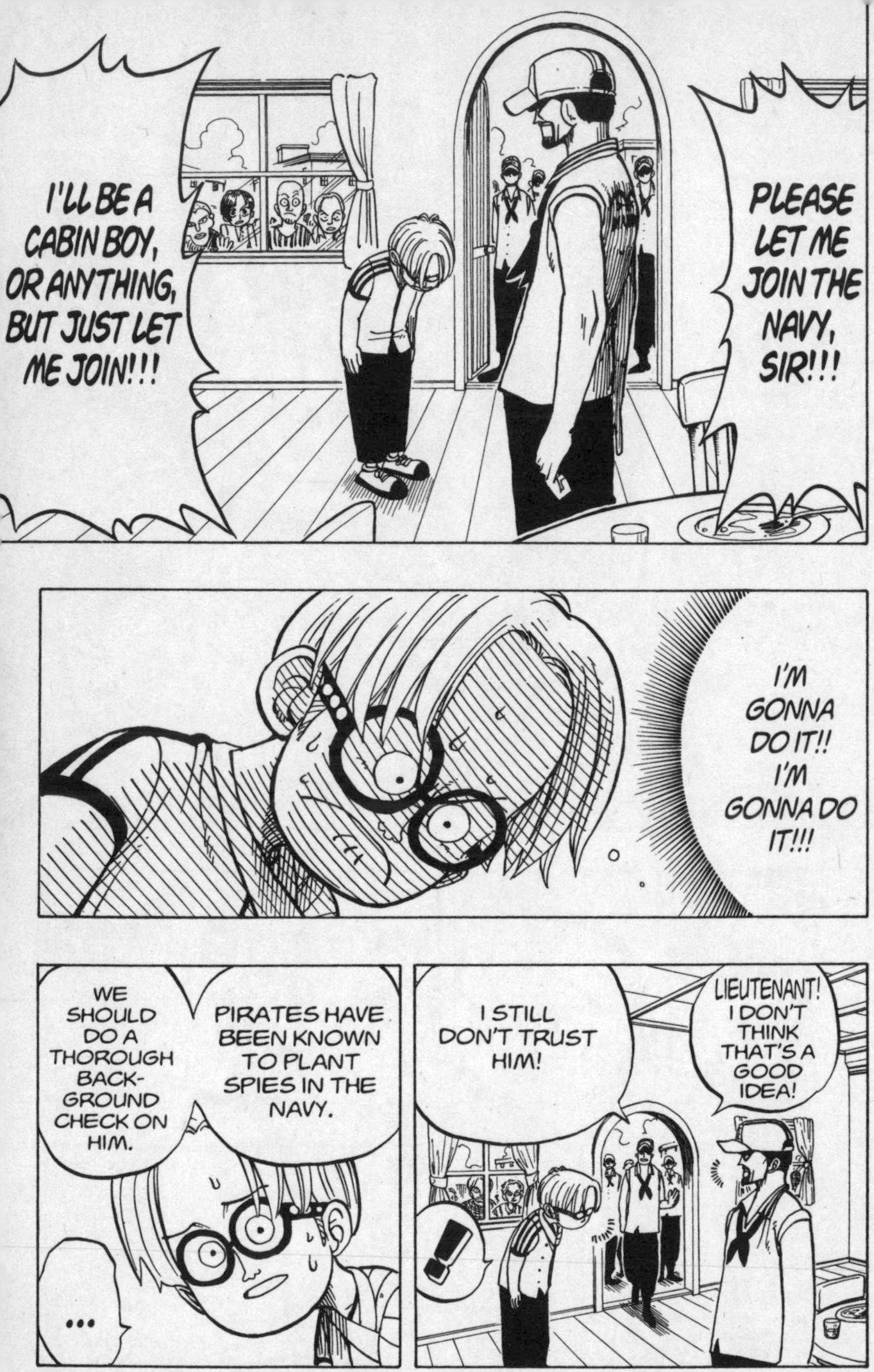
PLEASE LET ME JOIN THE NAVY, SIR!!!
I'LL BE A CABIN BOY, OR ANYTHING, BUT JUST LET ME JOIN!!!
I'M GONNA DO IT!! I'M GONNA DO IT!!!
LIEUTENANT! I DON'T THINK THAT'S A GOOD IDEA!
I STILL DON'T TRUST HIM!
!
PIRATES HAVE BEEN KNOWN TO PLANT SPIES IN THE NAVY.
WE SHOULD DO A THOROUGH BACK-GROUND CHECK ON HIM.
...

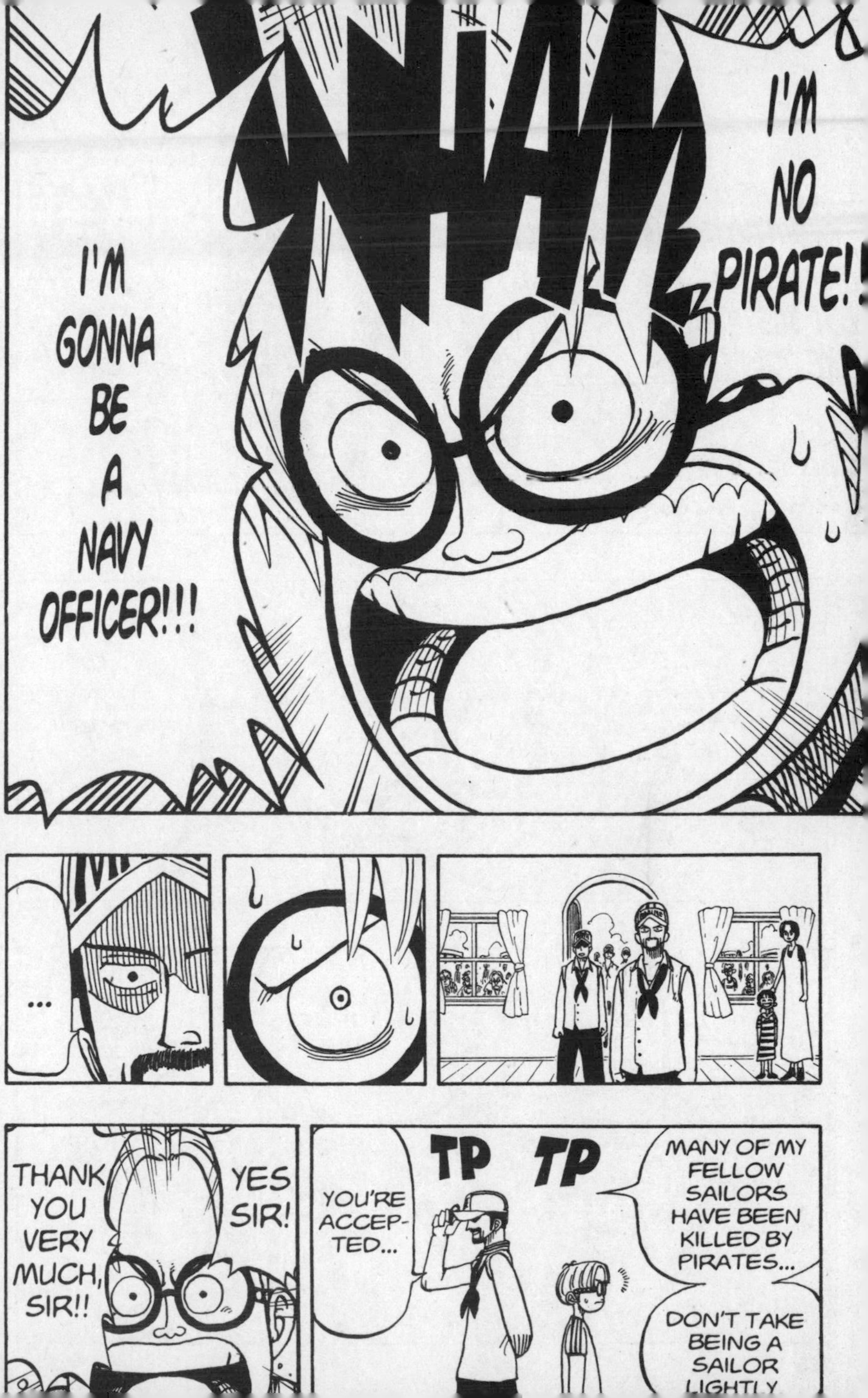
I'M NO PIRATE!!
I'M GONNA BE A NAVY OFFICER!!!
...
MANY OF MY FELLOW SAILORS HAVE BEEN KILLED BY PIRATES...
DON'T TAKE BEING A SAILOR
TP TP
YOU'RE ACCEP-TED...
YES SIR!
THANK YOU VERY MUCH, SIR!!

READ THIS WAY

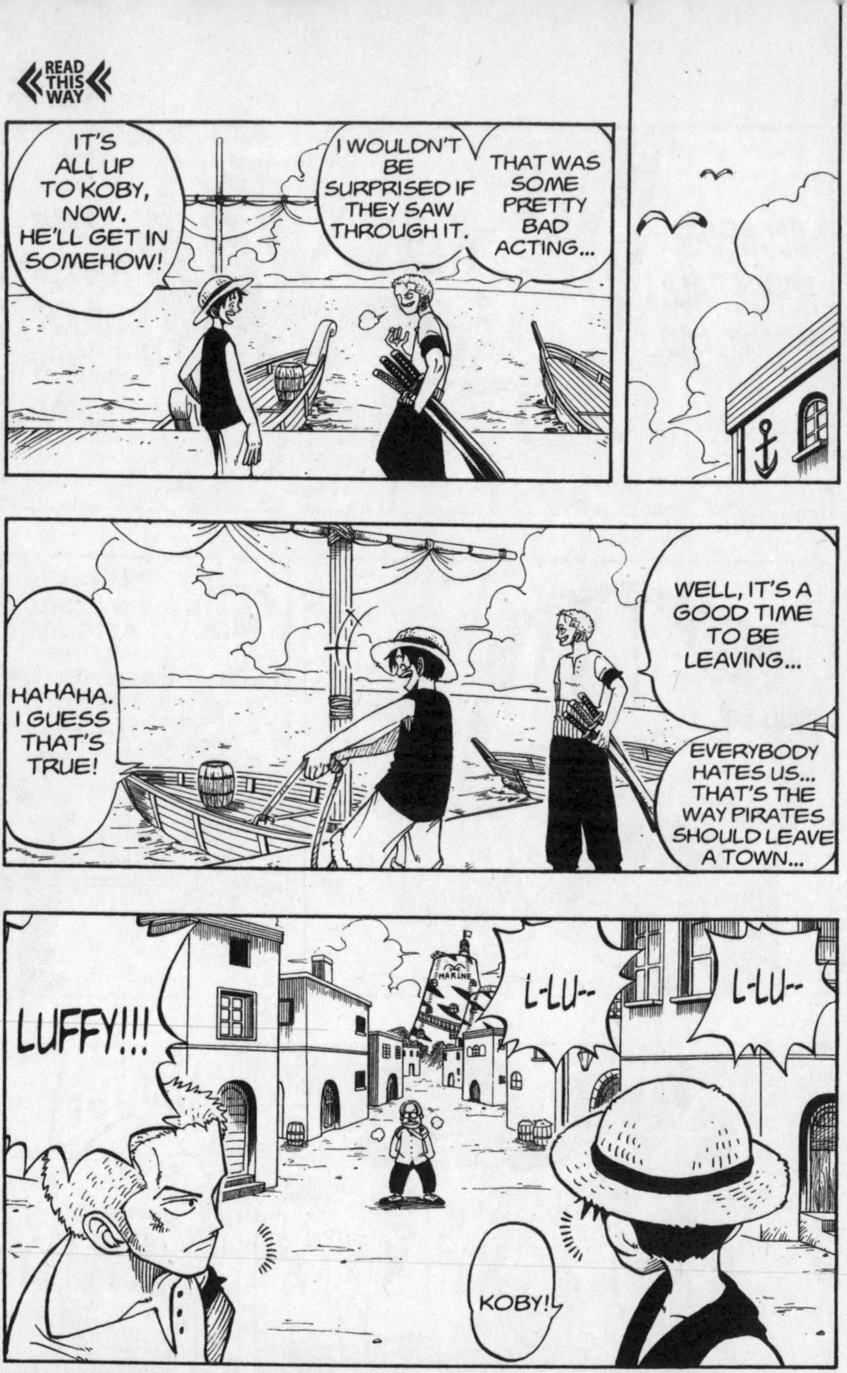
THAT WAS SOME PRETTY BAD ACTING...
I WOULDN'T BE SURPRISED IF THEY SAW THROUGH IT.
IT'S ALL UP TO KOBY, NOW. HE'LL GET IN SOMEHOW!
WELL, IT'S A GOOD TIME TO BE LEAVING...
EVERYBODY HATES US... THAT'S THE WAY PIRATES SHOULD LEAVE A TOWN...
HAHAHA. I GUESS THAT'S TRUE!
L-LU--
L-LU--
MARINE
LUFFY!!!
KOBY!

READ THIS WAY

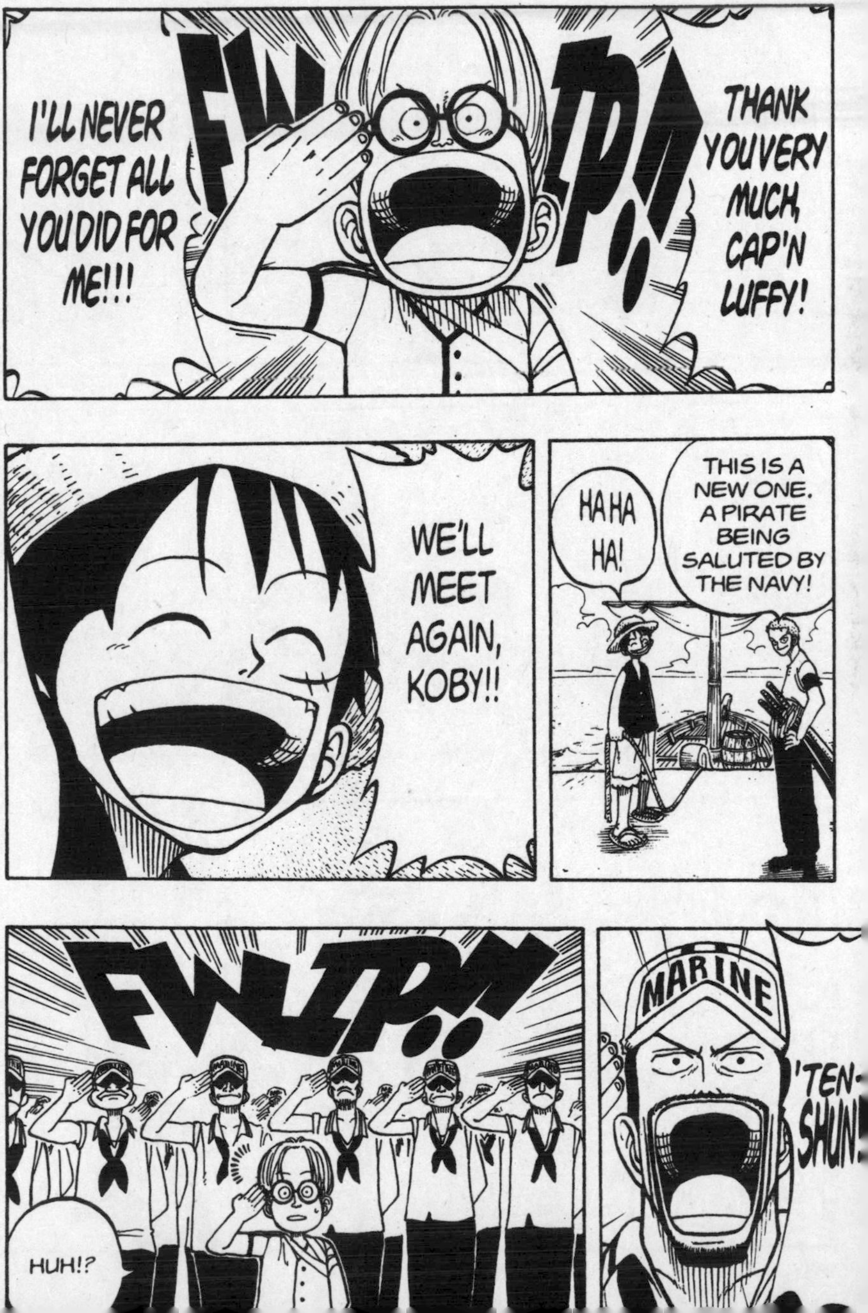
THANK YOU VERY MUCH, CAP'N LUFFY!
I'LL NEVER FORGET ALL YOU DID FOR ME!!!
THIS IS A NEW ONE. A PIRATE BEING SALUTED BY THE NAVY!
HA HA HA!
WE'LL MEET AGAIN, KOBY!!
MARINE
'TEN-SHUN!
FWIP!!
HUH!?

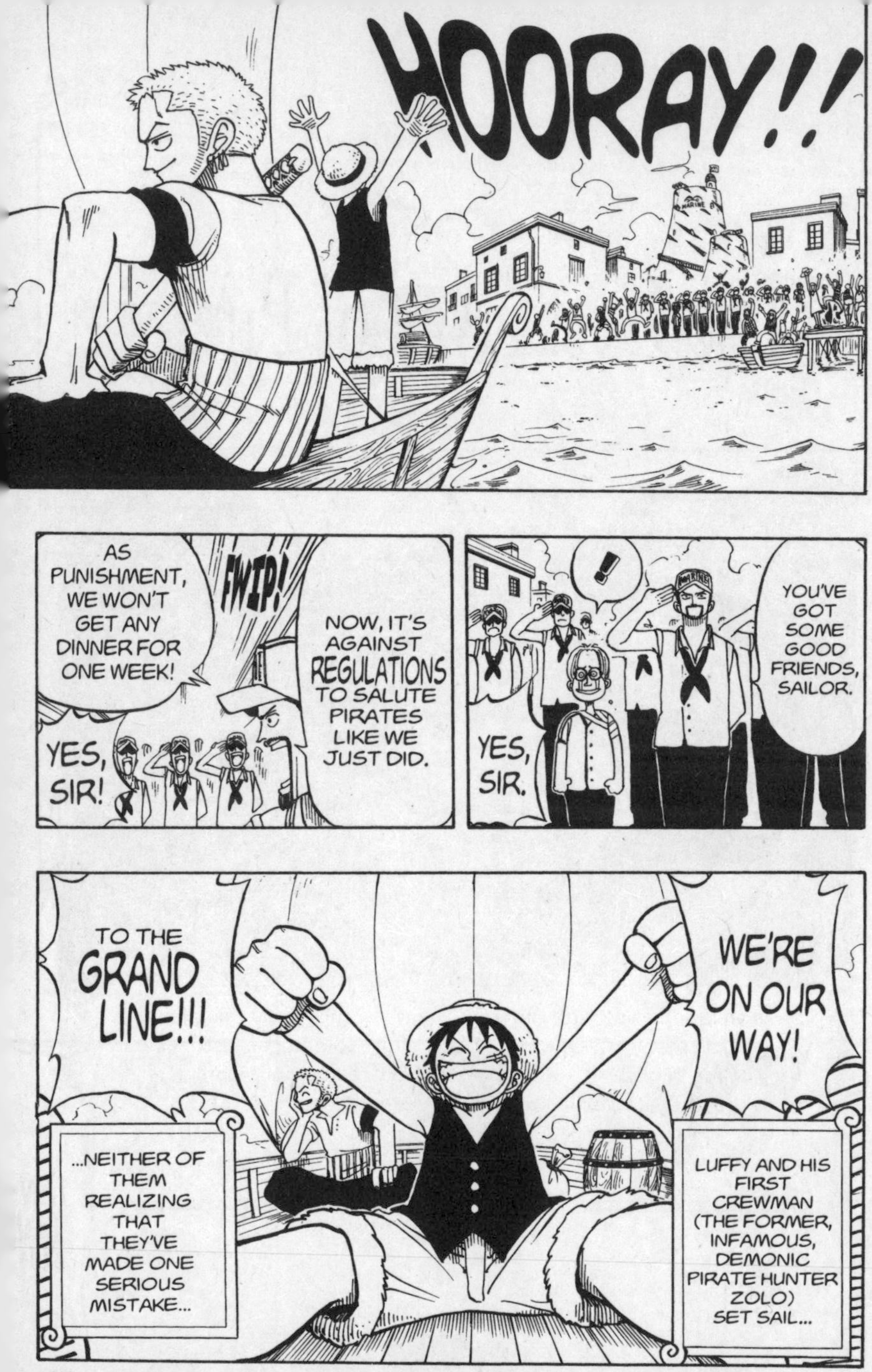
HOORAY!!
YOU'VE GOT SOME GOOD FRIENDS, SAILOR.
!
YES, SIR.
NOW, IT'S AGAINST REGULATIONS TO SALUTE PIRATES LIKE WE JUST DID.
FWIP!
AS PUNISHMENT, WE WON'T GET ANY DINNER FOR ONE WEEK!
YES, SIR!
WE'RE ON OUR WAY!
TO THE GRAND LINE!!!
LUFFY AND HIS FIRST CREWMAN (THE FORMER, INFAMOUS, DEMONIC PIRATE HUNTER ZOLO) SET SAIL...
...NEITHER OF THEM REALIZING THAT THEY'VE MADE ONE SERIOUS MISTAKE...

The Great Age of Piracy

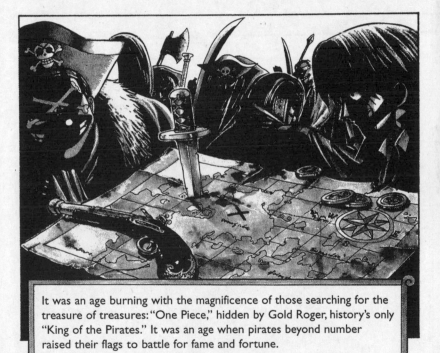

It was an age burning with the magnificence of those searching for the treasure of treasures: "One Piece," hidden by Gold Roger, history's only "King of the Pirates." It was an age when pirates beyond number raised their flags to battle for fame and fortune.

It was a Golden Age...

CHAPTER 8:

NAMI

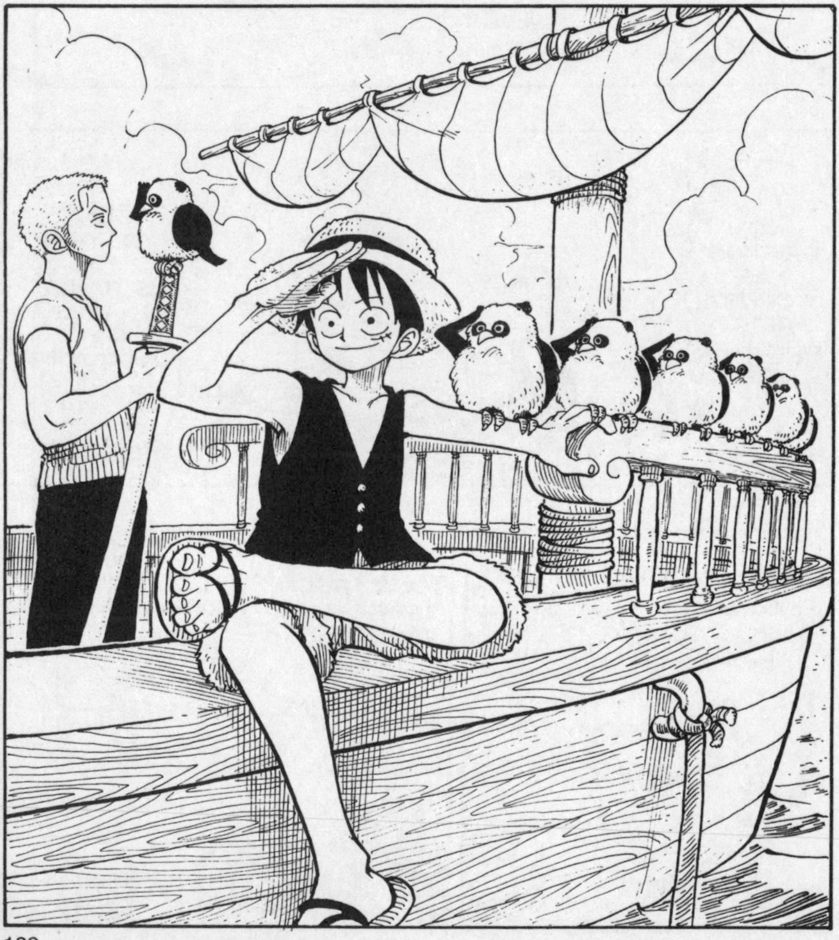

READ THIS WAY

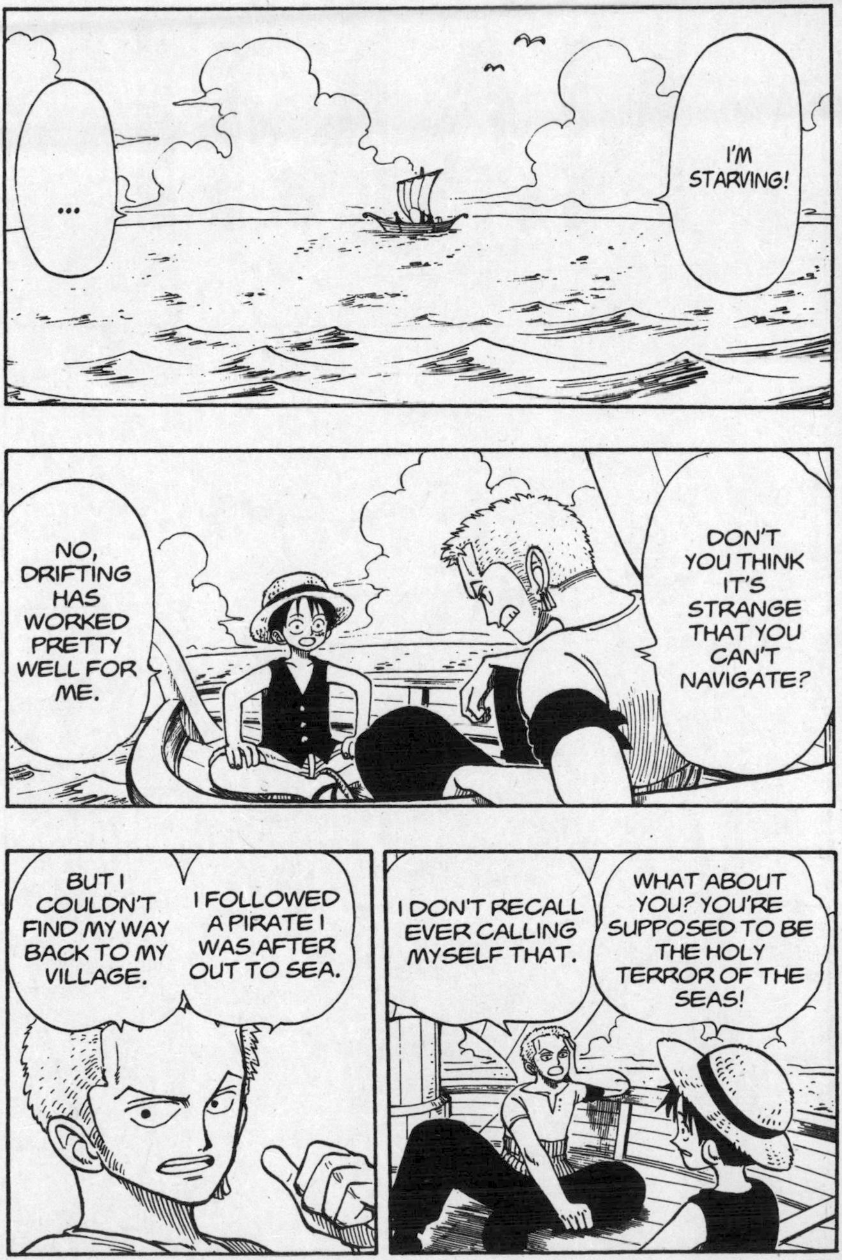
I'M STARVING!
...
DON'T YOU THINK IT'S STRANGE THAT YOU CAN'T NAVIGATE?
NO, DRIFTING HAS WORKED PRETTY WELL FOR ME.
WHAT ABOUT YOU? YOU'RE SUPPOSED TO BE THE HOLY TERROR OF THE SEAS!
I DON'T RECALL EVER CALLING MYSELF THAT.
I FOLLOWED A PIRATE I WAS AFTER OUT TO SEA.
BUT I COULDN'T FIND MY WAY BACK TO MY VILLAGE.

READ THIS WAY

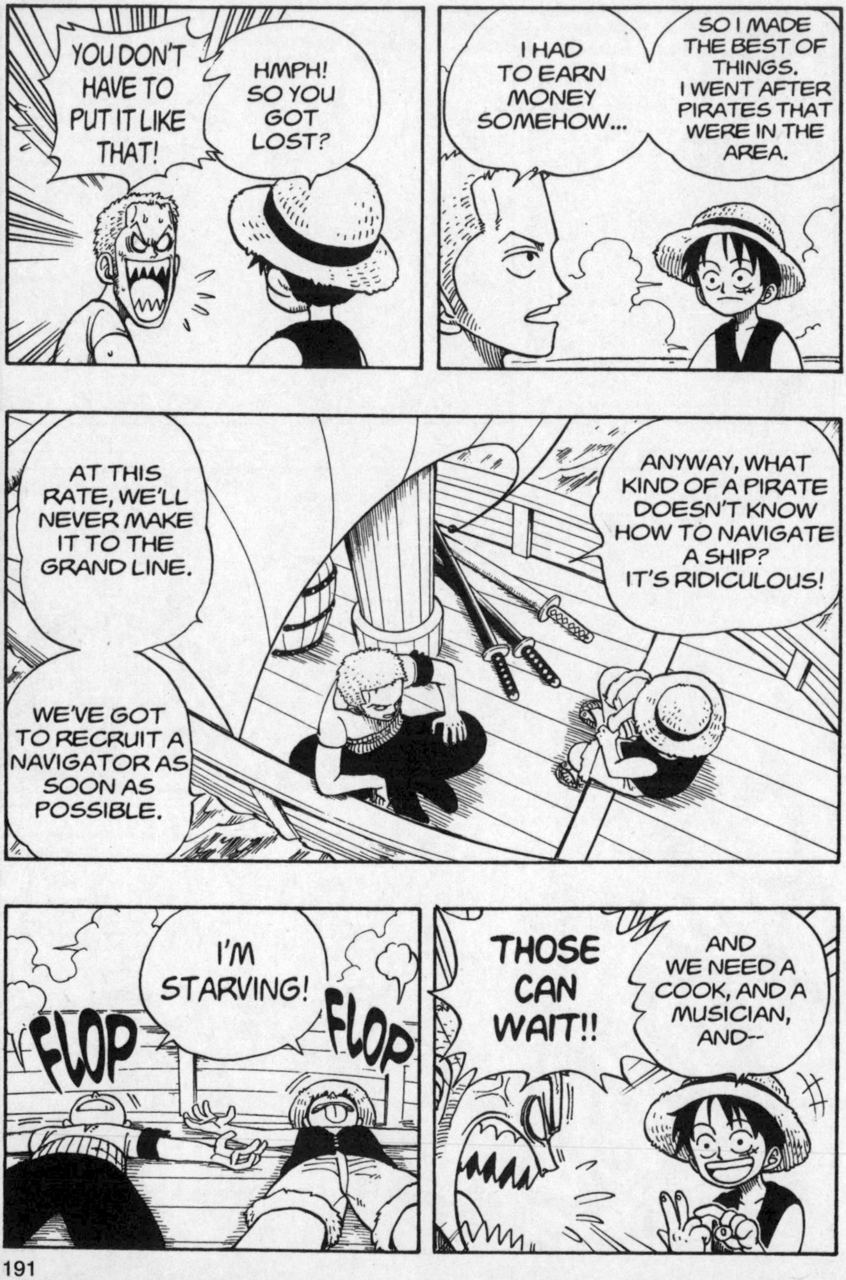
I HAD TO EARN MONEY SOMEHOW...
SO I MADE THE BEST OF THINGS. I WENT AFTER PIRATES THAT WERE IN THE AREA.
HMPH! SO YOU GOT LOST?
YOU DON'T HAVE TO PUT IT LIKE THAT!
ANYWAY, WHAT KIND OF A PIRATE DOESN'T KNOW HOW TO NAVIGATE A SHIP? IT'S RIDICULOUS!
AT THIS RATE, WE'LL NEVER MAKE IT TO THE GRAND LINE.
WE'VE GOT TO RECRUIT A NAVIGATOR AS SOON AS POSSIBLE.
AND WE NEED A COOK, AND A MUSICIAN, AND--
THOSE CAN WAIT!!
I'M STARVING!
FLOP
FLOP

READ THIS WAY

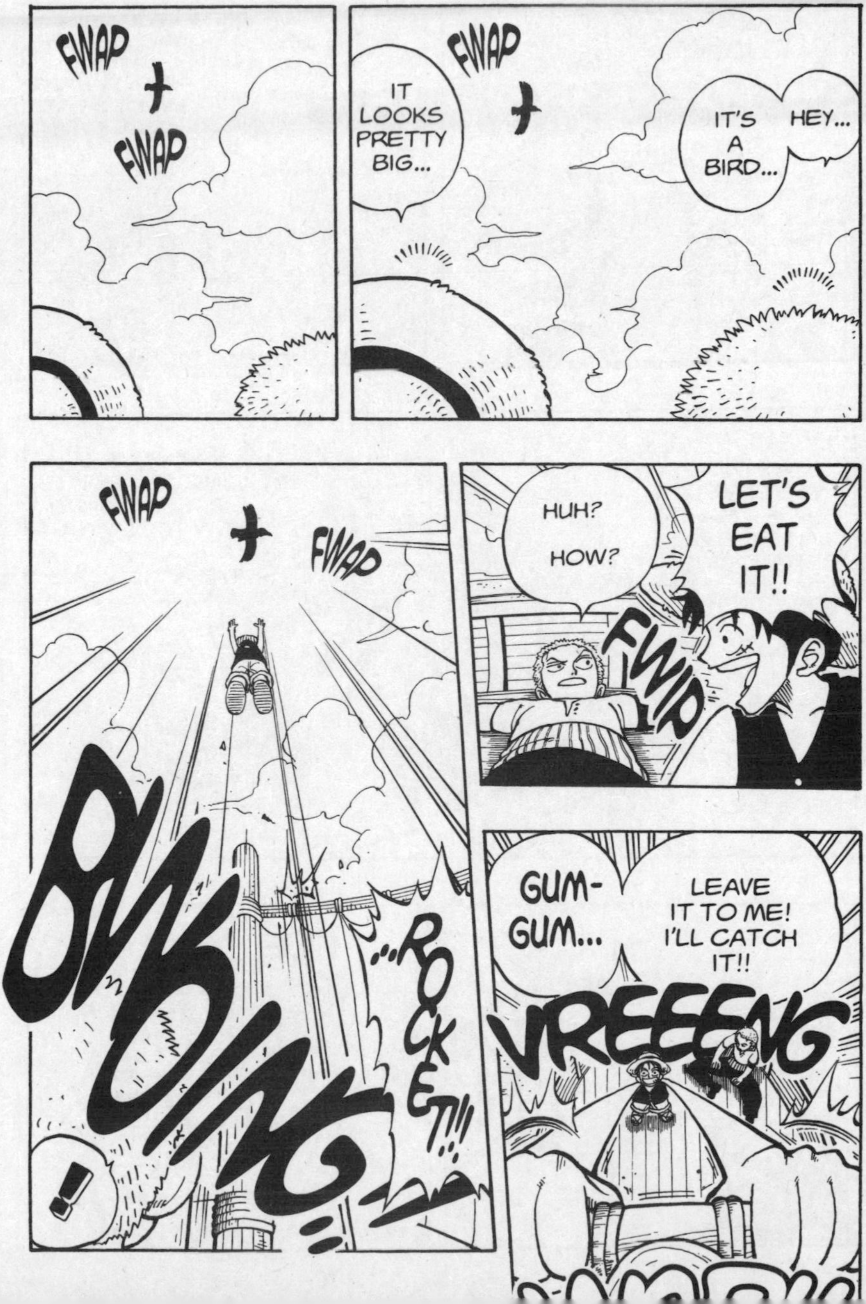
HEY...
IT'S A BIRD...
FWAP
IT LOOKS PRETTY BIG...
FWAP
FWAP
LET'S EAT IT!!
HUH? HOW?
FWIP
LEAVE IT TO ME! I'LL CATCH IT!!
GUM-GUM...
VREEENG
FWAP
FWAP
...ROCKET!!
BWOING!!
!

READ THIS WAY

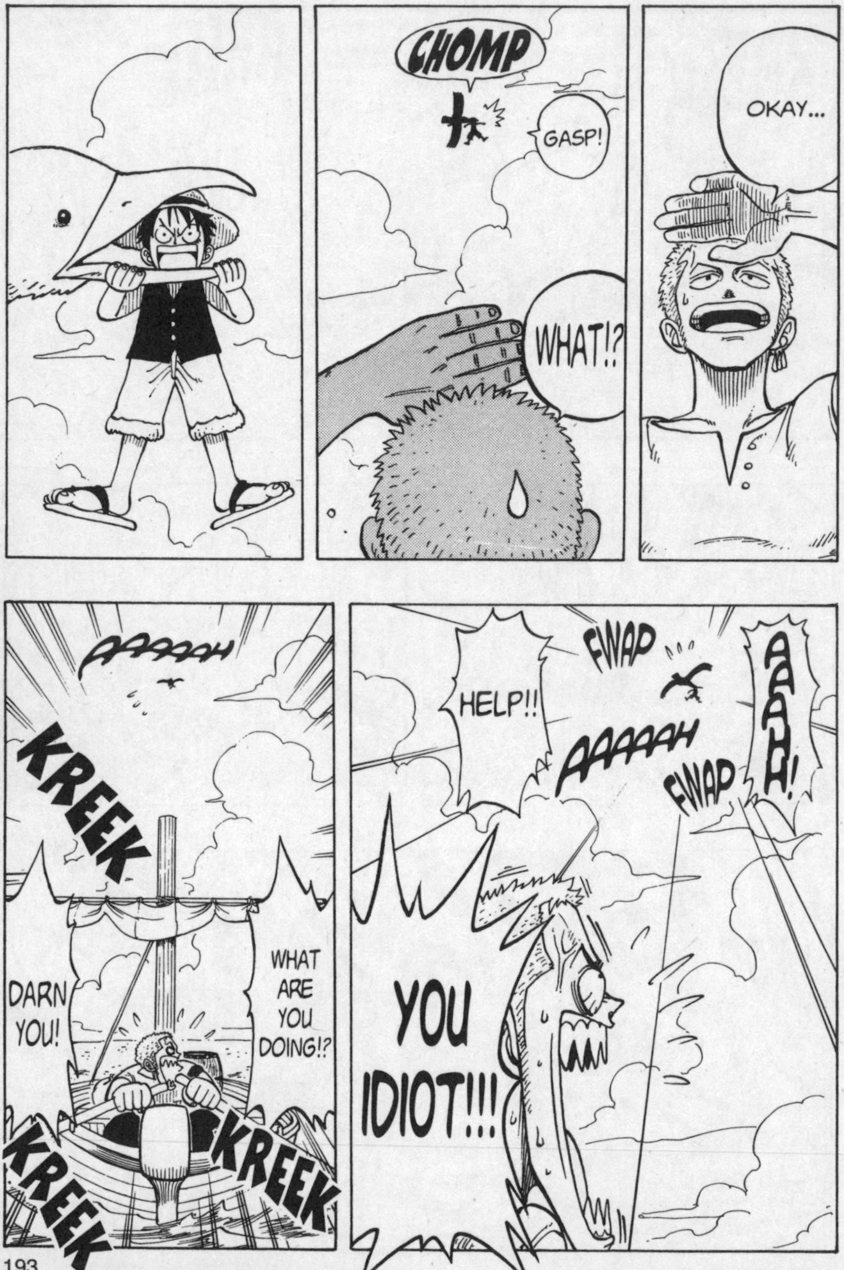

OKAY...
CHOMP
GASP!
WHAT!?
AAAAH!
FWAP
HELP!!
AAAAAH
FWAP
YOU IDIOT!!!
AAAAAH
KREEK
WHAT ARE YOU DOING!?
DARN YOU!
KREEK
KREEK

READ THIS WAY

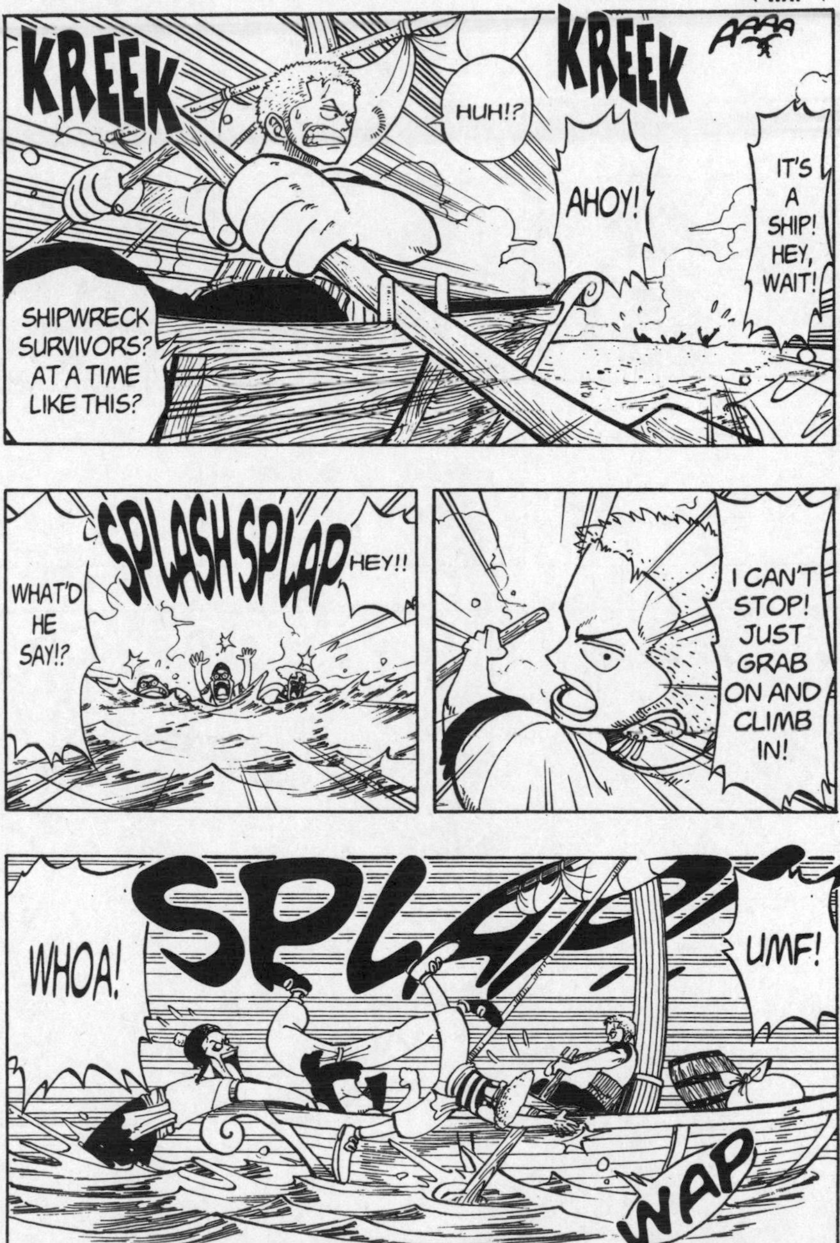
AAAA
IT'S A SHIP! HEY, WAIT!
KREEK
AHOY!
HUH!?
KREEK
SHIPWRECK SURVIVORS? AT A TIME LIKE THIS?
I CAN'T STOP! JUST GRAB ON AND CLIMB IN!
HEY!!
SPLASH SPLAP
WHAT'D HE SAY!?
UMF!
SPLAP
WHOA!
WAP

READ THIS WAY

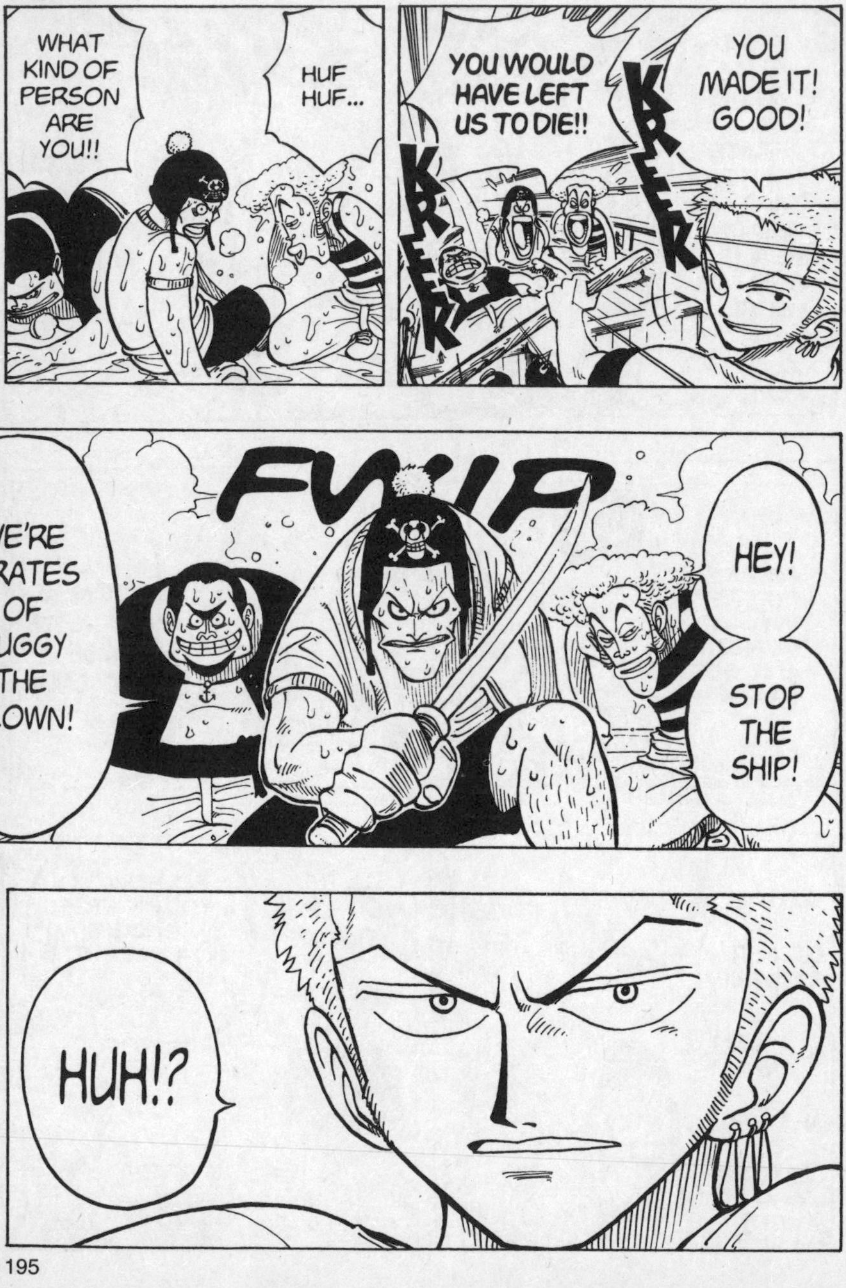
YOU MADE IT! GOOD!
KREEK
KREEK
YOU WOULD HAVE LEFT US TO DIE!!
HUF HUF...
WHAT KIND OF PERSON ARE YOU!!
HEY! STOP THE SHIP!
FWIP
WE'RE IRATES OF BUGGY THE CLOWN!
HUH!?

READ THIS WAY

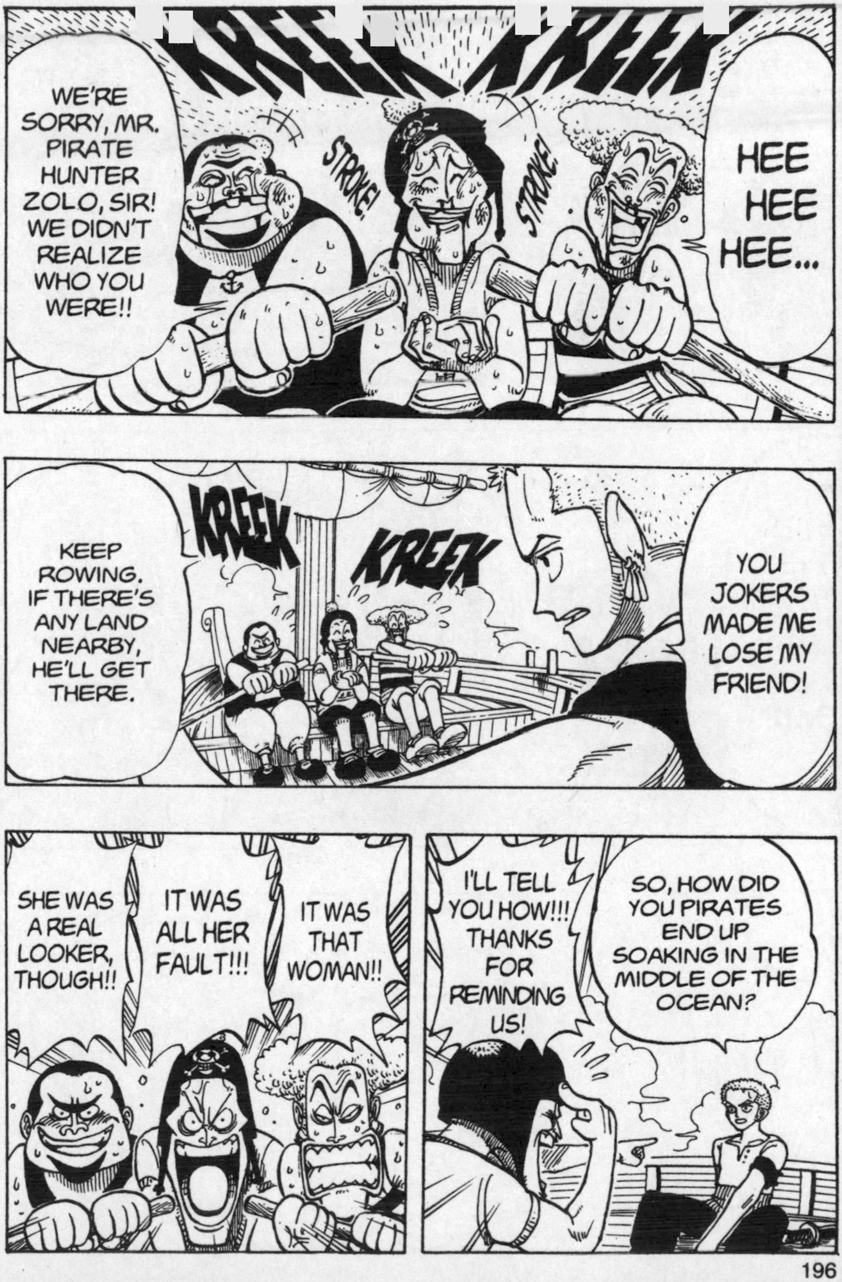
HEE HEE HEE...
STROKE!
STROKE!
KREEK KREEK
WE'RE SORRY, MR. PIRATE HUNTER ZOLO, SIR! WE DIDN'T REALIZE WHO YOU WERE!!
YOU JOKERS MADE ME LOSE MY FRIEND!
KREEK
KREEK
KEEP ROWING. IF THERE'S ANY LAND NEARBY, HE'LL GET THERE.
SO, HOW DID YOU PIRATES END UP SOAKING IN THE MIDDLE OF THE OCEAN?
I'LL TELL YOU HOW!!! THANKS FOR REMINDING US!
IT WAS THAT WOMAN!!
IT WAS ALL HER FAULT!!!
SHE WAS A REAL LOOKER, THOUGH!!

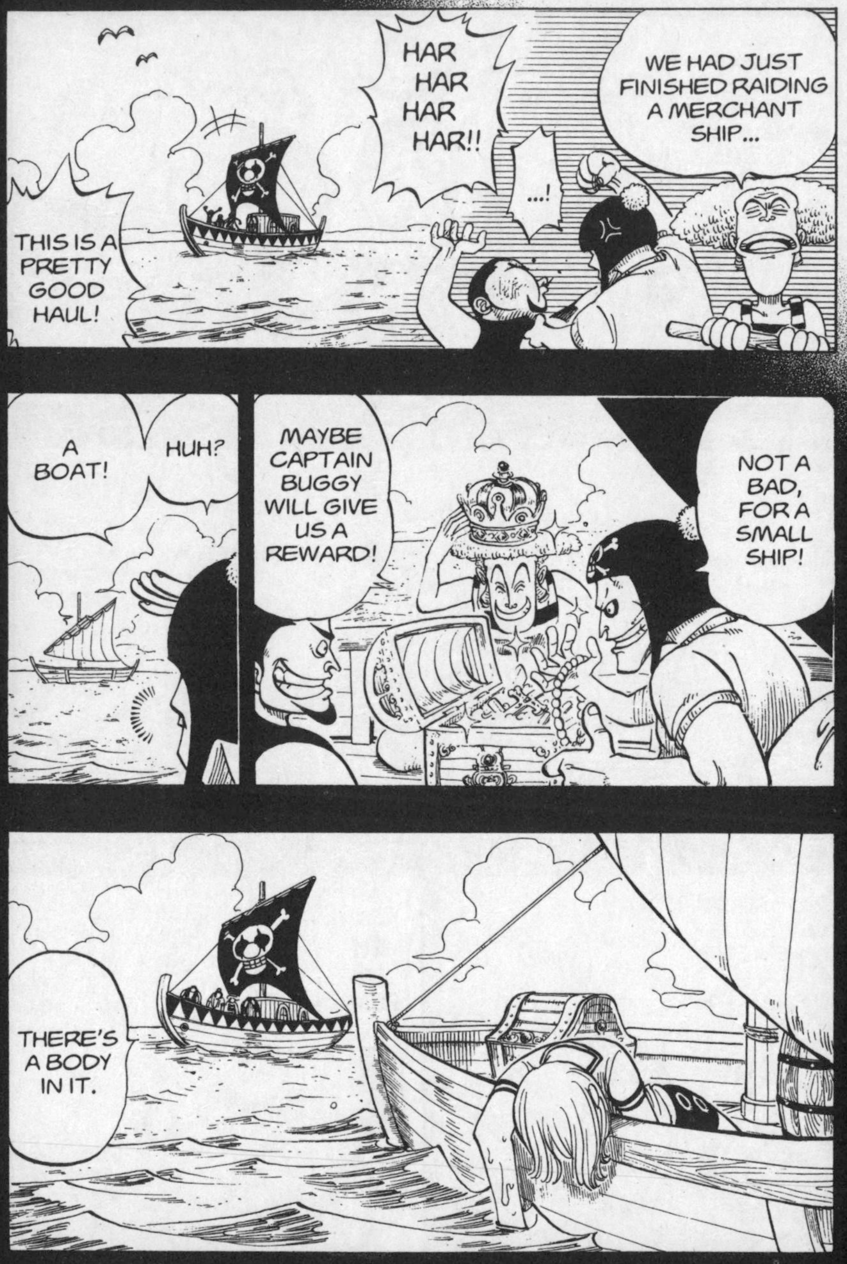
WE HAD JUST FINISHED RAIDING A MERCHANT SHIP...
...!
HAR HAR HAR HAR!!
THIS IS A PRETTY GOOD HAUL!
NOT A BAD, FOR A SMALL SHIP!
MAYBE CAPTAIN BUGGY WILL GIVE US A REWARD!
HUH?
A BOAT!
THERE'S A BODY IN IT.

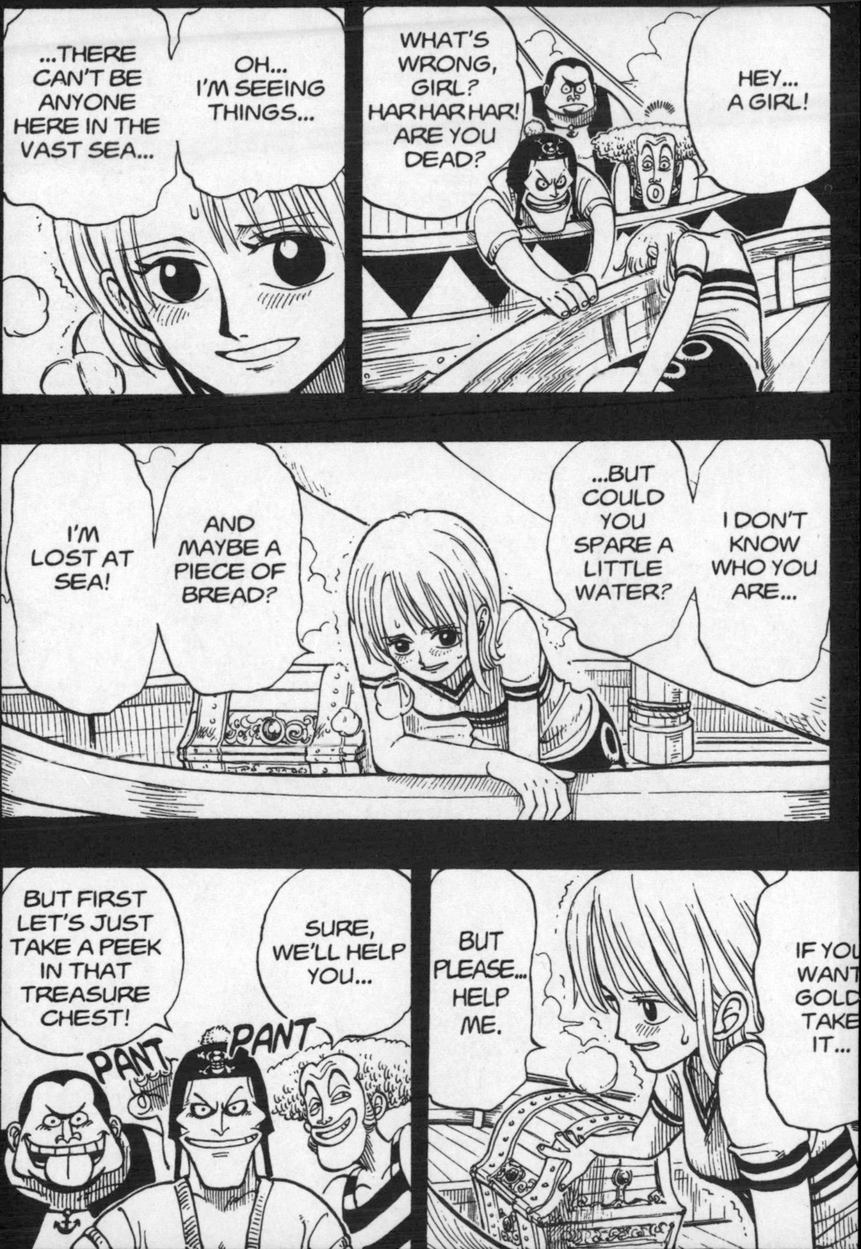
HEY... A GIRL!
WHAT'S WRONG, GIRL? HAR HAR HAR! ARE YOU DEAD?
OH... I'M SEEING THINGS...
...THERE CAN'T BE ANYONE HERE IN THE VAST SEA...
I DON'T KNOW WHO YOU ARE...
...BUT COULD YOU SPARE A LITTLE WATER?
AND MAYBE A PIECE OF BREAD?
I'M LOST AT SEA!
IF YO WANT GOLD TAKE IT...
BUT PLEASE... HELP ME.
SURE, WE'LL HELP YOU...
BUT FIRST LET'S JUST TAKE A PEEK IN THAT TREASURE CHEST!
PANT
PANT

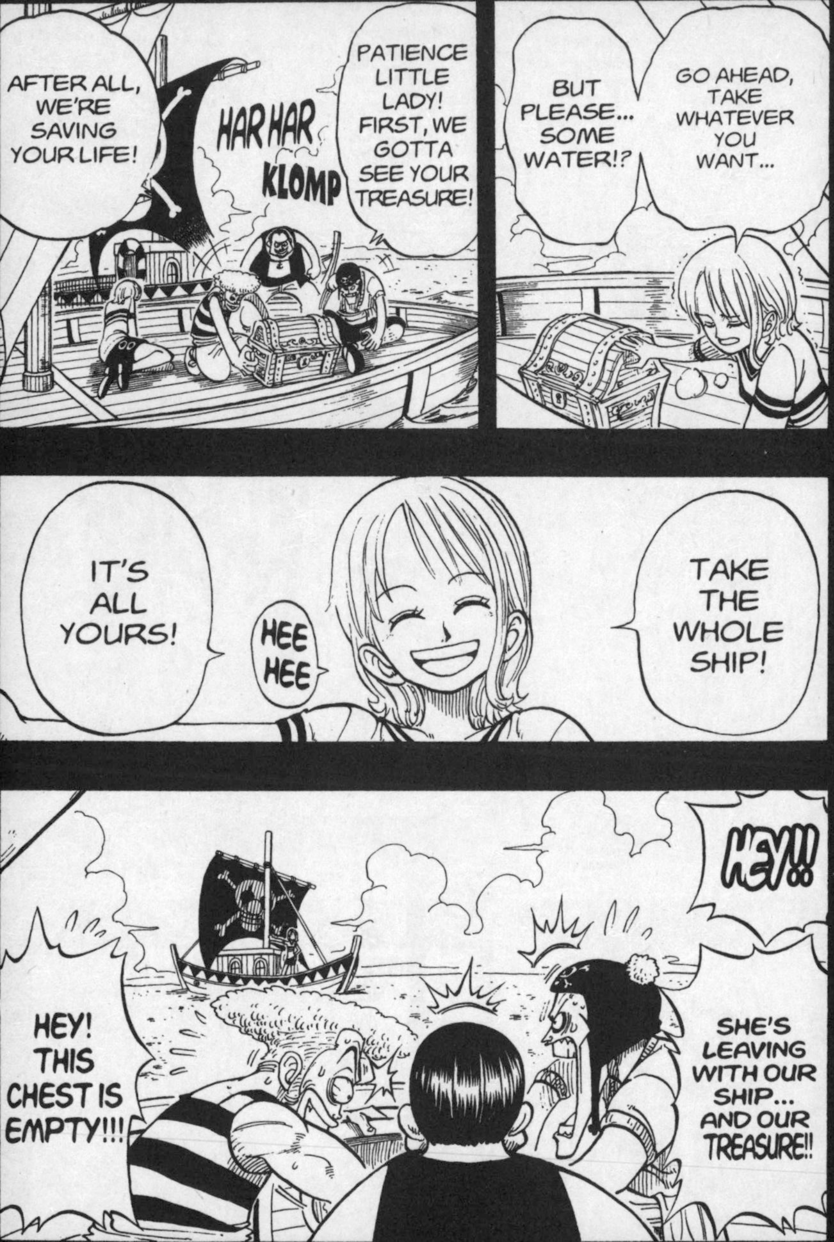
GO AHEAD, TAKE WHATEVER YOU WANT...
BUT PLEASE... SOME WATER!?
PATIENCE LITTLE LADY! FIRST, WE GOTTA SEE YOUR TREASURE!
HAR HAR
KLOMP
AFTER ALL, WE'RE SAVING YOUR LIFE!
TAKE THE WHOLE SHIP!
HEE HEE
IT'S ALL YOURS!
HEY!!
SHE'S LEAVING WITH OUR SHIP... AND OUR TREASURE!!
HEY! THIS CHEST IS EMPTY!!!

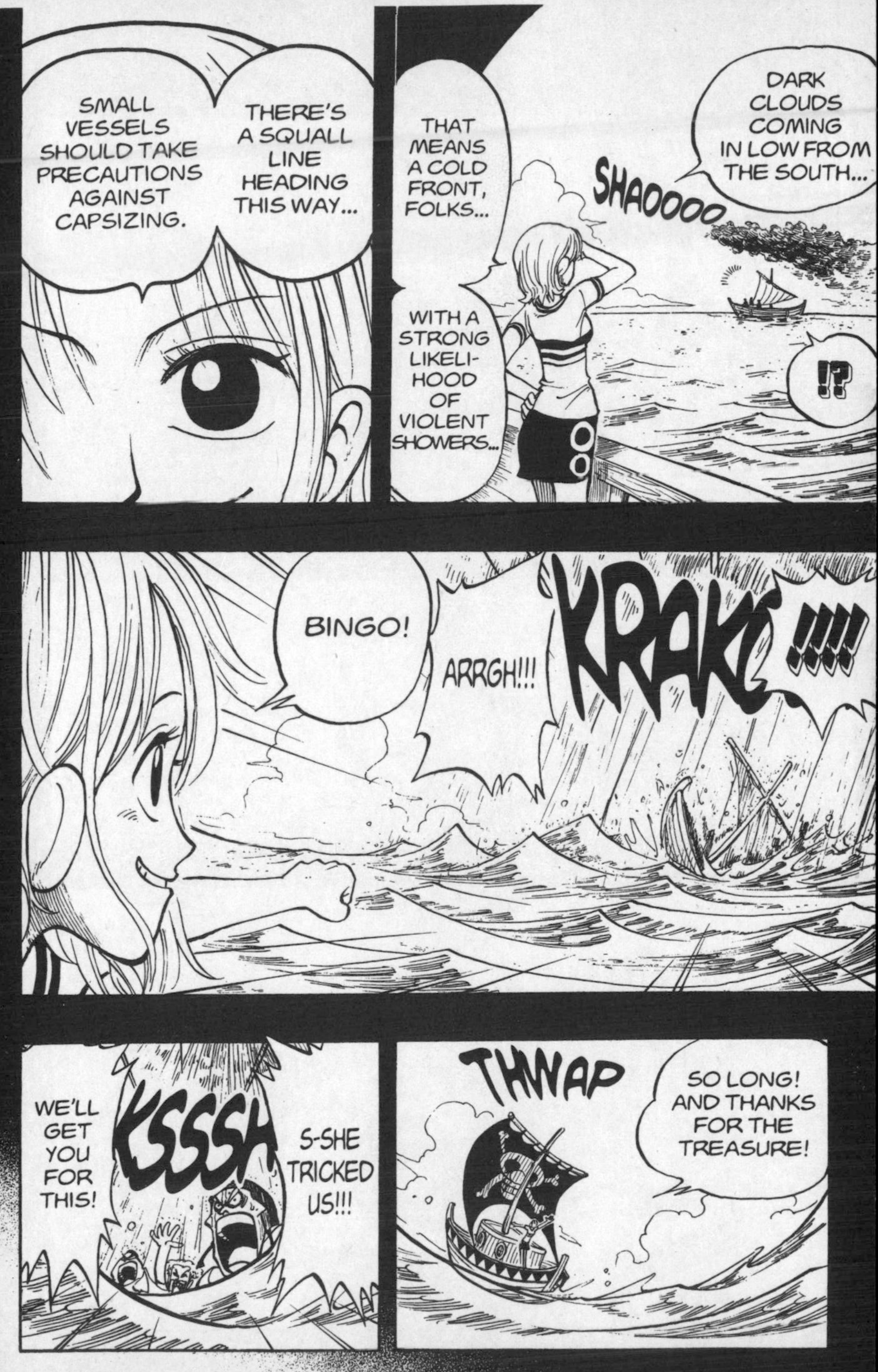
DARK CLOUDS COMING IN LOW FROM THE SOUTH...
SHAOOOO
!?
THAT MEANS A COLD FRONT, FOLKS...
WITH A STRONG LIKELI-HOOD OF VIOLENT SHOWERS...
THERE'S A SQUALL LINE HEADING THIS WAY...
SMALL VESSELS SHOULD TAKE PRECAUTIONS AGAINST CAPSIZING.
KRAKK!!!!
ARRGH!!!
BINGO!
THWAP
SO LONG! AND THANKS FOR THE TREASURE!
S-SHE TRICKED US!!!
KSSSH
WE'LL GET YOU FOR THIS!

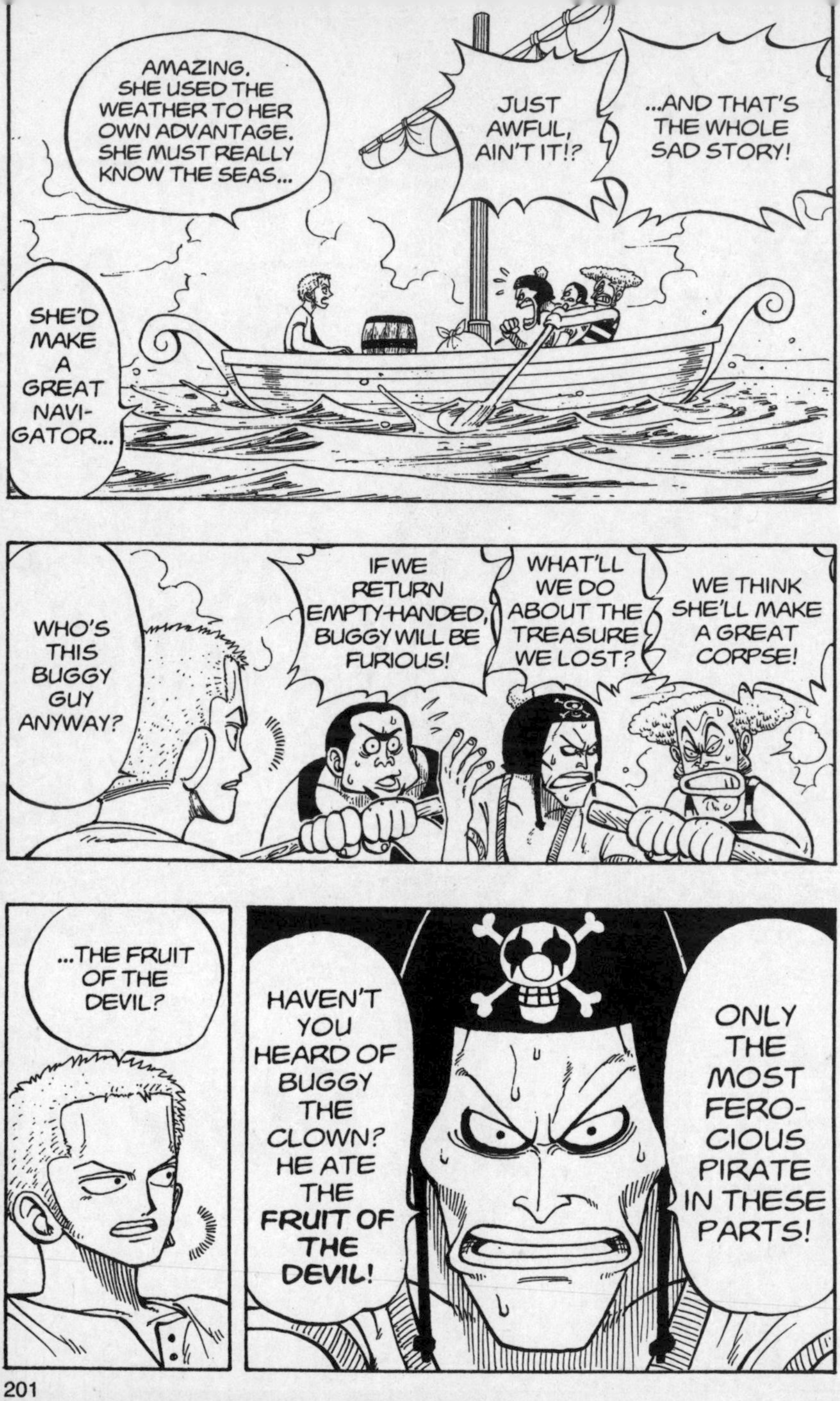
...AND THAT'S THE WHOLE SAD STORY!
JUST AWFUL, AIN'T IT!?
AMAZING. SHE USED THE WEATHER TO HER OWN ADVANTAGE. SHE MUST REALLY KNOW THE SEAS...
SHE'D MAKE A GREAT NAVI-GATOR...
WE THINK SHE'LL MAKE A GREAT CORPSE!
WHAT'LL WE DO ABOUT THE TREASURE WE LOST?
IF WE RETURN EMPTY-HANDED, BUGGY WILL BE FURIOUS!
WHO'S THIS BUGGY GUY ANYWAY?
ONLY THE MOST FERO-CIOUS PIRATE IN THESE PARTS!
HAVEN'T YOU HEARD OF BUGGY THE CLOWN? HE ATE THE **FRUIT OF THE DEVIL!**
...THE FRUIT OF THE DEVIL?

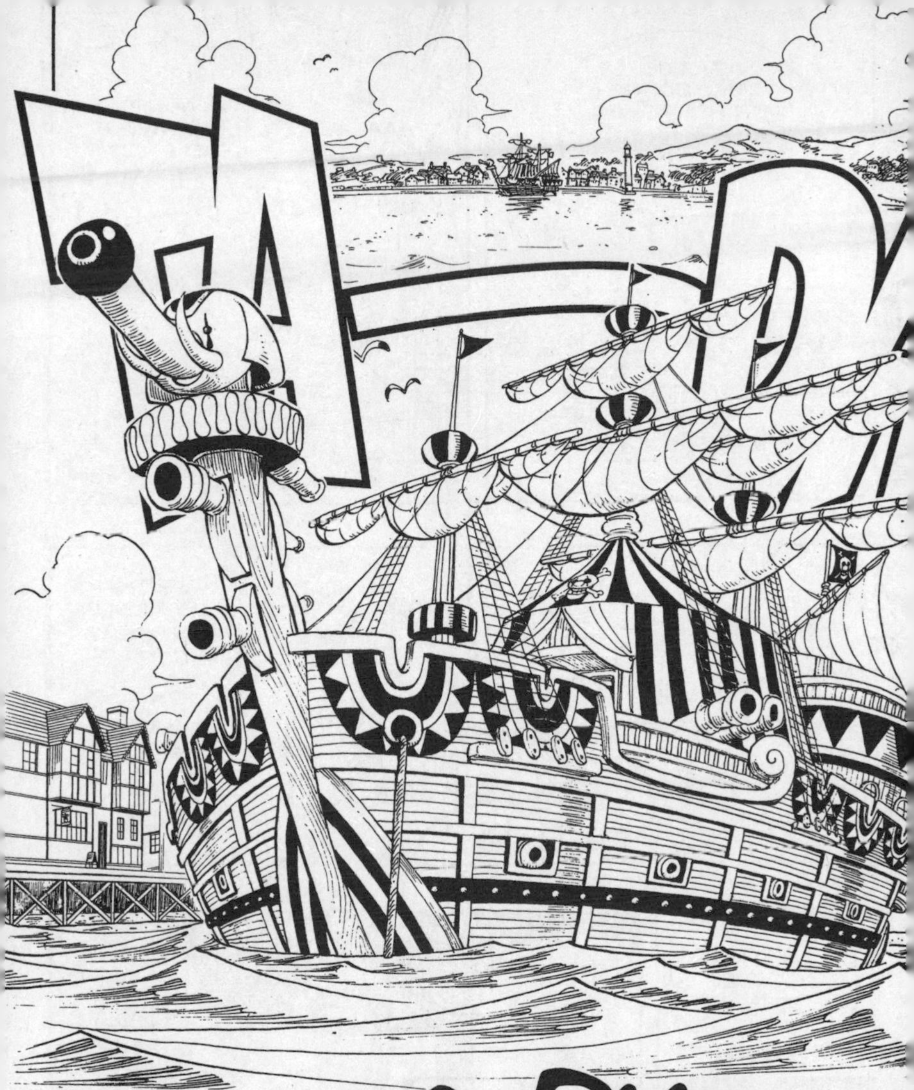

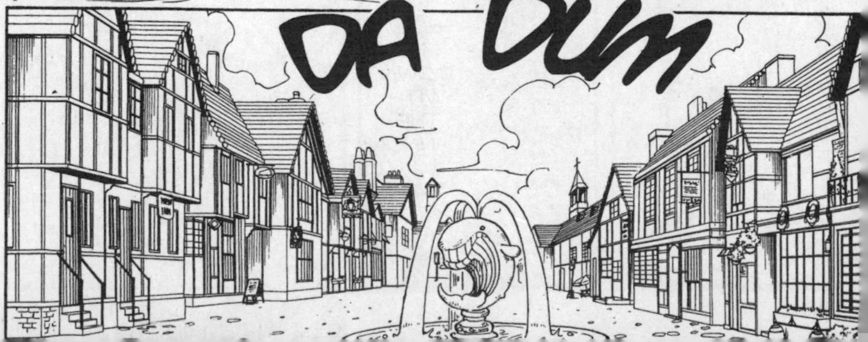
DA DUM

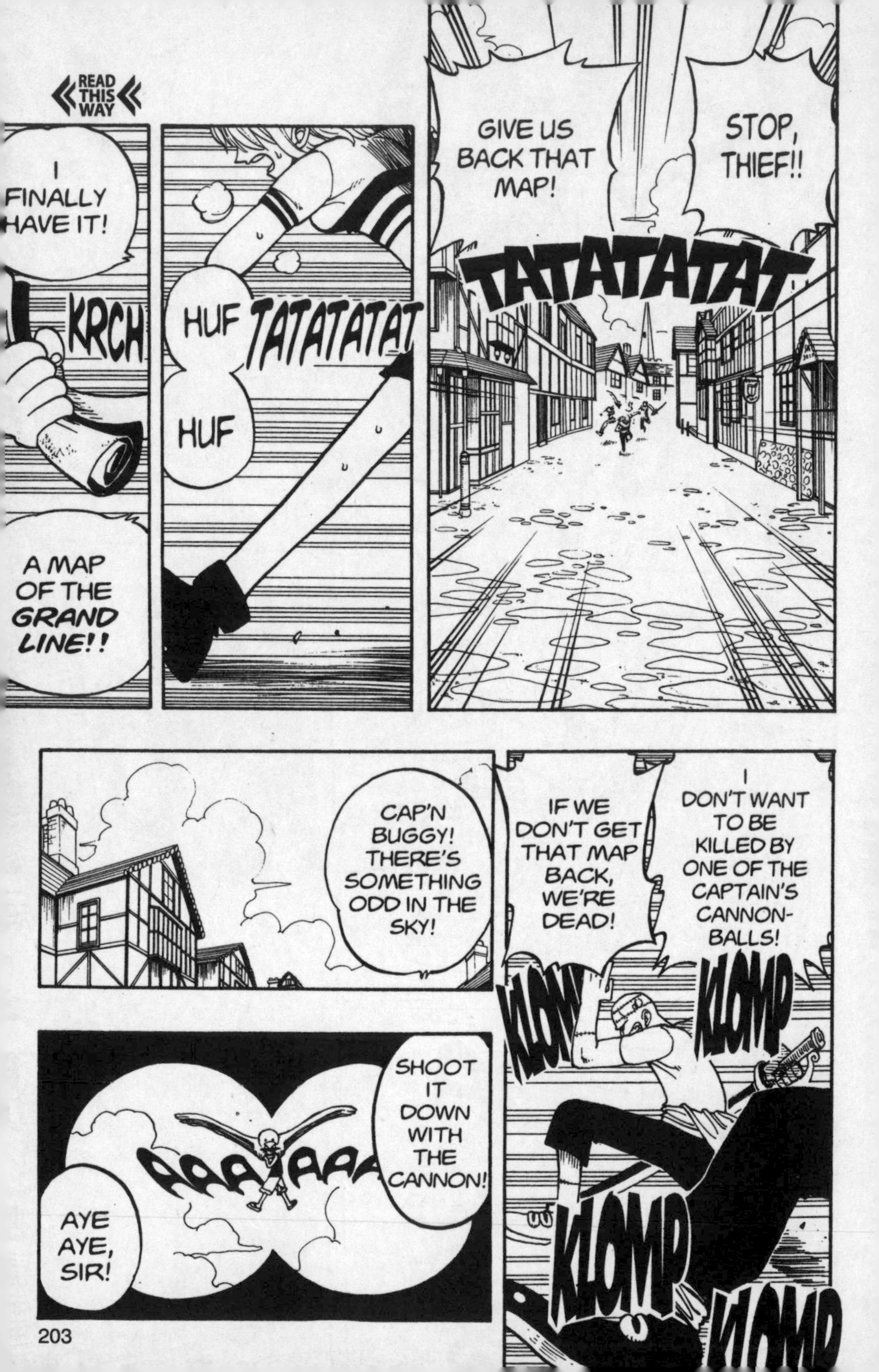
READ THIS WAY
STOP, THIEF!!
GIVE US BACK THAT MAP!
TATATATAT
HUF
HUF
TATATATAT
I FINALLY HAVE IT!
KRCH
A MAP OF THE GRAND LINE!!
I DON'T WANT TO BE KILLED BY ONE OF THE CAPTAIN'S CANNON-BALLS!
IF WE DON'T GET THAT MAP BACK, WE'RE DEAD!
KLOMP
KLOMP
CAP'N BUGGY! THERE'S SOMETHING ODD IN THE SKY!
SHOOT IT DOWN WITH THE CANNON!
AYE AYE, SIR!

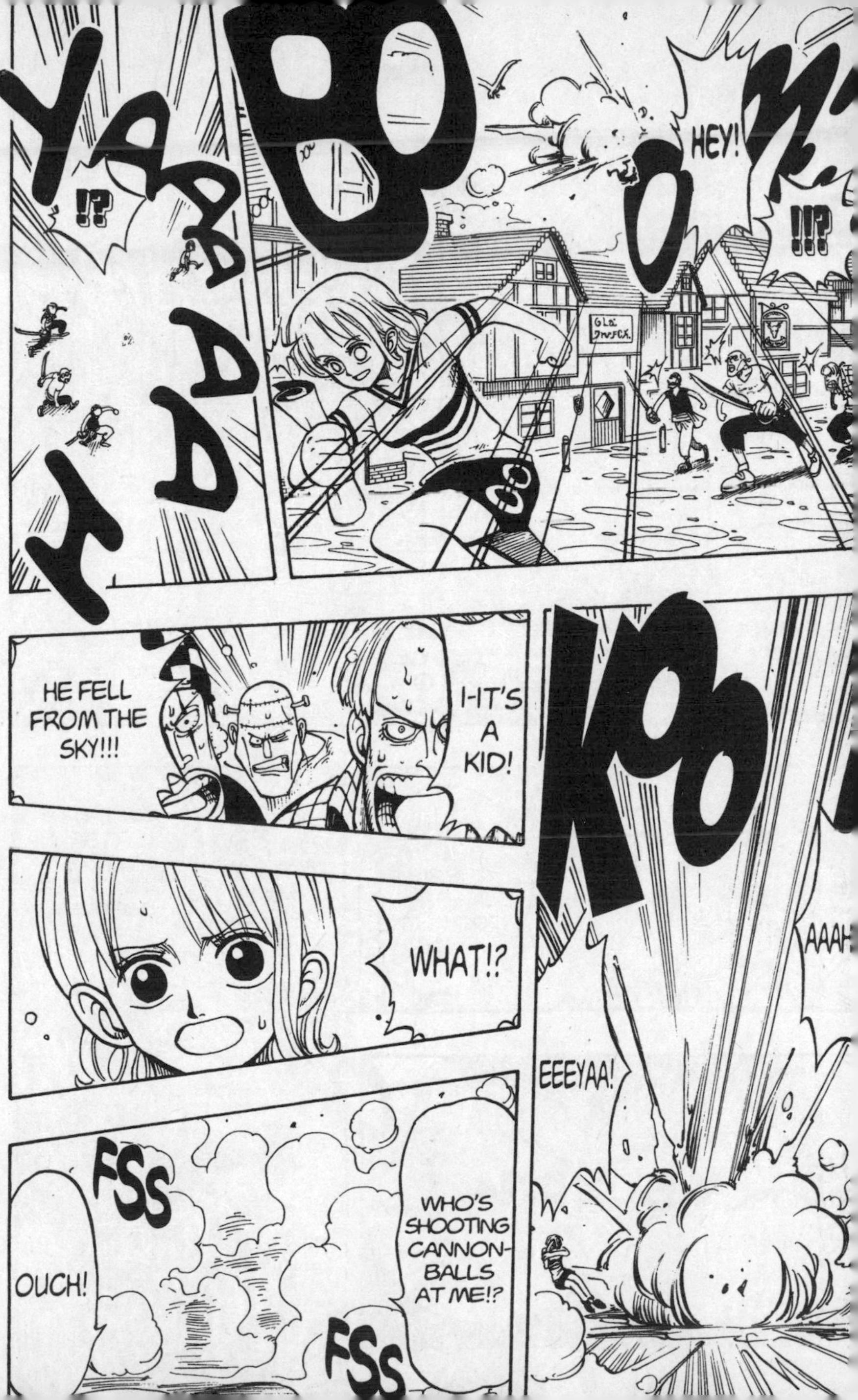
HEY!
!!?
!?
KBOO
AAAH
EEEYAA!
I-IT'S A KID!
HE FELL FROM THE SKY!!!
WHAT!?
WHO'S SHOOTING CANNON-BALLS AT ME!?
FSS
FSS
OUCH!

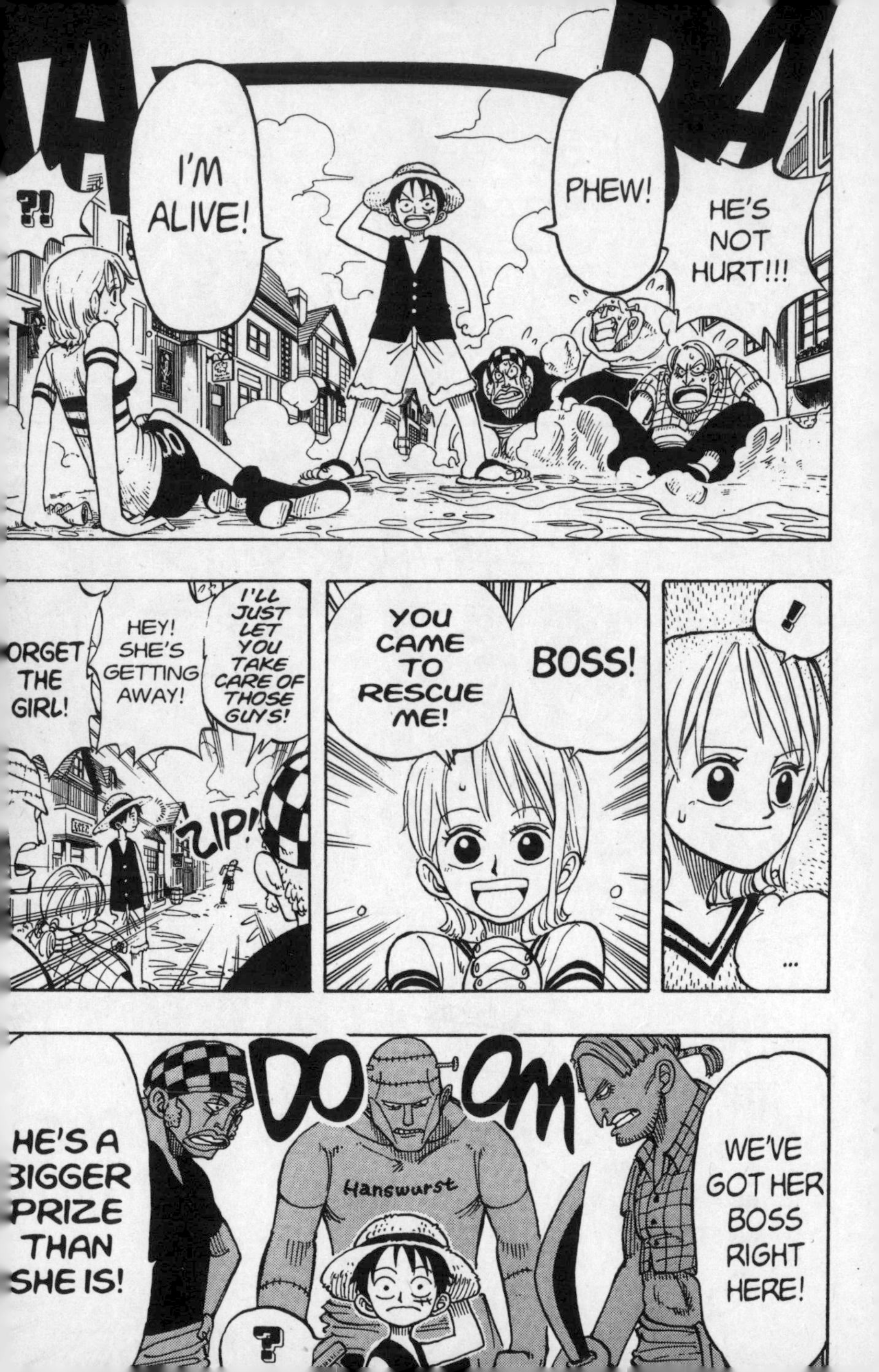
HE'S NOT HURT!!!
PHEW!
I'M ALIVE!
?!
!
...
BOSS!
YOU CAME TO RESCUE ME!
I'LL JUST LET YOU TAKE CARE OF THOSE GUYS!
ZIP!
HEY! SHE'S GETTING AWAY!
ORGET THE GIRL!
WE'VE GOT HER BOSS RIGHT HERE!
DOOM
Hanswurst
HE'S A BIGGER PRIZE THAN SHE IS!
?

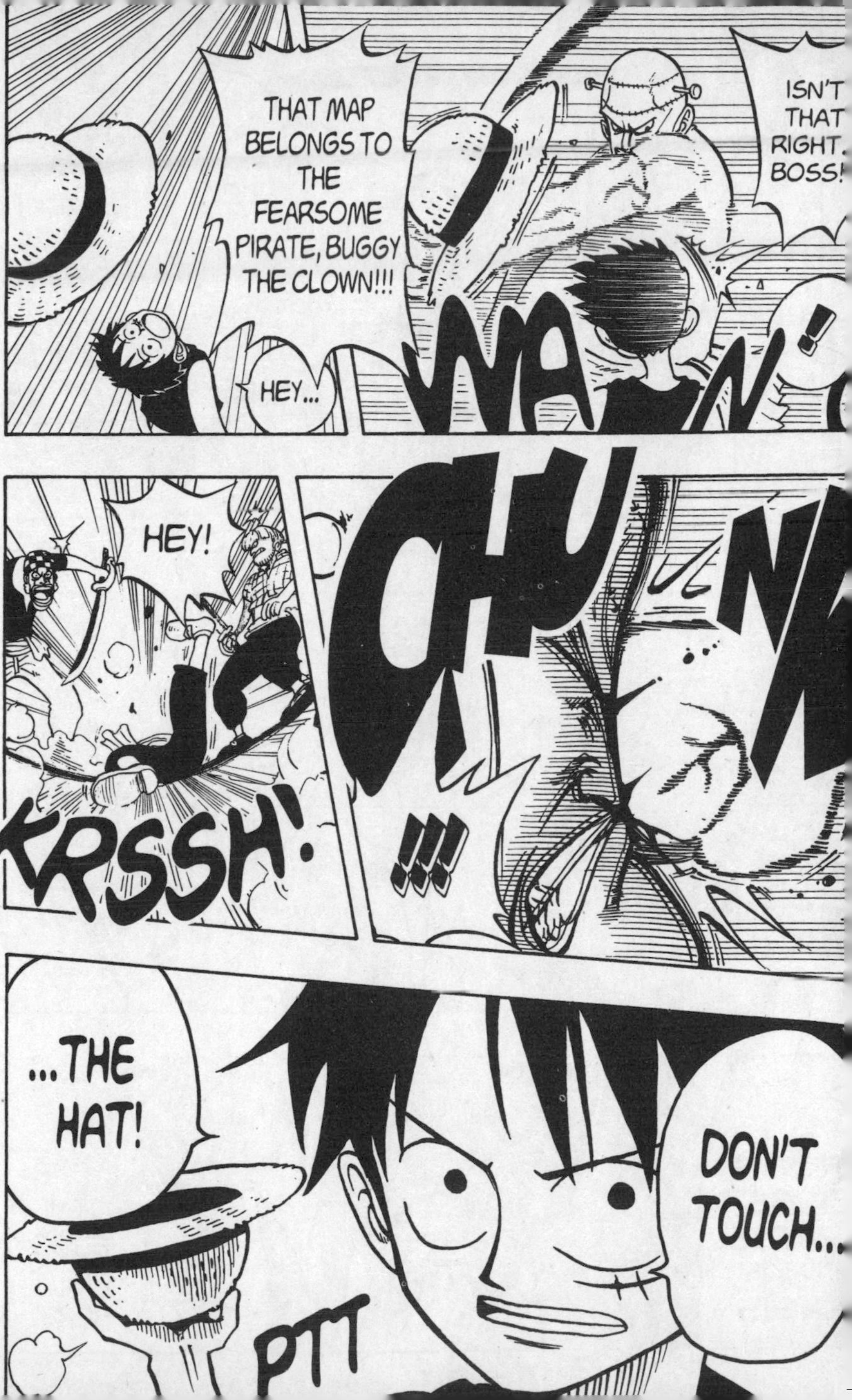
ISN'T THAT RIGHT. BOSS!
THAT MAP BELONGS TO THE FEARSOME PIRATE, BUGGY THE CLOWN!!!
WAN!
HEY...
CHUNK!!!
HEY!
KRSSH!
DON'T TOUCH...
...THE HAT!
PTT

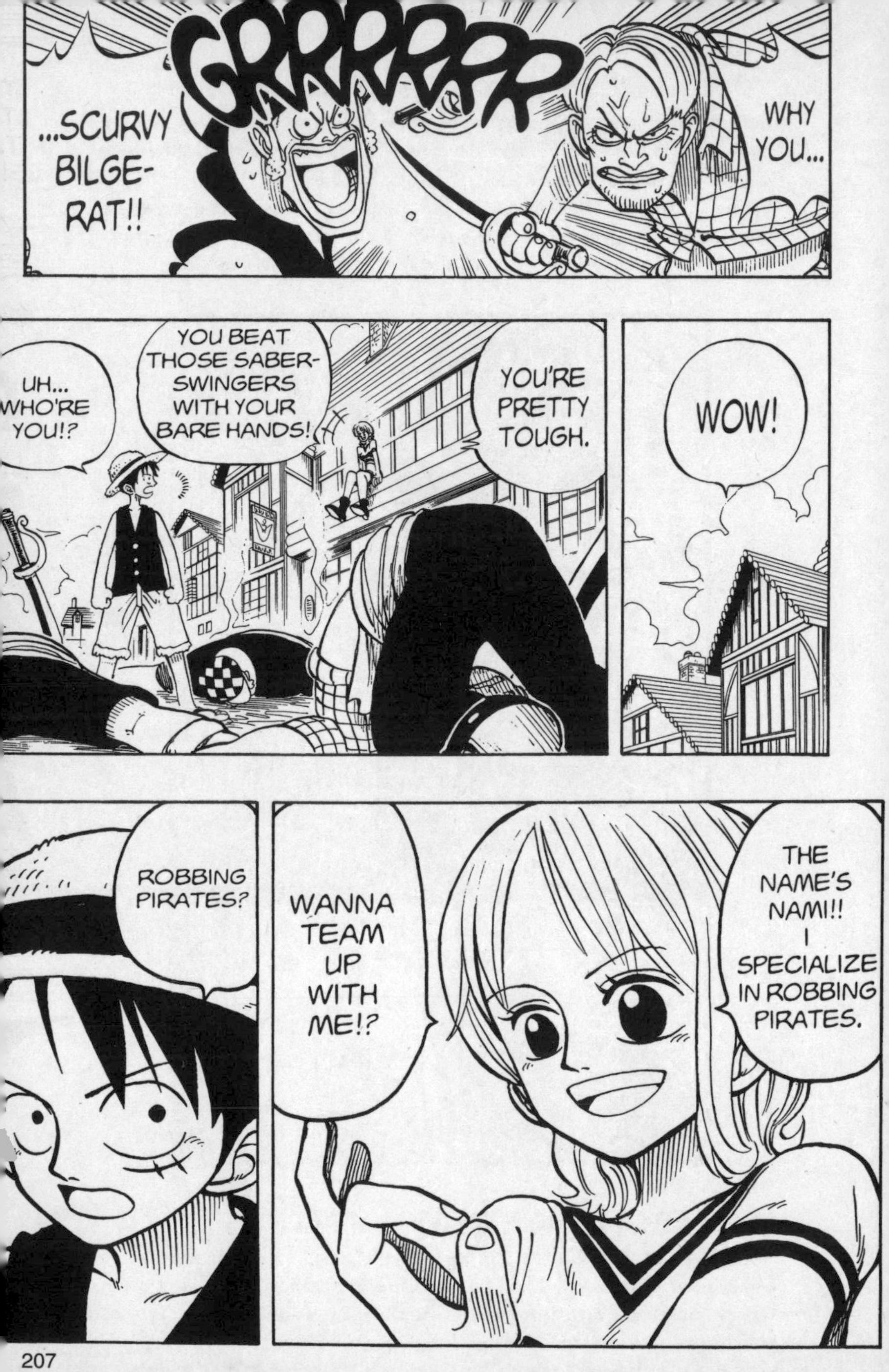
GRRRRRR
WHY YOU...
...SCURVY BILGE-RAT!!
WOW!
YOU'RE PRETTY TOUGH.
YOU BEAT THOSE SABER-SWINGERS WITH YOUR BARE HANDS!
UH... WHO'RE YOU!?
THE NAME'S NAMI!! I SPECIALIZE IN ROBBING PIRATES.
WANNA TEAM UP WITH ME!?
ROBBING PIRATES?

THE MAKING OF ONE PIECE

Before creating the final version of **One Piece** printed in this graphic novel, Eiichiro Oda drew two early one-shot stories starring Luffy, under the title **Romance Dawn** (the same title used for chapter 1 of the final version). These stories aren't part of the plot of **One Piece**—they're like "alternate universe" versions telling a similar story of Luffy's origin. Here's a page from each of the untranslated early versions.

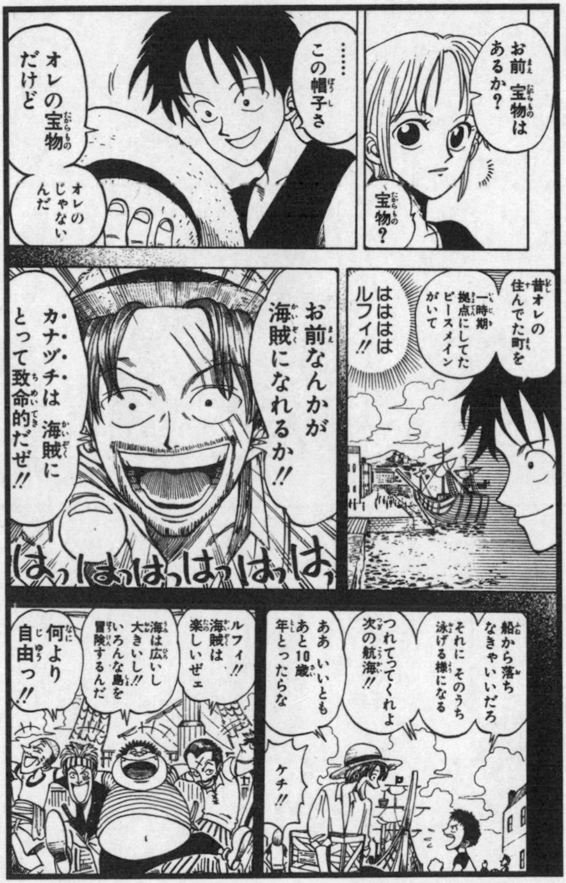

お前 宝物はあるか?
宝物?
……この帽子さ
オレの宝物だけど
オレのじゃないんだ
昔オレの住んでた町を
一時期拠点にしてたピースメインがいて
ははは ルフィ!!
お前なんかが海賊になれるか!!
カ・ナ・ヅ・チは 海賊にとって致命的だぜ!!
はっはっはっはっはっは
船から落ちなきゃいいだろ それに そのうち泳げる様になる
つれてってくれよ次の航海!!
ああ いいとも あと10歳年とったらな
ケチ!!
ルフィ!! 海賊は楽しいぜェ
海は広いし大きいし!! いろんな島を冒険するんだ
何より自由っ!!

ROMANCE DAWN: VERSION 1

Drawn about a year and a half before **One Piece** began, this version was printed in one of the **Shonen Jump Specials** showcasing upcoming artists. In it, Luffy fights a pirate named Jolly of the Crescent Moon. Luffy's origin is the same as in **One Piece**—he gets his treasured straw hat from his idol, Shanks.

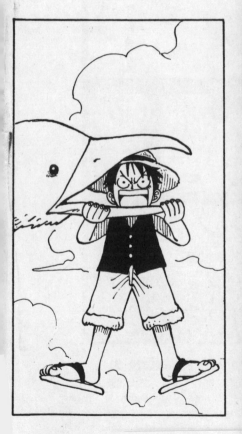

FACTS ABOUT EIICHIRO ODA
Creator, Artist and Author o
One Piece

Birthdate:
January 1, 1975
Greek Astrological Sign:
Capricorn
Chinese Astrological Sign
Rabbit
Blood Type:
A
Favorite Animals:
Big, gentle dogs
Favorite Video Game:
Puyo Puyo
Favorite Music:
'70s soul music
Hidden Talent:
Makes good coffee
Places He's Been:
Japan, America
Favorite Real-Life Pirate
Blackbeard (Edward Teach)
Interesting Possessions:
Legos, Playmobil, figures,
swords, flintlocks, a cow sku

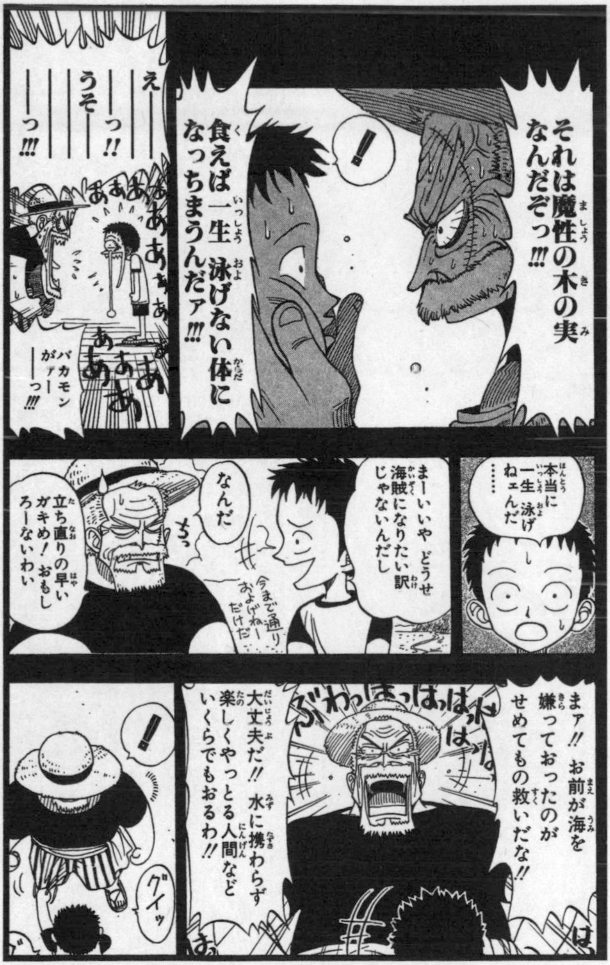
それは魔性の木の実なんだぞっ!!!
!
食えば一生泳げない体になっちまうんだァ!!!
えーーっ!! うそーーっ!!!
ああああああああああああ
バカモンがァーーっ!!!
本当に一生泳げねェんだ……
まーいいや どうせ海賊になりたい訳じゃないんだし
今まで通りおよげねーだけだ
なんだ
ちっ
立ち直りの早いガキめ! おもしろーないわい
まァ!! お前が海を嫌っておったのがせめてもの救いだな!!
ぶわっはっはっはっはっ
大丈夫だ!! 水に携わらず楽しくやっとる人間などいくらでもおるわ!!
!
グイッ

ROMANCE DAWN: VERSION 2

Now the art is more like **One Piece**. Printed as a one-shot in **Weekly Shonen Jump** itself, this version changes Luffy's origin: he gets the Gum-Gum Fruit, and his straw hat, from his grandfather. Oda's explanation: "I didn't want the readers of **Weekly Shonen Jump** to find out about the existence of Shanks because when serialization started, it would lose its impact. Yes, I am a cheeky new artist." In it, Luffy fights a pirate captain who uses magic, a plot element absent from **One Piece** itself.

DRAGON BALL SUPER

STORY BY **Akira Toriyama** ART BY **Toyotarou**

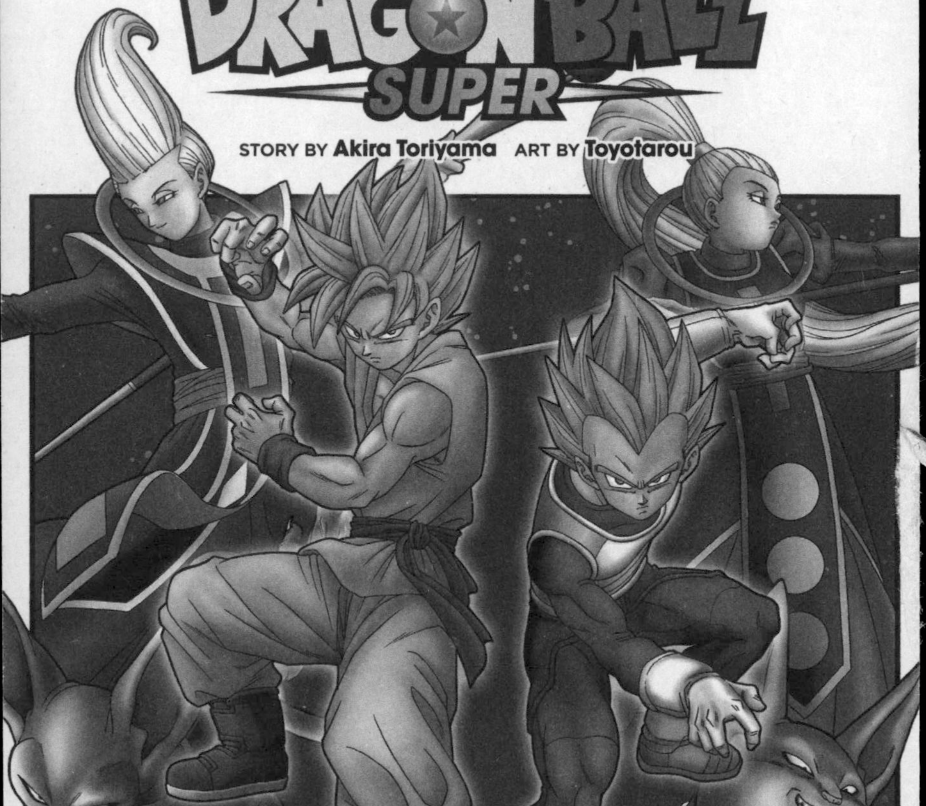

Goku's adventure from the best-selling classic manga *Dragon Ball* continues in this new series written by Akira Toriyama himself!

Ever since Goku became Earth's greatest hero and gathered the seven Dragon Balls to defeat the evil Boo, his life on Earth has grown a little dull. But new threats loom overhead, and Goku and his friends will have to defend the planet once again!

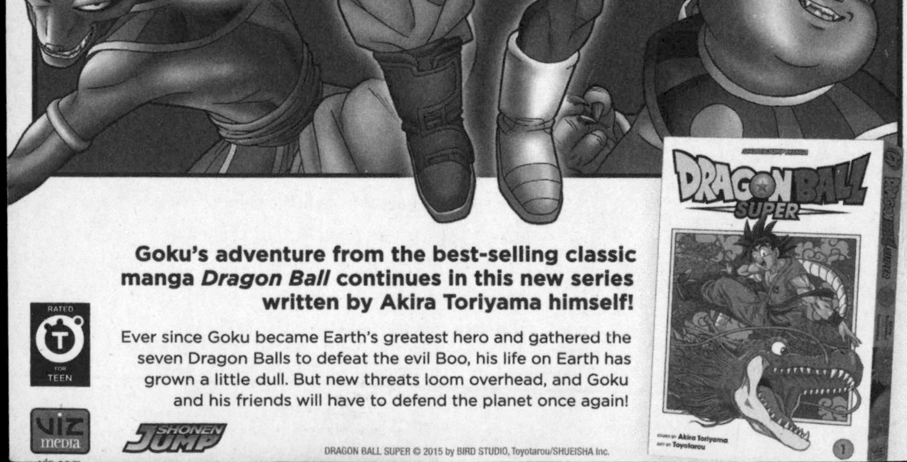
DRAGON BALL SUPER
Akira Toriyama
Toyotarou
1

RATED T FOR TEEN

VIZ media

SHONEN JUMP

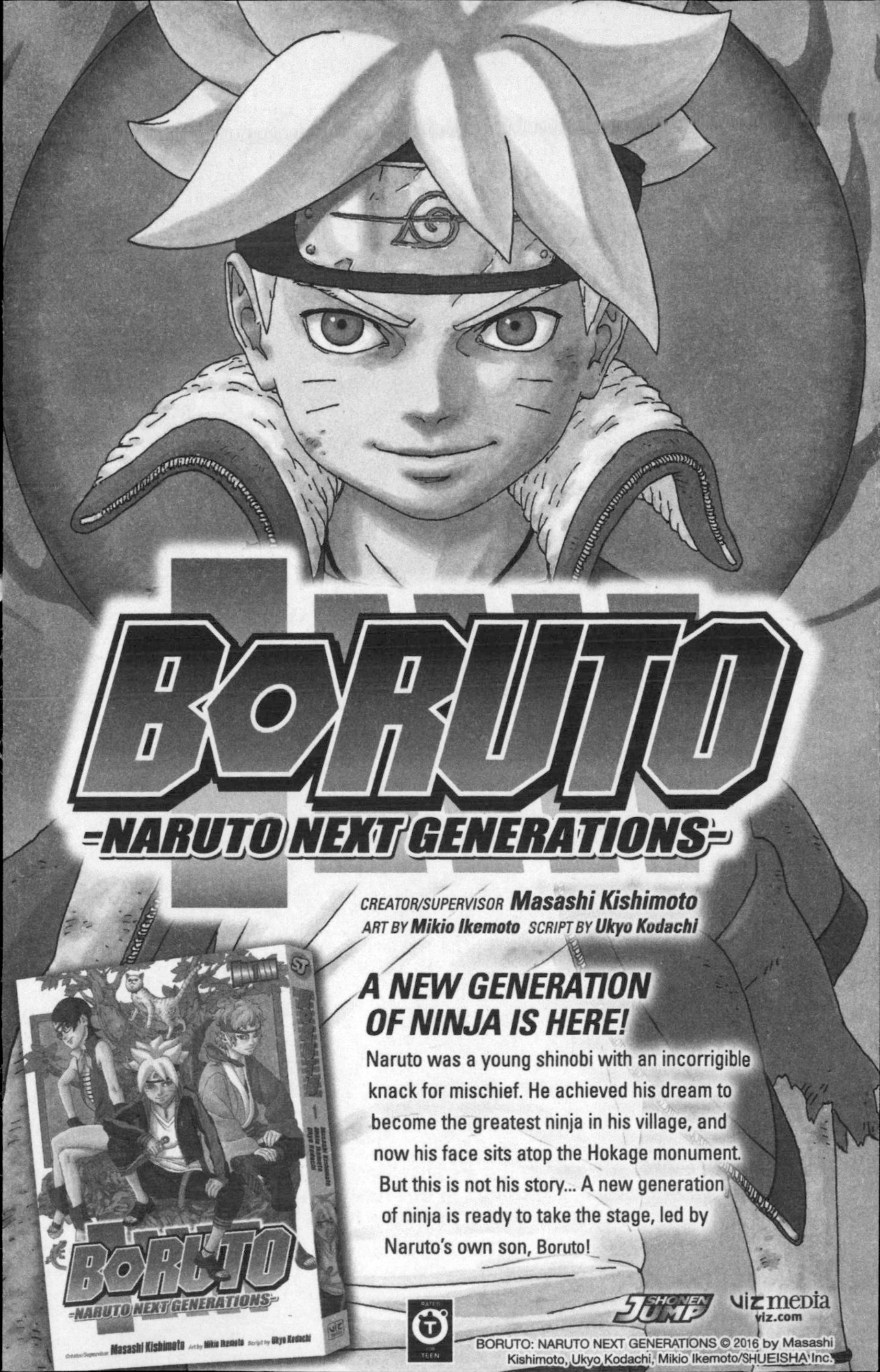
BORUTO
-NARUTO NEXT GENERATIONS-
CREATOR/SUPERVISOR Masashi Kishimoto
ART BY Mikio Ikemoto SCRIPT BY Ukyo Kodachi
A NEW GENERATION OF NINJA IS HERE!
Naruto was a young shinobi with an incorrigible knack for mischief. He achieved his dream to become the greatest ninja in his village, and now his face sits atop the Hokage monument. But this is not his story... A new generation of ninja is ready to take the stage, led by Naruto's own son, Boruto!
BORUTO
-NARUTO NEXT GENERATIONS-
Masashi Kishimoto
SHONEN JUMP
viz media
viz.com
BORUTO: NARUTO NEXT GENERATIONS © 2016 by Masashi Kishimoto, Ukyo Kodachi, Mikio Ikemoto/SHUEISHA Inc.

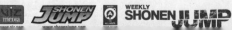

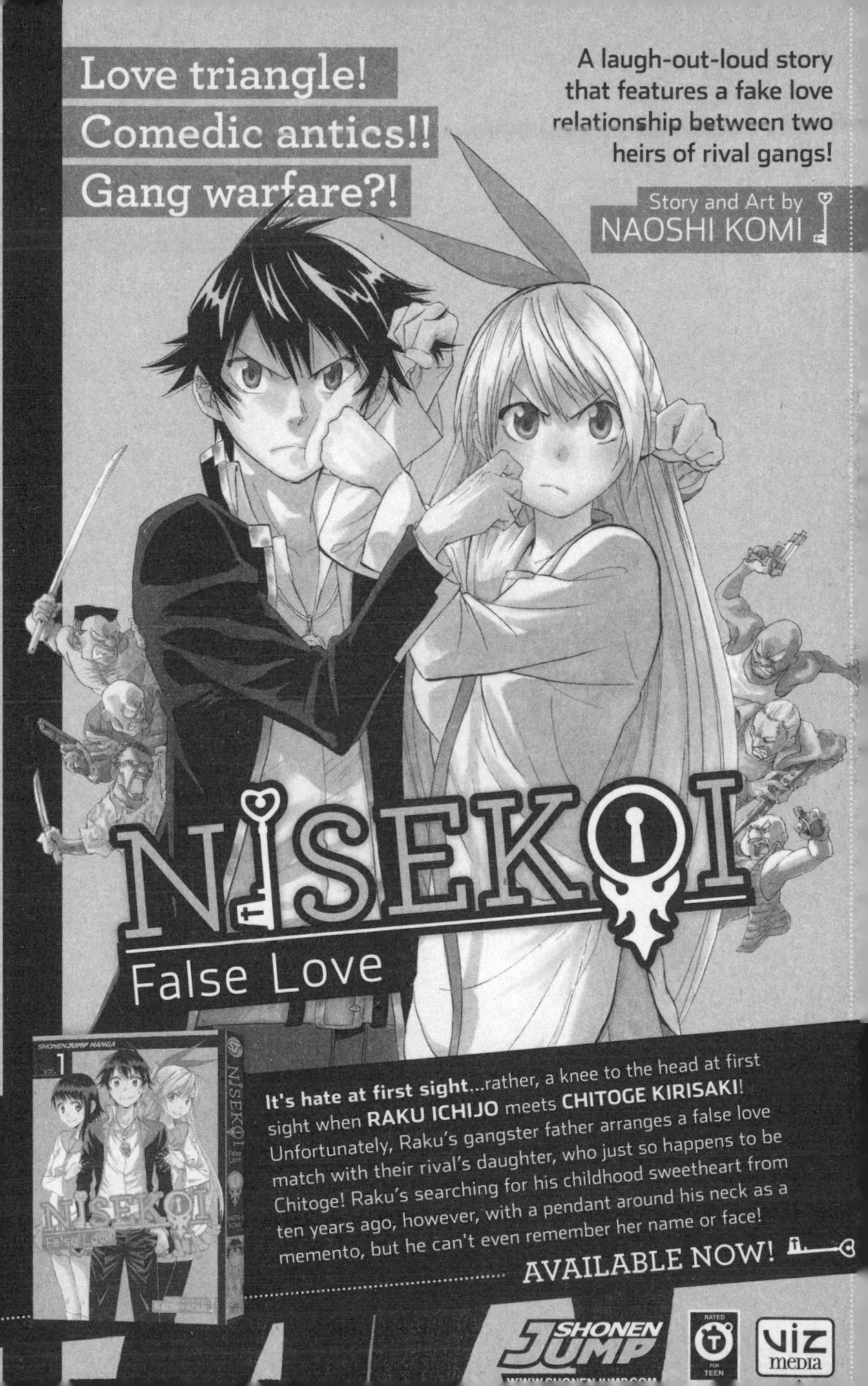
Love triangle!
Comedic antics!!
Gang warfare?!
A laugh-out-loud story that features a fake love relationship between two heirs of rival gangs!
Story and Art by
NAOSHI KOMI
NISEKOI
False Love
It's hate at first sight...rather, a knee to the head at first sight when RAKU ICHIJO meets CHITOGE KIRISAKI! Unfortunately, Raku's gangster father arranges a false love match with their rival's daughter, who just so happens to be Chitoge! Raku's searching for his childhood sweetheart from ten years ago, however, with a pendant around his neck as a memento, but he can't even remember her name or face!
AVAILABLE NOW!
SHONEN JUMP
RATED T FOR TEEN
VIZ media

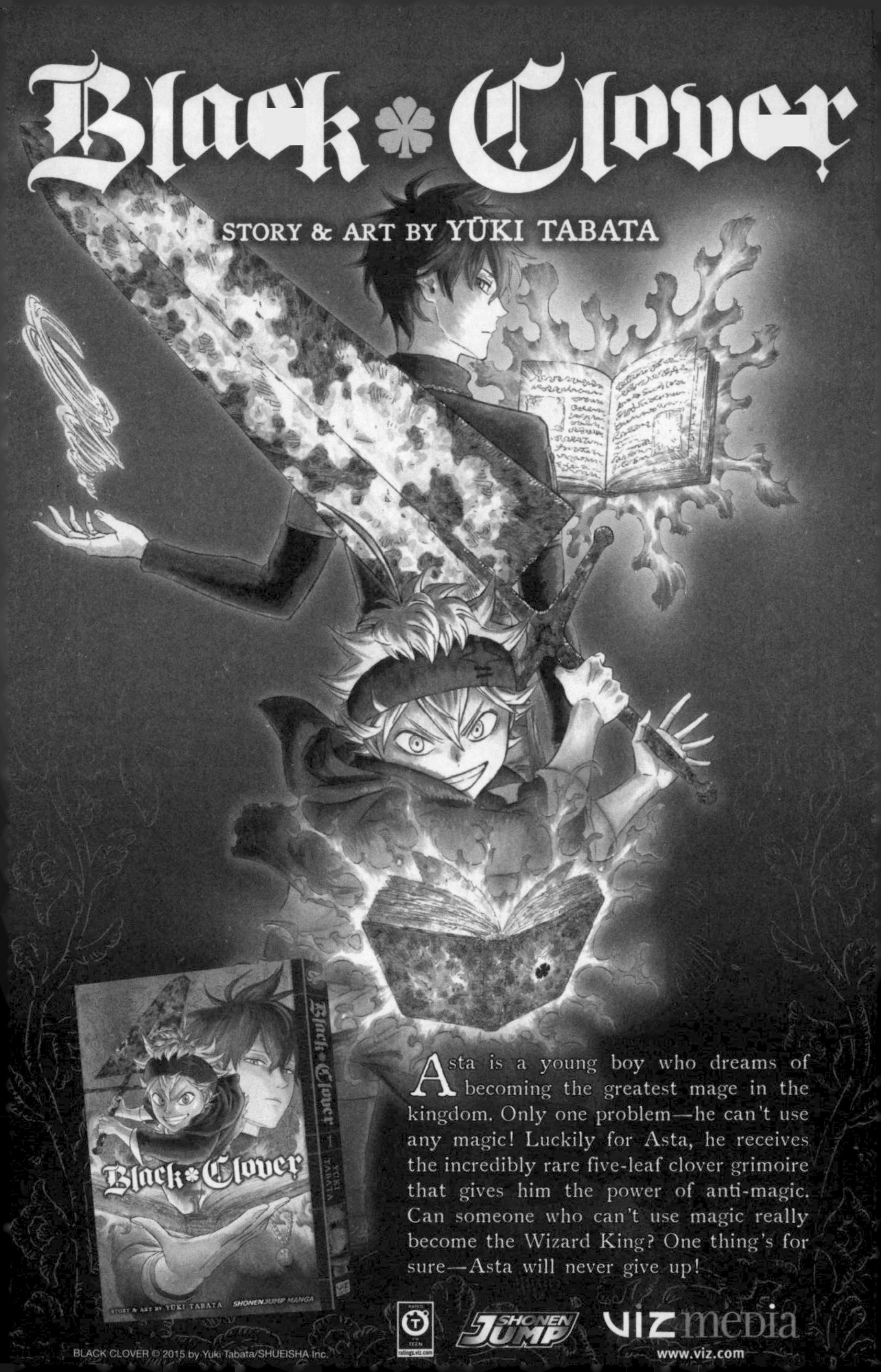
Black Clover
STORY & ART BY YŪKI TABATA
Asta is a young boy who dreams of becoming the greatest mage in the kingdom. Only one problem—he can't use any magic! Luckily for Asta, he receives the incredibly rare five-leaf clover grimoire that gives him the power of anti-magic. Can someone who can't use magic really become the Wizard King? One thing's for sure—Asta will never give up!
Black Clover
STORY & ART BY YUKI TABATA
SHONEN JUMP MANGA
TEEN
SHONEN JUMP
VIZ media
www.viz.com
BLACK CLOVER © 2015 by Yuki Tabata/SHUEISHA Inc.

You're Reading in the Wrong Direction!!

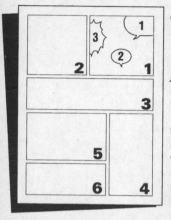

Whoops! Guess what? You're starting at the wrong end of the comic!

...It's true! In keeping with the original Japanese format, **One Piece** is meant to be read from right to left, starting in the upper-right corner.

Unlike English, which is read from left to right, Japanese is read from right to left, meaning that action, sound effects and word-balloon order are completely reversed...something which can make readers unfamiliar with Japanese feel pretty backwards themselves. For this reason, manga or Japanese comics published in the U.S. in English have sometimes been published "flopped"—that is, printed in exact reverse order, as though seen from the other side of a mirror.

By flopping pages, U.S. publishers can avoid confusing readers, but the compromise is not without its downside. For one thing, a character in a flopped manga series who once wore in the original Japanese version a T-shirt emblazoned with "M A Y" (as in "the merry month of") now wears one which reads "Y A M"! Additionally, many manga creators in Japan are themselves unhappy with the process, as some feel the mirror-imaging of their art reveals otherwise unnoticeable flaws or skews in perspective.

We are proud to bring you Eiichiro Oda's **One Piece** in the original unflopped format. For now, though, turn to the other side of the book and let the journey begin...!

—Editor

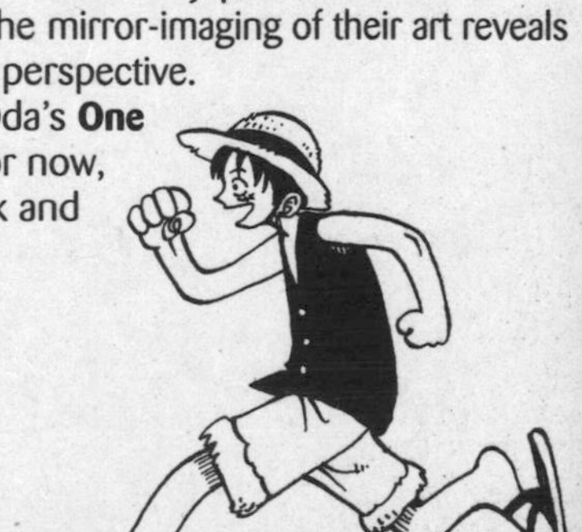